ALLIES OF CONVENIENCE

EVAN N. RESNICK

ALLIES OF
CONVENIENCE

A Theory of Bargaining in U.S. Foreign Policy

Columbia University Press / New York

Columbia University Press
Publishers Since 1893
New York   Chichester, West Sussex
cup.columbia.edu
Copyright © 2019 Columbia University Press
All rights reserved

Library of Congress Cataloging-in-Publication Data
Names: Resnick, Evan N., author.
Title: Allies of convenience : a theory of bargaining in U.S. foreign policy /
Evan N. Resnick.
Description: New York : Columbia University Press, [2019] |
Includes bibliographical references and index.
Identifiers: LCCN 2018050405| ISBN 9780231190589 (cloth : alk. paper) |
ISBN 9780231190596 (pbk. : alk. paper) | ISBN 9780231549028 (e-book)
Subjects: LCSH: United States—Foreign relations—1945–1989. | United
States—Foreign relations—China. | China—Foreign relations—United States. |
United States—Foreign relations—Pakistan. | Pakistan—Foreign relations—
United States. | United States—Foreign relations—Iraq. | Iraq—Foreign
relations—United States. | United States—Foreign relations—Great Britain. |
Great Britain—Foreign relations—United States.
Classification: LCC E840 .R42 2019 | DDC 327.73009/04—dc23
LC record available at https://lccn.loc.gov/2018050405

Columbia University Press books are printed on permanent
and durable acid-free paper.

Printed in the United States of America

Cover design: Elliott S. Cairns
Cover image: © Bettmann/Getty Images

For Barb, Lorelei, and Eileen

CONTENTS

ACKNOWLEDGMENTS

UNTIL QUITE RECENTLY, I was certain that this long-gestating book would never see the light of day. That you are now holding it is a testament to the combined efforts of many people, who provided me with the guidance, support, friendship, and love that I needed to stagger my way to the finish line.

To begin with, Deans Barry Desker and Joseph Liow, Ambassador Ong Keng Yong, and Professors Ralf Emmers and Tan See Seng at the S. Rajaratnam School of International Studies offered me one of the best academic jobs on the planet and then exhibited considerable patience as I painstakingly brought this project to fruition. RSIS is an extraordinarily collegial place to work and I have made many friendships in my six years there. Among the people who are most accustomed to hearing my knock on their office door are Ralf Emmers, Bhubhindar Singh, Anit Mukherjee, Sinderpal Singh, Ahmed Hashim, Bernard Loo, Farish Noor, Alan Chong, and the one and only Ong Weichong. I started work at RSIS on the same day as Pascal Vennesson, who has since become a close friend and limitless source of advice, wisdom, moral support, and humor. Pascal uncomplainingly read and offered astute critiques of multiple versions of my book proposal and the manuscript's introductory chapter. I have also been extremely fortunate to meet Ted Hopf and Yuen Foong Khong, both based at our crosstown rival, the National University of Singapore. Their comradeship and guidance have meant a great deal to me.

This book evolved out of a doctoral dissertation written at Columbia University under the supervision of three living legends in the field of International Relations: Bob Jervis, David Baldwin, and Jack Snyder. The first of these, the chair of my dissertation committee, has furnished me with so much help of so many different types since my grad student days that it is impossible to imagine I might have made it this far without him. Although Richard Betts and the late Kenneth Waltz were not on my dissertation committee, I was extremely fortunate to have them both as teachers and their influence has suffused everything I have written and taught about international politics and American foreign policy. Tim Crawford was my first TA in grad school, and since that time has adroitly juggled multiple roles as my mentor, role model, and good friend. Whenever I have been wracked with doubts about my ability to succeed in this career path, all it has taken is a brief conversation with Tim, whose confidence in me and enthusiasm for the field of IR is infectious, to dissipate them.

My academic debts extend to a small number of other scholars who have also had an outsized influence on this project. I met Steve Lobell, Jeff Taliaferro, and Norrin Ripsman well after I had become a devotee of their scholarship and have relished every minute that I have had the chance to spend with them since. One of the many perks of working at RSIS has been the opportunity to meet visiting IR luminaries from around the world, none of them as generous, helpful, and entertaining as T. V. Paul. T. V. insightfully guided me through the daunting process of academic book publishing and saved me from sending out a disastrous early draft of my proposal to prospective editors.

I undertook crucial research for this book during summer stints as a visiting scholar at both the George Washington University and Columbia University. Charlie Glaser graciously allowed me to spend a few extremely productive weeks during the summer of 2013 at the Institute for Security and Conflict Studies at GW's Elliott School of International Affairs. Dick Betts and the marvelous Ingrid Gerstmann similarly hosted me for multiple research visits in 2014, 2015, and 2017 to my old stomping ground, the Saltzman Institute of War and Peace Studies at Columbia.

Stephen Wesley, my editor at Columbia University Press, has stewarded the process of publishing my first book with remarkable efficiency, skill, and finesse. All of his editorial interventions have significantly improved the manuscript, down to and including its title. Three anonymous reviewers scrutinized the manuscript twice, in part and in full, offering a flood of useful critiques and comments that also greatly improved the final product. I am also grateful for Katherine Harper's skilled and meticulous copyediting. I would be remiss if I didn't note that I am delighted that this book carries the imprint of the university that changed my life and that I adore so much.

Finally, some of the people who have been most integral to this book's completion are not card-carrying International Relations scholars and have not read a word of the manuscript. This special category includes Asher Kahn, Sally David, P. Thiagarajan ("Dr. Raj"), Maria Thomas, Michelle Angela Gowans, Chris Robinson, Steve Fromhart, and Karl Kahandaliyanage. It also includes my loving parents Bob and Daria and my sister Allison and brother-in-law Charles. My satisfaction at having completed another career milestone is yet again counterbalanced by my sadness at having done it while living so far away from my family.

Most importantly, this book is dedicated to my wife Barbara and daughters Lorelei and Eileen, whom I love so much. Barb and I have experienced a series of adventures together since we first met at Café Taci on 110th Street and Broadway in the fall of 1997, and our incredible relationship has literally spanned the globe. During that time, we have helped each other succeed beyond our wildest dreams and endure through our most difficult moments. We have also managed to raise two spectacular children who fill us with pride and have made every single day a joy to live.

* * *

Portions of the introduction, chapters 1 and 4, and the conclusion appeared in Evan N. Resnick, "Strange Bedfellows: U.S. Bargaining Behavior with Allies of Convenience," *International Security* 35, no. 3 (Winter 2010/2011): 144–84, © 2010 President and Fellows of Harvard College and the Massachusetts Institute of Technology, reprinted courtesy of the MIT Press. I thank the journal's editors for granting me permission to use the material here.

ALLIES OF CONVENIENCE

INTRODUCTION

Alliances of Convenience in International Politics and U.S. Foreign Policy

If [international] pressures are strong enough, a state will deal with almost anyone . . . It is important to notice that states will ally with the devil to avoid the hell of military defeat.

—KENNETH N. WALTZ, *THEORY OF INTERNATIONAL POLITICS*

BARBARIANS AND THE LAW OF SELF-PRESERVATION

As recounted by Thucydides in his classic work *The History of the Peloponnesian War*, in 432 BC the Hellenic world teetered on the brink of war between the leading powers of Athens and Sparta. A fragile peace between the two archrivals was rocked when Athens established an alliance with the formerly neutral city-state of Corcyra (now Corfu), in opposition to Sparta's longstanding ally, Corinth. The Athenians further antagonized Sparta by imposing a trade embargo on neighboring Megara, another Spartan ally, and besieging the remote Corinthian colony of Potidea.[1] At the next meeting of Sparta's assembly, emissaries from several aggrieved states—including Corinth and Megara—rose to condemn these predations and enjoin Sparta to declare war against Athens.[2] Deliberations among Sparta's leaders quickly revealed that the "opinions of the majority all led to the same conclusion; the Athenians were open aggressors, and war must be declared at once."[3]

It was at this fraught moment when the Spartan monarch Archidamus, whom Thucydides records as a man of wisdom and moderation, rose to address the assembly. Archidamus cautioned that plunging into war against Athens would be disastrous because Sparta lacked the warships and money necessary to defeat the upstart maritime republic. Instead, he advised initiating diplomatic negotiations with the Athenians while at the same time quietly recruiting as many allies as possible to Sparta's side to ensure military victory if those talks collapsed.[4] As far as such prospective allies were concerned, Archidamus said, "Hellenic or barbarian it matters not, so long as they are an accession to our strength naval or financial." He added, emphatically, "I say Hellenic or barbarian because the odium of such an accession to all who like us are the objects of the designs of the Athenians is taken away by the law of self-preservation."[5] With this counsel, Archidamus became quite possibly the first political leader in recorded history to outline the logic behind what is now commonly referred to as an alliance of convenience.

Although the Spartan assembly impetuously rejected its king's counsel and voted to launch what history would remember as the Peloponnesian War (431–404 BC), Archidamus's comment on the value of barbarian allies proved prophetic. After the Athenian invasion of Sicily in 415 BC, Sparta desperately solicited the help of none other than the barbarian superpower of the ancient world, the Persian Empire, which had launched two large-scale invasions of Greece earlier in the century.[6] Although, as historians Victor Davis Hanson and David Berkey note, "Sparta hated Persia as much as did Athens,"[7] in 411 it nevertheless concluded a formal alliance with Persian king Darius II. Darius's son Prince Cyrus subsequently began dispensing the funds necessary for Sparta to undertake a large-scale naval buildup. With his new fleet, Admiral Lysander of the Spartans inflicted a devastating blow against the Athenians at Aegospotami in 405, and Athens would formally surrender the next year.[8] A decade later, however, Sparta's reckless attempt to liberate the Ionian Greeks in Asia Minor from their Persian overlords afforded Athens an excellent opportunity to exact revenge by establishing its own alliance with the barbarian empire. In 394, the Persian satrap Pharnabazus and the Athenian high admiral Conon led a fleet of Phoenician and Persian ships staffed by Greek mercenaries to Cnidus, where they destroyed the Spartan navy.[9] Historian Jennifer Roberts succinctly captured the irony of this momentous shift in the balance of power in ancient Greece: "Persian gold, which had once enabled Lysander to order the Long Walls [protecting Athens] destroyed, now aided in their reconstruction."[10]

ALLIANCES OF CONVENIENCE FROM KAUTILYA TO SHAKESPEARE

Nearly a century and a half after Archidamus lectured the Spartan assembly, the Indian philosopher Kautilya wrote *Arthashastra* (circa 300 BC), his renowned treatise on politics and statecraft. Kautilya was a senior advisor to the Indian king Chandragupta Maurya, who was the first monarch to successfully unite much of the Indian subcontinent into a single realm. Kautilya aimed to provide a handbook of sorts for kings to consolidate their rule and maximize the power of their kingdoms.[11] In *Arthashastra*'s most well-known section, he advanced his "Mandala theory" of foreign policy. It holds that a given state's geographical proximity to the monarch's kingdom alone should determine whether the monarch regards it as a friend or foe: "The king, endowed with personal excellences and those of his material constituents, the seat of good policy, is the would-be conqueror. Encircling him on all sides, with territory immediately next to his is the constituent called the enemy. In the same manner, one with territory separated by one (other territory) is the constituent called the ally."[12] Kautilya's theory is closely related to and may have even inspired the well-worn aphorism "the enemy of my enemy is my friend."[13]

Traditionally, however, the synonymous phrases "alliance of convenience" and "the enemy of my enemy is my friend" have been invoked to describe a newly cooperative relationship between rivals or adversaries, a context that is not explicit within those phrases, in Archidamus's remarks to the Spartan assembly, or in Kautilya's geographically rooted Mandala theory. It is more clearly conveyed in an oft-paraphrased snippet from Shakespeare's *The Tempest*, written around 1610. In the play's second act, a member of King Alonzo of Naples's shipwrecked royal party, the court jester Trinculo, encounters Caliban, a semihuman creature conceived in a

3

grotesque tryst between the devil and a witch. Caliban is slave to Prospero, the former Duke of Milan, who magically orchestrated the storm that wrecked Alonzo's ship on his remote island. Caliban mistakes Trinculo for one of Prospero's tormenting spirits and lies down to hide under his cloak, while Trinculo, having heard thunder rolling in the distance, scrambles to find shelter. Casting his gaze on the partially concealed figure lying in front of him, Trinculo is horrified by the prospect of huddling next to "this monster."[14] Still, he reasons that it is the lesser of evils: "Alas, the storm is come again! My best way is to creep under his gabardine; there is no other shelter hereabouts; *misery acquaints a man with strange bedfellows.* I will here shroud till the dregs of the storm be past."[15]

In *Safire's Political Dictionary*, former presidential speechwriter and columnist William Safire defines *strange bedfellows* as "Enemies forced by circumstances to work together; members of an unlikely alliance, often attacked as an unholy alliance."[16] Attributing the source of the phrase to *The Tempest*, Safire notes that in current usage, "politics" (as opposed to the "misery" of poor, frightened Trinculo) has been the most common motivation for enemies to become strange bedfellows.[17]

AN OPERATIONAL DEFINITION OF ALLIANCES OF CONVENIENCE

In international politics, the concept *alliance of convenience* should refer to security cooperation between states that are ideological and geopolitical adversaries in order to balance against a third party that the states view as a greater immediate danger.[18] This is rooted in alliance scholar Glenn Snyder's observation "Conflicts and common interests generate a pattern of alignment that exists prior to, and independently of, formal alliances. That is, *states will have some expectation of being supported in war or crises by states with whom they share interests and values, and opposed by states with whom they have conflicts.* These expectations will generate 'strategic interests' in defending states that are expected to be supportive and in blocking the accumulation of power resources by putative opponents."[19] Logically,

4

alliances of convenience should constitute the starkest exceptions to this rule and be established by the strangest of bedfellows: those states that perceive one another as so repellent that they would be enemies in all but the most exigent circumstances. As Snyder insinuates, the states least likely to form alliances will be those that exhibit conflicting domestic political values and foreign policy interests.

There are three elements to our definition here. The first, which refers to "security cooperation between states," implies that an alliance of convenience need not be formalized to exist. Since alliances of convenience are formed among highly antagonistic states that are unlikely to enshrine their partnership in a treaty, they are not captured by most definitions of military alliances proposed by international relations (IR) scholars, which stipulate that alliances must be formalized.[20] The second element stipulates that the parties to an alliance of convenience must be both ideological and geopolitical adversaries. The partners can be called ideological adversaries if, at the time the alliance was formed, they possessed widely divergent political ideologies.[21] (Ideological conflicts since the French Revolution have pitted liberal democracy against illiberal autocracy, free-market capitalism against communism, communism against fascism, and liberal democracy against illiberal democracy.[22]) The partners can be called geopolitical adversaries if, at the time the security cooperation was initiated, they possessed ongoing or unresolved conflicts of interest in national security–related foreign policy.[23] The final element holds that the chief motivation behind the creation of the alliance is the rise of an overarching third-party threat.[24] In this regard, alliances of convenience are distinct from *tethering alliances*, in which two rivals form an alliance primarily to avoid war with each other or to otherwise restrain or control each other's actions.[25]

ALLIANCES OF CONVENIENCE, AMBIVALENT ALLIANCES, AND SPECIAL RELATIONSHIPS

By defining alliances of convenience in this way, we can conceptually differentiate them from other defensive or balancing alliances in which the partners are *neither* geopolitical *nor* ideological rivals, as well as those in which they are *either* geopolitical *or* ideological rivals, which we can call *special relationship alliances* and *ambivalent alliances*, respectively (figure 0.1).

The term *special relationship* is borrowed from Winston Churchill's famous March 1946 "Iron Curtain" speech in Fulton, Missouri, in which he referred to the "fraternal association of the English-speaking peoples . . . a special relationship between the British Commonwealth and Empire and the United States."[26] Since then, the term has become ubiquitous in references by both policymakers and scholars to the Anglo–U.S. relationship, though it has also been used to describe U.S. bilateral relationships with other friendly democracies, such as Canada, Australia, and Israel.[27] During the Cold War, the United States made several ambivalent alliances with repressive authoritarian regimes that strongly shared Washington's aversion to the Soviet Union and global communism and pursued general foreign policies that were closely aligned with U.S. interests. Among the charter members of this group of "friendly tyrants" were Iran under Shah Mohammed Reza Pahlavi, the Philippines under Ferdinand Marcos, and Nicaragua under Anastasio Somoza.[28]

The extent to which mutually threatened states are divided by ideological or geopolitical animosities or both will generally determine their

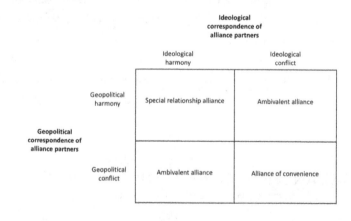

FIGURE 0.1

Typology of balancing alliances

FIGURE 0.2

Continuum depicting relative difficulty of formation, management,
and perpetuation of different alliance types

difficulty in forming an alliance in response to that threat, managing the
alliance once it is formed, and perpetuating it to the point of victory and
perhaps beyond. Of the three alliance types, alliances of convenience
should generally be the most difficult and special relationship alliances the
easiest to form, manage, and perpetuate, while ambivalent alliances
should range between these two extremes (figure 0.2).[29]

ALLIANCES OF CONVENIENCE IN U.S. HISTORY

The doctrine of "American exceptionalism" stems from the premise that
U.S. foreign policy is uniquely influenced by the creedal values of democracy, liberalism, individualism, and egalitarianism that have formed the core
of the republic's political culture since before its founding.[30] According to
political scientist Colin Dueck, the American people and their leaders
adhere strongly to the belief that the United States "has a special mission
or destiny in world affairs; classical liberal ideals will ripple and spread
worldwide from the United States; [and] the result will be a more open and
peaceful international system, characterized by democratic governments
and open exchange."[31] This mission was conceived as an antidote to the
benighted practice of international politics by the great powers of Europe,
which embodied a toxic stew of "militarism, autocracy, war, secret alliances,

corruption, and balance of power politics."[32] Notwithstanding the persistent efforts of U.S. leaders to pursue a foreign policy guided by lofty moral imperatives as opposed to cynical material ones, they have recurrently confronted emergent threats that have necessitated the sacrifice of the former at the altar of the latter. On such occasions, policymakers have engaged in the most cynical and potentially self-defeating tactic of *realpolitik* behavior, embracing one untrustworthy autocratic adversary to balance the growing danger posed by another.

In two especially noteworthy instances, such unholy alliances had the distinction of shielding the republic against threats to its survival. Not long after the thirteen American colonies declared their independence from Britain, they made a fateful alliance with France to prevent King George III's forces from strangling the American Revolution in its crib. In February 1778, the fledgling United States of America signed a Treaty of Alliance with the French king Louis XVI, though in actuality the security partnership had been consummated nearly two years earlier, when France began to surreptitiously funnel military aid to the American rebels.[33] As historian Mark Grimsley avers, the Franco-U.S. alliance exemplified the "triumph of *realpolitik* over historical, religious, and ideological considerations."[34] The ideological gap between the allies was perhaps most striking, as the nascent American republic was paradoxically waging a war of liberation against a constitutional monarchy by making common cause with "the most powerful absolute monarchy on the European continent."[35] The relationship had also been marred by recurring conflict. In the century before the 1776 Declaration of Independence, the colonists had fought no fewer than four wars against France, the last of which (the Seven Years War or French and Indian War of 1756–1763) resulted in the collapse of French power in North America. These frictions were exacerbated by the deep religious divide between the mostly Protestant American colonies and mostly Catholic France.[36]

The alliance yielded steadily increasing dividends for the revolutionaries. From the outset of the war, France's formidable navy confronted the British in the North Atlantic, Mediterranean, and Caribbean, preventing London from concentrating its forces on the North American front.[37] In August 1781, Admiral François Joseph Paul de Grasse helped turn the tide of the conflict by redeploying his formidable twenty-nine-ship fleet—carrying three thousand infantrymen—from the West Indies to Chesapeake Bay to confront the British forces that were on the verge of overrunning Virginia. Upon receiving this momentous news, General George Washington, the commander in chief of the Continental army, marched a combined allied force of eighteen thousand troops from New York to Yorktown, where they laid siege to the ten-thousand-strong Redcoat army of General Charles Cornwallis as they awaited the arrival of supply ships. Cornwallis's October 19 surrender compelled London to suspend offensive operations in North America.[38] In Grimsley's estimation, France's economic and military subvention "had sustained the [revolutionary] cause for most of the conflict, and had been absolutely indispensable to the [strategic] triumph at Yorktown."[39]

A second alliance, forged a century and a half later with Joseph Stalin's Soviet Union, proved vital to defeating the threat posed by Nazi Germany and its Axis partners during World War II. The advent of the world's first communist regime in Moscow in 1917 sparked acute fears of ideological contagion in the United States.[40] Stalin's stunning conclusion in August 1939 of a nonaggression treaty with Germany, followed by the Red Army's successive invasions of eastern Poland and Finland, added an intense geopolitical conflict with the United States to the already smoldering ideological one. Following the Soviets' "dreadful rape of Finland," a furious President Roosevelt wrote that "people are asking why one should have anything to do with the present Soviet leaders because their idea of civilization and human happiness is so totally different from ours."[41]

After Adolf Hitler double-crossed Stalin by launching an all-out invasion of the Soviet Union in June 1941, the Roosevelt administration embraced the very Soviet regime that the president had only recently denounced as "a dictatorship as absolute as any other dictatorship in the world."[42] In September, Roosevelt began providing Stalin's regime with extensive military assistance under the aegis of the Lend-Lease program. Three months later, the Japanese attack on Pearl Harbor and Hitler's subsequent declaration of war against the United States prompted the United States to join the Soviets and British in what Churchill memorably referred to as "the Grand Alliance" that would eventually win the war.[43] Over the course of the conflict, the Roosevelt administration strove to make America's alliance with the murderous communist leader as palatable as possible to domestic audiences by referring frequently to Stalin as "Uncle Joe," concealing evidence of Soviet wartime brutalities, and playing down the stark differences between the U.S. and Soviet political systems.[44] However distasteful, such propaganda helped maintain domestic support for an ally whose contributions to the war effort were invaluable and irreplaceable. Between Germany's invasion of the Soviet Union in June 1941 and its eventual surrender in May 1945, the Red Army confronted between 67 and 98 percent of the Wehrmacht's combat divisions.[45] Additionally, the Soviet Union's eventual declaration of war against Japan on August 9, 1945 compelled Emperor Hirohito to cast a tie-breaking vote in the Imperial Council in favor of immediate surrender to the Allies, bringing the Pacific War to a close less than a month later.[46]

AMERICA'S ALLIES OF CONVENIENCE SINCE 1945

Although the United States emerged from World War II with what historian Melvyn Leffler has described as a "preponderance of power,"[47] Washington's subsequent determination to contain Soviet expansionism led to a range of formal alliances and informal alliances of convenience. Scholars have tended to concentrate on the former, particularly the North Atlantic Treaty Organization (NATO) alliance with Canada and Western Europe and the bilateral alliances in Asia with Japan and South Korea. However, a narrow focus on these formal security partnerships, mostly with fellow democracies, obscures the pivotal role played during the Cold War by ad hoc and informal alliances of convenience struck with autocratic adversaries of both the Left and Right. For example, NATO's task of deterring a Soviet invasion of Western Europe was eased by the Truman and Eisenhower administrations' provision of economic and military aid to Marshal Josip Broz Tito's communist government in Yugoslavia after Tito's monumental split with Stalin in 1948.[48] During the 1980s, the Central Intelligence Agency tempted Nicolae Ceaușescu's neighboring communist regime in Romania into secretly transferring to the United States various advanced Soviet weapons systems in exchange for desperately needed hard currency.[49]

These U.S. alliances with disaffected European satellites of the Soviet Union pale in significance, however, by comparison with the one struck in the early 1970s with the communist juggernaut in Asia, Mao Zedong's People's Republic of China. President Richard Nixon's landmark visit to Beijing in February 1972 instantaneously reversed America's steadily deteriorating strategic position in East Asia, mitigating the strategic consequences of its looming military defeat in Vietnam. Nixon and his successors would increasingly ensconce the world's second most powerful communist state in the anti-Soviet bloc, intensifying the military and economic strains that would eventually result in the Soviet Union's collapse and dissolution.[50] The Carter and Reagan administrations' decision to arm the *mujahedin* insurgents fighting the Soviet Red Army in Afghanistan only exacerbated these strains. The U.S. government could only mount this ambitious covert operation in Afghanistan, however, by simultaneously collaborating with Zia ul-Haq's repressive Islamist regime in neighboring Pakistan.[51]

Tito, Ceauşescu, Mao, and Zia were joined in the rogues' gallery of America's least savory Cold War alliances by other unfriendly despots around the world who found their national security interests suddenly and surprisingly overlapping with those of Washington. In Europe, the United States allied with General Francisco Franco's fascist regime in Spain. In the Middle East, it made common cause with a succession of Saudi monarchs to thwart the Soviets and their most dangerous regional proxy of Gamal Abdel Nasser's Egypt. In Africa, it partnered with Mobutu Sese Seko's Zaire, Mengistu Haile Mariam's Ethiopia, Siad Barre's Somalia, and P. W. Botha's apartheid government in South Africa.[52] Finally, during the 1980s, Reagan established the United States' first Cold War–era alliances of convenience that were not directed against the Soviet Union or one of its proxies when it linked arms with Saddam Hussein's especially odious regime in Iraq, and again with the Saudis, this time to counter Ayatollah Khomeini's Iran during the Iran-Iraq War.[53]

As the Soviet Union plunged into internal turmoil and the Cold War wound down in the late summer of 1990, the United States' former Iraqi ally brazenly invaded and occupied Kuwait to seize its enormous oil resources. In response, President George H. W. Bush assembled a broad international coalition that successfully liberated the tiny Gulf emirate from Iraq's clutches early the next year. Although the coalition comprised a wide range of states—including the Syrian regime of Hafez al-Assad, one of Washington's bitterest foes in the Middle East—its geographic and financial linchpin was America's most prolific ally of convenience: Saudi Arabia.[54]

Despite the United States' elevation from superpower to hegemon since the end of the Cold War, alliances of convenience have still recurred in its national security policy. Most prominently, after the catastrophic September 11, 2001, attacks against New York and Washington, DC, by Osama bin Laden's Al Qaeda terrorist organization, the second Bush administration opened clandestine intelligence-sharing channels on Al Qaeda with two reviled regimes in the Middle East that had previously been the targets of U.S. airstrikes: Mu'ammar Gaddhafi's Libya and Omar al-Bashir's Sudan.[55] The administration also cooperated briefly with America's longstanding regional antagonist, Iran, to overthrow the Taliban regime in Afghanistan, which was providing sanctuary to bin Laden and Al Qaeda.[56] After Al Qaeda suicide bombers launched multiple attacks on residential apartment complexes in Riyadh in 2003 and early 2004, Saudi Arabia awkwardly joined the administration's Global War on Terrorism. Relations between Washington and Riyadh had been extremely tense since 9/11: the discovery that fifteen of the nineteen Al Qaeda hijackers were Saudi nationals had turned a glaring spotlight on the kingdom's extreme Wahhabi ideology and its history of subsidizing organizations that promoted violent strains of Sunni Islam abroad.[57]

Although Bush's successor, Barack Obama, viewed the longstanding U.S.-Saudi alliance with considerable distaste, even calling the kingdom one of America's "so-called allies in the Middle East,"[58] he nevertheless perpetuated it in response to the emergence of new adversaries. Following the rise of the Islamic State of Iraq and Syria (ISIS) in 2014, the Obama administration formed a global anti-ISIS coalition, which included the Saudis.[59] Despite Obama's remark in an April 2016 interview that Saudi Arabia needed to "share the neighborhood and institute some sort of cold peace"[60] with its regional nemesis, Iran, the White House quietly aided Riyadh's military intervention in Yemen in 2015 to defeat the Iran-backed Houthi rebels that had seized control of much of that country.[61]

The 2016 U.S. presidential election delivered an unexpected victory to the Republican candidate, Donald Trump, who has exhibited fewer inhibitions about linking arms with repressive and otherwise hostile dictatorships than any of his predecessors. During a televised debate against his Democratic opponent, Hillary Clinton, Trump stunned his own advisors and outraged many veteran Republican foreign policy hands when he claimed that the Syrian, Russian, and Iranian governments were forces for good in the ongoing and bloody Syrian civil war: "I don't like [Syrian president Hafez al-] Assad at all, but Assad is killing ISIS. Russia is killing ISIS and Iran is killing ISIS."[62]

Since his inauguration, Trump has acted less consistently than his campaign rhetoric indicated he would. On the one hand, he has actually adopted a more confrontational policy than Obama's toward Syria and Iran, launching airstrikes against Syria and withdrawing the United States from the Joint Comprehensive Plan of Action, the 2015 agreement that rolled back international sanctions against Iran in exchange for Tehran's acceptance of tight restrictions on its nuclear program.[63] On the other hand, Trump has moved to bolster the longstanding alliance of convenience with Saudi Arabia and revitalize U.S. relations with Russia in the face of strong domestic political headwinds. Soon after entering office, he sent an unmistakable signal by making his first foreign trip not to neighboring Canada or Mexico but rather to Saudi Arabia, defying the tradition of all incoming presidents since Ronald Reagan. There, he agreed to a massive $110 billion arms deal with the kingdom, though critics subsequently pointed out that this impressive sum was largely illusory, consisting mostly of nebulous letters of interest or intent, as opposed to actual contracts. In any event, Trump refused to suspend even the much smaller-scale delivery of U.S. arms to Saudi Arabia in the wake of credible allegations that Saudi crown prince Mohammed Bin Salman orchestrated the October 2018 assassination of U.S.-based Saudi journalist Jamal Khashoggi.[64] Trump has also consistently lavished praise on Russian president Vladimir Putin and taken some small if still controversial steps to improve Russo-U.S. relations. However, these efforts have run up against intense resistance from Congress, the general public, and even the president's own cabinet, which has been galvanized by the intelligence community's assessment that the Kremlin mounted cyber operations to influence the outcome of the 2016 U.S. presidential election in Trump's favor.[65]

THE PUZZLE OF U.S. BARGAINING WITH ALLIES OF CONVENIENCE

America has always negotiated alliances of convenience, and there is every indication that it always will. This raises a crucial question: how have its leaders managed these especially volatile and potentially dangerous alignments? Every alliance involves bargaining among the partners to determine who will bear the higher material and behavioral costs of sustaining the relationship through to its objective. The stakes attached to such bargaining should be considerably higher in alliances of convenience among recent enemies than in other, less fractious alliances, because the achievement of their objectives will likely mean a return to the tense, mutually threatening status *quo ante*. The partner that pays greater costs to maintain the alliance will be in a relatively disadvantaged position vis-à-vis its adversary-turned-ally after the partnership ends.

Two venerable bargaining theories seek to account for the outcome of U.S. negotiations with allies of convenience since America's rise to superpower status at the end of World War II. *Neorealist alliance theory* claims that intra-alliance bargaining power derives from the relative international systemic positions of the respective allies, as measured by the intra-alliance balances of dependence, commitment, and interests. Under this theory, the United States should have bargained successfully with all of its post-1945 allies of convenience, at least in disputes affecting its vital interests. This is because America was exponentially stronger than all of its allies, less immediately threatened by their shared enemies, and only weakly and informally committed to its allies' defense. *Tying hands theory* counterintuitively proposes that the outcome of international bargaining will favor the state whose negotiators' autonomy is most constrained domestically. This theory similarly predicts that the United States should have prevailed because it is an internally "weak state" whose political leadership possess little policy-making autonomy, as compared with the "strong state" autocrats that dominated political decision-making in all of America's allies of convenience.

This book pits against these two approaches a novel theory of alliance bargaining that is drawn from the neoclassical realist research program in IR. It proposes that if the systemically advantaged partner in an alliance of convenience possesses an internally weak state, it will bargain passively and unsuccessfully with its systemically disadvantaged ally. This is because its leaders will feel compelled to disarm domestic opponents of the relationship by casting the ally and the alliance in the most benign light possible, sacrificing their bargaining leverage. This theory expects U.S. policymakers to have recurrently found themselves in the precarious position of Goethe's sorcerer's apprentice, who magically animates a broom to fetch water on his behalf, only to discover that the workshop is soon flooded.[66] Like the apprentice, under this theory American officials would eventually find that their ally of convenience has become a formidable menace in its own right.

STRUCTURE OF THE BOOK

The rest of the book proceeds as follows. Chapter 1 shows that the IR literature on alliance management has almost entirely neglected the study of the United States' most nettlesome alliances, namely, those struck with unfriendly autocracies. It then describes in detail the three rival theories of U.S. bargaining with post-1945 allies of convenience and discusses the project's research design. Chapters 2, 3, and 4 examine the U.S. alliances of convenience with the People's Republic of China (1971 to 1989), Pakistan (1981 to 1988), and Iraq (1982 to 1988). In each case, as predicted by neoclassical realist theory alone, persistent domestic opposition to the alliance drove senior officials to adopt a velvet-gloved negotiating strategy with the ally, resulting in failed bargaining on salient national security–related disputes.

In order to avoid selecting on neoclassical realism's dependent variable, a fourth case study is included in which the theory conversely predicts aggressive and successful U.S. bargaining. Whereas it expects the formation of an alliance of convenience to generate heavy domestic opposition, a special relationship alliance with an ideologically and geopolitically friendly partner should conversely engender minimal opposition. As a result, even if the systemically favored ally has an internally weak state, its leaders should nevertheless find it relatively easy to mobilize domestic support on behalf of an aggressive and ultimately successful alliance policy. Chapter 5 tests this proposition by examining bargaining between the United States and the United Kingdom during the Korean War (1950–1953). Across a wide range of salient bilateral disputes, a relatively muted domestic opposition to the alliance with Britain enabled U.S. officials to drive a series of hard bargains with their counterparts in London, and the latter glumly conceded in virtually each instance. The conclusion addresses the implications of the book's key arguments and findings for the practice of American foreign policy.

1

CONTENDING THEORIES OF U.S. BARGAINING WITH ALLIES OF CONVENIENCE

Because allies are governments, each is a more or less complex arena for internal bargaining among the bureaucratic elements and political personalities who collectively comprise its working apparatus. Its action is the product of their interaction. They bargain not at random but according to the processes, conforming to the perquisites, responsive to the pressures of their own political system.

—RICHARD NEUSTADT, *ALLIANCE POLITICS*

HOW EFFECTIVELY DOES the United States bargain with its most treacherous allies, particularly when important national security interests are at stake? Alliance scholars have almost entirely ignored the phenomenon of alliances of convenience, focusing their empirical studies predominantly on America's formal alliances with friendly democracies and, to a much lesser extent, friendly autocracies. Two prominent bargaining theories, neorealist alliance theory and the two-level games theory of tying hands, propose that, at least since 1945, the United States should have bargained successfully with all of those allies, albeit for different reasons. Neorealism attributes this outcome to the nation's favorable international systemic position compared to that of its allies of convenience, which were all far less powerful and more immediately endangered by the shared threats that precipitated the formation of the alliances. Tying hands attributes U.S. success to the large disparity in formal decisionmaking power between U.S. leaders and the exclusively autocratic leaders of its allies of convenience. By contrast, I advance a novel theory of alliance bargaining that is drawn from the neoclassical realist research program in International

Relations (IR), which makes the opposite prediction. It hypothesizes that heavy domestic opposition to the formation of alliances of convenience should have compelled U.S. leaders to squander America's advantageous international systemic position by adopting a passive bargaining posture toward those allies, resulting in bargaining failure.

AN INCONVENIENT GAP IN THE ALLIANCE LITERATURE

Over the past several decades, a burgeoning academic literature has sought to explain the origins, management, and effectiveness of military alliances. Several recent contributions have thickened a previously thin canon pertaining to their management or bargaining dimension. Although many, if not most, advance theories and arguments that are applicable to alliances of convenience between the United States and hostile autocracies, their authors have exhibited a strong bias in favor of testing their propositions in U.S. alliances with fellow democracies.

This tendency is evident in five major works on alliance politics published in recent years. In *Warring Friends: Alliance Restraint in International Politics* (2008), Jeremy Pressman devises a neoclassical realist theory that somewhat resembles the one I propose below to account for the ability and willingness of powerful states to restrain the foreign policy behavior of weaker allies. He tests the four propositions derived from the theory in the two cases of (formal) U.S. alliance relations with Britain during the 1950s and (informal) U.S. alliance relations with Israel between the early 1960s and the early 2000s.[1] In *America's Allies and War: Kosovo, Afghanistan, and Iraq* (2011), Jason Davidson advances a different neoclassical realist theory to explain variations in the commitments of America's NATO allies of Britain, France, and Italy to seven U.S.-led military interventions since the end of World War II.[2] Stefanie von Hlatky similarly deploys a neoclassical realist theory in *American Allies in Time of War: The Great Asymmetry* (2013) to account for the unipolar United States' mixed record in bargaining with Canada, the United Kingdom, and Australia during the Afghanistan and

Iraq wars that followed the September 11, 2001, terrorist attacks.[3] In *NATO in Afghanistan: Fighting Together, Fighting Alone* (2014), David Auerswald and Stephen Saideman seek to explain the varying proclivity of America's NATO allies to impose restrictions or caveats on their military activities during the post-9/11 U.S.-led war in Afghanistan.[4] In an important recent article in the flagship journal *International Security*, Gene Gerzhoy tests his argument that under certain conditions a nuclear-armed state can successfully coerce an ally into aborting the pursuit of nuclear weapons by examining U.S. bargaining with its NATO ally West Germany between 1954 and 1969.[5]

Although some works have focused on U.S. military cooperation with autocratic states, a number of these have been atheoretical. Prime examples are two edited volumes, *Friendly Tyrants: An American Dilemma* (1991), edited by Daniel Pipes and Adam Garfinkle, and *Dealing with Dictators: Dilemmas of U.S. Diplomacy and Intelligence Analysis, 1945–1990* (2006), edited by Ernest May and Philip Zelikow.[6] Both books consist of several historical case studies of U.S. alliances with various right-wing anticommunist dictatorships during the Cold War. Their usefulness is limited, however, by their lack of a unifying theoretical framework. In addition, neither book explores the United States' Cold War alliances with anti-Soviet left-wing dictatorships. This latter critique obviously also applies to David Schmitz's *Thank God They're on Our Side: The United States and Right-Wing Dictatorships, 1921–1965* (1999) and *The United States and Right-Wing Dictatorships* (2006).[7] In this sweeping two-part history, Schmitz broadly contends that the United States established alliances with right-wing anticommunist dictatorships of various stripes from the 1920s through the end of the Cold War because they "promised stability, protected American trade and investments, and aligned . . . with Washington against the enemies of the United States."[8]

Two more theoretically self-conscious contributions to the literature on U.S. alliances with autocracies are Douglas MacDonald's *Adventures in Chaos: American Intervention for Reform in the Third World* (1992) and Victor Cha's *Powerplay: The Origins of the American Alliance System in Asia* (2016).[9] MacDonald argues that U.S. efforts to induce right-wing authoritarian allies to implement domestic reforms during the Cold War were constrained, primarily by the intensity of Washington's commitment to those states' security. Cha contends that the United States negotiated formal bilateral alliances in East Asia after World War II in order to maximize its leverage and control over much weaker but potentially troublesome small-power partners. However, none of the alliances studied by MacDonald (Nationalist China, 1946–1948; the Philippines, 1950–1953; and South Vietnam, 1961–1963) or Cha (South Korea and Taiwan in the early 1950s) meet my criteria for categorization as alliances of convenience. According to my typology, the U.S. allies surveyed in these two books fall under the more benign category of ambivalent allies, which had autocratic political systems but possessed geopolitical interests that were closely aligned with those of the United States.[10] In addition, MacDonald's argument explains U.S. efforts to modify its authoritarian allies' domestic politics, whereas the present study focuses on attempts by the United States to modify the behavior of its allies on salient national security–related issues.

Only two relatively recent theoretical works on U.S. alliance management—Alexander Cooley's *Base Politics: Democratic Change and the U.S. Military Overseas* (2008) and Tongfi Kim's *The Supply Side of Security: A Market Theory of Military Alliances* (2016)—include brief discussions of allies of convenience.[11] Cooley is not interested in alliance politics broadly defined, but rather in the conditions under which U.S. military bases in foreign states are accepted domestically in those states. He argues that the host country's response to U.S. basing hinges on the degree to which the host regime is politically dependent on the security contract with Washington and the contractual credibility of the host state's political institutions. One of several cases that Cooley examines, which I classify as an alliance of convenience, is the basing agreement signed by the United States in 1953 with General Francisco Franco's Spain (Treaty of Madrid). Although Cooley touches on some of the compromises made by both sides in negotiating and later renegotiating the treaty, he is primarily interested in showing both that it brought legitimacy (and American economic assistance) to the Franco regime and that this legitimacy was weakened following Franco's death and the advent of democratic rule in Madrid.[12] Kim examines the trajectory of the U.S. alliance with Spain from the Treaty of Madrid through 2004. In accordance with Kim's market theory of alliances, which proposes that an ally will have to make fewer concessions to a pro-alliance leader in the partner state whose hold on power is secure, he claims that Washington had to make few concessions to Franco in order to maintain the alliance.[13]

In sum, IR scholars have not yet subjected alliances of convenience and U.S. relations with such allies to rigorous scrutiny. Since the United States has frequently partnered with allies of convenience to thwart impending threats, only to subsequently wage hot and cold wars against them, it is imperative that scholars and policymakers achieve a more refined understanding of the dynamics attendant to these uniquely complex and challenging bilateral relationships.

RIVAL THEORIES OF ALLIANCE BARGAINING

This book restricts the temporal scope of study to the period 1945–2015. Prior to 1945 the relative power of the United States vis-à-vis its allies of convenience varied widely over time from relative weakness to relative parity, complicating the analysis. At the time of its first such alliance, struck with Louis XVI's France during the American Revolutionary War, the thirteen rebelling colonies together constituted a minor actor in the great power system centered in Europe. By the time of its final pre-1945 alliance of convenience with Stalin's Soviet Union during World War II, the United States had risen to become one of several great powers—along with the USSR—in a multipolar international system. Since 1945, however, it has been one of two superpowers in a bipolar Cold War system and subsequently the sole great power in a post–Cold War unipolar system, while all of its allies have been small powers. This configuration seems more likely to resemble U.S. alliances in the near-term future than does the pre-1945 model. Although the gap in power and wealth between the United States and "the rest" has shrunk in recent years, a considerable body of evidence indicates that it should remain predominant for several years to come. Even if the upward trajectory of China's relative rise in power is steeper than these data predict, the international system will resemble the two-superpower bipolar order that prevailed during the Cold War.[14]

Glenn Snyder defines alliance management as "a continuous bargaining process in which the members seek to maximize their alliance benefits while minimizing their risks and costs."[15] Since the end of World War II, the United States has established twenty-one distinct alliances of convenience, which are listed in table 1.1. The dependent variable of this study is the outcome of U.S. bargaining with these allies on salient national security–related issues in which the United States and its partners had divergent preferences. Specifically, did the outcome lie closer to the ideal point of the United States

TABLE 1.1 UNIVERSE OF THE UNITED STATES' ALLIANCES
OF CONVENIENCE, 1945–2015

ALLY OF CONVENIENCE	SHARED THREAT	ALLIANCE TIME SPAN
COLD WAR		
Spain	Soviet Union	1947–1976
Saudi Arabia	Soviet Union	1950–1991
Yugoslavia	Soviet Union	1951–1958
Saudi Arabia	Egypt	1962–1967
China	Soviet Union	1971–1989
Zaire	Soviet Union/Angola	1974–1991
Ethiopia	Soviet Union/Somalia	1976–1977
Somalia	Soviet Union/Ethiopia	1978–1989
Romania	Soviet Union	1979–1989
Pakistan	Soviet Union	1981–1988
South Africa	Soviet Union	1981–1986
Saudi Arabia	Iran	1981–1988
Iraq	Iran	1982–1988
Saudi Arabia	Iraq	1990–2003
Syria	Iraq	1990–1991
POST–COLD WAR		
Iran	Taliban/Al Qaeda	2001
Libya	Al Qaeda	2001–?
Sudan	Al Qaeda	2001–?
Saudi Arabia	Al Qaeda	2003–present
Saudi Arabia	Islamic State	2014–present
Saudi Arabia	Houthis in Yemen/Iran	2015–present

(i.e., successful U.S. bargaining) or that of its ally (i.e., failed U.S. bargaining)?[16] Below, I introduce three broad theories of alliance bargaining and their respective hypotheses addressing this question.[17]

NEOREALIST THEORY OF ALLIANCE BARGAINING

The neorealist research program consists of works that attempt to explain international political behavior or foreign policy behavior or both by reference to the structure of the international system.[18] Neorealists share a set of theoretical assumptions: that the international system is anarchic; that the most important actors are nation-states; that states seek, at minimum, to survive; that state behavior is primarily a response to international systemic pressures or opportunities; and that states are generally able to efficiently mobilize domestic resources in response.[19] Glenn Snyder has advanced the most influential and comprehensive neorealist theory of alliance management. It proposes that bargaining power within alliances hinges on three variables, namely the intra-alliance balances of dependence, commitments, and interests.[20]

An alliance member's influence will vary inversely with its dependence on the alliance. Greater bargaining power will be possessed by the member that is less dependent than its partner on the alliance, and vice versa.[21] More specifically, Snyder depicts the military dependence as an amalgam of three factors: "(1) a state's need for military assistance; (2) the degree to which the ally fills that need, and (3) alternative ways of meeting the need."[22]

In his seminal neorealist work *Theory of International Politics*, Kenneth Waltz employs the concept of the balance of dependence to explain why a shift from a multipolar international system to a bipolar one affects the bargaining power of the great powers over their allies dramatically. In multipolarity, individual great powers cannot secure themselves via domestic efforts to increase their military power (i.e., internal balancing) and therefore must court other great powers—and to a lesser extent, small powers—as allies (i.e., external balancing).[23] Since military interdependence is so high in this system, "the politics of power turn on the diplomacy by which alliances are made, maintained, and disrupted."[24] Under this configuration, allies therefore possess considerable inherent bargaining power: "Flexibility of alignment narrows one's choice of policies. A state's strategy must please a potential or satisfy a present partner . . . strategy is at least partly made for the sake of attracting and holding allies."[25] By contrast, in a bipolar system, allies of the two superpowers are considerably less powerful and influential. Military interdependence is low, as the two great power poles or superpowers are highly independent; each is able to effectively balance the other's power via internal means alone, thereby rendering alliances with other states largely superfluous.[26] Meanwhile, whereas alliances in multipolarity consist predominantly of great powers, alliances in bipolarity always consist of a superpower and one or more lesser powers. Since the distribution of power in such alliances is highly asymmetric, "the contributions of the lesser members are at once wanted and of relatively small importance."[27]

Waltz's deductions regarding the balance of dependence in bipolar alliances apply even more strongly to unipolar systems. A unipole possesses more security and autonomy than great powers possess in either bipolar or multipolar systems because there are no peer competitors to challenge or threaten it. As Stephen Walt notes, since the unipole possesses enormous, unrivaled power, both its allies and its adversaries are necessarily much weaker.[28] It should therefore need allies much less than is the case even with superpowers in a bipolar system, affording the unipole an overwhelming bargaining advantage over its allies.[29] In addition, unlike its much smaller allies, the unipole confronts no existential threats. This asymmetry of threat compels those allies to "work harder" to ensure that the less-imperiled unipole lives up to its promises.[30] By contrast, in a bipolar system, the small and medium power allies of a superpower can derive at least some leverage from both the implicit or explicit threat to defect to the other superpower's camp and the degree of symmetry in the vital interests of the superpower and its allies, which are all threatened gravely by the rival superpower.[31]

The second determinant of alliance bargaining power is the balance of commitment. Snyder defines commitment in the context of alliance politics as "an arrangement of values that disposes one to act in a certain way"[32] and explains that it emerges from two sources: the verbal promise rendered in the original alliance treaty and subsequent elaborations of that promise and the inherent interest that a state would have in assisting its ally in the absence of a formal pledge to do so. Bargaining power will vary inversely with the extent of commitment. The advantage will be held by the alliance partner that is less committed to the alliance owing to its formal alliance pledge or inherent interest, or both.[33]

Snyder identifies the balance of interests as the theory's third independent variable. Interest pertains to the valuation or stakes attached by each of the allies to the outcome of bargaining in a given issue-area. Snyder draws a direct relationship between intensity of interest and bargaining power: the more that an ally values what its partner is demanding that it relinquish (and the less it values what the partner would relinquish in turn), the more bargaining power it will possess vis-à-vis the partner, and the less power the partner will possess.[34]

NEOREALIST THEORY AND U.S. BARGAINING WITH POST-1945 ALLIES OF CONVENIENCE

Since the end of World War II, the United States has been one of two great power poles in the Cold War bipolar international system (1945–1991) and the only pole in the post–Cold War unipolar international system (1991–present).[35] Meanwhile, all of its allies during this period have been exponentially weaker small powers. In addition, because the United States is geographically situated in a benign Western hemisphere separated from all of its post–World War II adversaries by thousands of miles of ocean, it has been geographically less proximate to the sources of the shared threats— and thereby less threatened by them—than have all of its allies of convenience.[36] Furthermore, many of those allies experienced an even more hostile relationship than the United States did with the shared enemies that precipitated the alliances, which should have minimized their likelihood of defecting to those adversaries. Consequently, the United States has been the less-dependent partner in all of its post-1945 alliances of convenience.

The balance of commitment between the United States and its postwar allies of convenience has also favored the former. Since all of its postwar alliances of this kind have been informal, the United States has not had an explicit and binding legal commitment to defend those allies.

This means that the reputational and prestige consequences, let alone the legal and political ones, that would have been associated with defecting from those alliances were considerably lower than would have been the case with America's formal alliances.

The United States' refusal to strike formal treaties with its allies of convenience also implies strongly that it did not consider its "inherent interest" in these allies' security to be as high as was the case with those states that Washington joined in formal alliances, particularly NATO and the bilateral alliance with Japan. In the absence of rival great powers in the Western hemisphere, which America has dominated since the late nineteenth century, the only threats to U.S. survival have emanated from great powers in Europe and Asia that could only undertake an economic blockade or military invasion if they first managed to subdue all of the local rivals in their home region. Consequently, as successive generations of realist scholars have argued, the most vital U.S. national interest is the maintenance of a balance of power in both Europe and Asia to prevent the emergence of a regional hegemon on either continent.[37]

As the Soviet threat intensified in the aftermath of World War II, the Truman administration shored up its inherent interest in maintaining a balance of power in both regions by signing the North Atlantic Treaty with the states of Western Europe (and Canada) and the Treaty of Mutual Cooperation and Security with Japan. With these formal alliances serving as linchpins of the balance of power in Europe and Asia, respectively, all other alliances established by the United States, including its alliances of convenience, were less important, as they merely supplemented these core regional balances.[38] After the demise of the Soviet Union, the absence of rival great powers anywhere in the world meant that the nation's inherent interest in defending even NATO and Japan diminished considerably.[39]

Although it is possible to generalize about the overall balances of dependence and commitment between the United States and its postwar allies of convenience, it is not possible to do so about the balance of interests. In each alliance, the United States and its partner likely exhibited divergent preferences in a number of issue-areas, and the intensity with which each held its respective preferences almost certainly varied widely. While it is possible that favorable balances of dependence and commitment enabled

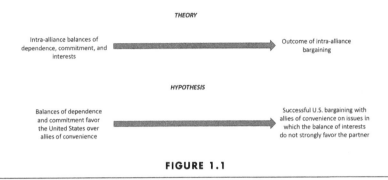

FIGURE 1.1

Neorealist theory of alliance bargaining and hypothesis on U.S. bargaining with post-1945 allies of convenience

the United States to prevail in bargaining with its allies even on those issues in which the balance of interests strongly favored the latter, it is also possible that Washington would have been inclined to compromise or even capitulate on those matters. The neorealist theory can therefore only make a deterministic prediction of clear-cut U.S. success relating to issues in which the balance of interests did not strongly favor the partner. In the following empirical chapters, I focus on disputes between the United States and its allies that entailed salient national security implications for the former (i.e., those in which it had a strong interest in prevailing), and therefore in which the balance of interests could not strongly favor its partner.

In sum, since the balances of dependence and commitment have asymmetrically favored the United States over all of its post-1945 allies of convenience, neorealist theory strongly predicts that it should have bargained successfully with those allies on issues in which the balance of interests did not grossly favor the ally (figure 1.1).

TYING HANDS THEORY

Another popular theory of interstate bargaining, tying hands theory, derives from the two-level games research program in IR, which was launched by Robert Putnam in a 1988 article, "Diplomacy and Domestic Politics: The Logic of Two-Level Games."[40] The program consists of works that attempt to explain international bargaining outcomes by reference to the combination of international and domestic circumstances that simultaneously confront state leaders during bilateral or multilateral negotiations. As Putnam relates, "At the national level, domestic groups pursue their interests by pressuring the government to adopt favorable policies and politicians seek power by constructing coalitions among those groups. At the international level, national governments seek to maximize their own ability to satisfy domestic pressures, while minimizing the adverse consequences of foreign developments. Neither of the two games can be ignored by central decision-makers, so long as their countries remain interdependent, yet sovereign."[41] The "two-level" metaphor permits scholars to assess the innovative and dynamic strategies by which leaders exploit their position in international negotiations to manipulate domestic political constraints at home and in other countries and use those internal constraints to manipulate the outcomes of international negotiations.

An intriguing and counterintuitive theory that emerged from the two-level games literature is tying hands theory. It derives from a paradoxical insight first captured by Thomas Schelling in his landmark 1960 work *The Strategy of Conflict*: "The well-known principle that one should pick good negotiators to represent him and then give them complete flexibility and authority—a principle commonly voiced by negotiators themselves—is by no means as self-evident as its proponents suggest; the power of a negotiator often rests on a manifest inability to make concessions and meet demands."[42]

Putnam elaborated in his path-breaking article that a given state's domestic "win-set," defined as its range of domestically acceptable international agreements, is a function of the magnitude of formal or informal policymaking power possessed by its senior foreign policy decision-makers vis-à-vis their domestic constituents (e.g., parliament, bureaucratic agencies, interest groups, social classes, or the general public). The more decisionmaking power they possess, the larger their win-set. Highly autonomous leaders will therefore be capable of agreeing to and ratifying a wider range of agreements than highly constrained leaders with smaller win-sets. This implies that an inverse relationship exists between the size of a state's domestic win-set and the bargaining power possessed by its leaders.

According to Putnam, "a small domestic win-set can be a bargaining advantage: 'I'd like to accept your proposal, but I could never get it accepted at home.'"[43] In sum, greater bargaining leverage will accrue to leaders whose hands are tied more tightly by their domestic constituencies. The enhanced leverage possessed by highly constrained negotiators is counterbalanced, however, by an elevated risk of involuntary defection. As both Schelling and Putnam observed, a domestic constituency can establish such a rigidly narrow win-set for its political leaders that they are precluded from reaching agreement with the other parties to the negotiation.[44]

TYING HANDS THEORY AND U.S. BARGAINING WITH POST-1945 ALLIES OF CONVENIENCE

Tying hands theory makes the same prediction as neorealist theory: namely, that the United States should have engaged in successful bargaining with its post-1945 allies of convenience. Initially Schelling suggested that the tying hands strategy is not equally available to all parties to an international negotiation, as "the ability of a democratic government to get itself tied by public opinion may be different from the ability of a totalitarian government to incur such a commitment."[45] Putnam somewhat more broadly echoed that "diplomats representing an entrenched dictatorship are less able than representatives of a democracy to claim credibly that domestic pressures preclude some disadvantageous deal."[46]

Whereas, by definition, all of America's allies of convenience were dictatorships exhibiting highly concentrated political power, the United States is a liberal democracy whose central feature, according to Stephen Krasner, is "the fragmentation and dispersion of power and authority."[47] The framers of the U.S. Constitution sought deliberately to limit presidential autonomy in foreign affairs by separating foreign policymaking powers between the executive and legislative branches and instituting numerous checks and balances between these branches.[48] In addition, legislative power in the United States is itself highly fragmented and dispersed, with the implication that legislation sought by the president can be scuttled at several different "veto points" or decisionmaking nodes in the labyrinthine legislative process involved in passing a bill. As Krasner describes,

In the House these include subcommittees, full committees, the Rules Committee, the full House, the Rules Committee again before for a bill going to a conference committee, and the conference committee itself. The situation is similar in the Senate except that there is no direct parallel with the Rules Committee. The Appropriations Committees of both branches can change programs by not approving funds or by issuing reports that tell agencies precisely what to do . . . The jurisdictional authority of individual committees is often not clearly differentiated: the Appropriations and Government Operations Committees, the House Rules Committee, and the Joint Economic Committee all have virtually universal scope in the matters they can consider. There is usually little cooperation between committees with the same jurisdiction in the two Houses.[49]

Since many of the crucial elements of an alliance policy cannot be implemented by the president without congressional acquiescence, the legislative branch plays a central role in alliance management. Congress can use its inherent powers, particularly those of ratifying treaties, making laws, and appropriating money, to constrain security partnerships initiated by the executive branch. It can refuse to formalize an alliance, eschew the provision of military and economic subvention to alliance partners, approve but later reduce the scope or amount of such subvention, and attach stringent behavioral conditions to its provision.

An administration's alliance policy can also be influenced by renegade actors within its own extensive executive bureaucracy. The proliferation since World War II of executive departments and agencies involved in the formulation and execution of foreign policy has multiplied the number of potential veto points at which dissenting bureaucratic actors can also frustrate the will of the White House.[50] As Krasner claims,

Within the executive branch, it cannot be assumed that the President can control all bureaus. Even here the state [which Krasner defines as "the President and those bureaus relatively insulated from societal pressures, which are the only institutions capable of formulating the national interest"] must struggle against the legislature and the private sector. Many presidential appointments are subject to ratification by the Senate. Budgets require legislative approval. The legal structures of many agencies reflect the desire of Congressional committees to maintain some formal control. Some agencies can get support from Congress against the preferences of the President. Many federal regulatory agencies are controlled by the groups that they are supposed to regulate.[51]

In sum, as Putnam relates, "the US separation of powers imposes a tighter constraint on the American win-set than is true in many other countries. This increases the bargaining power of American negotiators, but it also reduces the scope for international cooperation."[52]

The already prominent gap in win-sets between the United States and its allies of convenience should have been even further widened by the generation of substantial domestic political opposition to those alliances. As is likely to be the case with any dramatic, controversial, and potentially hazardous shift in foreign policy, an administration's initiation of security cooperation with a previously estranged ideological and geopolitical adversary will elicit considerable skepticism and resistance in Congress and among the executive bureaucracy and the general public. Opponents will protest that the United States should not align with a state that is not only a repressive dictatorship, but has also recently engaged in hostile foreign policy behavior toward the United States. As a result, opponents in Congress and the executive bureaucracy should have sought to prevent or restrict U.S. material cooperation with allies of convenience. This should have had the effect of even further reducing the negotiating autonomy of senior officials, compelling them to drive even harder bargains with those allies. Consequently, the United States should have frequently and effectively relied on a highly credible tied-hands negotiating posture toward allies of convenience (figure 1.2).

In this particular subset of cases, Schelling's and Putnam's admonition that a negotiator's relatively small win-set can just as readily result in bargaining miscarriage—due to involuntary defection—as bargaining success should not apply. As mentioned above, all of the United States' allies of

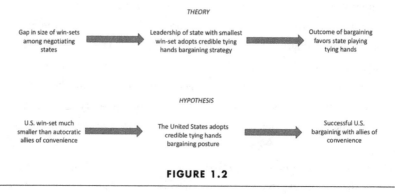

FIGURE 1.2

Tying-hands theory and hypothesis on U.S. bargaining with post-1945 allies of convenience

convenience have been far smaller powers that were located closer to the respective sources of shared threat and typically experienced an even more hostile relationship with the shared adversary than did the United States. As a result, they should have been extremely unlikely to defect from the alliance in order to avoid making concessions to Washington on disputed issues.

Although both neorealism and tying hands theory advance identical hypotheses on the outcome of U.S. bargaining with allies of convenience, they do so on the basis of discrete causal mechanisms. Neorealism predicts that favorable international systemic conditions produce U.S. bargaining success. Thus, during process-tracing of individual cases, a neorealist approach would expect policymakers to emphasize these structural advantages in their negotiations with allied representatives. By contrast, the identical tying hands prediction is premised on the United States' relatively narrow domestic win-set. That theory would therefore expect policymakers to emphasize their lack of domestic maneuverability during their negotiations with allied counterparts.

NEOCLASSICAL REALISM

I pit the neorealist and tying hands bargaining theories against a novel theory deriving from the increasingly prominent neoclassical realist research program in IR. The term neoclassical realism (NCR) was coined in a 1998 review article by Gideon Rose to categorize several recent books which explained great power foreign policy behavior by combining neorealism's theoretical parsimony and focus on the international systemic distribution of power with classical realism's multifarious insights into the effective conduct of statecraft.[53] According to Rose, neoclassical realists subscribe to the traditional realist assumptions that the international system is anarchic, the most important actors in the system are states, and states' foreign policy behavior is motivated primarily by the desire to promote national security by "seeking to control and shape their external environment."[54] On the basis of these assumptions, the paradigm's generic theoretical logic proceeds as follows:

> It explicitly incorporates both external and internal variables, updating and systematizing certain insights drawn from classical realist thought. Its adherents argue that the scope and ambition of a country's foreign policy is driven first and foremost by its place in the international system and specifically by its relative material capabilities. This is why they are realist. They argue further, however, that the impact of such power capabilities on foreign policy is indirect and complex, because systemic pressures must be translated through intervening variables at the unit level. This is why they are neoclassical.[55]

In contrast to neorealists, neoclassical realists interpose "an imperfect 'transmission belt' between [international] systemic incentives and constraints, on the one hand, and the actual diplomatic, military, and foreign economic policies states select, on the other."[56] International systemic variables may be compelling over the long term but over the short and medium term may be misperceived by foreign policymakers, or those policymakers may be prevented from adequately responding to them by domestic political obstacles. Alternatively, the international system may present ambiguous or otherwise indeterminate signals, necessitating the consideration of domestic political variables in order to explain the precise response that a given state adopts in response to them.[57]

A NEOCLASSICAL REALIST THEORY OF ALLIANCE BARGAINING

The neoclassical realist theory of alliance bargaining that is introduced and tested in this book represents both an extension of and alternative to the neorealist theory described above. The theory diverges from neorealism by maintaining that the outcome of bargaining among balancing allies will not always closely reflect the intra-alliance balances of dependence, commitment, and interest.[58] Even if these three international systemic variables align to favor a particular alliance member, that state's proclivity to exploit this advantage will additionally hinge on both the type of ally with which it is partnered and the degree of foreign policymaking autonomy possessed by its leaders.[59]

Alliance Types and Domestic Opposition

In accordance with neoclassical realism's stress on the primary causal role played by international systemic variables in foreign policy behavior, the theory begins with the presumption that the rising threat posed by a third-party adversary will put pressure on mutually threatened states to engage in security cooperation to balance against it. Importantly, however, not all prospective allies will be considered equally attractive. To paraphrase Glenn Snyder, a threatened state will be disposed to align with similarly threatened states that share its values and interests and extremely wary of joining with similarly threatened states that exhibit conflicting values and interests.[60] Thus, a threatened state will perceive special relationship allies that broadly share its ideological and geopolitical orientation as relatively friendly, trustworthy, reliable, and innocuous. Conversely, it will view allies of convenience that possess divergent ideological values and geopolitical interests as unfriendly, untrustworthy, unreliable, and dangerous. It will view ambivalent allies that manifest conflicting values or interests, but not both, as less benign than special relationship allies but more so than allies of convenience.

In any state, the most consequential national security decisions, including the formation and stewardship of military alliances, are made by the foreign

34

policy executive (FPE), defined as "the head of government and the ministers and officials charged with making foreign security policy."[61] Of all domestic actors, the FPE is uniquely capable of interpreting and pursuing the national interest, construed as the state's optimal response to the constellation of pressures and opportunities presented by the international system. This is due to its formal-legal position at the nexus of the domestic and international political systems, exclusive responsibility for the pursuit of interests that transcend those of any other substate actor, and possession of privileged information (i.e., intelligence) about the international system.[62]

Although the emergence of an overarching third-party threat should engender a modicum of domestic support for the FPE's establishment of a balancing alliance with any similarly endangered state, the relative breadth and depth of this support will nevertheless vary depending on the two security partners' ideological and geopolitical relationship. The formation of special relationship alliances should precipitate a low level of opposition, ambivalent alliances moderate opposition, and alliances of convenience high opposition. Alliance opponents will include hardliners who are against it entirely and urge its dissolution, as well as moderates who support the alliance but advocate a punitive and conditional bargaining strategy toward the ally in order to modify aspects of its foreign or domestic policy behavior or both.

The level of domestic opposition to the formation of a given alliance can be coded in the following manner. A low level of opposition should be characterized by consistently strong public support for the alliance, the absence of dissent from the alliance policy within the executive bureaucracy, and legislative efforts to constrain the alliance that are extremely rare, weakly supported, and mild in severity. A moderate level of opposition should be characterized by tepid public support for the alliance, occasional expressions of dissent from the alliance policy within the executive branch, and legislative efforts to constrain the alliance that are infrequent, erratically supported, and of varying severity. Finally, a high level of domestic opposition will be characterized by intense public opposition to the alliance, frequent expressions of dissent from the alliance policy in the executive branch, and legislative efforts to constrain the alliance that are frequent, widely supported, and severe.

Internal State Strength and the Task of Mobilizing Domestic Support for an Alliance

Notwithstanding its magnitude, domestic opposition to the formation of a balancing alliance will be relevant only if it is effectual in terms of its policymaking power. Several neoclassical realist scholars have identified "states' extractive and mobilization capacity as a crucial intervening variable between systemic imperatives and the actual foreign and defense policies states pursue."[63] In internally strong states, the FPE possesses substantial autonomy from other domestic actors and is thereby able to easily extract national resources in pursuit of its foreign policy goals. By contrast, in internally weak states the FPE possesses little policymaking autonomy from other domestic actors; this makes it difficult for leaders to extract national resources on behalf of their foreign policy objectives.[64]

NCR holds that the intensity and effectuality of domestic opposition to an alliance will modulate the inclination of the ally that is advantaged by the international system—as determined by the intra-alliance balances of dependence, commitment, and interests—to exploit this leverage to drive hard bargains with its partner. If domestic opposition to an alliance is low, ineffectual, or both, the FPE will be able to easily establish and formalize the alliance and extract military and economic resources on its behalf. Importantly, it will also therefore possess the autonomy to bargain *aggressively* with the systemically disadvantaged partner by deploying those resources or transferring them to the partner on a strictly conditional basis. An aggressive strategy requires that the FPE consistently provide accurate images to domestic audiences of both the partner's actual benignity (or lack thereof) and the extent of actual intra-alliance conflict or frictions.

At the tactical level, aggressive bargaining necessitates that the FPE articulate clear and extensive demands of the partner that adequately meet its preferences on the issues in dispute and threaten to impose commensurate punishments against the partner if it does not comply fully with those demands. Such threats may range from the nonexpansion of material subvention to the ally to the retraction of such subvention. If the partner fails to comply with the FPE's demands, the FPE must assay the extent of its noncompliance precisely and impose the threatened punishment(s) until the partner modifies its behavior. Since the FPE represents the systemically advantaged ally, this aggressive bargaining stance will typically result in successful bargaining with its (systemically disadvantaged) partner.

The first two NCR hypotheses stem from the relative ease of mobilizing domestic support for any alliance in an internally strong state and support for an uncontroversial alliance in an internally weak state, both of which dovetail with neorealism. First, *if the systemically advantaged ally is an internally strong state, irrespective of alliance type, it will bargain aggressively, and thereby successfully, with its systemically disadvantaged partner(s).* Because an internally strong state possesses considerable extractive autonomy, the FPE will be able to easily mobilize national material resources on behalf of the alliance, irrespective of the amount of domestic opposition the relationship engenders. Thus, it is immaterial whether the partner is a special relationship ally, ambivalent ally, or ally of convenience, as domestic opponents will be minimally capable of constraining or abrogating the alliance owing to their lack of policymaking power vis-à-vis the FPE. Since the FPE possesses an internally strong state and represents the ally that is advantaged by the international system, it will be able to freely manage its alliance with the systemically disadvantaged partner and be highly inclined to bargain aggressively with it, while the partner will be highly disposed to concede to its demands. Second, *if the systemically advantaged ally is an internally weak state, it will bargain aggressively, and thereby successfully, with its systemically disadvantaged partner if it is a special relationship ally.* Even if the internal state strength of the systemically advantaged ally is weak, its FPE will be able to readily exploit its favorable bargaining position to bargain tenaciously and successfully with its systemically disadvantaged partner because special relationships generate little, if any, domestic opposition.

The difficulties of mobilizing domestic support for a balancing alliance will be greater if the systemically favored ally is an internally weak state and the alliance in question is a more controversial alliance of convenience or ambivalent alliance. In the case of an alliance of convenience, domestic political opposition will be *both* high *and* effectual. For any given nation-state, an ally of convenience is simultaneously a friend and foe. It is a friend insofar as it is similarly endangered by an overarching third-party adversary and can meaningfully contribute toward the adversary's deterrence or defeat. At the same time, however, it is also an ideological and geopolitical rival that poses national security challenges in its own right. The optimal alliance strategy for the systemically advantaged ally of convenience is a carefully calibrated mix of inducements and punishments that is aimed at generating effective security cooperation with the partner against the enemy of the alliance while at the same time coercing it into making a series of concessions on disputed issues. Although the international systemic context is extremely auspicious for the FPE to manage the alliance of convenience by adopting an aggressive bargaining strategy toward its partner, if it possesses an internally weak state the domestic context will be extremely inauspicious for such a strategy. Domestic opposition will be both high and capable of easily constraining, crippling, or even terminating the alliance.

The FPE will experience enormous domestic political difficulties if it pursues an aggressive bargaining strategy toward an ally of convenience. This is because aggressive bargaining necessitates that the FPE convey to domestic audiences the true breadth and depth of its ongoing disputes with the ally. This lends credence to the arguments of domestic opponents of the alliance. In the public discourse pertaining to the alliance, the FPE will be at a fundamental disadvantage because an aggressive bargaining strategy entails projecting a complex image of the ally and the means required to deal successfully with it. The public message the FPE will inevitably send is confusing and difficult to justify: the ally is simultaneously a friendly state with which the more powerful nation must cooperate and a hostile state which it must reform by withholding or restricting cooperation. The former signal facilitates the FPE's efforts to extract domestic resources for the alliance, but undercuts its subsequent efforts to coerce the ally into making concessions. The latter facilitates the FPE's efforts to coerce the ally into making concessions but undercuts its efforts to extract domestic resources for the alliance.[65]

An aggressive bargaining strategy would inevitably bolster both hardline opponents, who seek the outright abrogation of the alliance, and moderate opponents, who seek to retract security assistance for the ally or attach stringent behavioral conditions to the provision of security assistance security to it. While it may appear at first glance that only the hardline opponents pose a danger to the alliance policy, in actuality the FPE will be at least as concerned about fanning the flames of moderate opponents. Although it ostensibly shares the general goals of the moderates, who support the alliance yet also seek to reform the behavior of the ally, it will be preoccupied with achieving the former aim and the moderate opposition with the latter. This is because the FPE bears exclusive responsibility for extracting domestic resources for the purpose of establishing and perpetuating the alliance, while moderate opponents have the luxury of focusing their attention and efforts on resolving particular conflicts with the ally that affect their more narrow-gauged interests and concerns. Thus, for the FPE in an internally weak state, any and all domestic opposition poses an acute danger of spiraling out of control and leading to the alliance's dissolution. From its vantage point, the imperative of effectively balancing against the third-party enemy must be fulfilled even if that comes at the expense of fulfilling the less urgent priority of resolving its ongoing disputes with the ally favorably. This means that the FPE's highest priority will be to maximize domestic support for the alliance policy. Andrew Moravcsik refers generically to this type of strategy as "cutting slack," which he defines as "the attempt to *expand* the domestic win-set to accommodate an international agreement that might otherwise be rejected."[66] This is the opposite of a tying hands strategy, which aims to either exploit a narrow domestic win-set or further shrink it in an effort to secure a favorable international agreement.

Instead of adopting an aggressive bargaining strategy that complicates the task of securing domestic legitimacy for the alliance, the FPE will prefer to adopt a passive strategy that facilitates it. The task of extracting national resources for the alliance will be eased if the FPE can purvey a consistently positive and reassuring image of both the ally and the alliance. To the extent that it can broadly persuade domestic audiences that the ally is friendly and benign and that the alliance relationship is characterized by comity rather than conflict, it will be able to marginalize domestic opponents. The problem with this strategy is that it is necessarily deceptive and misleading and prohibits the FPE from holding the ally scrupulously accountable for its misbehavior.[67]

A passive bargaining strategy that is aimed at projecting exaggerated images of allied benignity and of intra-alliance comity will entail the resort to one or more of the following political tactics. First, the FPE can exploit its privileged access to classified intelligence about the ally by ignoring, downplaying, or concealing evidence of the ally's misbehavior. If rival domestic actors such as the national legislature or media manage to acquire such evidence, the FPE's informational advantage and possession of the "bully pulpit" also enable it to authoritatively contest the embarrassing revelation(s).

Second, the FPE's formal position atop the executive branch of government also enables it to marginalize policy dissidents within the national security bureaucracy. Efforts by the FPE to project positive impressions of the ally and the alliance are highly likely to run afoul of officials within the bureaucracy who acquire evidence of the actual magnitude of the ally's misbehavior and possess an organizational or moral interest, or both, in curbing it. Senior officials can neutralize the adverse influence of these dissident bureaucrats in several ways. The head of state can rebuke or remove troublesome cabinet officials, agency heads, and other senior-level political appointees. Short of outright dismissal, the head of state and other members of the FPE can labor to weaken the influence of obstructive agency heads (or politically appointed senior bureaucrats) by, for instance, excluding them from important meetings and discussions relating to the alliance. Meanwhile, if the dissidents are permanent civil servants, members of the FPE can instruct their agency superiors to order or otherwise pressure them to desist.

Third, the FPE can oversell flimsy cosmetic concessions by the ally. As discussed above, an aggressive bargaining strategy necessitates that the systemically advantaged ally accurately acknowledge the extent to which the partner has acquiesced to its demands. This is because the latter can attempt to skirt those demands by rendering small-scale, symbolic, and easily retractable behavioral concessions that furnish the veneer of compliance yet are not indicative of a fundamental or lasting shift in its behavior. In such circumstances, as part of a passive bargaining strategy aimed primarily at shoring up domestic support for the alliance, the FPE can oversell the magnitude of the partner's concessions, portraying minor concessions as major ones.[68]

Fourth, the FPE can cynically extend secret concessions to the alliance partner to induce it to adopt a more outwardly supportive attitude toward the alliance. Ostensibly, the systemically advantaged ally should not have to make any concessions to the systemically disadvantaged partner. In light of the preoccupation of its senior leaders with fending off domestic opponents and critics of the alliance, however, it will be tempted to trade substantive concessions on disputed issues clandestinely for the partner's agreement to symbolically endorse the alliance relationship. The partner government can do this by issuing public statements of support for the alliance, agreeing to hold friendly bilateral summit meetings, and refraining from using disparaging and overly confrontational rhetoric that could be construed as embarrassing to the FPE of the systemically advantaged state. Related fifth and sixth tactics to which the FPE can resort are to either quietly backslide on prior threats to punish the partner for its misbehavior or beseech it to change its behavior in an exceedingly nonconfrontational manner that avoids threatening to impose serious retaliatory punishments if it fails to concede.

Seventh, since the FPE stands atop an internally weak state in which societal actors possess considerable influence over policymaking, it can actively promote the activities of private interest groups eager to maximize contacts with the allied state. Such groups will usually reflect narrow economic or ethno-nationalist interests, both of which share the aim of strengthening the alliance on an unconditional basis. Economic interests oppose any restrictions on contacts with the ally because the greater their access to the allied state's market for exports and investment, the more profit those groups will accrue. Similarly, ethno-national interests hold a deeply rooted identity-based attachment to the allied state, which will spur them to advocate unstinting support for the allied state. These groups can facilitate the extractive efforts of the FPE by vigorously combating the efforts of domestic opponents and critics to impose any constraints on the alliance.[69] The FPE will provide succor to these groups by publicly endorsing their activities and coordinating its own efforts to mobilize political support for the alliance with theirs. The obvious dilemma with this tactic is that the maximalist orientation of these pro-alliance private interest groups will only reinforce the FPE's temptation to bargain anemically with an ally of convenience.

NCR's third hypothesis is therefore that *if the systemically advantaged ally is an internally weak state, it will bargain passively, and thereby unsuccessfully, with its systemically disadvantaged partner if it is an ally of convenience*. Faced with the possibility that domestic opponents will cripple or even sever the alliance, the FPE of the systemically advantaged ally will adopt a passive bargaining strategy aimed primarily at bolstering the alliance's domestic legitimacy to keep it afloat in the face of the third-party enemy.

Finally, the advent of ambivalent alliances with ideological or geopolitical adversaries can be expected to engender greater domestic controversy than special relationship alliances, but not as much as alliances of convenience. If the systemically advantaged ally has an internally weak state, its FPE should be concerned, though not entirely preoccupied, with establishing sufficient domestic legitimacy for the alliance. It should therefore proceed to adopt a schizophrenic bargaining strategy characterized by alternating passive and aggressive postures toward the systemically disadvantaged partner. Either the FPE will bargain passively in some issue-areas but aggressively on others, or it will oscillate between passive and active stances in the same issue-area. This mixed strategy should produce mixed results, resulting in either thoroughgoing success in some intra-alliance disputes but failure in others or uniformly suboptimal, partially successful results in all disputes. Thus, the theory's fourth hypothesis is that *if the systemically advantaged ally is an internally weak state, it will bargain passive aggressively, and thereby with partial success, with its systemically disadvantaged partner if it is an ambivalent ally*.

Successful bargaining on the part of the systemically advantaged ally can occur only if it adopts a consistently aggressive bargaining posture, as predicted only by the first and second hypotheses.[70] If the FPE adopts a passive or passive-aggressive bargaining strategy, however, as predicted by the third and fourth hypotheses, it will, respectively, fully or partially constrict its ability to exact major concessions from an alliance partner on the basis of its favorable systemic position. This will inevitably produce bargaining outcomes that fall short of complete success. This is because even a minimally self-interested partner will avoid making costly concessions on salient national security issues unless the systemically advantaged ally scrutinizes its behavior carefully and punishes it consistently for defiance. If the latter adopts a passive strategy, the result will invariably be failed bargaining; if a passive-aggressive strategy, the result will be mixed. Consequently, whereas the first and second hypotheses dovetail with neorealism, the third and fourth hypotheses run contrary to the neorealist prediction that the systemically advantaged ally will always bargain successfully with its systemically disadvantaged partner. To summarize, the four NCR hypotheses are:

Hypothesis 1: If the systemically advantaged ally is an internally strong state, irrespective of alliance type it will bargain aggressively, and thereby successfully, with its systemically disadvantaged partner.

Hypothesis 2: If the systemically advantaged ally is an internally weak state, it will bargain aggressively, and thereby successfully, with its systemically disadvantaged partner if it is a special relationship ally.

Hypothesis 3: If the systemically advantaged ally is an internally weak state, it will bargain passively, and thereby unsuccessfully, with its systemically disadvantaged partner if it is an ally of convenience.

Hypothesis 4: If the systemically advantaged ally is an internally weak state, it will bargain passive aggressively, and thereby with partial success, with its systemically disadvantaged ally if it is an ambivalent ally.

These propositions comport with the belief generally shared by classical realists, and assimilated by a number of neoclassical realists, that internally weak states, typically democracies, operate at a disadvantage in foreign policy relative to internally strong states, typically autocracies.[71] This general skepticism about the capacity of democratic governments to play the game of power politics as shrewdly and effectively as their autocratic counterparts differentiates classical and neoclassical realists from tying hands theorists, who propose that democratic regimes will frequently exploit their relative lack of autonomy from domestic political pressures and opinion to drive hard bargains at the negotiating table with their autocratic interlocutors.

NEOCLASSICAL REALIST HYPOTHESIS ON U.S. BARGAINING WITH POST-1945 ALLIES OF CONVENIENCE

NCR predicts that the United States, an internally weak state, should have squandered its favorable international systemic position vis-à-vis its post-1945 allies of convenience by bargaining passively, and consequently unsuccessfully, with them (NCR Hypothesis 3). The same domestic political structure that affords the United States a relatively small win-set in international negotiations also presents especially formidable obstacles to U.S. leaders intent on allying with an ideological and geopolitical adversary. Whereas Schelling and Putnam focus on the foreign policy advantages bestowed by the internal "weakness" of the American state, Krasner more pessimistically holds that it ensures that attempts by U.S. leaders to extract resources for foreign policy can be easily frustrated by opposing forces within the polity. Thus, "in trying to promote the national interest, the American state often confronts dissident bureaus, a recalcitrant Congress, and powerful private actors."[72] The relative permeability of democratic states to private pressures renders them "weaker" than autocracies in their ability to mobilize internal resources and the exceptionally high level of permeability of the American state arguably renders it particularly weak. The FPE in the United States possesses "relatively little command of material resources . . . that can be used to offer incentives or to make threats [to glean the support of other domestic actors]."[73]

The decisions by post–World War II U.S. administrations to establish alliances of convenience should have generated intense, widespread, and effectual domestic opposition. Confronted in each instance by strong public disapproval of the alliance and persistent efforts by legislative and bureaucratic critics to bridle or scuttle it, the FPE should have been compelled to adopt a passive bargaining strategy toward its alliance partner. In order to cast favorable and reassuring images of the ally to domestic audiences, the FPE should have adopted at least some of the following tactics: ignoring, downplaying, or concealing evidence of the partner's misbehavior; marginalizing dissident voices in the national security bureaucracy; overselling symbolic or tactical behavioral concessions by the ally; making secret gratuitous concessions to the ally to induce it to adopt a more outwardly

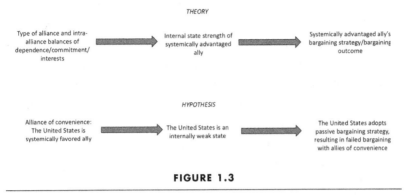

THEORY

Type of alliance and intra-alliance balances of dependence/commitment/interests ⟹ Internal state strength of systemically advantaged ally ⟹ Systemically advantaged ally's bargaining strategy/bargaining outcome

HYPOTHESIS

Alliance of convenience: The United States is systemically favored ally ⟹ The United States is an internally weak state ⟹ The United States adopts passive bargaining strategy, resulting in failed bargaining with allies of convenience

FIGURE 1.3

Neoclassical realist theory of alliance bargaining and hypothesis on U.S. bargaining with post-1945 allies of convenience

supportive attitude toward the alliance; backsliding on prior threats to punish the partner's noncompliance; beseeching the partner to modify its behavior in an exceedingly nonconfrontational manner; or promoting the activities of private interest groups eager to maximize contacts with the allied state. In so doing, the FPE should have forfeited its capacity to secure major concessions from the partner, resulting in U.S. bargaining failure (figure 1.3).

RESEARCH DESIGN

In the next three chapters, I test the rival neorealist, tying hands, and neoclassical realist hypotheses in a set of historical case studies drawn from the universe of twenty-one U.S. alliances of convenience spanning the years 1945 to 2015. In all of these cases, neorealism and tying hands theories uniformly predict successful U.S. bargaining with its allies, while NCR predicts uniformly passive and failed U.S. bargaining. I subject three of these alliances to detailed historical process-tracing: (1) the alliance with the People's Republic of China against the Soviet Union (1971–89); (2) the alliance with Pakistan against the Soviet Union in Afghanistan (1981–88); and (3) the alliance with Iraq against Iran (1982–88).[74]

I chose these three cases from the larger universe for several reasons. A central role was played in all of them by hardline Republican presidents whose national security credentials were widely considered to be domestically unimpeachable. Since the early years of the Cold War, Republicans have generally been perceived by the U.S. public to be more reliable and trustworthy on matters of national security and defense than Democrats.[75] Ronald Reagan, inarguably the most hawkish of America's Cold War presidents, was commander-in-chief for the entirety of the U.S.-Pakistan and U.S.-Iraq cases. He was also president for eight of the eighteen years of the U.S.-China case, while another hardline Republican anticommunist, Richard Nixon, was president for the first four years of that alliance, totaling a majority of twelve of the alliance's eighteen years. Meanwhile, of the three major national security–related disputes that emerged between the United States and China over the course of that alliance, two were managed exclusively by the Nixon and Reagan administrations.[76] Because hardline Republican administrations were in office for the entirety of two alliances and accounted for most of the bargaining with the ally in the third, these constitute what Harry Eckstein referred to as "crucial" cases because they were "least likely" from the vantage point of neoclassical realist theory.[77] Reagan and Nixon should have been the post-1945 presidents most highly insulated from domestic opposition to the formation and maintenance of alliances of convenience with hostile autocracies. If even these administrations nevertheless proved susceptible to the domestic political pressures identified by the theory, and vulnerable to the pathological bargaining behaviors resulting from them, this should indicate strong confirmatory evidence for the theory.[78]

These three cases are also crucial insofar as they are "most likely" from the perspective of both neorealism and tying hands. In each of the three alliances, the ally of convenience, but not the United States, was either directly engaged in military hostilities with the shared adversary (Pakistan, Iraq) or had recently engaged in war with the adversary and was on the cusp of a reignited conflict (China). For both theories, the allies' embroilment in ongoing or recent military hostilities with the shared enemy only enhanced a marked U.S. bargaining advantage. For neorealism, this added to an already lopsided balance of dependence that grossly favored the United

States due to its allies' relative military and economic weakness and closer proximity to the source of the shared threat.[79] Meanwhile, from the vantage point of tying hands theory, because each ally was engaged in a state of ongoing or recent (and possibly imminent) war with the shared adversary, they could not as credibly threaten to defect from their alliance with the United States and bandwagon with the shared adversary.

These cases were lengthy in duration, spanning seven years (U.S.-Iraq), eight years (U.S.-Pakistan), and eighteen years (U.S.-China). This allows for the collection of many observations of the posited causal dynamics of each of the three contending theories.[80] Related to the previous point, empirical research into all three cases benefits considerably from extensive declassified government document collections that have been made available by the George Washington University's Digital National Security Archive.[81]

These cases evince considerable variation in both the allied regime type and the object of the alliance. Although all three allies were autocratic, they differed widely in their political orientations. The People's Republic of China under Mao Zedong and Deng Xiaoping was a communist dictatorship, Saddam Hussein's Ba'athist regime in Iraq espoused a left-wing Arab nationalist ideology, and Zia ul-Haq's putschist regime in Pakistan had a conservative theocratic bent. The three alliances of convenience also varied in terms of their shared adversary: while the U.S.-China and U.S.-Pakistan alliances were directed against the Soviet Union, a global superpower, the U.S.-Iraq alliance was directed against revolutionary Iran, a nonaligned small power. Since Iran posed an existential threat to neighboring Iraq but little danger to the United States, this case should have been an even more likely one for neorealist theory than the China and Pakistan cases.

As chapters 2 through 4 demonstrate, each of the three cases strongly validates the NCR prediction of passive and failed U.S. bargaining while undercutting the neorealist and tying hands prediction of (aggressive and) successful U.S. bargaining. Domestic opposition to each alliance was high, and repeated efforts were initiated by dissidents in both the executive bureaucracy and Congress to inhibit or derail them. In response, the FPE (which in the U.S.-China case transcended a single administration) strove to maximize domestic legitimacy and support for the alliance by adopting at least some of the seven specified tactics associated with a passive bargaining strategy. Across the three cases, the FPE adopted all of these tactics. On all major national security disputes with each of the three allies—three with China, one with Pakistan, and two with Iraq—the United States failed abjectly to secure outcomes that more closely met its preferences than those of its ally.

In the book's concluding chapter, I supplement these full-fledged case studies with a brief survey of the U.S. alliance of convenience with Libya following the September 11, 2001 Al Qaeda terrorist attacks against New York and Washington, DC. I include this mini-case because it is the exception that proves the neoclassical realist rule that systemically advantaged but internally weak states will bargain passively and unsuccessfully with allies of convenience. As the United States and Libya engaged in close cooperation to counter Al Qaeda, the George W. Bush administration struck a surprisingly aggressive and successful bargaining posture toward the regime of Mu'ammar Gaddhafi on the matters of Libyan restitution for past sponsorship of terrorism and its ongoing proliferation of chemical and nuclear weapons. I contend that this anomalous outcome can be explained within the parameters of NCR: the White House was able to negotiate effectively with Gaddhafi only because the U.S.-Libya alliance was narrowly focused on clandestine intelligence cooperation, and therefore the relationship was completely shielded from domestic political opposition.[82]

AVOIDING SELECTION BIAS: EXAMINING U.S. BARGAINING WITH A SPECIAL RELATIONSHIP ALLY

Even if the record of U.S. bargaining with post-1945 allies of convenience supports the neoclassical realist hypothesis of passive and failed U.S. bargaining, doubts will remain about the theory's persuasiveness. By testing the theory exclusively in cases of alliances of convenience, the research design falls victim to selection bias by selecting on a single value of the dependent variable.[83] By examining only cases of passive and failed U.S. alliance bargaining, I cannot establish that the causal variables identified by neoclassical realism (namely, the magnitude and effectuality of domestic opposition to the alliance in the systemically advantaged ally) actually co-vary with the outcomes they predict (the bargaining strategy adopted by that ally and its consequent success or failure). This leaves the theory vulnerable to the charge that its seemingly supportive empirical results are spurious.

In order to avert this pitfall, I include a fourth case study that establishes the covariation needed to perform a more robust test of the theory. According to Hypothesis 2, if the systemically advantaged ally has an internally weak state but enters into a special relationship alliance, then it will bargain aggressively and successfully with its partner. Even though the FPE of the advantaged ally presides over a political system in which it possesses little policymaking autonomy, it will nevertheless encounter minimal domestic opposition to its formation of a special relationship alliance with a partner that is neither an ideological nor a geopolitical adversary. Consequently, it will not be compelled to adopt a passive bargaining strategy in order to extract the national resources needed to maintain the alliance. Assured of solid domestic support, the FPE will be able to freely exploit its favorable international systemic position to adopt an aggressive bargaining posture toward the special relationship ally, resulting in successful bargaining.[84]

A case study of the United States bargaining with its archetypal special relationship ally, the United Kingdom, during the Korean War (1950–1953) serves to test this antipodal proposition. I chose this case for two principal reasons. First, during the period spanning the Korean War, U.S. and British leaders differed on several issues related to the prosecution of both the "hot war" on the Korean Peninsula and the burgeoning "Cold War" against the Soviet Union. Thus, the case contains a substantial number of observations of intra-alliance bargaining. Second, it constitutes a least likely one for neoclassical realism owing to the prevailing international systemic and domestic political conditions during the war. From the international systemic vantage point, Britain was less dependent on the United States than all of Washington's other allies and the United States was firmly committed, in both the contractual and inherent senses, to the defense of the United Kingdom. From a domestic political perspective, the case was also least likely because for most of the Korean War (June 1950–January 1953), the United States was led by Democratic president

Harry S. Truman, whose administration became increasingly unpopular as the war dragged on. As a result, the administration should have been highly motivated to bargain passively with Britain in order to insulate the relationship from domestic critics. The findings of the case nevertheless validate the neoclassical realist prediction of aggressive and successful U.S. bargaining with the United Kingdom. It demonstrates that the alliance with London produced minimal domestic opposition, which freed both the Truman and Eisenhower administrations to adopt a highly aggressive and uniformly successful bargaining strategy with Whitehall on all salient national security disputes.[85]

2

THE U.S. ALLIANCE WITH
THE PEOPLE'S REPUBLIC OF CHINA,
1971–1989

V. Nam:

1. We are ending our involvement—

2. We had hoped you would help—but now it doesn't matter

3. We must end it honorably— + will.

—PRESIDENT RICHARD M. NIXON'S HANDWRITTEN NOTES IN ANTICIPATION OF

HIS FORTHCOMING MEETING WITH CHINESE PRIME MINISTER ZHOU ENLAI,

DRAFTED TWO DAYS BEFORE HE DEPARTED ON HIS LANDMARK TRIP TO

CHINA ON FEBRUARY 17, 1972. QUOTED IN JAMES MANN, *ABOUT

FACE: A HISTORY OF AMERICA'S CURIOUS RELATIONSHIP WITH

CHINA, FROM NIXON TO CLINTON*

THE UNITED STATES' relationship with the People's Republic of China (PRC) during the 1970s and 1980s stands as both the least likely and most consequential of its post-1945 alliances of convenience. Following the victory of Mao Zedong's Chinese Communist Party (CCP) in the Chinese civil war in 1949, relations between the United States and its former World War II ally descended rapidly into deep antagonism and hostility. For American leaders, the "loss" of China tipped the precarious balance of power in the burgeoning Cold War between the United States and the Soviet Union in Moscow's favor. By the mid-1960s, Mao's revolutionary fervor and foreign policy adventurism had actually convinced many officials that China posed an even greater danger to America's national security than the Soviet Union itself. By the time that Richard Nixon entered the White House in 1969, however, the tectonic plates of international geopolitics had shifted dramatically. A resurgent Soviet Union achieved strategic nuclear parity with a flagging United States that was still mired in a stalemated war in Vietnam. Meanwhile, Moscow's relationship with the PRC had deteriorated so precipitously that the two communist giants were engaging in military hostilities along the eastern fringe of the expansive Sino-Soviet border. These developments generated a powerful impetus for the United States and China to reach out to one another across a gulf of mutual mistrust and hostility that had previously appeared insurmountable. As Prime Minister Zhou Enlai remarked to Nixon at the outset of the president's momentous February 1972 trip to Beijing, "Your handshake came over the vastest ocean in the world—twenty-five years of no communication."[1]

Five successive presidential administrations—four Republican and one Democratic—managed an increasingly robust if informal alliance of convenience with China that effectively counterbalanced the Soviet Union. Although this cooperation was halted in the wake of the Chinese government's infamous 1989 crackdown on pro-democracy demonstrators in Beijing's Tiananmen Square, within months the Soviet empire in Eastern Europe collapsed. Even as the two unlikely allies worked to contain Soviet expansionism during the 1970s and 1980s, the alliance was riven by several crucial disputes. First, no meaningful improvement in Sino-U.S. relations could transpire absent some negotiated agreement on the smoldering irredentist dispute between the PRC and America's formal treaty ally of Taiwan, both of which claimed sovereignty over the whole of China. The Taiwan question overshadowed the Sino-U.S. alliance from its advent in 1971 until the two countries signed a joint communiqué in August 1982 that temporarily eased tensions across the Taiwan Strait. Second, in 1971 and 1972, the Nixon administration desperately sought China's help to pressure the communist government of North Vietnam into accepting a peace deal with Washington to end the Vietnam War. Third, during the 1980s, the Reagan administration strove to curb China's sale of nuclear weapons–related technologies to Pakistan, antiship missiles to Iran, and ballistic missiles to Saudi Arabia, Syria, Pakistan, and Libya.

Both the neorealist and two-level games theories predict relatively aggressive and successful U.S. bargaining with the Chinese on all three issues. From the vantage point of neorealist theory, this is because the intra-alliance balance of dependence and commitment strongly favored the United States. Meanwhile, according to tying hands theory, the liberal democratic United States possessed a far weaker state and therefore, a much smaller domestic win-set than China, which was a totalitarian communist autocracy. This disparity should have been exacerbated by considerable opposition to improved relations with the PRC—and concomitant downgrading of relations with Taiwan—in the U.S. Congress and executive branch and among the general public. By contrast, neoclassical realist theory predicts passive and failed U.S. bargaining with China. The extractive weakness of the U.S. state, compounded by heavy domestic opposition to security cooperation with the People's Republic, should have compelled senior officials to strive mightily to cut domestic slack for the tenuous alliance policy, in the process allowing Beijing to attain much of what it wanted in its disputes with the United States.

Across all three issue-areas, the behavior of U.S. administrations from Nixon to Reagan (the Tiananmen Square uprising occurred less than six months after George H. W. Bush took office) closely matched the neoclassical realist hypothesis. Senior White House, State Department, and Pentagon officials' profound fear that domestic opponents might upset the burgeoning alliance led them to minimize conflicts between the two allies and project a deceptive and misleading image of Chinese cooperativeness. Specifically, they did so by ignoring, downplaying, and concealing evidence of Chinese misbehavior; overselling cosmetic Chinese concessions; marginalizing dissident voices in the executive branch; making gratuitous secret concessions to China; beseeching Chinese concessions in an exceedingly nonconfrontational manner; and relying on the actions of private interests eager to maximize economic contacts with the PRC. Ultimately these efforts helped prevent the alliance from being subverted by domestic opponents, but did so at the expense of sacrificing U.S. goals relating to Taiwan, Vietnam, and nonproliferation of nuclear weapons and missiles.

THE U.S. ALLIANCE OF CONVENIENCE
WITH CHINA, 1971–1989

SOURCES OF IDEOLOGICAL AND
GEOPOLITICAL ANTAGONISM

The Sino-U.S. relationship from the early 1970s to the late 1980s can be considered an alliance of convenience because the two states were both ideological and geopolitical adversaries and their leaders perceived the Soviet Union as an overarching national security threat. At the outset of the alliance, the ideological divide between the two states was yawning. Politically, whereas the United States was a liberal democracy, China was an extraordinarily repressive communist autocracy.[2] Over the course of the alliance, the PRC fell under the personalist rule of two men, Mao Zedong and Deng Xiaoping. Mao, who led China from the CCP's 1949 triumph in the Chinese civil war until his death in September 1976, established a totalitarian dictatorship that was based on a carefully crafted personality cult. Mao was a devout revolutionary whose ardor was reflected in repeated efforts to mobilize the country behind massive campaigns of economic collectivization in the late 1950s ("the Great Leap Forward") and political indoctrination in the mid to late 1960s ("the Cultural Revolution"), which caused the deaths of millions of Chinese citizens.[3] Following Mao's death, the ideological gulf between the United States and China narrowed to some extent. Mao's handpicked successor, Hua Guofeng, held the reins of power only briefly before he was dislodged in 1977 by the dynamic and visionary Deng Xiaoping, who soon began instituting an ambitious program of liberalizing economic reforms.[4] Although he also tempered some of the egregiously totalitarian elements of Mao's regime, Deng remained steadfastly committed to the retention of an authoritarian political system based on firm one-party rule, as evidenced most dramatically in his brutal suppression of the pro-democracy demonstrations in 1989.[5]

By the early 1970s, the Sino-American relations were also roiled by multiple geopolitical conflicts. Most fundamentally, Mao's 1949 victory in the Chinese revolution moved China out of the U.S. camp in the burgeoning

Cold War, a shift that led one year later to China's entry into the Korean War in opposition to the U.S.-led United Nations coalition. For the first decade after the revolution, Mao allied closely with the Soviet Union, a grand strategic orientation he referred to as "leaning to one side."[6] By 1959, however, Sino-Soviet military cooperation began to stall when the Kremlin reneged on an agreement to provide Beijing with advanced military and nuclear technologies. The consequent rift eventually deepened into a split as Moscow became increasingly enraged by China's refusal to follow the Soviet lead on various political, ideological, and economic matters and Mao became more and more resentful of Soviet efforts to subordinate China's interests to those of Moscow.[7]

Even though China's alignment with the Soviet Union fractured over the course of the 1960s, there was no concomitant thaw in its relations with the United States, in part because two other lingering sources of geopolitical friction between the two states remained unresolved. The first of these was Taiwan. After Mao's CCP overthrew China's Nationalist government in October 1949, ousted Chinese president Chiang Kai-shek and his compatriots fled across the Taiwan Strait to regroup and plot their return to the mainland. Immediately following North Korea's invasion of South Korea the next year, President Harry Truman ordered the U.S. Seventh Fleet into the Taiwan Strait to deter a PRC invasion of Taiwan. Soon thereafter, Washington began dispensing military assistance to Chiang's regime and in 1954, the Eisenhower administration concluded a mutual defense treaty with Chiang's Republic of China (ROC) and adopted the position that China's legal status was undetermined.[8] The PRC tested this commitment in 1954–1955 and again in 1958 when it shelled the Quemoy-Matsu island chain just offshore Taiwan.[9] Over the course of the next decade, Taiwan served as a key base for U.S. military operations during the Vietnam War. Between 1964 and 1970, America's military presence there grew from one thousand troops to ten thousand.[10]

The growing U.S. military presence in Taiwan only added to Mao's already strong motivation to support the communist Democratic Republic of Vietnam (DRV), or North Vietnam, in its ongoing war against the Republic of Vietnam (RVN), or South Vietnam, which was allied with the United States. After Washington began to take a more active and direct role in the conflict in late 1964, Beijing began transferring MiG-15 and MiG-17 fighter jets to the DRV, training North Vietnamese fighter pilots, and constructing supply and repair stations in Chinese territory along the border with North Vietnam. In 1965, as the number of U.S. troops in South Vietnam swelled from 23,000 to 184,500, Mao also began reluctantly allowing Soviet arms shipments to the DRV to be transported through Chinese territory. In December of that year, China signed a military assistance treaty with North Vietnam, which triggered Mao's deployment of hundreds of thousands of People's Liberation Army (PLA) soldiers into DRV territory.[11] China's staunch support for Hanoi placed it in direct opposition to the United States, which was determined to help noncommunist South Vietnam prevail in its war of survival against North Vietnam and its insurgent faction operating in the South, the National Liberation Front.

THE OVERARCHING SOVIET THREAT

During the 1960s, the already high level of mutual antagonism between the United States and China actually increased. Despite clear signs of discord between the PRC and Soviet Union in the early part of the decade, the Democratic administrations of John F. Kennedy and Lyndon Johnson concluded that, although China was much weaker than the USSR, it represented the "more aggressive and dangerous adversary."[12] Both administrations contemplated military action, perhaps even in collusion with the Kremlin, to attack China's nuclear installations.[13] Meanwhile, although China's alliance with the Soviet Union was deteriorating steadily, Mao adopted a "dual adversary" grand strategy that viewed the United States and Soviet Union as equally dangerous security threats.[14]

By the decade's end, however, leaders in both Washington and Beijing began to perceive the Soviet Union as the foremost danger to their respective states. For the former, the shift in threat perception was driven primarily by rapid growth in the Soviet strategic nuclear arsenal. By the time that Richard Nixon entered office in early 1969, the Soviets had surpassed the United States in total number of deployed land-based intercontinental ballistic missiles (ICBMs). Although Moscow continued to field fewer submarine-launched ballistic missiles (SLBMs) and nuclear-armed bombers, the aggregate disparity in the size of the two rivals' nuclear arsenals had dwindled from a four-to-one gap favoring the United States in 1964 to two-to-one.[15] Although the 1972 Strategic Arms Limitation Treaty (SALT) imposed quantitative limits on both superpowers' deployment of nonmobile land-based ICBMs, SLBMs, and nuclear-armed submarines, the Kremlin nevertheless continued to deploy ICBMs with heavy payloads that would be useful only for counterforce purposes (i.e., a surprise first strike against U.S. land-based missiles).[16] In terms of conventional military capabilities, by the early 1970s the Soviets had not only increased their quantitative superiority over the United States in tanks, armor, artillery, and total military personnel, but also reduced the gap favoring the United States in total number of both naval and air forces.[17] Finally, during the early 1970s, the Nixon administration became extremely concerned about Soviet adventurism in the underdeveloped world, particularly in the volatile and geopolitically crucial Middle East region. Massive Soviet transfers of cutting-edge weaponry to Egypt and Syria set the stage for their joint surprise attack against Israel in October 1973.[18]

By the end of the 1960s the Kremlin had also substantially expanded its military presence along the Sino-Soviet and Soviet-Mongolian borders and bolstered its naval presence in the Pacific.[19] Less than a year after Soviet forces invaded neighboring Czechoslovakia in the summer of 1968 in order to forestall that country's defection from the Eastern Bloc, Soviet and Chinese frontier units clashed on remote Zhenbao Island on the frozen Ussuri River dividing northeast China from eastern Siberia.[20] Although a September 11 cease-fire brought an end to the fighting on Zhenbao, tensions along the border continued to rise. Mere weeks later, the Chinese conducted two hydrogen bomb tests, to which Moscow responded by both conducting offensive military exercises directed at the PRC and moving nuclear-tipped medium-range ballistic missiles to the shared border. For the entirety of the next decade, Chinese troops "undertook extensive defensive exercises targeted toward a potential Soviet attack."[21]

ELEMENTS OF THE U.S.–PRC ALLIANCE
OF CONVENIENCE

Even prior to the establishment of high-level diplomatic contacts between the United States and China, the Nixon administration began to assist the People's Republic by attempting to deter the Soviet invasion that Mao and his coterie acutely feared. After the outbreak of the Ussuri River skirmish, Nixon instructed Secretary of State William Rogers, Secretary of Defense Melvin Laird, and Director of Central Intelligence Richard Helms to spread the word that the administration would not allow the Red Army to "smash" China.[22]

In 1971 and 1972, successive visits to China by National Security Advisor Henry Kissinger and President Nixon laid the groundwork for the alliance. During his secret trip to Beijing on July 9–11, 1971, which was intended to discuss a prospective presidential-level summit the next year, Kissinger provided Chinese premier Zhou Enlai with a "full intelligence briefing on the array of Soviet forces along the Chinese border."[23] During a follow-up trip in October, Kissinger furnished additional intelligence to Chinese leaders, including communications intercepts and high-resolution satellite photographs. He also promised Zhou that the White House would inform China about any understandings it reached with the Soviets that impinged on Beijing's interests.[24] Nixon affirmed this pledge in writing and expanded its scope to encompass understandings reached "with other Socialist countries [i.e., Eastern Europe and North Vietnam]."[25] In February 1972, the potent signal conveyed to Moscow of the U.S. president travelling to Beijing to confer with Chinese leaders, including Mao himself, was reinforced by the admonitory wording of the summit's final communiqué, which declared that the United States and China would oppose the efforts of any country to establish "hegemony" in the Asia-Pacific region.[26]

In the aftermath of Nixon's China trip, the White House took several additional steps to bolster China's security vis-à-vis the Soviets. Acting on Kissinger's private depiction of the post-summit bilateral relationship as one in which "we have now become tacit allies,"[27] in March 1973 Nixon sent Mao a letter affirming that China's territorial integrity represented a "fundamental element" of U.S. foreign policy, and that the "viability and independence of China" was necessary for world peace. Soon thereafter, Kissinger elaborated on the president's letter in a meeting in New York with PRC foreign minister Huang Hua, asserting that the "United States would consider any threat to the integrity of the PRC as incompatible with its own interests and with the interests of world peace," notably adding that this was "an American decision and without a request for reciprocity."[28] In June, while General Secretary Leonid Brezhnev was in Washington, DC for a summit with Nixon, both Nixon and Kissinger repeatedly briefed China's new liaison chief in Washington, Huang Zhen, on their secret discussions with the Soviet leader. Later that summer, Kissinger also told Huang that the White House had privately assured the British and French governments that it would not oppose their sale of modern jet engines and nuclear technology to China.[29] After Nixon resigned the presidency in disgrace in 1974, his successor, Gerald Ford, acquiesced to China's purchase of $200 million worth of U.S.-made jet engines from the United Kingdom for use in its fighter bombers. Ford allowed the transaction to bypass COCOM (Coordinating Committee for Multilateral Export Controls), the committee comprising the NATO members and Japan that was responsible for controlling exports of dual-use technologies to the communist bloc. Just after Mao's death in September 1976, Ford additionally permitted the direct sale to China of two advanced Cyber 72 computers, which had military applications.[30]

Although Democratic president Jimmy Carter initially hewed to a careful policy of "evenhandedness"[31] in high-technology exports to both the USSR and China after entering the White House in early 1977, his administration occasionally nodded in the direction of enhanced military contacts with China. During a visit to Beijing in May 1978, Carter's National Security Advisor Zbigniew Brzezinski went beyond the Nixon administration's declaration that the United States did not want to see China defeated in a war against the Soviets, instead professing that Washington desired nothing less than a "strong and secure China."[32] In addition, the White House approved the export of infrared airborne geological survey equipment to China and allowed France to sell China a nuclear reactor containing several components that were manufactured in the United States. Further, it announced publicly that it would not object to arms sales to China by fellow NATO states.[33] In January 1979, the administration formally normalized diplomatic relations with the People's Republic, and the next month, the president authorized Brzezinski to initiate "special negotiations" with Chinese leaders to expand bilateral defense cooperation.[34] The next month, after China invaded Soviet-backed Vietnam, Brzezinski met almost nightly with China's newly installed ambassador to the United States, Chai Zemin, during the brief conflict to provide the CCP with the latest satellite intelligence on Soviet deployments near China.[35]

The Soviet invasion of Afghanistan in late December 1979 prompted Carter to scrap his evenhandedness policy. Within days of the invasion, Carter dispatched Harold Brown to Beijing, marking the first-ever trip to the People's Republic by a U.S. defense secretary. Brown conveyed to China's leaders that Carter had decided to authorize the sale of nonlethal military equipment to the PRC on a case-by-case basis.[36] This directive afforded the Chinese government access to several items that would prove integral to the modernization of the People's Liberation Army, especially "a ground station to receive data from Landsat satellites, transport aircraft, military helicopters, and communications equipment."[37] While in Beijing, Brown's delegation also provided Chinese leaders with a full intelligence briefing on Soviet deployments near China and the two governments agreed to begin regular exchanges of high-level military officials and working-level military delegations. Chinese leader Deng Xiaoping also proposed to Brown that the two countries cooperate to "turn Afghanistan into a quagmire for the Soviets."[38] This proposal yielded an arrangement maintained over the course of the next decade whereby the Central Intelligence Agency purchased Chinese-made light arms, which were then shipped to Pakistan for distribution to the Afghan rebels fighting the Red Army. Reciprocally, the Chinese agreed to provide the insurgents with U.S.-made Stinger shoulder-launched antiaircraft missiles, as well as to send mules packed with small arms into Afghanistan via the Karakoram Highway.[39] In the months that followed Brown's visit to China, the Pentagon and CIA began airlifting equipment to construct two sophisticated electronic listening posts in western China to replace similar installations in Iran that had had to be abandoned after that country's recent revolution.[40]

Bilateral defense cooperation reached its zenith during Ronald Reagan's administration. Although Reagan was vociferously anticommunist and an ardent supporter of Taiwan, soon after entering the Oval Office he became persuaded of China's geopolitical utility vis-à-vis the Soviets. A 1981 Defense Department memo laid this bare: "The Chinese tie down 47 [Soviet Red Army] Divisions along the 3,000 mile Sino-Mongolian-Soviet border. About 25% of the Soviet defense effort, or $40 billion annually, is devoted to counter the direct Chinese threat."[41] In June 1981, Reagan signed a directive establishing a "two-times" technology transfer policy for China, meaning that the administration would begin approving high-technology exports for China at levels of technological sophistication that were twice as high as those that had been permitted for the USSR prior to the Carter administration's imposition of sanctions against the Soviets in retaliation for the Red Army's invasion of Afghanistan.[42] In May 1983, the administration proceeded to classify China as a "friendly non-allied country," thereby moving it into the category of states that was subject to the least stringent restrictions on technology transfer.[43] The next year, the White House made China eligible to purchase weapons directly from the U.S. government, albeit on a cash-only basis, via the Foreign Military Sales program. Finally, between 1985 and 1987, the United States and the rest of COCOM loosened the organization's restrictions on exports to China.[44] The only hiccup in this process occurred in October 1987, when (as discussed in further detail below) the State Department desisted temporarily from further loosening technology transfer restrictions in response to China's sale of antiship missiles to Iran.[45]

By the time Reagan left office in January 1989, bilateral trade in high technology and arms was soaring. The dollar value of U.S. exports of high-technology goods to China had ballooned from $630 million in 1982 to $1.7 billion in 1988, while the dollar value of U.S. export licenses approved for China similarly grew from $500 million to $2.9 billion over the same period. Also, between 1981 and 1989 the value of U.S. arms sales to China grew from $0 to $106.2 million.[46] Among the more noteworthy weapons systems exported to the PRC were twenty-four Sikorski S-70 helicopters, five

General Electric LM-2500 gas turbine engines for two naval destroyers, six Boeing Chinook helicopters, AN/TPQ-37 artillery-locating radars, avionics equipment to modernize fifty F-8 interceptor aircraft (the so-called Peace Pearl program), Hughes I-TOW antitank and I-HAWK antiair missiles, Mark-46 Mod 2 antisubmarine warfare torpedoes, Phalanx close-in weapons systems, and the Large Caliber-Ammunition Modernization Program.[47]

The alliance of convenience ended almost instantaneously following the Deng regime's violent suppression of pro-democracy demonstrations in Tiananmen Square in June 1989. In response, President George H. W. Bush suspended all arms sales to the PRC and introduced a moratorium on high-level bilateral military exchanges. Two weeks later, he authorized a second tranche of sanctions, including mandatory U.S. opposition to all lending to China by international financial institutions and a prohibition against bilateral exchanges of all senior officials. The administration also suspended export guarantees by the Overseas Private Investment Corporation, financing by the Commerce Department's Trade Development Program, licenses for U.S. satellites to be launched by Chinese rockets, and implementation of a 1985 nuclear cooperation agreement between the United States and the People's Republic. In 1990, the U.S. Congress passed legislation suspending export licenses for the sale of police equipment to China and recommending the suspension of loans to China by the Export-Import Bank of the United States.[48]

In any event, the alliance's *casus foederis* had largely disappeared by the time of the tumultuous events of June 1989. Prior to the uprising in China, Chairman Mikhail Gorbachev of the Soviet Union had already concluded a treaty with the United States banning intermediate-range nuclear forces, ordered drastic cuts in Soviet defense spending, and begun withdrawing his country's forces from Afghanistan. Then, within months of the abrogation of U.S. defense cooperation with China, the Kremlin stood aside as one Eastern European satellite after another defected from the Soviet bloc and adopted noncommunist, democratic governments.[49] Sino-Soviet tensions had also dissipated by the summer of 1989. The previous year, Gorbachev had systematically addressed each of China's major outstanding conflicts with the USSR, namely its war in Afghanistan, alliance with

Vietnam, and extensive military deployments in the Far East. In addition to agreeing to end the Afghanistan war, Gorbachev helped to secure Vietnam's military withdrawal from Cambodia—which Hanoi had invaded in 1978—and initiated a large-scale withdrawal of Red Army forces from Asia and Mongolia.[50]

The nearly two-decade-long Sino-American partnership had intensified external pressures on the USSR significantly, thereby exacerbating the domestic economic strains that would eventually precipitate its collapse in December 1991. In the short term, Nixon's trip to China in 1972 represented a "critical factor"[51] in motivating the Kremlin to pursue nuclear arms control agreements with the United States. Thus, despite a ferocious U.S. bombing campaign against North Vietnam in the spring of 1972, Leonid Brezhnev invited Nixon to Moscow for a presidential summit. Brezhnev emphasized that consistent long-term dialogue with Washington would preclude the establishment of a united Sino-American front against the USSR. By the end of the year, the Soviets had signed on to two landmark superpower arms control pacts: the Strategic Arms Limitation Treaty and Anti-Ballistic Missile Treaty.[52] Over the longer term, the alliance compelled Moscow to undertake an "unprecedented military buildup"[53] along the border with China and provide increased military and economic assistance to client states throughout the Third World that were at heightened risk of defecting to either the United States or China. These efforts diverted critical resources away from the urgent task of resuscitating the moribund Soviet economy.[54]

INTRA-ALLIANCE DISPUTES BETWEEN THE UNITED STATES AND CHINA

Over the course of the alliance, three major national security–related disputes arose between the two partners. These concerned the fate of America's treaty ally of Taiwan, China's steadfast support for North Vietnam in its war against the United States, and Chinese nuclear and missile sales to the Middle East and South Asia.

The U.S. interest in prevailing on all three issues was strong. With respect to Taiwan, the embattled island was a keystone in America's anticommunist containment policy in Asia and occupied a crucial position along the maritime shipping routes that connected Japan, America's foremost Asian ally, with its lucrative export markets in Southeast Asia. Moreover, any fraying of the formal U.S. defense commitment to Taiwan could sow doubts on the part of America's other allies around the world, and especially in Europe, regarding the credibility of Washington's commitments to their defense against communist aggression. Meanwhile, for the CCP, Taiwan represented nothing less than a renegade province, which, along with British-held Hong Kong, topped the list of "lost territories" that the Chinese communists were determined to recover in order to reunify the country and restore it to its historical glory as the "Middle Kingdom." Located a mere hundred miles offshore, an independent Taiwan allied to an enemy great power, as had been the case since 1954, also posed a mortal threat to the security of the mainland.[55]

Although the U.S. interest in Taiwan was unquestionably strong, it can be persuasively argued that the PRC's interest was (and remains) even stronger because the island's disposition was (and continues to be) viewed by Chinese leaders as a matter of existential importance to the sovereign integrity of the People's Republic. This does not mean that substantial Chinese compromises on Taiwan were unfathomable, however, given the nation's abject military and economic weakness vis-à-vis the United States and its far greater vulnerability to the mutual threat posed by the USSR, as discussed below. Robert Ross notes that "China aimed at full achievement of its objectives and could not change them, but it had a considerable range of other potential policy options. Without prejudice to its goals, it could defer negotiations on Taiwan in order to consolidate U.S.-PRC cooperation. It might also reach partial agreements, thereby preserving its ability to address its outstanding concerns at a later date. In this way, it could try to achieve its ultimate objective in a step-by-step process."[56]

Meanwhile, President Nixon's hope that Mao would help the White House negotiate an end to its long-running war in Vietnam represented one of the principal motives behind his initial decision to court China. Nixon owed his narrow electoral victory in 1968 in large part to his campaign pledge that he would achieve "peace with honor" in Vietnam.[57] By early 1972, however, his efforts to end the war had failed.[58] This placed enormous pressure on the White House, which had authorized the "Vietnamization" of the war (i.e., a steady stream of troop withdrawals from South Vietnam) in order to deflate the surging antiwar movement at home.[59] According to journalist Patrick Tyler, "Nothing was of greater concern [to Nixon] than finding an exit strategy in Southeast Asia. There would be no second term if Nixon did not end the Vietnam War."[60] Meanwhile, although China was closely allied with North Vietnam, it did not have nearly as great a stake in the matter as the United States, which was actually waging (and losing) the war and stood to benefit geopolitically from an American military withdrawal from Indochina. Even so, the CCP was ideologically committed to the defense of its communist neighbor in its efforts to secure a decisive victory against the RVN and the United States, and sought to prevent the DRV from falling under the Soviet sphere of influence.[61]

The third dispute regarding China's nuclear and missile proliferation activities during the 1980s was also a matter of considerable importance to the U.S. government. In addition to the United States' general commitment to nuclear nonproliferation as evinced by its stewardship and subsequent ratification of the 1968 Nuclear Non-Proliferation Treaty, the Reagan administration adopted a firm stance on the issue. In June 1981, Reagan declared that "our position is—and it is unqualified—that we're opposed to the proliferation of nuclear weapons and do everything in our power to prevent it."[62] A month later, the president signed a secret national security decision directive that stated that nuclear counterproliferation constituted a "fundamental security and foreign policy objective."[63] Reagan was viscerally motivated by a strong desire to completely eliminate nuclear weapons from the face of the earth.[64]

Reagan's administration was also determined to limit the spread of ballistic missiles capable of delivering nuclear weapons, which was at issue in Beijing's sale of intermediate-range ballistic missiles (IRBMs) to Saudi Arabia and short-range ballistic missiles (SRBMs) to Syria, Pakistan, and Libya. In 1982, it participated in negotiations with Canada, France, West Germany, Italy, Japan, and the United Kingdom to create a Missile Technology Control Regime (MTCR) prohibiting the export of missile systems capable of delivering a 500-kilogram (1,110-pound) or heavier warhead and possessing a range of greater than 300 kilometers (186 miles). According to a July 1988 State Department briefing paper, the regime's goal was to "limit the risks of nuclear proliferation by controlling the transfers of equipment and technology which could make a contribution to nuclear weapons delivery systems, other than manned aircraft."[65] Revealingly, in March 1985 the White House instructed all relevant government agencies to begin enforcing the regime's rules, even though the agreement was still in the process of being finalized and would not be officially inaugurated for another two years.[66]

Although the Silkworm shore-to-ship missiles that China sold to Iran did not fall under the aegis of the MTCR, they had the potential to tilt the momentum in the ongoing Iran-Iraq War away from America's ally of convenience, Iraq (chapter 4), and toward its bitter enemy, Iran. The Silkworms additionally posed a direct threat to U.S. naval vessels, which in the spring of 1987 began convoying Kuwaiti oil tankers through the Persian Gulf. Although Beijing clearly had a major economic stake in these various nuclear and missile sales, and had a geopolitical interest in arming Pakistan with nuclear weapons and ballistic missiles to balance against both countries' shared enemy and neighbor, India, they were hardly matters of existential salience to the Chinese regime commensurate with the Taiwan issue.

RIVAL PREDICTIONS ON U.S. BARGAINING WITH CHINA

Both neorealism and tying hands theory propose that the United States should have bargained successfully with China on all three disputes, while neoclassical realist theory predicts that Washington's bargaining should have been passive and thereby unsuccessful.

Neorealist theory bases its prediction on the United States' favorable international systemic position vis-à-vis China. Specifically, the intra-alliance balances of dependence and commitment were both highly advantageous to the United States. The United States was much less dependent on the alliance because it was exponentially more powerful than China, even as China was more gravely threatened by their shared Soviet adversary. In the early to mid-1970s, although the United States was overstretched militarily by the grueling war in Vietnam and beset by economic "stagflation," it still dwarfed China in aggregate material capabilities. In 1971, the year that the two states began to align, U.S. military spending amounted to $128 billion, while its Gross National Product (GNP) was $1.8 trillion. Chinese military spending, by contrast, was $36.7 billion and its GNP a mere $271.9 billion. By 1989, the year the alliance ended, these gaps remained yawning. Whereas U.S. military spending was $304.1 billion and its GNP $5.2 trillion, Chinese military spending was $22.3 billion and its GNP $603.5 billion.[67]

China was also more vulnerable than the United States to Soviet depredations. Whereas the United States was located an ocean and half a highly armed continent away from its superpower rival, China shared a massive 7,500-mile (12,000-kilometer) border with the USSR and Soviet-dominated Mongolia, the longest in the world. Along that border, during the 1970s and 1980s the Soviets deployed "massive numbers of troops to launch multidirectional assaults against Chinese territory."[68] The Chinese capital of Beijing lay a mere 560 kilometers from the city of Erenhot on the Mongolian border, well within range of frontline Soviet mechanized divisions that were capable of traversing up to 725 kilometers without auxiliary fuel tanks.[69] In terms of nuclear capabilities, China's arsenal was scant compared with those of both the United States and Soviet Union. In 1971, whereas the United States and Soviet Union possessed 25,830 and 13,092 nuclear warheads respectively, China had only managed to build 100. By 1989, the USSR had taken the quantitative lead with a staggering 39,000 warheads as compared with the United States' 22,217 and China's 238.[70] In sum, as Robert Ross contends, "despite China's impressive size and military capability, and despite its importance to U.S. security, it remained a significantly weaker state in international affairs and in its ability to contend with Soviet power . . . Even at the best of times, this fact severely limited China's negotiating leverage with the United States."[71]

As with all of America's postwar alliances of convenience, the balance of commitment here favored the United States. Security cooperation between the two states was never formalized in a treaty, which meant that the United States was not legally obliged to defend the PRC. Washington also did not have a strong inherent interest in defending China, as evidenced by the Truman administration's earlier refusal to intervene militarily in the 1945–1949 Chinese civil war to prevent Mao's CCP from toppling Chiang Kai-shek's Nationalist government.[72] So long as the United States remained allied to Asia's wealthiest power, Japan, it could effectively ensure a regional balance of power against the USSR.

Generally tying hands theory also predicts aggressive and successful U.S. bargaining with China, owing to the large gap in domestic win-sets between the two governments. For the entirety of the alliance, the United States was a weak state democracy in which the formal policy-making powers of executive leaders were tightly constrained, particularly by Congress. Successive administrations' domestic win-sets should have been further narrowed by heavy opposition both in Congress and by the general public to any uptick in relations with the People's Republic of China, a longtime ideological and geopolitical adversary. Meanwhile, for nearly the entire lifespan of the alliance, the Chinese government was rigidly authoritarian. With the exception of a chaotic leadership transition between the summer of 1976 and the end of 1978, Chinese political authority rested firmly in the hands of a single leader, first Mao and then Deng, and both should have therefore been highly vulnerable to frequent and effective tying hands threats and demands issued by U.S. leaders.

In sharp contrast to the neorealist and tying hands theories of alliance bargaining, neoclassical realist theory predicts that U.S. leaders should have engaged in passive and ultimately failed bargaining with China across all four administrations of Nixon, Ford, Carter, and Reagan. In response to high domestic opposition to the alliance with China, each administration's foreign policy executive should have placed a premium on cutting domestic slack for the policy. This should have entailed its resort to a passive bargaining strategy aimed at casting the PRC and the bilateral alliance in the most benign possible terms.

THE FATE OF TAIWAN

EARLY CONTACTS AND SIGNALS, 1969–1971

To signal Beijing of its desire to begin reversing the twenty-year deep-freeze in Sino-U.S. relations, during its first year the Nixon administration began making preemptive concessions on Taiwan. In October 1969, Nixon agreed to cancel regular naval patrols of the Taiwan Strait in order to induce China to renew ambassadorial-level secret talks that had been conducted on a sporadic basis since 1955.[73] In early 1970, after China agreed to reopen the talks in Warsaw, U.S. Ambassador to Poland Walter Stoessel announced to China's chargé d'affaires, Lei Yang, that "it is our hope that as peace and stability in Asia grow we can reduce those [U.S. military] facilities on Taiwan that we now have."[74] Lei's reply to Stoessel that China was ready to receive a high-level envoy in Beijing was received skeptically by Assistant Secretary of State for East Asian and Pacific Affairs Marshall Green. Green presciently warned Secretary of State William Rogers that the visit would probably have an "unsettling and potentially damaging impact on some of our friends and allies," and would communicate to Beijing that "we are prepared to make more fundamental policy changes than is the case."[75]

Although Nixon and Kissinger decided to bypass the State Department by opening up their own secret channel of communication with Beijing, the president nevertheless shared the department's hesitations. He feared the possibility that the PRC intended to "embarrass [him] by staging a propaganda show about Taiwan the moment his special envoy arrived,"[76] which would devastate Nixon's chances for reelection in 1972.[77] He recognized that a still-vocal pro-Taiwan "China Lobby" anchored in his own Republican Party in Congress would undoubtedly pounce on any hint of perceived weakness vis-à-vis Beijing. The influence of Republican hardliners was amplified by public opinion polls showing that a plurality of Americans opposed formal recognition of the People's Republic and its accession to the United Nations.[78] The domestic political stakes grew in April 1971, when Vice President Spiro T. Agnew announced that he was incensed by the "apparent thaw" in U.S. relations with China and Treasury Secretary John Connelly enjoined the president to adopt a "principled" (i.e., anticommunist) position in opposition to the PRC's campaign to supplant Taiwan at the United Nations.[79]

Notwithstanding the inauspicious domestic political context, Nixon agreed to dispatch National Security Advisor Henry Kissinger to Beijing in July. Kissinger's two-day trip was shrouded in secrecy. The general public, Congress, and the executive bureaucracy, even the State Department, were all left in the dark by the White House.[80] Upon landing in Beijing, Kissinger adopted a strikingly conciliatory stance with Premier Zhou Enlai. Astutely apprehending that Nixon needed "a successful outcome of the negotiations to bolster his presidential campaign,"[81] Zhou demanded that the administration acknowledge that Taiwan was a province of China, recognize the PRC as the sole legitimate government of China, establish a deadline for removing all troops from Taiwan, and sever the U.S. military alliance with Taipei. In response, Kissinger "went a long way toward meeting Chinese expectations."[82] He promised that the administration would not support an independent Taiwan, "two Chinas," or "one China, one Taiwan," and would never support a military invasion of the mainland by Nationalist forces. This went well beyond the State Department's official position that the status of Taiwan was "undetermined." Kissinger also promised that the administration would reduce troop levels in Taiwan by two-thirds once the Vietnam War ended and withdraw the remaining third as Sino-U.S. relations improved.[83] Journalist Patrick Tyler notes that the fact that Kissinger's promises were proffered in secret "reflected Nixon's unwillingness to confront his conservative wing openly. Instead he would try to ride the wave of popular goodwill on China over the heads of his opponents."[84]

In return, Kissinger received from Zhou an invitation for the U.S. president to visit China. Although this represented the "single tangible, political benefit Nixon sought the most,"[85] it was coupled with Zhou's categorical refusal to pledge that China would resolve its dispute with Taiwan peacefully.[86] Notwithstanding this lack of substantive progress, on July 15 an ebullient Nixon revealed to the American public that Kissinger had just visited China in order to arrange his own visit the next year for a presidential summit. Nixon maintained, however, that his efforts to craft a "new relationship" with the PRC would "not be at the expense of our old friends" (i.e., Taiwan).[87]

In October, as Kissinger planned a return visit to Beijing in order to continue preparations for the forthcoming summit meeting, the administration's UN delegation began lobbying in the General Assembly to protect Taiwan's endangered seat. The annual vote on China's UN status was scheduled for October 25, five days after Kissinger was to arrive in Beijing. Kissinger persuaded Nixon to allow him to depart for China prior to the UN vote on the logic that it would "hurt you more with right-wingers if I go to Beijing after Taiwan has been kicked out [of the UN]."[88] In a meeting with Kissinger and Nixon on September 30, the administration's UN ambassador, George H. W. Bush, protested that he thought the UN fight was still "winnable," but that Kissinger's forthcoming trip to China would "not be helpful at all."[89] As expected, Kissinger's trip dealt a lethal blow to Bush's efforts at the UN. On October 25, the U.S. delegation narrowly failed to secure the two-thirds majority vote of the General Assembly required to prevent reconsideration of China's UN membership. This vote was followed by the passage of an Albanian-sponsored resolution ejecting Chiang Kai-shek's Republic of China from the United Nations and admitting the People's Republic in its place.[90] Prior to these monumental UN votes, as Kissinger was on his flight to Beijing, he fumed that Secretary of State Rogers's dogged efforts to protect Taiwan at the UN were motivated by the desire "to ruin the China trip."[91]

The combination of Kissinger's return visit to Beijing and the removal of Taiwan from the UN precipitated a domestic backlash. Coming on the heels of a public opinion poll showing that 62 percent of the American people opposed Taiwan's ouster from the UN, the successive General Assembly votes were received with widespread hostility in Congress.[92] Republicans were especially outraged, and the White House discovered that Senators Barry Goldwater (R-AZ) and James Buckley (R-NY) were planning an organized effort to reverse the UN decision.[93]

While in Beijing, Kissinger continued to make unilateral concessions to the PRC. Although initially he warned Zhou Enlai that there were "many elements in the U.S. who are violently opposed to the policy we are pursuing," he subsequently told the Chinese premier not to be concerned about the U.S. delegation's ongoing efforts at the UN to save Taiwan's seat because "it has not [yet] been possible to instill the discipline [in the foreign policy bureaucracy] that will be the case as the years go on." In any event, Kissinger conveyed the administration's hope that the PRC would settle the Taiwan dispute by peaceful means, "but whether you do or not, we will continue in the direction which I indicated," by which he meant the steady reduction of U.S. troops from Taiwan.[94] These concessions vitiated his subsequent attempt on October 22 to subtly signal Zhou of China's relative military vulnerability to the Soviets by averring obliquely that the Kremlin was seeking détente with the West because of its "great desire to free itself in Europe so it can concentrate on *other areas.*"[95]

"THE WEEK THAT CHANGED THE WORLD"

In early January 1972, Kissinger dispatched his deputy, Brigadier General Alexander Haig Jr., to Beijing for the purpose of finalizing various outstanding logistical issues relating to the summit. Haig reiterated Kissinger's previous warnings about both the dangers posed to the PRC by the Soviet Red Army and the existence of domestic elements in the U.S. government and Congress that were implacably opposed to a rapprochement with the PRC.[96] Just as his boss had done a few months before, Haig then immediately sacrificed his bargaining leverage by explaining to Zhou that in light of the domestic political pressures confronting the administration, Nixon and Kissinger were "all the more concerned" about making the presidential summit "a success not only in reality [i.e., in substantive terms] *but also in the appearance of the visit.*" He elaborated that it was "crucial that there be no public embarrassment to the President as a result of his visit to Peking," and that it was "in our mutual interest that the visit reenforce [*sic*] President Nixon's image as a world leader."[97]

During his monumental weeklong visit to China in February 1972, to which he would memorably refer as "the week that changed the world,"[98] Nixon was extremely careful not to disrupt the atmospherics of the landmark summit by demanding too much of the Chinese. Although initially the president warned Zhou about the military perils confronting China and the domestic political perils facing the White House, he nevertheless proceeded to dilute the impact of these warnings by offering a gratuitous concession to the PRC. Nixon proposed an agenda for the complete withdrawal of U.S. troops from Taiwan, dropping a requirement he had articulated mere days earlier at the outset of his visit that the withdrawal of the final third of U.S. forces from Taiwan would occur "as progress is made on the peaceful resolution of the problem."[99]

In Beijing, Nixon and Kissinger also fought a rearguard action against the State Department. Nixon excluded Secretary Rogers and Assistant Secretary Green from the important negotiations regarding the joint communiqué to be released at the conclusion of the summit, which were being conducted by Kissinger and China's Vice Minister for Foreign Affairs, Qiao Guanhua. Consequently the two State Department officials were only given the final version of the draft communiqué after China's Politburo had already approved it and the presidential party had departed Beijing for a final stop in Shanghai. Green noticed that a passage listing America's continuing alliance and security commitments in Asia excluded the 1954 Mutual Security Treaty with Taiwan. He frantically alerted Rogers, who in turn apprised Nixon of the error. When Kissinger appealed to the Chinese to amend the communiqué, Zhou would only allow the American delegation to delete the entire passage reaffirming U.S. support for its Asian allies, which Nixon and Kissinger glumly accepted. Although Rogers and Green had saved the administration from making a potentially grievous error, Nixon angrily charged that "State Department people seemed to be telling everyone about the flawed document and lining up in opposition to it."[100]

The summit communiqué, which was released while Nixon was in Shanghai, has served as the linchpin of U.S. relations with the People's Republic to the present day. It stated that the United States "acknowledges that all Chinese on either side of the Taiwan Straits maintain there is but one China and that Taiwan is a province of China." It also stipulated that "the ultimate objective" of the United States was to withdraw all troops from Taiwan, and that it would "progressively reduce its forces and military installations on Taiwan as the tension in the area diminishes."[101] Although the Chinese had sought a specific timetable for a U.S. withdrawal, they were able to make this and other small concessions to the administration because, according to journalist James Mann, "in the larger context, they were obtaining so much of what they wanted."[102] The administration had gone well beyond the State Department's official policy that Taiwan's status was "undetermined," and gave up on its effort to secure in the communiqué an explicit Chinese commitment to peaceful resolution of its dispute with Taiwan. In private, Nixon went even further, delinking a U.S. military withdrawal from Taiwan with a peaceful resolution of the cross-strait dispute, opposing Taiwanese independence, and promising to dissuade Japan from dispatching troops to Taiwan after U.S. forces vacated the island.[103]

Upon his arrival back at Andrews Air Force Base in Maryland, Nixon announced disingenuously that he had concluded "no secret deals of any kind" with the Chinese and insisted that he did not "negotiate the fate of other nations behind their backs."[104] Also, in a series of carefully orchestrated briefings of the cabinet, White House staff, congressional leaders, the press, and Taiwanese officials, Nixon and Kissinger repeatedly professed that their new policy toward China did not adversely affect the U.S. relationship with Taiwan in any way.[105]

On the whole, Nixon's China summit was "well received"[106] by Congress, the media, and the general public, to a large degree because they were not privy to the raft of secret concessions made by the president in Beijing. In any event, public opinion toward China would prove to be highly antagonistic for the next several years. During the sixteen years spanning 1972 and 1987 (excepting the years 1974, 1981, and 1982) annual public opinion polling revealed that a majority of Americans held a favorable view of China in only four of those years (1979, 1980, 1985, and 1987), a narrow plurality held a favorable view of China in one year (1973), and a majority held an unfavorable view of China in six years (1972, 1975, 1976, 1977, 1978, and 1983). Also, in an annual poll conducted between the years 1982 and 1988 (excepting 1986) that asked Americans whether China should be considered a close ally or friend, neutral, or unfriendly or an enemy, in every survey a plurality of those polled considered China a neutral state or worse.[107]

THE FORD INTERREGNUM

After Vice President Gerald Ford assumed the presidency following Nixon's August 1974 resignation, Chinese leaders placed enormous obstacles in the way of continued improvement in Sino-American relations. In November 1974, during yet another Kissinger trip to Beijing, this time in his new capacity as Ford's secretary of state, Deng Xiaoping, who had replaced the ailing Zhou, told Kissinger bluntly that to proceed with the normalization of diplomatic relations with the PRC, the United States had to completely sever diplomatic relations with Taiwan, withdraw all of its military forces from the island, and abrogate the Mutual Security Treaty.[108] Remarkably, in the face of Deng's intransigence, Kissinger proposed that Deng invite President Ford to Beijing for a presidential summit. While this gesture allowed Kissinger to save face and project the appearance that he had actually accomplished something in his high-profile visit to China, he sacrificed the bargaining leverage that a presidential summit might have afforded the White House to break the stalemate on Taiwan.[109]

In the months leading up to Ford's December 1975 summit trip to China, the domestic political headwinds confronting the administration strengthened considerably. By 1975, only 28 percent of Americans viewed the PRC favorably, while a 58 percent majority viewed it unfavorably.[110] Chiang Kai-shek's death in April also reenergized the conservative opposition to the PRC. Senator Goldwater, who led the U.S. delegation to Chiang's funeral, fumed to a reporter that if the Ford administration was intending to change the U.S. relationship with Taiwan, "as I told the President and as I told Kissinger, they've got a hell of a fight on their hands."[111] On November 19, Ford's political straitjacket tightened even further when California governor Ronald Reagan called to tell the president that he was going to enter the contest for the Republican presidential nomination.[112] Ford went ahead with the trip even though the two sides could not even agree on language for a final communiqué, on the grounds that "to cancel it would be a disaster, both internationally and with the left and right."[113] Despite the summit's lack of substantive progress, it projected an image of Sino-U.S. comity. As recounted by Ross, "appearances were everything. When Ford and Mao found nothing more to say with more than a half hour remaining in their meeting, they kept to schedule rather than suggest to the world less than harmonious relations."[114]

CARTER AND NORMALIZATION

Seeking to differentiate his China policy from those of his Republican predecessors, newly elected Democratic president Jimmy Carter dispatched Secretary of State Cyrus Vance to Beijing in August 1977 to present the administration's "maximum position"[115] on Taiwan: namely, that it intended to maintain an official consulate in Taipei after normalization. In response, Deng angrily pointed out that this marked a "retreat" from the Nixon/Ford understanding that the United States would completely abrogate official contacts with Taiwan, as Japan had already done in order to normalize diplomatic relations with the mainland.[116] In the aftermath of Vance's contentious visit, however, the administration began to backslide. Similar to Nixon, Carter confronted a deep divide between his secretary of state and national security advisor on China. Vance supported a cautious, hard-nosed approach toward Beijing that would not disrupt the administration's pursuit of strategic arms limitation talks with the Soviets.[117] By contrast, Carter's hawkish national security advisor, Zbigniew Brzezinski, was eager to court Beijing in order to maximize external pressure on the Soviets.[118]

In May 1978, over Vance's objections, Carter dispatched Brzezinski to China to meet with Deng.[119] After arriving in Beijing, Brzezinski announced that the White House was ready to completely sever official government-to-government contacts with Taipei in exchange for a Chinese pledge to resolve the cross-strait dispute peacefully.[120] Notably, during his trip, Brzezinski sidelined the two senior State Department colleagues who accompanied him, Assistant Secretary of State for East Asian Affairs Richard Holbrooke and Holbrooke's deputy, William H. Gleysteen. Not only did he refuse to share his prepared talking points with Holbrooke and Gleysteen, but he also excluded them from his meeting with Deng, and later barred all State Department personnel from reviewing the meeting's transcripts.[121]

After Brzezinski returned to Washington, Carter agreed to set a December 15 deadline for concluding the process of normalizing diplomatic relations with the People's Republic. Carter swore his lead negotiator,

Leonard Woodcock, the director of the U.S. liaison office in Beijing, to complete secrecy, explaining, "I don't trust (1) Congress (2) White House (3) State, or (4) Defense to keep a secret."[122] Despite Carter's efforts, media reports began to circulate that the administration had put the U.S. alliance with Taiwan on the chopping block in secret normalization discussions with the Chinese. This infuriated Senator Goldwater, who responded by introducing a concurrent resolution stipulating that Senate advice and consent would be required to abrogate the mutual security treaty (MST). Although the Democratic majority in the Senate forestalled a vote on Goldwater's measure, it passed a less strident bipartisan resolution introduced by Senators Robert Dole (R-KS) and Richard Stone (D-NY), which requested that the president consult with Congress before modifying the treaty. Carter nevertheless defied the resolution by continuing to conduct the normalization discussions "in absolute secrecy in order not to arouse concerted opposition from Taiwan's supporters [in the United States], as well as to avoid building up excessive expectations."[123]

Once the White House secured Deng's agreement, on December 15, that Washington could provide limited defensive weapons to Taiwan following the abrogation of the MST, Carter announced publicly that the United States and the People's Republic of China had agreed to normalize relations as of January 1, 1979. On that date, the U.S. government would formally withdraw from the MST and terminate diplomatic relations with Taiwan, and would pull its remaining troops from the island within four months.[124] Notably, in order to secure this agreement with Deng's regime, Carter abandoned his prior demand that the PRC commit formally to a peaceful resolution of its dispute with Taiwan.[125] Carter's stunning announcement unleashed a flurry of criticism at home. Goldwater shrilly accused Carter of "lying, thumbing his nose at the Constitution and the U.S. Congress, and selling out Taiwan," Reagan condemned the agreement as a "betrayal" and immediately scheduled a trip to Taiwan, and the ultra-conservative Republican senator Jesse Helms of North Carolina charged the president with attempting to "sell Taiwan down the river."[126] Goldwater even filed a lawsuit against the president in U.S. district court, on the grounds that Carter had illegally terminated the MST without obtaining Senate approbation. Although the court ruled in Goldwater's favor, the judgment was later overturned on appeal.[127] Even the relatively moderate George Bush published an op-ed in the *Washington Post* accusing Carter of paying a steep price for normalization that "has not only diminished American credibility in the world but has also darkened the prospects for peace," despite the fact that "China needs us more than we need them."[128]

The domestic backlash against normalization intensified in late January when the administration submitted the Taiwan Enabling Act to Congress. The bill, which created an American Institute in Taiwan (AIT) to manage unofficial relations between the two countries and included the administration's tepid declaration that "the United States continues to have an interest in the peaceful resolution of the Taiwan issue," was met with nearly unanimous outrage in Congress. Even stalwart Democratic allies of the White House, such as Clement Zablocki (WI) in the House and Richard Stone (FL), John Glenn (OH), Edward Kennedy (MA), and Dale Bumpers (AR) in the Senate, joined the fray.[129]

Although initially the White House opposed any modifications to the language of the legislation, it had no choice but to bend in the face of overwhelming congressional pressure. Carter used a veto threat to fend off a Republican amendment in the Senate that would have transformed the AIT into a full-fledged liaison office, but was compelled to accept Congress's insertion into the bill of language construing "any effort to determine the future of Taiwan by other than peaceful means . . . a threat to the peace and security of the Western Pacific area and of grave concern to the United States." Even more importantly, the White House also yielded to the insertion of a provision stating that the United States would "provide Taiwan with arms of a defensive character" and "maintain the capacity of the United States to resist any resort to force or other forms of coercion that would jeopardize the security, or the social or economic system, of the people on Taiwan."[130] The rechristened Taiwan Relations Act (TRA) passed both houses by enormous, veto-proof majorities of 339–50 in the House and 85–4 in the Senate. Tellingly, after signing the act, Carter took steps to dilute its impact on the PRC by reassuring Chinese leaders that he would have considerable flexibility in interpreting and enforcing the law and would do so in strict accordance with the agreements his negotiators had reached with Beijing.[131]

ENTER REAGAN

In the 1980 presidential election, Carter was beaten decisively by Reagan, who had been one of Taiwan's fiercest defenders over the course of the previous decade. During the early stages of his campaign for the Republican nomination, Reagan promised on several occasions that if he won the presidency he would reestablish "official relations" with Taiwan.[132] Upon taking office, the new administration was riven by deep divisions on China, which mirrored those of its predecessors. Several senior officials, including President Reagan, National Security Advisor Richard Allen, Secretary of Defense Caspar Weinberger, and James R. Lilley, the senior National Security Council staffer responsible for China policy, endorsed a robust defense relationship with Taiwan. Arrayed against this faction was Secretary of State Alexander Haig, who had previously served as Kissinger's NSC deputy and Nixon's chief of staff. Haig subscribed to the belief that all outstanding disagreements with China had to be subordinated to the larger goal of strengthening the alliance to more effectively contain the USSR.[133]

During the North-South Summit held in Cancún, Mexico, in late 1981, Chinese foreign minister Huang Hua presented Haig with a note demanding that the administration set a specific date for the complete cessation of arms sales to Taiwan. Until that date, these sales would not be able to exceed those provided during the Carter administration in quality or quantity, and had to be lowered progressively in each successive year. Huang told Haig bluntly that if the administration balked, China would downgrade bilateral diplomatic relations and withdraw its ambassador from Washington.[134] During his visit to Washington a few days later, Huang leveled an even more brazen ultimatum against President Reagan in the Oval Office, threatening a downgrade in bilateral relations unless the administration agreed to immediately suspend all arms transfers to Taiwan and begin negotiating a deal with Beijing to phase them out permanently.[135]

In early January 1982, Haig exploited the recent resignation of National Security Advisor Richard Allen to convince Reagan to eschew selling Taiwan the advanced FX fighter jet, and instead continue transferring to Taipei the older generation F-5E.[136] He summarily dispatched Assistant Secretary of State for East Asian and Pacific Affairs John Holdridge to

Beijing to share the FX news with Chinese leaders.[137] At a welcome banquet for Holdridge, however, an unimpressed Vice Foreign Minister Zhang Wenjin threatened that the bilateral relationship would be imperiled if the White House failed to accept an immediate moratorium on arms sales to Taiwan and enter negotiations with China to phase them out by a specific deadline. State Department officials tried desperately to squelch any evidence of discord between Holdridge and his hosts by informing the media that that the visit was "useful and a success" and "positive and productive."[138] When Vice President George H. W. Bush subsequently flew to Beijing that spring, he tried to reassure China's leadership that, although the White House could not establish a specific date for ending arms sales to Taiwan, it did not contemplate transferring arms to Taipei indefinitely. Foreign Minister Huang then "stunned" Bush by lamenting that nothing whatsoever had been accomplished since his trip to Washington the previous November.[139]

Inside the State Department, Haig's director of policy planning, Paul Wolfowitz, repeatedly expressed concern that the administration had "vastly overestimated China's strategic importance to the United States." According to Wolfowitz, "the bottom line . . . was that China needed the United States far more than the United States needed China. It was China, not the United States, that was being threatened by a Soviet invasion. Washington had considerable leverage in negotiations with Beijing but wasn't making use of it . . . By overestimating China's importance, America was making concessions it didn't have to make."[140] After Wolfowitz drafted an internal memo in the spring of 1982 accusing the State Department of being far too conciliatory toward China on the issue of arms sales to Taiwan, an irate Haig ordered his exclusion from ongoing bilateral negotiations with the PRC.[141] Meanwhile, Haig's increasingly imperious behavior toward other senior administration officials, including Reagan, led the president to demand the secretary's resignation in late June 1982. Haig's removal occurred against a backdrop of growing agitation not only in Haig's own agency over the administration's appeasement of the PRC, but also in Congress.[142] Specifically, Senator Goldwater told the president personally that he was "profoundly disturbed by the mounting evidence that we do not intend to honor our commitments [to Taiwan]," while firebrand Republican senator Strom Thurmond of South Carolina distributed to fellow legislators a draft letter demanding that the White House sell cutting-edge fighter jets to Taiwan.[143]

After Haig's departure, Reagan sent Deng a letter containing his "final offer,"[144] namely that the United States would agree to reduce arms sales to Taiwan over time on condition that China renounce the use of force against Taiwan. Subsequent negotiations proceeded quickly and on August 17, the two states concluded a joint communiqué on U.S. arms sales to Taiwan. Deng mounted little resistance to Reagan's proposal because the latter had "agreed to most of the demands that China had originally raised."[145] Specifically, the communiqué stipulated that the United States "does not seek to carry out a long-term policy of arms sales to Taiwan, that [U.S.] arms sales to Taiwan will not exceed, either in qualitative or quantitative terms, the level of those supplied in recent years since the establishment of diplomatic relations between the United States and China, and that it intends to reduce gradually its sale of arms to Taiwan, leading over a period of time to a final resolution." As for Deng, he not only rebuffed yet another U.S. attempt to persuade the CCP to renounce the use of military force against Taiwan, but also refused to explicitly acknowledge any linkage between China's behavior toward Taiwan and the magnitude of U.S. arms transfers to the island.[146]

On Capitol Hill, the signing of the joint communiqué engendered a "flurry of skepticism and opposition."[147] Many legislators agreed with the declaration of Senator John Glenn (D-OH) that the tenets of the communiqué "contravene the spirit and purpose of the [Taiwan Relations Act]" and that in the eyes of China's leaders, it ostensibly committed Washington to completely cut off arms shipments to its former ally.[148] Administration officials swarmed the Hill to reassure enraged members of Congress that there was no fundamental discrepancy between the communiqué and the TRA. Specifically, they insisted that so long as the threat to Taiwan from the PRC diminished, the United States could reduce arms sales to Taiwan without endangering the island's security and thereby violating the act. They also reminded skeptical lawmakers that the communiqué was not a legally binding document. Moreover, the White House pledged to congressional opponents that it would adjust the maximum level of arms sales to Taiwan upward for inflation, sell Taiwan newer weapons systems as older ones became obsolete or their production was discontinued, and observe no restrictions on the sale to Taiwan of defense production technologies, as opposed to finished weapons.[149]

Within the parameters set by the 1982 communiqué, cross-strait tensions diminished in intensity over the course of the decade, as cultural and economic contacts between the mainland and Taiwan proliferated.[150] Although neither side had completely capitulated to the other on Taiwan between 1971 and 1982, of the two the United States had moved much farther from its original bargaining position. Across four presidential administrations representing both major political parties, it had removed all of its troops from Taiwanese soil, abrogated its bilateral military alliance with Taiwan, terminated all official government-to-government relations with Taipei, conceded that there was only one China, and agreed to tightly circumscribe and gradually reduce arms deliveries to the island. By contrast, the PRC's only concession to the United States was allowing Washington to continue selling limited defensive arms to Taiwan.[151]

ENLISTING CHINESE HELP IN ENDING THE VIETNAM WAR

As the Sino-American alliance began to take shape, the Nixon administration began appealing to the CCP to exercise its influence over Hanoi in order to expedite a negotiated end to the Vietnam War. While on a visit to Japan in the summer of 1970, Secretary of State Rogers declared that a peace agreement in Vietnam could be concluded "very quickly" if China was willing to exercise its diplomatic influence over the Vietnamese communists.[152] Rogers's assertion was underscored by the fact that, although the Soviet Union was North Vietnam's chief source of arms, most of that weaponry made its way to the DRV by transiting Chinese territory. In addition, since the large-scale U.S. deployment of ground forces to Vietnam in 1965, Beijing had deployed antiaircraft units and construction brigades to North Vietnam and protected the railway that connected the two countries with

PLA troops.[153] Not only did Mao refer to China as North Vietnam's "base area," but he also had long enjoined North Vietnam's leaders to maintain a hard line with the Americans at the peace table.[154]

PRELIMINARY APPEALS FOR CHINA'S HELP

Indicative of the high priority the White House placed on Vietnam, when Kissinger set off on his secret trip to China in July 1971 he included his aide on Vietnam, Dick Smyser, in his small delegation.[155] During his first discussion with Premier Zhou Enlai after arriving in Beijing on July 9, Kissinger explicitly linked a rapid end to the war in Indochina to a more rapid pace in Sino-U.S. rapprochement.[156] The initial Chinese response to Kissinger's proposal was inauspicious, however, as Zhou proclaimed that the Vietnam and Taiwan situations were incommensurable.[157] He also questioned why the White House was resisting Hanoi's demand that South Vietnam's president, Nguyen Van Thieu, be removed as a precondition for a peace agreement.[158] During deliberations over the wording of the joint communiqué summarizing Kissinger's visit, Zhou even refused to include a sentence stating obliquely that the talks would "favorably influence peace in Asia and the world," for fear that it would convey to the DRV that Beijing and Washington were colluding against it.[159] When Kissinger prepared to return to China in late October, the CCP refused to allow Ambassador David K. E. Bruce to be part of Kissinger's delegation because Bruce had most recently served as the administration's chief envoy to the Vietnam peace negotiations in Paris.[160]

In the weeks leading up to Nixon's February 1972 summit in Beijing, administration officials made two last-ditch attempts to wring some concessions from China on Vietnam. First, when the head of Nixon's advance team, Deputy National Security Advisor Alexander Haig met with Zhou in Beijing in January, he insinuated heavily that the United States was prepared to counter Soviet aggression against China so long as the CCP persuaded the North Vietnamese to reach acceptable peace terms.[161] Zhou pointedly replied that if Nixon broached the matter with Chinese officials during the summit, this would introduce "an unfavorable element" into the proceedings.[162] Later that month, General Vernon Walters, the U.S. military attaché in Paris, approached Chinese embassy officials to request the CCP's assistance in softening North Vietnam's peace demands. They replied that China would not allow Washington to "enmesh" the PRC in the Vietnam dispute and spurned Walters's request for a possible meeting between Nixon and North Vietnam's lead peace negotiator, Le Duc Tho, in Beijing during the president's visit.[163] In early February, after Nixon delivered a public address articulating the administration's peace terms, Kissinger wrote to Zhou, this time pleading that the Chinese use their "good offices" to ease North Vietnam's demands for an unconditional withdrawal of U.S. combat forces and elimination of the "puppet" Thieu government. Zhou once again rebuffed the administration's appeal for help.[164]

NIXON DEMURS IN BEIJING

As he prepared for face-to-face meetings with the CCP leadership, Nixon became increasingly determined to press Mao's regime on Vietnam. Initially, the handwritten notes that he scribbled just before leaving Washington, which are cited in this chapter's epigraph, implied that he would not push too hard on the matter. While the president was on board Air Force One en route to Beijing, however, he reconsidered, jotting the following:

> *What we want*:
> 1. Indochina (?)
> 2. Communists—to restrain [Chinese Communist] expansion in Asia.
> 3. In future—Reduce threat of a confrontation by Chinese Super Power.

These notes evince the high priority that the president placed on obtaining Chinese help on Vietnam, though his lingering anxieties about achieving that aim were also evident in the question mark that followed that notation. After arriving in China, as Nixon sat in the Diaoyutai State Guest House awaiting a meeting with Zhou, he even less ambivalently scribbled:

Taiwan = Vietnam = trade off

1. Your people expect action on Taiwan.

2. Our people expect action on Vietnam.

Neither can act immediately—But both are inevitable—Let us not embarrass each other.[165]

In his much-anticipated meeting with Zhou, however, Nixon adopted a far more acquiescent stance than his most recent handwritten notes indicated. After Zhou remarked that Vietnam was the "most pressing question" confronting the two countries, he added that China could not furnish any assistance on the matter, as they were "not in a position to settle it." In reply, Nixon stated meekly that he was under "no illusion" that he could end the war in Beijing, adding that the only party benefitting from the war's perpetuation was the Soviet Union. To this, Zhou angrily rejoined that his nation had "a responsibility to sympathize with [the North Vietnamese] and support them; we have no right to interfere with them, to make suggestions to them, or to speak for them."[166] After Nixon unleashed a massive strategic bombing campaign against the DRV and began mining its ports in the spring of 1972, Beijing doubled the size of its program of military and economic aid to Hanoi.[167]

"SUBTLE CHANGES" IN CHINA'S POSTURE

In the immediate wake of the May 1972 superpower summit in Moscow between President Nixon and General Secretary Leonid Brezhnev of the USSR, the Chinese government introduced "subtle changes" in its policy toward Vietnam.[168] Beijing began to actively promote a negotiated peace between the United States and North Vietnam, advising Hanoi's lead peace negotiator, Le Duc Tho, to initiate direct talks with Thieu.[169] The North ignored Zhou's counsel and ramped up its war effort, prompting Mao to intercede on his premier's behalf by instructing Hanoi to "send away the [U.S.] demon"[170] and reignite hostilities after the last American troops left Indochina. Le Duc Tho yielded to Mao's logic and in early October at the peace talks with the Americans in Paris duly introduced a peace plan that for the first time did not require Thieu's ouster.[171] During a November 13 meeting in New York, Kissinger asked China's vice foreign minister, Qiao Guanhua, to press Hanoi to accept a number of minor changes to the proposed peace plan that had been demanded by Saigon. Qiao angrily retorted that it was the United States that had to make concessions because as a great power it had less to lose than the DRV.[172] Two weeks later, Kissinger repeated the request in Paris during a meeting with China's ambassador to France, Huang Zhen. This time, though, he insinuated that if the United States conceded too much to secure a peace agreement in Vietnam, it would subsequently experience greater difficulty in confronting "greater pressures": that "if the American people are told that the U.S. will do anything to have peace [in Vietnam], then if *some great power with aggressive tendencies* engages in aggression, it will be very difficult to appeal to our people to resist them as we in the White House believe we should resist them."[173] Then, on January 3, 1973, Kissinger approached Huang Hua in New York and explained that if America's "minimum conditions" were met by the North, the administration would arm-twist Saigon into accepting the deal.[174] Huang obstreperously replied that "if the U.S. side truly wished a settlement, this opportunity should not be missed."[175] Five days later, Kissinger and Le resumed the recently stalled peace talks without Chinese help and on January 27, the warring parties signed the Paris Peace Agreement, thereby bringing the U.S. war in Vietnam to an end.[176]

In his memoir, Nixon recalled of his trip to China in 1972 that he had "no illusions about being able to settle the Indochina war in Peking."[177] What is surprising about the Nixon administration's behavior throughout the final two years of his first term in office is the tentativeness with which it bargained with China on an issue considered the president's most urgent foreign policy priority. At no point in their discussions with China's leaders did Nixon or Kissinger issue a definitive quid pro quo of U.S. help vis-à-vis the Soviets, or Taiwan (as the president's preparatory notes explicated) in exchange for Chinese help on Vietnam. They repeatedly beseeched Chinese help on Vietnam, but never overtly demanded it as a condition of rapprochement with the PRC to balance against the Soviet Union. Only during the war's final stages, in November 1972, did Kissinger begin to subtly imply that there might be costs associated with a lack of Chinese help.

By this juncture, Chinese leaders had resolved independently to press both sides to conclude a rapid peace agreement that would result in a U.S. military withdrawal and subsequent communist takeover of South Vietnam. In any event, between 1971 and 1973, Chinese military and economic aid to North Vietnam skyrocketed, exceeding the amount it had dispensed over the course of the previous two decades combined.[178] As historian Li Danhui concludes, "China stood firm in aiding Vietnam and did not adjust its relations with the United States at the expense of principle. It was able to develop its relations with the great power while at the same time remaining steadfast in its relations with the smaller nation."[179]

CHINESE NUCLEAR AND MISSILE PROLIFERATION ACTIVITIES

During the next decade bilateral tensions also developed regarding China's sale of nuclear weapons–related technologies to Pakistan, antiship missiles to Iran, and ballistic missiles to Saudi Arabia, Syria, Pakistan, and Libya.

CHINESE NUCLEAR COOPERATION WITH PAKISTAN

In late 1982, the White House began to convey its suspicions to Chinese leaders that Beijing was providing assistance to Pakistan's clandestine nuclear weapons program.[180] In a December 17 briefing memo prepared by U.S. Ambassador to China Arthur Hummel for Secretary of State George Shultz, Hummel noted that the Chinese had "refused to give us an unequivocal answer that they are not assisting Pakistan's reported efforts to manufacture a nuclear explosive device."[181] He dispatched a follow-on memo to Shultz the next day in which he conveyed the Chinese government's preference for U.S. corporations to fulfill its massive need for nuclear energy, but stated that Washington had to carefully exploit this leverage due to "suspicions" that the PRC had "facilitated Islamabad's acquisition of [nuclear] weapons-related know-how."[182] On the same day, *Newsweek* magazine cited official U.S. sources claiming that China had provided Pakistan with raw uranium and blueprints for constructing an atomic weapon.[183]

In June 1983, Assistant Secretary of State for Near Eastern and South Asian Affairs (NEA) Robert Gallucci disseminated a secret briefing paper reporting that NEA had "concluded that China has provided assistance to Pakistan's program to develop a nuclear weapons capability" by providing assistance in the areas of fissile material production and, possibly, actual weapons design.[184] Even more ominous, U.S. and Israeli intelligence also suspected that China had transferred two bombs' worth of weapons-grade, highly enriched uranium (HEU) to Pakistan. One U.S. intelligence source reported that Pakistani technicians had already managed to convert the HEU into a metal core that would eventually be inserted into the Chinese bomb design that was still in development at a secret nuclear installation located at Kahuta, just outside the Pakistani capital of Islamabad.[185]

In light of the recent replacement of Reagan's exceedingly pro-China Secretary of State Haig with the more circumspect George Shultz, it could have been expected that the administration would bristle in response to these explosive allegations. As recounted in his memoir, Shultz believed that U.S. administrations since Nixon's had overstated China's geostrategic importance, thereby rendering them exceedingly pliant in response to Chinese demands: "[M]uch of the history of Sino-American relations since the normalization of relations in 1978 could be described as a series of Chinese-defined "obstacles"—such as Taiwan, technology transfers, and trade—that the United States had been tasked to overcome in order to preserve the overall relationship."[186]

As it happened, however, Shultz would almost immediately fall victim to that same self-injurious tendency in his own dealings with the Chinese (not to mention the administration's two other foremost allies of convenience, Iraq and Pakistan, as chapters 3 and 4 show). To wit, notwithstanding the compelling evidence of nuclear cooperation between China and Pakistan, in July 1983 Shultz's State Department initiated negotiations with the Chinese on a draft nuclear cooperation agreement.[187] This decision led Senators Gordon Humphrey (R-NH), William Roth (R-DE), and William Proxmire (D-WI) to send a letter to Shultz demanding that the bilateral nuclear agreement with China include an explicit promise by the

Chinese government not to transfer nuclear weapons–related equipment or information to any other country.[188]

At this juncture, China took some small steps to allay U.S. concerns. In addition to formally applying for membership in the International Atomic Energy Agency (IAEA) in September 1983 (though it continued to boycott the Nuclear Non-Proliferation Treaty), during a visit to Washington in January 1984, Chinese premier Zhao Zhiyang pledged in a toast at a White House banquet that "we do not engage in nuclear proliferation ourselves, nor do we help other countries develop nuclear weapons." The marginal comments on a cable to Shultz from the U.S. embassy in Beijing praising Zhao's toast correctly indicate, however, that Zhao's statement did not address future activities.[189] When State Department officials attempted to obtain clarification on this point, the Chinese agreed that the declaration did apply to the future but refused the U.S. request to put this clarification in writing.[190] The administration's enthusiastic reception to Zhao's cryptic declaration did not extend to Gallucci, who later recalled that in its rush to embrace China, the White House failed to act on incriminating intelligence "of every conceivable nature using most of our agents and facilities."[191]

Domestic controversy over the U.S.-China nuclear deal erupted soon after President Reagan initialed a draft version of the agreement in April. In late May, Senators Proxmire and Alan Cranston (D-CA) responded by sending Reagan a sharply worded letter exhorting the president to "personally investigate" media reports alleging that China had "helped Pakistan develop a capacity to enrich uranium for nuclear weapons use and had provided Pakistan with sensitive information about the design of nuclear weapons."[192] In mid-June, the White House instructed Ambassador Hummel to ask Chinese officials whether the bilateral understanding contained within the draft nuclear agreement about the need to abstain from spreading nuclear weapons was "mutual" in light of a "particular" activity between China and Pakistan. Importantly, Hummel was explicitly instructed to avoid making any specific accusations against China.[193]

Later that month, Cranston turned up the heat on the administration by revealing on the Senate floor that it had been actively concealing from Congress intelligence showing that China was helping Pakistan to develop nuclear weapons. Cranston averred that disgruntled administration sources had divulged to him that China had provided Pakistan with a nuclear explosive device and was providing troubleshooting assistance with the approximately eight thousand centrifuges that were enriching uranium at the Kahuta complex.[194] The next day, a White House spokesperson announced that lingering concerns about China's role in Pakistan's unsafeguarded nuclear program meant that the bilateral nuclear agreement would not be sent to Congress for ratification until the United States received stronger nonproliferation assurances from Beijing.[195] The administration's predicament deepened in December, when a number of senators sent a letter to the secretaries of state, defense, and energy decrying "the absence of clarification of PRC pledges made at the initialing of the proposed United States-PRC cooperative agreement not to help other nations develop nuclear weapons."[196] In order to cover its domestic flank, the administration dispatched Ambassador-at-Large for Non-Proliferation Richard Kennedy to Beijing with a classified memorandum containing various undisclosed assurances that China's nonproliferation policy was consistent with that of the United States, to which the Chinese government provided verbal but not written assent. On the basis of these assurances, the administration gleaned interagency consensus in favor of the agreement, which it signed and submitted to Congress for ratification in late July.[197]

At this juncture, the White House joined forces with influential private business interests to push the accord through Congress. Ambassador Kennedy and other administration officials testified that the agreement fully satisfied the legal requirements of the 1978 Nuclear Nonproliferation Act and did not undermine U.S. nonproliferation policy. In addition, they warned that if Congress scuttled the agreement, China would merely purchase nuclear technology from other countries on less onerous terms.[198] The administration's efforts were bolstered by the heavy lobbying pressure exerted by the nuclear power industry, which was set to make an estimated $7 billion in profits from China if the pact was successfully ratified. This pressure proved "instrumental" in achieving congressional acquiescence.[199]

In this atmosphere, Congress engaged in "little vigorous pursuit of reports of continuing Chinese assistance to the Pakistani weapons program,"[200] even though closed-door intelligence briefings for the committees stewarding the legislation revealed that in 1983 China had tested a nuclear device that had been constructed by Pakistan. As the pact was winding its way through both the House and Senate, however, Senator Cranston announced to the media that he was in possession of information from several executive branch sources indicating that China was "either engaged in serious nuclear trade negotiations with or actually has continued a series of nuclear exports" to Pakistan and four other "nuclear outlaw" nations: Brazil, Argentina, South Africa, and Iran. Cranston also claimed that the State Department, and specifically Ambassador Kennedy, had "systematically withheld, suppressed, and covered up information—known virtually throughout the executive branch—which Congress might find worrisome as it reviewed the draft agreement now before us." He added that multiple requests by senators "for an unfiltered, uncolored briefing on this issue from intelligence analysts still have not been met."[201] Despite Cranston's bombshell allegations, on November 21 the Senate passed a resolution containing the text of the bilateral agreement by voice vote and a few weeks later the House passed it by a lopsided 307–112 margin.[202]

The passage of the agreement did not end the political dispute over nuclear cooperation with China. Just after the House passed the measure, Senators Glenn and William Cohen (R-ME) introduced an amendment prohibiting all nuclear exports to China until it adopted strict IAEA standards for safeguarding nuclear imports from the United States. After the amendment passed by a 59–28 margin, the State Department protested that this would seriously impair U.S. relations with China and threatened a presidential veto of the entire omnibus spending bill to which it was appended. This persuaded a House-Senate conference committee to strike the amendment from the legislation. It nevertheless inserted a compromise measure stipulating that before any export licenses for nuclear materials could be granted to the PRC, the president had to certify that he had made "effective" arrangements with China to ensure "that nuclear exports . . . are used solely for intended peaceful purposes" and that China was no longer aiding states seeking to develop nuclear weapons.[203]

CHINA'S SILKWORM SALES TO IRAN

Not long after Reagan secured legislative passage of the nuclear deal with China, another proliferation-related controversy erupted, this time involving Chinese missile sales to America's adversary, Iran. Although China had already sold Iran a wide array of arms during the Iran-Iraq War (1980–1988), the export that engendered particular U.S. concern was the HY-2 Silkworm antiship missile.[204] In February 1987, the U.S. intelligence community began to "pick up signs" that Iran was moving Silkworm batteries to positions alongside the Strait of Hormuz, the chokepoint of the Persian Gulf. Iran's deployment of the Chinese-made missile constituted a major escalation of the "Tanker War," in which each of the two belligerents engaged in reciprocal attacks against merchant vessels servicing the other.[205] The Silkworm possessed a range of 80 kilometers (50 miles) and held a warhead that could carry up to 454 kilograms (1,000 pounds) of explosives. This payload marked a fivefold increase over the shore-to-ship missiles previously employed by Iran to attack merchant shipping in the Gulf.[206]

Iran's Silkworm deployment became a matter of direct military concern to Washington in May 1987, when the Reagan administration accepted Kuwait's request to convoy its oil tankers transiting the Gulf. In June, a Chinese Foreign Ministry spokesperson claimed that U.S. reports that China was selling Iran the Silkworms were "sheer fabrication," as the missiles were of North Korean origin.[207] Undersecretary of State for Political Affairs Michael Armacost, the third-ranking official in the State Department, subsequently showed Chinese officials pictures of the Silkworms leaving China and later arriving on the same ship at the Iranian port of Bandar Abbas. Even in the face of this indisputable photographic intelligence, the Ministry of Foreign Affairs and People's Liberation Army continued to deny the accusation, even going so far as to deny that China had made *any* weapons sales to *either* belligerent in the war.[208]

According to Eden Y. Woon, who was then tasked with helping to manage the Pentagon's relationship with the PRC, "the frustration level at the

Pentagon in the latter half of 1987 rose steadily as the Chinese continued to avoid the Silkworm issue."[209] The combination of China's disingenuousness and the concern that the Silkworms posed a significant danger to U.S. naval vessels operating in the Gulf "eroded the earlier goodwill toward China felt by many in the U.S. defense establishment. Some even questioned the basic worth of a military relationship with China. The frustration was by no means limited to the military; it extended to other U.S. government agencies, the press, and most notably the Congress."[210] In September, Secretary of Defense Caspar Weinberger issued a "strongly worded"[211] communiqué to his Chinese counterpart protesting the Silkworm sales to Iran. The dangers posed by the missile system ceased to be merely hypothetical in mid-October, when a Liberian-flagged oil tanker that was being escorted by the U.S. Navy was hit by an Iranian Silkworm, resulting in significant damage to the ship. The next day, a U.S.-flagged Kuwaiti tanker was also targeted by a Silkworm, which injured eighteen crew members.[212]

These incidents prompted the administration to take only the mildest of punitive actions against China. On October 22, the State Department announced that due to "rising tensions in the Persian Gulf," it was an "inappropriate time"[213] to further liberalize the rules regarding technology transfers to China. Although U.S. officials maintained in discussions with their Chinese interlocutors that the "presence of Chinese-made weapons in the Gulf [has] seriously undermined political support in Congress and the administration for further relaxation of restrictions on technology transfers to China," they also made sure to extend "assurances about continued long-term U.S. support for China's modernization and no change in existing export licensing procedures."[214] Importantly, even these mild sanctions aroused the ire of private business interests. On November 30, Eben S. Tisdale, chairman of the Industry Coalition on Technology Transfer (ICOTT), sent off an angry letter to the State Department protesting the sanctions. Tisdale conveyed the organization's opposition to retributive "actions that effectively single out the United States businesses for punishment."[215]

In early November, Shultz dispatched Armacost to Beijing to urge Chinese leaders to stop selling Tehran the Silkworms. Although senior Chinese Foreign Ministry officials continued to deny that the PRC had transferred arms of any kind to Iran, they assured Armacost that China intended to "prevent the diversion of Chinese-origin equipment to Iran."[216] This assurance was belied by subsequent U.S. satellite intelligence, which identified Chinese-manufactured Silkworms at a North Korean port and then later showed that those missiles had disappeared, along with an Iranian ship that had previously been used to transport Silkworms.[217]

As late as February 1988, declassified U.S. government documents imparted that China was continuing to sell Silkworms to Iran. In a heavily redacted February 4 cable dispatched by U.S. Ambassador to China Winston Lord to the State Department, Lord affirmed that the matter of Chinese missile sales to Iran would be the "most difficult issue we will face" during Chinese Foreign Minister Wu Xueqian's forthcoming visit to Washington. Lord equivocally surmised that China's behavior on the Iran Silkworm issue since the imposition of the U.S. sanctions was "mixed":

> [the Chinese government had made] *some effort* to
> —halt the supply of anti-naval missiles to Iran, as well as the training and spare parts needed to use them;
> —ensure that Iran does not use the missiles it already has against the U.S. and other non-belligerents[218]

Although Hu was intent on pressuring the administration to lift the sanctions on the grounds that "for several months the Chinese have not delivered Silkworms to the international market," Lord advised Shultz that "we should demonstrate appreciation for the positive steps the Chinese have taken without at the same time implying that the issue is behind us, as much as we wish it were, [REDACTED] Recent visitors, for example, sharpl[y] questioned Wu, on the basis of press reports, about Chinese Silkworms being shipped to Iran through North Korea."[219]

In a speech at the National Press Club in Washington at the end of his three-day visit to the United States, Foreign Minister Wu announced that China "has adopted strict measures to prevent what you call the Silkworm missiles from flowing into Iran through the international arms market." Importantly, Wu implicitly denied that China had previously shipped Silkworms to Iran and therefore made no mention of any Chinese effort to ensure that Iran did not use any Silkworms already in its possession. In return, a State Department spokesperson informed the media that the sanctions on technology transfer were being lifted because "we are encouraged by Chinese statements and actions regarding Iran's acquisition of Chinese antiship missiles, such as the Silkworm." Contrary to Lord's equivocal assessment of the previous month, an unnamed U.S. official added that "we have every reason to believe the Chinese have lived up to their assurances" concerning the Silkworms.[220] In actuality, however, China continued to transfer Silkworms to Iran through the end of the Iran-Iraq War in August 1988 and into 1989.[221]

THE CSS-2 SALE TO SAUDI ARABIA

The administration's hasty retraction of the technology sanctions imposed against China the previous October was questionable not merely on the basis of China's unabated sale of Silkworm missiles to Iran, but also in light of the U.S. government's discovery that China was concurrently engaged in another, "considerably more serious"[222] missile transaction in the Middle East. In March 1988, the State Department confirmed to the *Washington Post* that Saudi Arabia had covertly purchased CSS-2 (East Wind) intermediate-range surface-to-surface ballistic missiles from China.[223] The missiles in question—estimates placed the number transferred at between thirty-five and sixty, along with nine launchers—were developed by the PRC as a delivery vehicle for nuclear weapons and possessed a range of 2,494 to 3,138 kilometers (1,550 to 1,950 miles).[224] The clandestine transfer not only marked the first time that a ballistic missile of such an extensive range had been transferred by one country to another, but it also provided Riyadh with the longest-range missile system deployed by any country other than the five permanent members of the UN Security Council.[225]

That the Chinese and Saudi governments conducted the prolonged negotiations for the sale in the utmost secrecy over the course of two and a half years in order to avoid discovery by the United States attests to the deal's adverse implications for U.S. national security interests.[226] First, the transaction took place in the immediate aftermath of the establishment of the Missile Technology Control Regime. Second, by suddenly granting Riyadh the capability to strike Iran and Israel, the purchase would inevitably exacerbate tensions in an already volatile and war-prone Middle East.[227] Not surprisingly, after learning of the sale, the Israeli government threatened to launch preemptive strikes against Saudi Arabia's CSS-2 sites.[228]

During Foreign Minister Wu's visit to Washington in March 1988, Secretary of State Shultz and National Security Advisor Colin Powell confronted Wu about the Saudi sale. Pressed for an explanation, he assured Shultz and Powell that the missiles had been modified so that they could not deliver nuclear warheads and that the Saudis had pledged both that they would not transfer the missiles to other countries and would only use them in self-defense.[229]

The proliferation controversy deepened considerably in the spring of 1988, when U.S. intelligence discovered that China had reached a tentative deal with Syria to sell Damascus its new M-9 Short Range Ballistic Missile and was seeking deals to sell Iran, Pakistan, and Libya its M-11 SRBM. Not only did the Reagan administration consider Syria, Iran, and Libya to be bitter enemies and Pakistan a highly problematic ally of convenience (see chapter 3), but China's introduction of the M-9 and M-11 to the region would be no less destabilizing than its prior introduction of the CSS-2. Although the recently developed M-9 possessed a range of only 600 kilometers (375 miles) and the M-11 an even shorter range of 290–300 kilometers (180–186 miles), they marked a significant technological improvement over the much older CSS-2. The CSS-2 was liquid-fueled, which made it difficult, dangerous, and time-consuming to transport, and necessitated at least two hours of fueling prior to launch. By contrast, the M-9 and M-11 were solid-fueled, which made them highly mobile and necessitated a mere half hour of pre-launch preparation. They were also highly accurate and capable of carrying a conventional or nuclear payload.[230]

In mid-July, a bipartisan group of 116 members of the House of Representatives signed a letter to Shultz expressing "profound concern" over reports of the prospective Chinese missile sale to Syria, which was suspected of possessing chemical weapons. The signatories noted that over the preceding year and a half, China had "demonstrated an apparent disregard for the implications of its arms transfers to the Middle East," referencing both the Silkworm sales to Iran and the CSS-2 sales to Saudi Arabia. In light of these activities and the "ineffectiveness of previous [U.S.] protests," the legislators urged the administration to "inform China that future United States cooperation in technological and military sales will be jeopardized" unless the PRC immediately halted the flow of all weapons to Iran and Iraq, abstained from selling ballistic missiles to all Middle Eastern countries, and joined the MTCR.[231]

With the sternly worded House letter in hand, Shultz set off on a scheduled trip to Beijing, where he cautioned Deng about the "particularly destabilizing potential" of China's missile sales to the Middle East. He later relayed to the media that the Chinese had vaguely assured him that they had not "yet" made any final missile sales to the region aside from the CSS-2s to Saudi Arabia.[232] Not long after Shultz returned to Washington, the Senate unanimously passed a nonbinding resolution sponsored by Republican senator Robert Dole of Kansas, which condemned Chinese missile sales to the Middle East as a "serious threat to American interests, and to regional peace and stability." It advised that if Beijing did not immediately stop transferring offensive arms to the region, the administration should "reassess bilateral relations with the PRC and reexamine agreements or contemplated agreements providing for arms and technology transfers to the PRC."[233]

On August 1, Shultz tried to calm the congressional waters on China in a written response to the House letter of the previous month. Although he acknowledged that during his recent visit to Beijing the Chinese government had given him "no commitments with regard to future [arms] sales," he emphasized nebulous assurances by Chinese leaders "to discuss the issue in regular diplomatic channels" and to follow "a prudent and responsible attitude toward arms sales." In lieu of punishing China for its reckless missile sales to the Middle East, Shultz stated that "the most effective way of addressing this issue with China is within the constructive relationship which we have developed with Beijing which enables us to discuss our differences in a straight-forward and businesslike fashion." He cautioned his congressional critics that "we must work to ensure that this issue does not undermine unrelated aspects of our relationship with China in ways that would be damaging to broader US interests."[234]

During a September trip to Beijing, Secretary of Defense Frank Carlucci struck a deal with Deng. The administration agreed to approve export licenses permitting American-made commercial satellites to be launched in China on Chinese Long March rockets, in exchange for the Chinese government's promise that "their future [missile] sales . . . will be very prudent and very serious." Administration officials later interviewed by investigative journalist James Mann elaborated that in private, Deng promised Carlucci that China would not sell "intermediate-range missiles," a prohibition that technically did not apply to the short-range M-9 and M-11 missiles that lay at the center of the latest bilateral dispute. Carlucci nevertheless exclaimed that he was "[t]otally satisfied with these discussions [about Chinese missile exports], and I am hopeful that as a result . . . we can put this issue behind us."[235] Whereas the Chinese concession was vague and incomplete, the U.S. concession was concrete and substantial: not only was China desperate for the massive sums of foreign exchange it could earn from launching commercial satellites, but until then Washington had allowed only NATO allies to launch U.S. satellites on their rockets.[236] Although the George H. W. Bush administration would pressure China into ostensibly cancelling its M-9 contract with Syria in 1991, reports surfaced later in the decade that China had actually transferred the missiles to Damascus in kit or partially assembled form.[237] In 1991, both U.S. and Indian intelligence sources also reported that Beijing had transferred M-9s to Pakistan.[238]

CONCLUSION

A now commonplace maxim in foreign policy circles holds that "only Nixon could go to China," which implies that only a president possessing incontestably hardline anticommunist foreign policy credentials could summon the domestic political capital to pursue a rapprochement with as odious a regime as Mao's People's Republic of China. While accurate insofar as Nixon was able to take risks in diplomatically engaging Mao that his immediate Democratic predecessors John F. Kennedy and Lyndon Johnson would not, the now-ubiquitous expression is nevertheless misleading. Perhaps only Nixon could have gone to China, but the hardline U.S. president paid an inordinately heavy price to deliver the rapprochement he so desperately sought with the communist regime in Beijing. Preoccupied with keeping domestic opponents of the nascent security partnership with China at bay, Nixon and his foreign policy consigliere Henry Kissinger scrambled to contain dissent in the executive branch, Congress, and the general public by taking a number of steps to cast their new Chinese ally in the most benign possible terms. This meant downplaying their disagreements with Beijing on Taiwan and Vietnam. Nixon's next three successors, the less hawkish Gerald Ford and Jimmy Carter and the ultra-hawkish Ronald Reagan, employed the same playbook of adopting an egregiously soft line in negotiations with China in order to avoid inflaming domestic opposition.

The long-term implications of these administrations' relaxed bargaining posture toward Beijing have been most problematic with respect to the issues of Pakistan's proliferation of nuclear weapons and the still-unresolved status of Taiwan. As the next chapter discusses in greater detail, China's nuclear cooperation with Pakistan during the early 1980s helped expedite Islamabad's efforts to develop a nuclear arsenal, which achieved fruition by the end of the decade. This, in turn, led to Pakistan's sale of nuclear components to an array of rogue states and raised the risk of both a nuclear exchange between Pakistan and India and the acquisition of nuclear materials by Islamist terrorist groups based in Pakistan. Even more ominously, the reluctance of the above administrations to strike a favorable deal with the CCP on Taiwan during the 1970s and 1980s has left the issue festering since the end of the Cold War, during which time China's wealth and military power have grown exponentially and Taiwan has transitioned to democracy.[239] According to Richard Betts, "The possibility of war over Taiwan could be the biggest danger that American security policy faces. No other flashpoint is more likely to bring the United States into combat with a major power, and no other contingency compels Washington to respond with such ambiguous commitment."[240]

3

THE U.S. ALLIANCE WITH PAKISTAN, 1981–1988

Our repeated warnings and demarches to Pakistan on nuclear issues have had little significant effect so far. Still more words, without some action to back it up, will only further reinforce Zia's belief that he can lie to us with impunity.

—KENNETH ADELMAN, DIRECTOR OF THE U.S. ARMS CONTROL AND DISARMAMENT AGENCY, SECRET MEMORANDUM FOR THE ASSISTANT TO THE PRESIDENT FOR NATIONAL SECURITY AFFAIRS, JUNE 16, 1986

FOR MUCH OF the Cold War, Pakistan served as the United States' on-again, off-again proxy in South Asia. By the late 1970s, however, Pakistan's suspected efforts to develop nuclear weapons and the advent to power in Islamabad of a repressive Islamist autocrat, General Muhammad Zia ul-Haq, produced a marked deterioration in that country's relationship with the United States. The downward spiral in bilateral relations was only halted in December 1979, when the sudden Soviet invasion of Afghanistan prompted the Carter administration to reengage the newly christened "frontline state"[1] that it had previously shunned as an international pariah. A reinvigorated security partnership was consolidated under Carter's successor, Ronald Reagan, whose administration began dispensing several billions of dollars in desperately needed military and economic assistance to Pakistan. This aid shored up Pakistan's defenses against Soviet attack and invasion, enabling it to continue playing a crucial intermediary role in funneling U.S.-procured arms and supplies to the anticommunist Afghan rebels, or *mujahideen.* By 1988, the mujahideen bled the Red Army into submission, spelling victory for the United States' alliance of convenience with Pakistan.

Even as Washington and Islamabad cooperated closely to successfully thwart Soviet aggression in Afghanistan, the Zia regime's concurrent efforts to manufacture nuclear weapons threatened the vital U.S. interest in countering nuclear proliferation. The neorealist and tying hands theories of intra-alliance bargaining expect that the Reagan administration should have engaged in fruitful nuclear bargaining with Zia during the war, due to the marked asymmetries of dependence and commitment in the alliance, which greatly favored the United States. Of the two partners, Pakistan was far weaker, more directly threatened by the Soviet military presence in Afghanistan, and more desperate to formalize the informal alliance of convenience. Tying hands theory advances the same prediction, albeit on the basis of the large gap in domestic win-sets between the United States, an internally weak state democracy, and Pakistan, an internally strong state autocracy. This gap should have been compounded by the considerable domestic opposition which the alliance should have provoked in the United States. Contrarily, neoclassical realist (NCR) theory expects U.S. nuclear bargaining with Pakistan to have been passive and unsuccessful. It predicts that the establishment of an alliance of convenience by the United States, an internally weak state, with Zia's Pakistan should have generated considerable domestic opposition, thereby compelling senior administration officials to spare no effort in mobilizing domestic support for the alliance. This overriding imperative should have driven them to adopt a passive bargaining posture toward Islamabad, which entailed presenting Pakistan's behavior on the nuclear issue in the most favorable possible light.

The empirical record provides strong support for NCR. Over the course of the Afghanistan War, decisionmakers—primarily based in the White House and State Department, but also in the Defense Department and Central Intelligence Agency (CIA)—made strenuous efforts to defuse all domestic criticism of Pakistan in both the U.S. Congress and the executive bureaucracy. They did so by suppressing evidence of Pakistan's proliferation activities, overselling cosmetic Pakistani concessions, reneging on prior threats to punish Pakistan for its misbehavior, and marginalizing alliance skeptics in the executive bureaucracy. These tactics enabled the Zia regime to enjoy enormous sums of U.S. assistance even as it hurtled relentlessly toward the acquisition of the bomb. By the end of the

Afghanistan War, Pakistan had crossed the threshold of nuclear weaponization, unleashing a host of regional and global dangers that would imperil America's national security for decades to come.

THE UNITED STATES, PAKISTAN, AND THE SOVIET WAR IN AFGHANISTAN, 1979–1989

The Soviet invasion of Afghanistan on Christmas Eve 1979 stunned the world and dealt a death blow to the détente that had been carefully nurtured by both superpowers since the middle of the previous decade.[2] Growing fears in Moscow about the loyalty and competence of Afghanistan's communist leader, Hafizullah Amin, spurred the ailing Soviet leader Leonid Brezhnev to order the invasion of Afghanistan with eighty thousand Red Army troops. After immediately assassinating Amin, Soviet forces aligned with the newly installed head of state, Babrak Karmal, to combat a fast-spreading anticommunist insurgency.[3] In immediate response to the Soviet invasion, President Carter approved a Top Secret presidential finding authorizing the CIA to clandestinely furnish arms and supplies to the mujahideen. Pakistani president Zia ul-Haq allowed the insurgents to establish base areas in Pakistani territory and authorized Pakistan's Inter-Services Intelligence agency to distribute weapons and supplies purchased by the CIA to the various rebel factions.[4]

As the United States' core objective in Afghanistan evolved over the course of the war from the mere "harassment" of Soviet forces to their outright "removal," the quantity and quality of arms delivered by the CIA to the rebels increased dramatically.[5] The most potent addition to the rebel arsenal was the battery-powered, heat-seeking Stinger antiaircraft missile system, which the agency began distributing to the mujahideen in late 1986.[6] The catastrophic damage inflicted by the shoulder-fired Stinger on Red Army aircraft coincided with the consolidation of political power in Moscow by reformist leader Mikhail Gorbachev. In April 1988, Gorbachev finally capitulated by formally agreeing to withdraw all Soviet troops from Afghanistan by February 15, 1989.[7]

THE U.S. ALLIANCE OF CONVENIENCE
WITH PAKISTAN

The Soviet intervention in Afghanistan set the stage for a thoroughgoing transformation of the relationship between the United States and Pakistan, short-circuiting a downward spiral of escalating mutual hostility. Immediately following the war's outbreak, diplomatic relations between Washington and Islamabad were revitalized and extensive security cooperation soon followed. This cooperation meets both of the criteria that distinguish an alliance of convenience from other types of alliances: (1) the pre-alliance relationship between the United States and Pakistan was characterized by both ideological and geopolitical antagonism; and (2) the Soviet intervention in Afghanistan posed an overarching threat to both the United States and Pakistan.

SOURCES OF IDEOLOGICAL AND
GEOPOLITICAL ANTAGONISM

During the entirety of the Afghanistan War, the ideological gap between the United States and Pakistan was vast. In contrast to the liberal democratic United States, Pakistan was led during the war by the most repressive regime to have held power in that country's tumultuous history. In July 1977, Chief of Army Staff General Mohammed Zia ul-Haq launched a bloodless coup against the democratically elected president, Zulfikar Ali Bhutto, and imposed martial law on Pakistan.[8] In the months that followed, Zia arrested Bhutto, reneged on an earlier pledge to hold national elections, and—spurning the exhortations of President Carter and many other world leaders—refused to stay Bhutto's execution after Pakistan's Supreme Court found the former president guilty of murder and sentenced him to death.[9] Zia alienated himself even further from the United States by foisting a strict code of Islamic law on the Pakistani populace.[10] To the Carter administration, the increasingly theocratic bent of the new Pakistani government appeared disturbingly redolent of the revolutionary Islamist regime that had just seized power in Iran. In another disturbing echo of recent events in Tehran, on November 21 an angry mob attacked the U.S. embassy in

Islamabad, resulting in the deaths of two Americans and leaving the embassy complex "a charred ruin."[11] In the aftermath of this incident the U.S. relationship with Pakistan was, in the estimation of one National Security Council (NSC) staff member, "as bad as with any country in the world, except perhaps Albania or North Korea."[12]

The Soviet invasion of Afghanistan also transpired against a backdrop of steadily worsening geopolitical relations between the United States and Pakistan. During the 1950s, the increasingly acute U.S. fear of Soviet expansion into the oil-rich Middle East compelled President Dwight Eisenhower to offer Pakistan membership in regional collective security alliances for the Middle East (the Central Treaty Organization or CENTO) and Southeast Asia (the Southeast Asia Treaty Organization or SEATO), inaugurate a large-scale military and economic aid program for Pakistan, and sign an executive order in 1959 pledging to defend Pakistan against communist invasion. In the years that followed, however, the bilateral relationship oscillated wildly.[13] President Lyndon Johnson imposed an arms embargo against Pakistan following its initiation of a reckless war against India in 1965, but President Richard Nixon diplomatically "tilted" back toward Pakistan during its subsequent 1971 war against India.[14] Nixon's successor, Gerald Ford, rescinded the 1965 arms embargo, but subsequently imposed stringent controls on high-technology exports to Pakistan after U.S. intelligence began to suspect that Bhutto had embarked on a nuclear weapons program following India's landmark nuclear test in May 1974.[15]

The simmering nuclear dispute between the two countries broke out into the open in late 1977. In September, President Carter declared Pakistan to be in breach of the just-passed Glenn Amendment to the International Security Assistance Act, which mandated a complete cutoff of military and economic assistance to any nonsignatory to the 1968 Nuclear Nonproliferation Treaty (NPT) that either imported or exported plutonium reprocessing equipment, materials, or technology.[16] Although the administration removed the Glenn Amendment sanctions in November 1978 after the French government backed out of a deal to build a plutonium reprocessing facility in Pakistan, U.S. intelligence began to suspect that Pakistan was also seeking to build nuclear weapons via uranium enrichment.[17] This prompted Carter to once again suspend aid to Pakistan, as mandated by the Symington Amendment to the International Security and Arms Control Act of 1977, which prohibited U.S. aid to states that imported or exported unsafeguarded uranium enrichment equipment, materials, or technologies.[18]

THE SHARED SOVIET THREAT

Although U.S. relations with Pakistan had soured by late 1979, neither state's leaders perceived the other as an urgent national security threat. By contrast, both states viewed the Soviet Union in precisely such minatory terms. In his January 1980 State of the Union address to Congress, President Carter decried the Soviet invasion of Afghanistan as "the most serious threat to the peace since the Second World War."[19] In response, the White House not only secretly approved the covert action program to arm the Afghan mujahideen, but also proposed a major increase in U.S. defense spending, imposed an array of economic and diplomatic sanctions against the Soviet Union, and withdrew the Strategic Arms Limitation Treaty II nuclear arms control agreement from consideration by the U.S. Senate.[20] The Soviet invasion also rattled Pakistan's leadership. Zia's army chief, General K. M Arif, imparted retrospectively that the Pakistani president "felt very acutely . . . [that] [e]ven if we were on a weak wicket, should we wait and let Afghanistan be crushed and then wait our turn to be crushed or should we act now, accept the wrath of the Polar Bear and, at least, if we have to go down, go down fighting."[21] Zia and his coterie feared that the invasion raised the ominous near-term possibility of "concerted Indo-Soviet action meant to intimidate, destabilize, or even dismember Pakistan."[22]

ELEMENTS OF SECURITY COOPERATION BETWEEN THE UNITED STATES AND PAKISTAN

Security cooperation between the United States and Pakistan during the Afghanistan War comprised two elements. The first was the joint program of covert action undertaken by the two countries to arm, supply, and shelter the mujahideen. The second consisted of the extensive military and economic subvention provided by the United States to Pakistan in order to bolster its capacity to withstand Soviet incursions and coercion. Carter immediately offered to provide Pakistan with $200 million in military and economic aid over two years, contingent on a congressional waiver of the Symington Amendment sanctions. This offer—which notably excluded the sale of cutting-edge F-16 fighter-bombers that Pakistan's government was desperate to acquire—was infamously dismissed by Zia as "peanuts."[23] Although Carter slightly increased the value of the proposed aid package and relented on the F-16 sale, Zia again declined, anticipating that he would get a more generous offer if Republican candidate Ronald Reagan were to win the upcoming U.S. presidential election, as was widely expected.[24]

As Zia predicted, Reagan defeated Carter in a landslide and in June 1981, the new administration announced a massive six-year $3.2 billion aid package to Pakistan, consisting of equal parts military and economic assistance.[25] Reagan not only agreed to sell Pakistan forty F-16 fighter jets, but also yielded to its demand that they be delivered on an expedited schedule. Over the course of the war, the administration sold Pakistan several other advanced weapon systems, including M-109A2 and M-110A2 self-propelled howitzers, M-198 towed howitzers, M-48A5 tanks, TOW antitank missiles, AH-1S Cobra attack helicopters, Harpoon submarine- and surface-launched antiship missiles, AIM-9L Sidewinder air-to-air missiles, and Stinger portable antiaircraft missiles.[26] In March 1986, the White House announced an even more generous follow-on assistance package, which would provide Pakistan with $4.02 billion in aid over six years (1988–1993).[27] The package was dispensed through the completion of the Soviet military withdrawal from Afghanistan in 1989.[28]

INTRA-ALLIANCE DISPUTES BETWEEN THE UNITED STATES AND PAKISTAN

Although the Reagan administration voiced concerns with several policies pursued by the Zia regime, the only one that remained a salient concern to U.S. policymakers over the course of the war was Pakistan's suspected effort to develop nuclear weapons.[29] As discussed in the previous chapter, the Reagan administration was generally committed to stanching the global spread of nuclear weapons and Reagan himself harbored an acute fear of nuclear war. More specifically, a secret memo drafted for the president by Secretary of State George Shultz in advance of Zia's visit to the White House in late 1982 delineated the high stakes attached to Pakistan's nuclear activities:

> If we implicitly or explicitly accept Pakistan's having nuclear weapons, it will be a major blow to our non-proliferation interests, make it more difficult to prevent proliferation elsewhere, and the administration would be seen at home and abroad as not taking the problem seriously.
>
> Pakistan's nuclear weapons activities, if carried to completion, will lead to a nuclear arms race on the Subcontinent. This would result in greater regional insecurity, including the possibility of pre-emption by India or Israel or even eventually a nuclear exchange . . . Moreover, eventual transfer of nuclear technology or weapons by Pakistan to unstable Arab countries cannot be excluded.[30]

Publicly, U.S. officials maintained that the nuclear issue had "the highest priority in our relationship with Pakistan."[31]

There can be no question that the Reagan administration's interest in stanching Pakistan's nuclear program was not as great as Pakistani leaders' existential interest in developing nuclear weapons to deter its mortal rival, India. India's 1974 nuclear test spurred Prime Minister Bhutto—who had infamously pledged that Pakistanis would "eat grass" if necessary to develop a nuclear deterrent should India acquire the bomb—to embark on a crash nuclear weapons program. After Zia ousted Bhutto from power, he assiduously continued his predecessor's nuclear program.[32] Even if it is virtually impossible to imagine that Zia could have been persuaded to completely dismantle Pakistan's nuclear program and join the 1968 Treaty on the Nonproliferation of Nuclear Weapons (NPT) in the absence of a reciprocal Indian commitment to do the same, that is not to say that tough bargaining by the White House could not have yielded a suboptimal but still favorable outcome.[33] To wit, an internal NSC memo drafted in 1987 noted that although "few in Pakistan would sacrifice the entire [nuclear] weapon's [sic] option, even for U.S. security assistance," this did not mean that the administration could not exploit its ample leverage over Pakistan to secure "limited" but nevertheless significant concessions, such as:

—verification of limits on [uranium] enrichment—[inspection] visits, [although] even one-time will be most difficult to obtain.

—identification of parties responsible for illegal procurement [operations inside the US].—action against those responsible.

—[government of Pakistan] decision (which it should know we monitor through intelligence) *and adherence* to its own [publicly professed] limit of five percent (5%) [uranium] enrichment.

—institutional measures, e.g., Pak legislation or [Prime Minister] Junejo/ [President] Zia written directive to relevant [Pakistani government] agencies on procurement, to be shared with the [US government] and with Congress.

—written commitment on the five percent (5%) enrichment limit by Zia/Junejo formally to the [US government].[34]

The likelihood that Pakistan might have complied with strident U.S. demands to limit, if not completely dismantle, its nuclear program was bolstered by the relative dormancy of the Indian nuclear program during the 1980s.[35]

RIVAL PREDICTIONS ON U.S. NUCLEAR BARGAINING WITH PAKISTAN

Both the neorealist and two-level games theories of alliance bargaining hypothesize that the United States should have achieved considerable success in restricting Islamabad's proliferation activities. Neorealist theory bases this prediction on the pronounced asymmetries of dependence and commitment that strongly favored Washington over Islamabad. In terms of the balance of dependence, whereas the United States was a military and economic superpower that was relatively unthreatened by the Soviet intervention in Afghanistan, Pakistan was militarily weak, poor, politically unstable, and highly threatened by the Soviet military presence in Afghanistan. Between 1979 and 1989, United States defense spending (as measured in constant 1989 U.S. dollars) rose from $196.6 billion to $304.1 billion, while Pakistan's defense budget grew from a mere $1 billion to $2.48 billion. During the same period, U.S. Gross National Product grew from $4 trillion to $5.2 trillion while Pakistan's grew from $19.1 billion to $36.8 billion.[36] Meanwhile, for U.S. leaders, the Soviet threat in Afghanistan was indirect; at worst, it represented the first step of a larger Soviet strategy to capture the vital oil-rich Persian Gulf.[37] By contrast, from Pakistan's perspective, the large-scale Soviet military deployment in neighboring Afghanistan constituted a direct and grave national security threat. Caught between the Soviet hammer and the Indian anvil, the Zia regime's "worst nightmare" was that a successful Soviet effort to pacify Afghanistan would in turn enable the USSR and India to launch a joint offensive to dismember Pakistan.[38] In the meantime, the Soviets attempted to cow Zia's government by engaging in an increasingly provocative campaign of cross-border reconnaissance overflights, air and artillery attacks, and sabotage operations against suspected Afghan insurgent bases and camps in Pakistan.[39]

Washington's bargaining leverage was further bolstered by the fact that the United States represented the only viable source of the massive amounts of military and economic subvention required by Pakistan. With regard to military aid, a 1982 CIA intelligence assessment claimed, "Islamabad is aware that only the United States can offset Soviet pressures and provide Pakistan with the sophisticated weapons it believes it needs."[40] A 1985 CIA analysis concurred that U.S. arms were "central" to Pakistan's military modernization drive, which was given extra impetus by India's extensive arms purchases from the USSR and by the Soviet war in Afghanistan.[41] Compounding Pakistan's military vulnerability to the Soviets was its economic frailty, which was exacerbated by the influx of millions of refugees from Afghanistan. The latter CIA analysis also indicated that Pakistani leaders regarded increased U.S. economic aid as "crucial . . . to avoid politically unpalatable reform to deal with serious economic difficulties."[42] It is also important to note that Zia had staked his political reputation on his ability to secure large amounts of military and economic assistance from the United States, which meant that its retraction would have posed a significant risk to Zia's domestic political position.[43]

The United States was not only much less dependent on the alliance of convenience than Pakistan, but it was also only informally and weakly committed to Pakistan's defense. The 1977 dissolution of SEATO meant that the only written commitment binding the United States to Pakistan's defense was the executive agreement signed by President Eisenhower in 1959. In contrast to formal alliance treaties, executive agreements are not submitted to the U.S. Senate for ratification and thereby do not enjoy the status of domestic law. The executive agreement was also quite vaguely worded, stipulating only that in the event of communist aggression against Pakistan, the United States was obliged to "take such appropriate action, including the use of armed forces, as may be mutually agreed upon." A 1980 State Department legal analysis "carefully distinguished U.S. obligations under these agreements as being 'basically an obligation to consult on possible U.S. or joint action,' as opposed to the 'legally binding commitment to take appropriate action' under our various mutual defense treaties."[44]

Events immediately following the outbreak of the Afghanistan War clearly showed that Pakistan desired a more robust U.S. commitment than the latter was willing to provide. During the same January 1980 press conference at which Zia contemptuously dismissed Carter's initial aid offer as "peanuts," the Pakistani strongman also beseeched the White House to convert the 1959 executive agreement into a full-fledged alliance treaty. Carter rebuffed Zia's request.[45] According to the CIA, as late as 1985, senior political and military leaders in Pakistan remained eager to secure a public U.S. commitment to their nation's defense.[46]

Tying hands theory also predicts successful U.S. nuclear bargaining with Pakistan, but attributes this outcome to the former's much narrower domestic win-set. Whereas the United States was a democracy with an internally weak state, Pakistan was an autocracy with an internally strong state.[47] The Reagan administration's already narrow win-set can be expected to have been even further constrained by the substantial domestic opposition that should have been engendered by its controversial decision to align with Pakistan.

From the vantage point of both the neorealist and two-level games theories, tough U.S. nuclear bargaining with Pakistan should also have been quite successful because Pakistan's outright defection from the alliance of convenience would have been prohibitively costly. Although U.S. intelligence analysts and policymakers warned periodically of the possibility that Pakistan might suddenly jump on the Soviet bandwagon, this was never more than a remote possibility. Not only did the Soviet Union enjoy a close relationship with Pakistan's arch-adversary, India, but Pakistan was also providing sanctuary in its already restive Northwest Frontier province to millions of heavily armed Afghan refugees who were fiercely opposed to Moscow and its communist client regime in Kabul.[48] On this score, it is crucial to note that even prior to the initial U.S. decision to provide large-scale aid to Pakistan, Zia had already decided not only to adopt a highly confrontational diplomatic posture toward the Soviets, but also provide arms, training, and sanctuary to the Afghan insurgents.[49] Any inclination by Zia's regime to defect from the United States in the face of strong pressure to constrain its nuclear program was also unlikely because Pakistan could not safely eschew U.S. conventional military aid and rely exclusively on nuclear weapons to ensure its national security. A February 1984 assessment by the State Department's Bureau of Intelligence and Research (INR) maintained that Pakistan's development of a nuclear weapon "would not displace the need for conventional arms," because Pakistan's lack of a conventional deterrent would force it into responding to any attack or incursion with either massive nuclear retaliation or acquiescence.[50]

In contrast to the neorealist and tying hands theories, neoclassical realism predicts that the foreign policy executive (FPE) in the Reagan administration should have engaged in weak and ultimately ineffectual nuclear bargaining with Islamabad. As the chief national security decisionmakers of a weak extractive state, the FPE should have been highly motivated to stanch heavy domestic criticism of the alliance by pursuing a passive bargaining strategy aimed at casting its Pakistani ally of convenience in the best possible light.

THE EMPIRICAL RECORD OF U.S. NUCLEAR BARGAINING WITH PAKISTAN

LOCKING HORNS WITH CONGRESS ON PAKISTAN

Pakistan's troubling nuclear activities threatened to immediately derail the newly elected Reagan administration's ambitious plan to dispatch several billions of dollars in military and economic aid to Islamabad. In the months leading up to Reagan's January 1981 inauguration, a flurry of media reports indicated that Pakistan was pursuing a wide range of sensitive technologies useful for uranium enrichment and plutonium reprocessing from several European countries, raising concerns on Capitol Hill.[51] During an April 1981 visit to Washington, Pakistani Foreign Minister Agha Shah and Chief of Army Staff General K. M. Arif gruffly informed Secretary of State Alexander Haig that Pakistan would not budge on the nuclear issue. With the new administration already placed on the defensive regarding Pakistan, Haig replied soothingly that Pakistan's nuclear program was a "private matter"[52] and dubiously assured Shah and Arif that Congress would only act against Pakistan if it were to detonate a nuclear device.[53]

As the administration's $3.2 billion aid request for Pakistan was being debated in the Senate Foreign Relations Committee (SFRC), where opponents of the initiative were putting up a "difficult fight,"[54] the administration misled legislators on the latest intelligence pertaining to Pakistan's nuclear program. A talking-points package disseminated by the State Department in March included the edifying claim that its own 1979 estimate that Pakistan was at least two to three years away from being able to conduct a nuclear test was erroneous and that the "schedule has since been delayed."[55] This prediction was in conflict, however, with contemporaneous intelligence reports that were predicting a Pakistani nuclear test "within 12 to 18 months."[56] The administration's campaign to line up congressional support for Pakistan was not helped by incendiary remarks made on the Senate floor by Senator Alan Cranston (D-CA), the senior Democrat on the SFRC's Arms Control Subcommittee. Cranston accused the White House of keeping Congress in the dark about Pakistan's construction of a nuclear test site and its completion of a pilot-scale facility to reprocess spent plutonium from its civilian nuclear reactor located in Karachi.[57]

In the House of Representatives, Undersecretary of State for Security Assistance, Science, and Technology James Buckley tried to allay the "considerable concern" exhibited by various members regarding Pakistan by holding a closed-door meeting with the members of the House Foreign Affairs Committee (HFAC). Buckley conveyed to the committee Zia's "assurance that Pakistan did not intend to make nuclear weapons." He also stated that he had personally made clear to Zia "that the US makes no distinction between so-called PNEs [Peaceful Nuclear Explosions] and nuclear weapons development."[58]

Ultimately, after a contentious legislative journey, in late December Congress promulgated the $3.2 billion aid package for Pakistan, but did not acquiesce to the administration's request to permanently repeal the Symington Amendment. Instead, it granted Pakistan a six-year waiver from the amendment and inserted a new provision barring U.S. military and economic aid to any nonnuclear state that either received or detonated a nuclear explosive device.[59]

MR. ZIA GOES TO WASHINGTON

In July 1982, Reagan dispatched a special envoy, former CIA Deputy Director and retired U.S. Army Lieutenant-General Vernon Walters, to Islamabad in order to directly address the concerns that had sparked the recent uproar in Congress.[60] Although Walters informed Zia that the administration possessed "intelligence of an incontrovertible nature"[61] showing Pakistani efforts to procure nuclear weapons components from abroad, Zia responded with incredulity. He also brusquely dismissed as bogus a satellite photo Walters showed him of a massive uranium enrichment facility located in the village of Kahuta on the outskirts of Pakistan's capital.[62] During a second trip later that year, Zia exclaimed to Walters that Pakistan was "not, repeat not, engaged even in a research program in the nuclear weapons field."[63]

Walters's frustrating encounters with Zia set the stage for the Pakistani leader's first meeting with President Reagan in Washington, which took place in December. In a memo prepared for Reagan in advance of Zia's visit, Secretary of State George Shultz—who had replaced Haig in June—referred to the U.S. government's possession of "overwhelming evidence that Zia has been breaking his assurances to us" by attempting to manufacture fissile material and a nuclear explosive triggering package, as well as by seeking to purchase relevant nuclear technologies from abroad.[64] During their one-on-one meeting in the Oval Office, Reagan warned Zia that the United States would be obligated to terminate the fledgling aid program for Pakistan if his regime assembled or tested a nuclear device, transferred technology for such a device, violated international nuclear safeguards, or conducted unsafeguarded reprocessing of spent reactor fuel. Notably, though, Reagan did not address the most pressing problems of Pakistan's already highly advanced uranium enrichment project at Kahuta and its extensive nuclear procurement operations abroad.[65] Later that day, an unidentified White House official informed the media on background that Zia had assured Reagan that Pakistan's nuclear program was dedicated exclusively to "peaceful purposes," adding that they believed "that [Zia] is telling us the truth."[66]

A secret State Department briefing paper drafted in June 1983 by Assistant Secretary of State for Near Eastern and South Asian Affairs (NEA) Robert Gallucci revealed the hollowness of the administration's public assurances. Gallucci specified that Pakistan "has already undertaken a substantial amount of the necessary design and high explosives testing of the explosive triggering package for a nuclear explosive device and we believe Pakistan is now capable of producing a workable package of this kind." The Chinese government had facilitated these efforts by sharing with Pakistan technical knowledge relating to "fissile material production and possibly also nuclear device design."[67] According to investigative journalists Adrian Levy and Catherine Scott-Clark, at this time U.S. and Israeli intelligence sources additionally suspected that China had shipped at least two bombs worth of weapons-grade uranium to Pakistan.[68]

MORE NUCLEAR CONSTERNATION IN CONGRESS

Notwithstanding the steadily accreting evidence that Pakistan was clandestinely developing nuclear weapons, between July 1983 and May 1984 Secretary of State Shultz, Secretary of Defense Caspar Weinberger, and Vice President George H. W. Bush made separate visits to Pakistan to extol the virtues of the newly improved bilateral relationship.[69] These high-profile trips transpired against a backdrop of growing consternation on Capitol Hill in the wake of several media reports alleging nuclear cooperation between China and Pakistan. According to Len Weiss, who was then a senior aide to Senator John Glenn (D-OH), these reports "came from nowhere" because the White House had been "burying the news from elected officials."[70] They were stoked further by a series of media interviews conducted with A. Q. Khan, the director of Pakistan's uranium enrichment facility at Kahuta, during which he boasted of successfully manufacturing weapons-grade uranium.[71]

In March 1984, Senators Glenn and Cranston drafted a stringent amendment to the 1984–1985 foreign assistance authorization bill that would cut off all U.S. aid and arms sales to Pakistan unless the president could certify that Pakistan "did not possess a nuclear explosive device," and that it "was not acquiring the equipment or technology, covertly or overtly, for a nuclear device."[72] This amendment, which was passed unanimously by the SFRC, would have effectively closed the legislative loophole that since 1981 had enabled the president to grant Pakistan aid so long as he could merely certify that it had not received or detonated a nuclear explosive device. According to then-SFRC staff member Peter Galbraith, following the committee's unanticipated passage of the Glenn-Cranston Amendment, "[t]he White House was incandescent. They could not let the amendment stand. They fought back."[73] Levy and Scott-Clark note that a "frenzy of bargaining and bullying" followed on the part of administration officials, who even at one point threatened to sever all U.S. foreign assistance programs if the committee did not withdraw the provision.[74] As part of this effort, Undersecretary of State for Security Assistance William Schneider disingenuously assured the committee that the administration had "made substantial strides with respect to Pakistan's nuclear program."[75] Officials also admonished committee members that the amendment was totally unacceptable because it would ruin already tenuous U.S. relations with Pakistan and thereby end up crippling the mujahideen.[76]

The donnybrook concluded with the committee's adoption of a heavily diluted compromise measure. After an "exhausting round of talks,"[77] on April 12 the committee decided by a single vote margin to supplant the Cranston-Glenn Amendment with one sponsored by three Republican committee members, Senators Larry Pressler (SD), Charles Percy (IL), and Charles Mathias (MD). The Pressler Amendment, as it subsequently became known, merely required that the president certify on an annual basis that Pakistan did not possess a nuclear device and that new U.S. aid would reduce significantly the risk of its acquiring such a device.[78] It bears noting that even this watered-down legislation—which was passed by Congress in August 1985—was less than ideal from the administration's perspective, as the SFRC spurned a White House demand to include a presidential waiver in the amendment.[79] The administration also moved to enervate the already weak Pressler Amendment by subsequently discounting its salience in private conversations with Pakistani leaders. According to Zia's aide Sharifuddin Pirzada, "we were repeatedly told by officials at State, 'Don't worry, Pressler will save you.'"[80]

Infuriated by the recent behavior of both Pakistan and the White House on the nuclear issue, Cranston delivered a blistering rejoinder on the Senate floor.[81] He declared that substantial nonclassified evidence gleaned from several government sources indicated that Pakistan "now has the designs, the hardware, the plans, and the personnel capable of producing several nuclear weapons per year."[82] This evidence revealed not only that Pakistan had recently expanded uranium enrichment operations at Kahuta, but also that it was operating a clandestine plutonium reprocessing facility. The evidence also indicated that the Zia regime had expanded its nuclear weapons design team, accelerated the importation of nuclear warhead components from abroad, and failed to rectify chronic failures in its safeguards system at its civilian nuclear reactor at Karachi.[83]

Cranston charged the White House with violating its statutory obligation to keep Congress "fully and completely" informed on counterproliferation developments by "systematic[ally] . . . ignoring—or withholding—the bad news" pertaining to Pakistan's nuclear activities. The senator disclosed that none of the intelligence he had received pertaining to Pakistan had "been volunteered to me in classified briefings by the administration." He also charged that the administration "dodged Congressional inquiries," "kept silent" regarding Pakistan's nuclear cooperation with China, and had "not been forthcoming about repeated [International Atomic Energy Agency] safeguards deficiencies in Pakistan." He specifically fingered Reagan's State Department with holding "a vested interest" not merely in "obscuring" and "withholding" information about Pakistan's nuclear program, but also with "downright misrepresenting the facts."[84]

The day after Cranston's stinging remarks in the Senate, three Pakistani nationals were arrested in Houston for attempting to illegally export fifty krytrons from the United States to Pakistan. Krytrons are small cathode gas–filled tubes used as high-speed switches in the triggering mechanism for nuclear explosives.[85] Although the Pakistani government publicly denied any association with the three suspects, Assistant United States Attorney Samuel G. Longoria told the judge presiding over the troika's June 28 bond hearing that "we strongly suspect that Mr. Vaid [i.e., the group's accused ringleader, Nazir Ahmed Vaid] is operating at the instance of the Pakistani government and that the purpose of the export of these krytrons was specifically for the Pakistani Government's use in obtaining a nuclear weapon."[86]

THE SCHIZOPHRENIC WHITE HOUSE RESPONSE TO THE VAID ARREST

Cranston's public accusations and the arrest of the nuclear smugglers in Houston aroused considerable anxiety in the White House. In a draft agenda prepared in advance of a September 7 meeting of the administration's top national security decisionmakers, National Security Advisor Robert "Bud" McFarlane remarked that "concern in Congress is mounting (as seen in Senator Cranston's recent pronouncements) and in the future we can expect stiff criticism and opposition on the Hill . . . until or unless Pakistan commits to safeguards."[87] At the meeting, Secretary of State Shultz counseled the president to write to Zia directly to demand that he commit in writing to a verbal promise he had already made to the U.S. ambassador in Islamabad that Pakistan would not enrich uranium beyond the 5 percent purity needed for the purpose of fueling a civilian nuclear reactor.[88] Reagan heeded Shultz's advice and on September 12 dispatched a personal letter to Zia warning that enrichment above 5 percent would "be of the same significance," and "have the same implications" as violation of the four nuclear redlines he identified during the two leaders' face-to-face meeting in 1982.[89]

Even as Reagan sternly admonished Zia to restrict his regime's nuclear activities, behind the scenes senior officials scrambled to obstruct intra-administration efforts to ratchet up pressure on Pakistan. Zia's belated reply to Reagan's letter, in which he denied that Pakistan was producing highly enriched uranium and categorically objected to the deployment of foreign monitors at Kahuta, rankled Reagan's NSC staff.[90] Two staff experts on South Asia, Donald Fortier and Shirin Tahir-Kheli, urged McFarlane to "press further . . . [on behalf of] a range of verifiable measures that span the distance between current GOP [Government of Pakistan] policy and our ultimate aim of full-scope safeguards."[91] To this end, they advised holding back on the sale of five hundred advanced Sidewinder air-to-air missiles to Pakistan in order to signal Zia of the administration's dissatisfaction. When Deputy National Security Advisor John Poindexter "made these points" to Undersecretary of State for Political Affairs Michael Armacost, the latter "expressed some skepticism as to whether we could get more out of [Pakistan]" and claimed that "we were in fairly good shape with the earlier 3% [sic] commitment." Poindexter thereupon "tried to disabuse him of this warm feeling."[92] In a March 1985 visit to Islamabad, Armacost was cleared by Secretary Shultz to announce the administration's decision to unconditionally sell Pakistan the requested Sidewinder missiles.[93]

Meanwhile, according to Levy and Scott-Clark, sources inside the U.S. Customs Service informed the office of Senator John Glenn that undisclosed senior officials had also interceded in the Justice Department's ongoing prosecution of Nazir Vaid in Houston.[94] This allegation provides a plausible explanation for Assistant U.S. Attorney Longoria's extensive efforts in the months following Vaid's arrest to "reduc[e] publicity about the case."[95] Specifically, Langoria failed to contest the federal judge's imposition of a gag order prohibiting all participants from commenting publicly on the case, redrafted the initial indictment of the three suspects to expunge any reference to the possible nuclear use of the krytrons, and permitted Vaid to plea-bargain to a much reduced charge, thereby avoiding the spectacle of a public trial. Remarkably, at Vaid's October 22 sentencing in Houston, the prosecution did not contest the presiding judge's assessment that Mr. Vaid was an innocent businessperson who was not acting on behalf of a foreign government.[96]

At this fraught juncture, the administration also sprang into action to cajole the government of the Netherlands into suspending a criminal investigation of A. Q. Khan, the director of the Kahuta nuclear facility. According to then-Dutch Prime Minister Ruud Lubbers, the CIA pressured his government to abort the prosecution of Khan for stealing classified information during the late 1970s from URENCO, the Dutch, British, and German nuclear research consortium where Khan had been employed.[97] This move was only the most intrusive element of a broader effort by the administration to downplay Pakistani nuclear procurement operations in Europe. Both Assistant Secretary of State Gallucci and Norman A. Wulf, the deputy assistant director for nonproliferation and regional arms control of the Arms Control and Disarmament Agency (ACDA), later alleged that top State Department officials had instructed U.S. embassies throughout Europe to issue only mild diplomatic reproaches when they uncovered evidence that European companies were furnishing nuclear supplies to Pakistan.[98]

These various efforts by the administration to contain the nuclear procurement controversy were not entirely successful in smothering Congress's ire on Pakistan. Majorities in both the House and Senate voted in favor of a stringent amendment sponsored by Representative Stephen Solarz (D-NY) that prohibited U.S. military and economic assistance to any country caught illegally exporting from the United States technologies that would "contribute significantly" to its ability to manufacture a nuclear explosive device. The White House exerted little effort to kill the measure because it included a waiver allowing the president to suspend the sanctions if he determined that a cutoff of aid would be "seriously prejudicial to the achievement of United States nonproliferation objectives and otherwise jeopardize the common defense and security."[99]

The passage of the Solarz Amendment in August 1985 once again prompted the administration to paradoxically warn Zia that his nuclear activities were endangering the bilateral relationship even as it strove to quash domestic opposition to that relationship. In July 1986, President Reagan welcomed Zia's newly appointed prime minister, Mohammed Khan Junejo, to the White House to sign a memorandum of understanding (MOU) that would allow Pakistan to purchase high-technology U.S. goods. A briefing memo prepared for Secretary Shultz in advance of the visit noted that Pakistan's actions were making "annual [Pressler] certification—and even [Symington] waiver—very problematic" and advised the secretary to "[e]nsure that . . . Junejo understands absolute criticality of actions, not pious words."[100] In a separate meeting on Capitol Hill with members of the SFRC, Junejo dissembled, insisting that "whatever nuclear work is going forward is for civil purposes" and that Pakistan was "abiding by the guidelines" of 5 percent enrichment set by Reagan in his 1984 letter to Zia.[101]

Although the MOU on dual-use exports to Pakistan contained strict language forbidding diversion of U.S. high-technology items to the Pakistani nuclear program, the White House almost immediately began circumventing its own requirements. Publicly, administration officials boasted that the MOU contained explicit prohibitions on the diversion of dual-use exports to nuclear activities that were "considered among the strongest" that the United States had imposed on Pakistan to date; they would "not allow Pakistan to circumvent US nuclear proliferation restrictions."[102] Stephen Bryen, the administration's under secretary of defense for technology security, later claimed, however, that although the Pentagon was granted "some access for a short time" to the export licensing process for Pakistan, "part of the arrangement [regarding the MOU] was that the Defense Department would no longer review export licenses for Pakistan."[103]

MORE EXECUTIVE BRANCH BRUSH FIRES

In the weeks preceding Reagan's meeting with Junejo, ACDA Director Kenneth Adelman dispatched an irate memo to National Security Advisor

McFarlane slamming the administration's hapless negotiations with Zia. Adelman made the charge cited in this chapter's epigraph. Instead, he said, it was imperative that the president "force Zia to face the choice between enrichment and security assistance before conceding him both," by refusing to certify that Pakistan had met the Pressler Amendment's stipulation that it did not possess a nuclear explosive. Reflecting White House fears, Adelman admitted that standing firm against Pakistan could encourage Congress to "overreact." He nevertheless counseled that this risk was outweighed by those associated with the current policy.[104]

In October, the president's decision to disregard Adelman's recommendation by issuing the Pressler certification for Pakistan touched off a "rebellion inside the White House and the State Department."[105] At a high-level State Department briefing, Assistant Secretary of State for Intelligence Morton Abramowitz conceded that the administration had not been tough enough on Pakistan, but immediately thereafter "insist[ed] there were to be no official papers on this discussion. Everyone was sworn to secrecy." As a result, according to Stephen Cohen, who was a member of the department's policy planning staff,

> The bottom line was that nobody could stand up and do anything to frighten the relationship with Pakistan and I was told by one very senior person at State that if we did what I wanted to do—for example try and rescind US military aid, like pulling back the F-16s—we would never get it through government. I was warned that we would lose our jobs tomorrow. One senior official in the Reagan administration told me, "Why are you talking about this? Keep your head down." It was not a suggestion.[106]

ACDA official Norm Wulf similarly recalled that the atmosphere within the administration following the October certification was quite tense, and he strongly believed at the time that Reagan's Pressler certification "was an outright lie."[107] A bombshell story in the *Washington Post* in early November lent credence to Wulf's harsh accusation, revealing that a recent Special National Intelligence Estimate (SNIE) requested by the White House had concluded that Pakistan was making "dramatic progress toward production of a nuclear weapon." The SNIE reportedly mentioned that

Pakistan had detonated a high-explosive device two months earlier and had successfully enriched uranium to weapons grade at Kahuta.[108]

At about the same time, Richard Barlow, a proliferation-intelligence officer at the CIA's Office of Scientific and Weapons Research, became alarmed at the scope of Pakistan's nuclear procurement activities. In his review of several classified State Department cables and files, Barlow also discovered that Foggy Bottom had repeatedly refrained from sharing crucial intelligence concerning Pakistan's nuclear program with both the Commerce Department, which was legally tasked with approving export licenses, and the Customs Service, which was responsible for enforcing U.S. export law. Even more disturbing, Barlow found that the department had dispatched a "steady pattern of demarches to Islamabad revealing classified material" pertaining to U.S. knowledge of Pakistani foreign procurement operations.[109] This precipitated a confrontation between CIA Deputy Director of Intelligence Richard Kerr and unnamed senior State Department officials, in which Kerr threatened to launch an internal investigation unless State immediately put an end to these surreptitious communications.[110]

THE PAKISTAN AID BATTLE ON CAPITOL HILL

As the first multiyear assistance package for Pakistan wound down in early 1987, the administration began to line up domestic political support for its intended $4.02 billion follow-on package. To this end, the White House approved a bristling speech in Islamabad by U.S. Ambassador to Pakistan Deane Hinton, in which he implored Pakistan's leaders to "accept full-scope [nuclear] safeguards."[111] In early March, however, after the Indian Army conducted its largest-ever military exercise (Operation Brasstacks, in the Rajasthan desert near its border with Pakistan), A. Q. Khan declared during an interview with an Indian journalist that Pakistan had produced a nuclear bomb.[112] Later that month, President Zia told *Time* magazine, "You can write today that Pakistan can build a bomb whenever it wishes."[113]

In congressional appearances accompanying the administration's formal aid request, officials firmly dismissed the likely effectiveness of any U.S. nuclear sanctions on Pakistan. For example, during a hearing of HFAC's

Subcommittee on Asian and Pacific Affairs, Deputy Assistant Secretary of State for Near Eastern and South Asian Affairs Robert Peck argued in his prepared statement that it would be a "mistake . . . to conclude that our non-proliferation efforts have been ineffective, or that our policies have failed," citing as evidence President Reagan's certification the previous October that Pakistan did not possess a nuclear device.[114] During his testimony, Peck also cautioned subcommittee members that the United States "should avoid public confrontations and legislative ultimata of standards Pakistan must meet." Such actions, he warned, would "create serious problems in our relationship . . . and put at risk a variety of larger interests in regard to Pakistan, including the influence which we have over Pakistan nuclear decision-making."[115] Revealingly, at the height of the administration's attempt to clear the way for the aid package on Capitol Hill, an unnamed "senior Pakistani official" exclaimed to the *New York Times*, "We expect the [Reagan] Administration to fight for every dollar" of the proposed $4 billion aid program.[116]

At this consequential moment for the U.S.-Pakistan alliance, Assistant Secretary of State for Near Eastern and South Asian Affairs Richard Murphy proposed an action plan for dealing with the Pakistan conundrum to Secretary Shultz. Murphy acknowledged candidly that the Pakistanis had "so far not responded constructively to our request that they take concrete actions to demonstrate compliance with their assurances on uranium enrichment and restraint in other key nuclear areas."[117] To defuse the "strong pressure" from Congress to impose tougher conditions on aid, Murphy insisted that the administration needed to persuade Pakistan to "rest on its oars."[118] He added that "to be credible, Pakistan will need to offer some arrangement for on-site inspections of its uranium enrichment facility."[119] Interestingly, although Murphy conceded that it was "unlikely" that Pakistan would make significant concessions on uranium enrichment in response to mere White House pleas, he nevertheless opposed establishing a "clear linkage" between U.S. security assistance and Pakistani nuclear restraint.[120] He also advised the secretary to "make calls to key members of the SFRC and the Senate leadership to discourage unacceptable amendments in the SFRC markup" of the foreign aid bill.[121]

By the end of April, the Pakistan aid package had successfully navigated HFAC by a wide 17–2 margin and SFRC by a less-comfortable 11–8.[122] The only constraint successfully attached to the bill by nonproliferation advocates was HFAC's substitution of the administration's request for another six-year waiver of the Symington Amendment for Pakistan with a more restrictive two-year waiver.[123] In a last-ditch effort to ensure successful passage by the Senate committee, Undersecretary of State Armacost assured its members that Pakistan "fully understands the consequences of acquiring or testing a [nuclear] device," and thereby cautioned that it would be "counterproductive" to level a public ultimatum toward Islamabad. Having failed to attach any conditions to the legislation at the committee level, congressional opponents vowed to redouble their efforts during consideration of the bill at the floor level in both chambers. In the Senate, Senator Glenn proposed an amendment calling for the complete cessation of all military aid to Pakistan unless the administration could provide Congress with "reliable assurances" that the country had stopped producing weapons-grade nuclear material. In addition, Senator Cranston co-sponsored an amendment requiring Pakistan to forfeit $100 million of the proposed $625 million aid program for fiscal year 1988 unless the president could make this certification.[124]

THE PERVEZ ARREST AND ITS AFTERMATH

Any hopes within the administration for the foreign aid bill's expeditious passage by the full House and Senate were shattered by the July 10 arrest of Arshad Pervez in Philadelphia by undercover federal agents. Pervez, a Pakistani-born Canadian citizen, was charged with attempting to illegally export to Pakistan fifty thousand pounds of Maraging 350 steel, a powerful alloy used almost exclusively to manufacture the tubular rotors that turn nuclear centrifuges for the enrichment of uranium.[125] Evidence presented in the affidavit filed in U.S. Federal Court by the Customs Service showed that Pervez was working for a retired brigadier general in the Pakistani army, Inam ul-Haq, who owned an import-export business in Lahore. This evidence included highly suspicious letters from Inam enjoining Pervez to complete the transaction for the sake of Pakistan's national interest.[126]

Further implicating Pervez was his concurrent attempt to purchase beryllium, an extremely light and flexible metal useful for constructing the shell that houses an enriched uranium core in a nuclear explosive device.[127] Pervez's arrest placed the administration's Pakistan policy in grave jeopardy, as the 1985 Solarz Amendment stipulated a complete cutoff of aid to any country that the president found had attempted to illegally export nuclear-related materials from the United States. Pakistan's Foreign Ministry issued a statement announcing that the Pakistani government had "no connection whatever" with Pervez, though it later announced that a warrant had been issued for the arrest of Inam, who had allegedly disappeared.[128]

The Pervez arrest provoked a furious reaction on Capitol Hill. SFRC chair Claiborne Pell (D-RI) publicly condemned "[o]ur record of accepting [Pakistan's] lies and transgressions," and avowed that this was "the time to show Pakistan we mean business." Meanwhile, two Democrats on the committee who had voted in favor of the Pakistan aid package, John Kerry (MA) and Christopher Dodd (CT), declared that they were reconsidering their position.[129] In the House, HFAC chair Dante Fascall (D-FL) and the chair of the Subcommittee on International Economic Policy and Trade, Don Bonker (D-WA) dispatched a letter to President Reagan urging him to temporarily suspend all aid to Pakistan pending good-faith efforts by Pakistan to "make good on its pledges of peaceful intent in the nuclear field."[130] Meanwhile, Stephen Solarz charged that the Pervez case was a "flagrant and provocative challenge to U.S. nonproliferation policy"[131] and reasoned that "[i]f the Department of Justice has sufficient evidence to seek an indictment [of Pervez], then presumably the President has ample justification for triggering the [1985 Solarz Amendment]."[132]

The incident also sparked intensified bureaucratic pressure on leading administration decisionmakers. On July 14, ACDA director Kenneth Adelman dispatched an angry memo to the State Department objecting to the "business as usual" tone of the talking points drafted for Undersecretary Armacost's forthcoming meeting with Pakistan's U.S. ambassador to discuss Pervez. Acknowledging the concern that the administration refrain from making "assertions to Congress and the media that could make it more difficult to deal with the Solarz Amendment later," Adelman nonetheless insisted that this concern should not apply to private conversations with

Pakistani officials.[133] A week later, an exasperated Adelman dispatched a second irate memo to Armacost warning that if "we now 'lawyer our way around' the Solarz Amendment, Zia will conclude once again that he need do nothing about his bomb project."[134]

Recognizing the high domestic political stakes attached to the Pervez scandal, the White House sprang into action to minimize the fallout. Publicly, even as administration officials claimed that it was "premature"[135] to conclude that the Zia regime had any involvement with the case, they nevertheless adopted harder-edged rhetoric toward Islamabad. For instance, State Department spokesperson Charles Redman announced that the administration "cannot, and will not, tolerate any clandestine, any illegal efforts to circumvent our export control laws."[136] Further, in testimony before a joint hearing of two HFAC subcommittees on July 22, Assistant Secretary Murphy announced that the administration intended to "intensify our efforts to produce concrete evidence of Pakistani nuclear restraint," and informed lawmakers that the administration had communicated to Pakistan that the Pervez case "increases the need for steps to demonstrate that Pakistan's nuclear program is 'peaceful.'"[137]

The administration was less than candid, however, in a closed-door, classified intelligence briefing delivered by General David Einsel, the national intelligence officer for nonproliferation, to the same subcommittees later that day. In response to a question by one of the dozen assembled legislators, Einsel remarked that the administration was "not sure" if Pervez and Inam were agents of the Pakistani government. CIA analyst Richard Barlow, who also represented the administration at the briefing, was stunned by Einsel's statement, which he judged to be "highly evasive, and deliberately so."[138] When he subsequently contradicted Einsel, the general insisted that Barlow "doesn't know what he's talking about."[139] Barlow additionally informed the subcommittees that there had been "scores of other cases" of Pakistani nuclear procurement operations abroad since 1985, prompting Einsel to interject that any additional procurement cases had yet to be definitively proven.[140] Following this incident, Einsel, Deputy Assistant Secretary of State Peck, and an unnamed assistant secretary of state all harangued Barlow's line managers at CIA and even lodged protests against Barlow with CIA Deputy Director for Intelligence Richard Kerr.[141]

Despite the administration's claims that it would more aggressively push Pakistan on the nuclear issue, by the end of the month Congress had begun to seize the reins on U.S. policy. On July 29, the House Appropriations Sub-committee on Foreign Operations inserted a provision in the 1988 foreign aid bill temporarily withholding $290 million in military sales credits and $250 million in economic support for Pakistan until January 15, 1988.[142] A State Department spokesperson expressed "regret" for the measure, insist-ing that "while we seek a more satisfactory understanding on the nuclear issue, we also wish to maintain the continuity of our crucial cooperation with Pakistan."[143] Both the House and Senate also passed a nonbinding resolution urging the president to inform Pakistan that the provision of additional U.S. military aid would be contingent on Pakistan's compliance with previously articulated nuclear commitments.[144]

ARMACOST IN ISLAMABAD

The White House took advantage of a previously scheduled trip to Islam-abad by Undersecretary Armacost to try to defuse the controversy sparked by the Pervez case. In light of growing restiveness toward Pakistan on Capitol Hill, Armacost told Zia that the White House had to "be able to show something concrete to the Congress."[145] To resolve the procurement controversy, Armacost requested that Zia furnish documentary evidence of procurement guidelines issued by Pakistani nuclear agencies, cooperate with the Justice Department on the Pervez/Inam case, and return illegally procured nuclear equipment originating from the United States.[146] Mean-while, on the matter of uranium enrichment, Armacost argued that Pakistani acquiescence to International Atomic Energy Agency inspection procedures at Kahuta would provide "the optimal solution" but conceded that an ad hoc bilateral inspection arrangement would be "satisfactory."[147]

Zia poured cold water on all of Armacost's suggestions. On procurement, he pledged melodramatically that he would step down from office if any connection was found between Pervez and the Pakistani government, claimed that Inam was under surveillance and would "get it in the neck" if found guilty of violating any laws, and promised not to procure any item in the future that the United States deemed illegal for export.[148] On enrichment, Zia not only categorically refused to allow on-site inspections of any kind unless India also agreed to them, but even dismissed as "impossible" the relatively innocuous proposal floated by Armacost to establish a bilateral working group to devise a mutually acceptable compromise solution to the enrichment dispute.[149] The next month, Prime Minister Junejo publicly ruled out any additional nuclear concessions to the United States and insisted that although his government knew the whereabouts of Inam ul-Haq, it would not act on that knowledge unless Pakistan received certain undisclosed documents pertaining to the Pervez/Inam case from Washington.[150]

RESCUING THE FOLLOW-ON AID PACKAGE FROM PURGATORY

The administration's awkward strategy of simultaneously enjoining Pakistan to make concessions on the nuclear issue while simultaneously shielding Pakistan from domestic critics was even more sorely tested in the months following the Pervez arrest. On September 21, Reagan approached Junejo at the annual inauguration session of the UN General Assembly and bluntly warned the Pakistani premier, "I have to certify on the nuclear program and you have to make it possible for me to do so."[151] An unnamed U.S. official informed the *New York Times* that the president had specifically demanded of Junejo that Pakistan open its nuclear installations to international inspections.[152] The next week Congress failed to extend the six-year waiver of the Symington Amendment's application to Pakistan, thereby preventing new aid to Pakistan from being appropriated for the fiscal year beginning on October 1. State Department spokesperson Phyllis Oakley charged that the cutoff "sends the wrong signal about the continuing U.S. commitment to Pakistan's security" and pressed Congress to immediately reopen the aid spigot in light of Pakistani leaders' assurances "that they do not intend to develop nuclear explosives."[153]

At a joint hearing of three HFAC subcommittees (Arms Control, International Security, and Science; Asian and Pacific Affairs; and International Economic Policy and Trade), Ambassador-at-Large for Non-Proliferation Richard Kennedy tried to break the congressional logjam on

Pakistan but was squarely confronted with the various fallacies and con-tradictions that continued to riddle the administration's policy. Kennedy assured legislators that the White House had "made it clear that Pakistan must show restraint in its nuclear program," but warned that it would be "extremely risky" for Congress to attach explicit behavioral conditions to U.S. aid because the Pakistani public would view such a move as a "discrimi-natory public ultimatum."[154] Kennedy also tried to dissuade the subcom-mittee from interfering with the administration's Pakistan policy by claiming that it had achieved "some success" in securing Pakistani compli-ance. On this score, he asserted that White House pressure had prevented Pakistan from conducting a nuclear test, transferring sensitive nuclear tech-nology to other countries, engaging in unsafeguarded plutonium repro-cessing, and violating its international safeguarding obligations.[155]

Kennedy's remarks did not mollify the proliferation hawks in attendance. Representative Solarz lambasted Kennedy for failing to "acknowledge sim-ple facts" in testifying that Pakistan's declarations regarding its nuclear program were reliable.[156] He also dismissed Kennedy's repetition of the administration's longstanding contention that the unconditional provision of large-scale military assistance diminished Pakistan's motivation to develop nuclear arms, objecting that "it is fairly clear that that effort has basically been a failure."[157] Further, Solarz scoffed at Kennedy's warning that Zia would not be able to comply with congressionally imposed condi-tions on Pakistan's continued access to U.S. aid because doing so would risk a public backlash: "[T]o stop enriching [uranium] over 5 percent . . . would not constitute a critical embarrassment to the government [of Pakistan] since they would simply be doing what they say they have been doing all along."[158] In a final salvo, Solarz inquired how Kennedy could logically state that U.S. legal provisions against the assembly or explosion of a nuclear device had "contributed to Pakistani decisions neither to test the device nor to assemble nuclear weapons," while also claiming that the U.S. adoption of a legal prohibition against enrichment risked driving Pakistan "to take the kind of step which is precisely the one we don't want them to take."[159]

Michigan Democrat Howard Wolpe joined the fray by questioning how the Zia regime's "persistent violations" of U.S. export control laws and con-travention of its promises not to produce highly enriched uranium could possibly be reconciled with Kennedy's assertion that Pakistan had demonstrated admirable restraint in its nuclear activities. Additionally, Wolpe contested Kennedy's declaration that the administration had exerted "all kinds of pressure" on Pakistan to curb its nuclear program:

MR. WOLPE. Is there any cost contemplated if they do not respond to an issue? Does the administration contemplate any kind of measure that would represent some cost in terms of Pakistan's relationship to the United States?

AMBASSADOR KENNEDY. We at this point don't want to look at that hypothetical. We want to look at the likelihood we are going to succeed [on the basis of diplomatic appeals alone].[160]

Dissident voices in the executive bureaucracy also continued to complicate the administration's attempt to push the embattled aid program through Congress. In early November, ACDA Director Adelman pressed Undersecretary Armacost to support an immediate presidential invocation of the Solarz Amendment.[161] When this appeal failed, Adelman dispatched another memo, this one addressed directly to President Reagan. He enjoined the president to maximize the pressure on Zia to stop uranium enrichment and foreign nuclear procurement not only by abstaining from issuing Pressler certification for Pakistan but also by invoking the Solarz Amendment.[162]

Despite these various congressional and bureaucratic efforts to harden U.S. policy toward Zia, the administration persisted in its blanket refusal to compromise on the issue. On December 17, Reagan issued the Pressler certification for Pakistan, carefully explicating that the amendment only necessitated the imposition of sanctions if the president judged that Pakistan "possesses a nuclear device, not whether Pakistan is attempting to develop or had developed various relevant capacities."[163] In spite of the mass of discrepant data and intelligence available to the U.S. government indicating that Pakistan's nuclear program had accelerated since the initiation of the administration's aid program in 1981, Reagan also reported that the second key condition imposed by the legislation, that continued U.S. assistance would "reduce significantly the risk that Pakistan will possess a nuclear explosive device," had also been met.[164] On the same day, a House-Senate conference committee agreed to allow a waiver of the Symington Amendment for another two and a half years and appropriate $260 million in military assistance and $220 million in economic aid to Pakistan for the remainder of the fiscal year.[165] This decision was preceded by a personal appeal from Secretary of State Shultz, who informed the committee that at the recently concluded superpower summit in Washington, Soviet leader Mikhail Gorbachev had told President Reagan that the Red Army was on the cusp of withdrawing from Afghanistan. Shultz exclaimed that at this potential turning point in the war, it was absolutely critical for Congress to continue funneling as much aid as possible to Pakistan.[166]

DENOUEMENT OF THE SECOND PAKISTAN AID BATTLE

Once again, the Zia regime leaped through the window that the White House had opened wide in its frantic efforts to blunt all attempts in Congress or the executive branch to restrict U.S. aid. In a secret December 29 memorandum to Armacost, INR director Morton Abramowitz reported that since the passage of the Solarz Amendment more than two years prior, there had been "no let-up in efforts by elements of the Pakistani nuclear weapons program to acquire U.S. [nuclear-related] goods and in some cases it appears they have succeeded."[167] He added that not only had Zia's promises to cooperate with the United States in investigating the Pervez case "thus far remained unfulfilled," but also that officials in the Pakistan Atomic Energy Commission continued to "concoct cover stories and clandestine plots to acquire U.S.-origin goods."[168] Then, on January 10, 1988, unnamed administration officials leaked to the *New York Times* that, according to recent intelligence reports, Pakistan was constructing a second uranium enrichment facility at Golra, just west of Islamabad.[169]

Within days of this latest development, President Reagan officially determined that Pakistan had run afoul of the Solarz Amendment, though he invoked the national security waiver, professing that the suspension of assistance there would adversely impact U.S. nonproliferation objectives and jeopardize the common defense and security.[170] In a public statement, Reagan justified this decision on the grounds that Pakistan had pledged that "procedures will be tightened to ensure an end to procurement activities in the United States."[171] In a February appearance before the HFAC Subcommittees on Asian and Pacific Affairs and International Economic Policy and Trade, Deputy Assistant Secretary of State Peck explained that the president's decision to waive the Solarz Amendment was made on the basis of "strengthened assurances from Pakistan as well as concrete evidence that those assurances were, in fact, being lived up to,"[172] though he declined to provide specific details of both the assurances and the evidence to which he alluded.

In Reagan's final year in office, as the Afghanistan War wound down, the administration finally began to strike a somewhat more confrontational tone with Pakistan's leadership. During a summer 1988 visit to Washington, a denial by Pakistan's newly reappointed foreign minister, Sahabzada Yakub Khan, that operations at Kahuta were continuing to expand prompted White House officials to whisk him to the State Department, where he was confronted with reams of photographic and technical intelligence data that thoroughly belied his claim.[173] Later that fall, although Reagan issued his third consecutive Pressler certification for Pakistan, his accompanying statement expressed deep concern about the country's nuclear activities.[174] These steps proved to be far too little, far too late to be consequential. By the spring of 1988, Pakistan had amassed enough highly enriched uranium to fill at least forty nuclear bombs.[175]

CONCLUSION

According to the conventional wisdom, straightforward geopolitics dictated the Reagan administration's policy toward Pakistan during the 1980s. Faced with the two competing imperatives of forestalling the Soviet conquest of Afghanistan and preventing Pakistan from going nuclear, it sacrificed the latter at the altar of the former.[176] This interpretation overlooks the United States' extremely favorable international systemic position vis-à-vis Pakistan, which should have enabled it to simultaneously achieve both geopolitical objectives. This chapter has argued that it was not geopolitics alone but the interaction of geopolitics with domestic politics that compelled the administration to give Pakistan a free pass on the nuclear issue. Caught between its strong desire to curb the Pakistani nuclear program and its deep concerns about domestic opposition, senior officials repeatedly temporized. They issued toothless admonitions to Pakistani leaders to curtail their nuclear activities while actively undercutting all attempts in Congress and the executive bureaucracy to tightly condition U.S. aid to Pakistani concessions on its nuclear program and punish Islamabad for its past transgressions. Over time, this strategy drained all credibility from the administration's repeated warnings to Pakistan that it would be penalized for continued misbehavior and induced the Zia regime to engage in increasingly brazen and risky actions to expedite Pakistan's quest for the bomb.

Whereas the short-term benefits of the U.S. alliance with Pakistan were immense, the long-term costs have proven nightmarish. In May 1998, India conducted a series of underground nuclear tests, which compelled Pakistan to do the same two weeks later in the face of desperate pleas by U.S. President Bill Clinton to hold fire.[177] One year later, an emboldened Islamabad undertook a risky military operation across the line of control in the Kargil Mountains of India's disputed Kashmir province, precipitating a skirmish that the Clinton administration feared might result in all-out nuclear war.[178] Then, in January 2005, Pakistani president General Pervez Musharraf placed A. Q. Khan under house arrest in response to revelations that Khan had run a private nuclear proliferation network that had secretly offered or provided uranium enrichment technology to North Korea, Libya, Iran, Iraq, possibly Syria, and other countries. The Khan network, which in all likelihood operated with the acquiescence of the Pakistani government, also allegedly sold the design of a workable nuclear weapon to Libya and offered to provide such a design to Iraq in 1990. Concern in Washington that Pakistan had facilitated the efforts by U.S. adversaries to develop nuclear weapons intermingled with the fear that Pakistan's nuclear arsenal was vulnerable to seizure by Al Qaeda or other jihadist terrorist groups based in the country.[179] The risks of nuclear war, nuclear proliferation, and nuclear terrorism have all increased dramatically as a result of the Reagan administration's behavior toward its Pakistani ally of convenience during the 1980s.

4

THE U.S. ALLIANCE WITH IRAQ, 1982–1988

Iraq has thus far been able to obtain from the U.S. essentially what it wanted while sacrificing few of its political ideals.

—U.S. DEFENSE INTELLIGENCE AGENCY, "DEFENSE ESTIMATIVE BRIEF: PROSPECTS FOR IRAQ," SEPTEMBER 25, 1984

T IS HARD to dispute the contention that Iraqi dictator Saddam Hussein was America's most nefarious post-1945 ally of convenience, especially considering that the United States subsequently waged two major wars against his regime, the second of which toppled him from power and resulted in his execution.[1] In early 1982, the Reagan administration began to cooperate with the then-newly ascendant strongman in Baghdad, after the invasion he had launched two years earlier against the United States' foremost regional enemy, Iran, faltered and the Iranians in turn mounted a ferocious counteroffensive into Iraq. As Iraq's position in the war steadily deteriorated, the administration unveiled a range of diplomatic, economic, and military measures intended to forestall Baghdad's defeat. These initiatives—which were temporarily undermined midway through the war by a covert White House operation to sell arms to Tehran in exchange for the release of American hostages being held by Shia terrorists in Lebanon—helped reinvigorate the Iraqi war effort. Iraq eventually rolled back the Iranian counteroffensive, and in August 1988, the two belligerents signed an armistice that ended the conflict without affording a decisive victory to either side.

Although the de facto alliance established between the United States and Iraq successfully contained Iranian expansionism, its management was complicated by serious disagreements between the partners regarding

Iraq's sponsorship of international terrorism and its proliferation of nuclear weapons and ballistic missiles. Both neorealist and tying hands theories strongly predict that the administration should have bargained success-fully with Iraq on both issues. For neorealism, this prediction rests on extremely lopsided balances of dependence and commitment that favored the United States, while the equally strong tying hands prediction rests on the enormous gap in domestic win-sets between the United States and Saddam's Iraq, which should have been magnified by heavy domestic opposition to the alliance in the former. By contrast, the neoclassical real-ist (NCR) theory of alliance politics predicts that U.S. bargaining with Iraq should have been passive and unsuccessful. Substantial domestic political opposition to the alliance should have led the foreign policy executive to adopt a passive bargaining strategy aimed at projecting an artificially benign image of Iraq.

As predicted by NCR, senior officials in the White House, State Department, and Commerce Department mounted an all-out campaign to stifle critics of the alliance by whitewashing Iraqi behavior. Specifically, they downplayed, ignored, and concealed evidence of Iraqi transgressions, oversold small-scale Iraqi concessions, reneged on prior threats to punish Iraqi misbehavior, marginalized policy dissidents in the executive bureau-cracy, and promoted the activities of private interests eager to maximize bilateral contacts with Iraq. Consequently, as the Iran-Iraq War dragged on, Iraq's sponsorship of international terrorism and development of unconventional weapons became increasingly brazen, and by the war's end Iraq had supplanted Iran as the gravest threat to U.S. interests in the Mid-dle East.

THE IRAN-IRAQ WAR

On January 16, 1979, a fragile détente between the longtime enemies of Iraq and Iran was shaken when the secular Iranian monarch, Shah Mohammed Reza Pahlavi, fled Iran in response to the outbreak of violent antigovern-ment demonstrations in Tehran. Two weeks later, the influential Iranian cleric Ayatollah Ruhollah Khomeini returned from exile in Paris and proclaimed himself to be the "Supreme Leader of the Revolution."[2] On April 2, Khomeini formally proclaimed the establishment of a Shia theocracy in Iran, which he renamed the Islamic Republic of Iran.[3] Iraqi president Saddam Hussein's subsequent decision to invade was largely attributable to the fear that the revolution would spread next door to Iraq. Not only did the two states share a lengthy border, but the majority of Iraq's population were Shia Muslims, who had experienced political exclusion and repression at the hands of the Sunni minority who had governed the country since its birth as a British mandate in 1920.[4]

Saddam's war aims were limited to the seizure of Iran's southwestern province of Khuzestan. This would in turn enable Iraq to establish complete control over the Shatt al-Arab River that feeds into the Persian Gulf, seize some of the surrounding oil-rich, predominantly Arab-populated Iranian territory, and coerce Iran's leaders into halting their support for a Shia uprising in Iraq. Immediately after Saddam initiated the war by launching a (botched) bombing raid against Iran's air defense network on September 22, he ordered a full-on ground invasion by ten Iraqi army divisions. By December, although the Iraqi forces had captured Iran's strategic port city of Khorramshahr and laid siege to its massive oil refinery complex at Abadan, the invasion sputtered to a halt. Iran launched a ferocious counteroffensive, and in September 1981 its forces managed to break the siege at Abadan. By the time Iran recaptured Khorramshahr in May 1982, Iraq had lost approximately 50 percent of the 100,000 troops initially committed to the invasion, as well as 60 percent of its tanks, 40 percent of its combat aircraft, and 20 percent of its artillery.[5]

A now-desperate Saddam declared a unilateral cease-fire on June 10. After Khomeini refused to reciprocate, the Iraqi leader frantically ordered his forces to vacate Iranian territory. The Ayatollah in turn ordered an advance into southern Iraq with the goal of seizing Iraq's second-largest city, Basra. This operation bogged down quickly, however, inaugurating a grinding four-year stalemate along the 1,200-kilometer front. In February 1986, Iran decisively broke the stalemate with its conquest of the Fao

Peninsula in southern Iraq, which contained major Iraqi oil installations and controlled the country's access to the Shatt. After the Iraqis blocked a follow-on Iranian attempt to conquer Basra, Iran's Supreme Defense Council decided to forgo additional costly land offensives and instead conduct all-out economic warfare against Iraq. By escalating naval and air attacks against merchant shipping in the Gulf, Iran's leadership hoped to coerce Iraq's Gulf Arab allies of Saudi Arabia, Kuwait, and the United Arab Emirates into curtailing their financing of Iraq's war effort. Iran's escalation of the "Tanker War" proved self-defeating, however, as it precipitated an even more vicious Iraqi retaliation against Iranian targets in the Gulf, and led the United States and other major powers to deploy a combat flotilla to protect neutral shipping. This intervention provoked several direct clashes between Iranian and U.S. warships, pulverizing Iran's naval capabilities.[6]

In early 1988, the war's momentum swung in Iraq's favor. On April 17, the Iraqi Army's Seventh Corps and elements of Saddam's elite Republican Guard assaulted Fao, wresting the peninsula from Iran's grip in a mere two days. Follow-on Iraqi offensives overran Iranian positions north of Basra. Iran's morale was also battered by the accidental downing of an Iran Air jetliner near the Strait of Hormuz by the American guided missile cruiser USS *Vincennes*, which resulted in 290 civilian fatalities. Two weeks later, the Iranian regime secretly notified the United Nations secretary general of its intention to accept UN Security Council Resolution 598, which called for an internationally supervised cease-fire. On July 20, Khomeini made the decision public, though the Ayatollah's subsequent refusal to allow his foreign minister to engage in direct negotiations with his Iraqi counterpart enabled Saddam to launch a massive reinvasion of Iran with all twelve of the Iraqi army's armored and mechanized divisions. This Iraqi blitzkrieg spurred the Ayatollah to finally acquiesce to face-to-face armistice negotiations. The two belligerents summarily concluded a cease-fire, which went into effect on August 20. Although the Iran-Iraq War exacted an enormous toll in terms of both blood (680,000 total combat deaths) and treasure ($1.1 trillion in total war spending by both sides in constant 1988 dollars), it ended almost exactly where it began, at the *status quo antebellum*.[7]

THE U.S. ALLIANCE OF CONVENIENCE
WITH IRAQ

The Reagan administration's "tilt" toward Baghdad began with its consequential decisions in early 1982 to remove Iraq from the State Department's
list of terrorism-sponsoring states, provide sensitive battlefield intelligence
to Baghdad, and enjoin America's allies in Western Europe and the Middle East to sell arms to Iraq. The consequent shift in bilateral relations meets
both of the conditions for classification as an alliance of convenience: the
pre-alliance relationship between the United States and Iraq was characterized by sharp ideological and geopolitical conflict, and Iran represented
an overarching threat to both.

Ideologically, whereas the United States was a liberal democracy, Iraq
was an extraordinarily repressive autocracy. While the formal ideological
program espoused by Iraq's ruling Ba'ath Party consisted of a mixture of
pan-Arabism and socialism, in practice Saddam Hussein constructed a
ruthless, totalitarian political system in which his arbitrary personalist rule
was absolute and permeated nearly all aspects of Iraqi society.[8]

Geopolitically, for more than two decades, Iraq's foreign policy had been
increasingly at odds with the United States' foremost global interest in containing the Soviet Union, as well as its chief regional interests in protecting
Israel and promoting a peaceful resolution of the Arab-Israeli conflict.
Iraqi-U.S. relations began to deteriorate in the aftermath of the 1958 military
coup in Baghdad that ousted the pro-Western Hashemite monarch
Faisal II. In short order, the new military regime led by General Abdul
Karim Qassim withdrew from the Central Treaty Organization (CENTO),
the U.S.-sponsored regional anti-Soviet collective security organization
created in 1955, canceled a bilateral military aid agreement with Washington, threatened to invade the British protectorate of Kuwait, and began
accepting deliveries of arms and economic credits from the Soviet Union.[9]

Bilateral tensions with the United States continued to rise after Qassim
was overthrown in a 1963 coup, which brought a succession of alternating
Ba'athist and military regimes to power in Baghdad. During the Six Day
War of June 1967, Iraq joined the Arab military coalition against Israel and,

following its resounding defeat, severed bilateral diplomatic relations with the United States. Then, in 1972, Iraq signed a fifteen-year friendship treaty with the Soviet Union, which was already furnishing it with virtually all of its military hardware.[10] In October 1973, Baghdad once again took up arms against Israel in the Yom Kippur War. In the aftermath of yet another Arab defeat, Iraq stood at the forefront of the bloc of radical Arab states that were vociferously opposed to Egyptian president Anwar Sadat's effort to pursue a U.S.-brokered peace with Israel. To bolster its credentials on this score, Iraq began providing political, financial, and material support to the most extreme militant groups associated with Yasser Arafat's Palestinian Liberation Organization (PLO).[11]

The threat posed by revolutionary Iran to both the United States and Iraq exceeded that posed by each of the allies to the other. For the United States, the Iranian revolution replaced the Shah of Iran, America's closest friend and security partner in the Persian Gulf region, with Ayatollah Khomeini, who transformed the Iranian polity into an Islamist theocracy. Khomeini railed against the United States (the "Great Satan") and Israel (the "Little Satan"), sponsored Shia terrorist groups operating throughout the region, and sought to export the revolution to surrounding Arab states.[12] Then, in November 1979, a student mob inspired and supported by Khomeini seized the U.S. embassy in Tehran and held dozens of its American employees hostage for the next fourteen months. This act, which horrified and infuriated the American public, marked the end of a dramatic, year-long transformation of Iran from the United States' closest ally in the Persian Gulf to its "bitterest foe."[13]

The Iranian threat to the United States reached its apogee during the summer of 1982, after Iran had repulsed the initial Iraqi thrust into its territory and begun mounting a counterattack into Iraq. In mid-July, Henry Rowen, chair of the National Intelligence Council, dispatched a memo to Geoffrey Kemp, the senior National Security Council (NSC) staff member responsible for the Middle East, in which he spelled out the implications of an Iranian victory: "We may soon be faced with a situation in which a significant portion of the oil supplies to the West are heavily influenced by Iran or by political forces hostile to the West or by forces unable or uninterested in maintaining the flow of oil."[14] In his 1993 memoir,

Reagan's Secretary of State, George Shultz, similarly claimed that, while there were "no stars in my eyes or in Ronald Reagan's" concerning Saddam Hussein's regime, an Iraqi collapse would nevertheless have been "a strategic disaster for the United States."[15] Richard Murphy, the U.S. ambassador to Saudi Arabia at the outset of the war, also recalled that the administration believed an Iranian victory would "become some sort of Middle East Armageddon."[16]

Meanwhile, as described above, the Iranian revolution and its aftermath stoked even deeper fears on the part of Iran's longtime Iraqi adversary. Saddam's decision to invade Iran was motivated primarily by the revolutionary government's exhortations to Iraq's majority Shia population to rise up and overthrow Saddam's regime and its provision of material support to Shia militants and Kurdish insurgents in Iraq. Although Saddam viewed the United States, the most powerful of his enemies, as the ultimate source of long-term danger, the most acute and immediate source was Iran.[17] To wit, in a February 1984 meeting with senior Iraqi officers, Saddam starkly admonished, "if we lose our morale and our ability to wage an attack [against Iran] then we could lose the whole of Iraq."[18]

THE ELEMENTS OF SECURITY COOPERATION BETWEEN THE UNITED STATES AND IRAQ

At the outset of the Iran-Iraq War, President Carter struck a position of firm neutrality vis-à-vis the belligerents.[19] Although the Reagan administration would officially maintain this position until the August 1988 armistice, during its first year in office it simultaneously began flirting with Baghdad while at the same time covertly hedging against an Iraqi victory. In April 1981, the president dispatched Deputy Assistant Secretary of State for Near Eastern and South Asian Affairs (NEA) Morris Draper on a goodwill mission to Baghdad to meet with Foreign Minister Saadoun Hammadi.[20] This diplomatic probe was soon followed by the new administration's unexpected condemnation of the Israeli Air Force's June 7 bombing raid against Iraq's Osirak nuclear reactor.[21] But even as it issued these unmistakably positive signals to Baghdad, the White House moved to forestall an Iraqi military victory by quietly allowing Israel to illegally ship billions of dollars' worth of U.S.-made arms, ammunition, and spare parts to Tehran.[22]

After Iran began its counteroffensive into Iraqi territory, the administration shed its initial ambivalence and began to favor Baghdad. On February 26, 1982, the State Department removed Iraq from its official list of terrorism-sponsoring states, thereby permitting it to both receive U.S. government-financed export credits and import dual-use high-technology U.S. goods on a case-by-case basis.[23] This initiative began paying concrete dividends to Saddam just a few months later when the Commerce Department approved the sale of six L-100 cargo planes to Iraq.[24] Around the same time, the Central Intelligence Agency began using the Jordanian government as an intermediary to furnish Iraqi military commanders with satellite images, Iranian communications intercepts, and intelligence analyses showing "where the Iranian [military] weaknesses were."[25] Thanks in large measure to this intelligence, when Iran invaded Iraq in July, Iraq's defenses had been "significantly fortified and the Iranians were repulsed with heavy casualties."[26] The White House also began to urge friendly Arab states to covertly transship U.S.-manufactured arms to Iraq. Jordan, Saudi Arabia, Kuwait, and Egypt responded with alacrity, selling Iraq Huey helicopters and various types of small arms and mortars, as well as thousands of HAWK antiaircraft missiles and Tube-launched, Optically tracked, Wire-guided (TOW) antitank missiles. Moreover, the White House reportedly encouraged the Egyptian government to provide Iraq with Soviet-made fighter planes and spare parts and coaxed its West European allies to arm it with billions of dollars' worth of their own indigenously produced weapon systems. [27]

As the front line stabilized, the Reagan administration steadily expanded bilateral diplomatic and economic contacts with Iraq. In October 1982, the Commerce Department approved the sale to Iraq of sixty Hughes light civilian helicopters.[28] Then, at the end of the year, the interagency National Advisory Council on International Monetary and Financial Policies (NAC) approved a request by the Department of Agriculture to disburse $210 million in Commodity Credit Corporation (CCC) export credit guarantees to Iraq.[29] Without these guarantees, the cash-strapped Ba'athist regime would have been unable to secure the private financing necessary to pay for its grain imports, which fulfilled a staggering 75 percent of Iraq's food needs. Critically, the CCC program enabled Saddam to devote the majority of his country's dwindling hard-currency reserves to waging the war against Iran.[30] The NAC significantly expanded the CCC program in the following months, allocating a total of $401.9 million in guarantees to Iraq by the end of the 1983 fiscal year.[31] In December 1983, the White House unveiled a diplomatic campaign to mobilize international support for a comprehensive arms embargo against Iran ("Operation Staunch"), which would prove highly effective in slowing the flow of foreign arms to Tehran.[32] Within days of this initiative, President Reagan dispatched his Special Envoy for the Middle East, Donald Rumsfeld, to Baghdad to meet personally with Saddam Hussein. Rumsfeld, who had served President Ford as both White House chief of staff and secretary of defense, conveyed the administration's hope that the Iran-Iraq War would not end in a manner that "weakened Iraq's role or enhanced [the] interests and ambitions of Iran."[33] In January 1984, the State Department placed Iran on its list of terrorism sponsors, thereby choking off Tehran's access to a wide array of crucial dual-use U.S. exports.[34] Soon thereafter, the administration approved the sale to Iraq of forty-five Bell 214 Super Transport helicopters and two thousand AM General heavy trucks.[35]

After making a follow-on visit to Iraq in March, however, Rumsfeld worriedly told Shultz that there "was a disaster on the horizon," as masses of Iranian troops pouring into Iraq "soon could threaten Kuwait and Saudi Arabia."[36] This gloomy report spurred the White House to take a number of additional steps on Saddam's behalf. On June 1, the United States voted in favor of UN Security Council Resolution 552, which condemned Iranian attacks on neutral shipping in the Gulf. Later that summer, the Export-Import Bank of the United States (Eximbank) approved a $200 million line of short-term export credit for Iraq and the NAC granted the country an additional $513.3 million in agricultural loan guarantees.[37]

In November, the alliance entered an entirely new phase as the State Department officially restored formal diplomatic relations with Iraq. Within a matter of weeks, the White House began to make intelligence available to it on a more regular basis by establishing a direct link between CIA headquarters and the new U.S. embassy in Baghdad. In March 1985, this channel proved critical in helping the Iraqis to successfully repulse a major Iranian offensive (Operation Badr) in the marshes north of Basra.[38] By late 1986, according to one unnamed NSC official, the nature of the intelligence that the CIA was feeding Iraq had become "difficult to characterize . . . as defensive assistance."[39]

Over the course of the next year, economic contacts between the two informal allies continued to balloon. The NAC disbursed $340.1 million in CCC credits for Iraq that it had approved for the fiscal year 1985, notwithstanding Saddam's rebuff of the CCC's request that his government became more forthcoming regarding its financial situation. It cleared an additional $392 million in credit guarantees for fiscal year 1986.[40] Additionally, in March 1985, the administration "opened the doors wide" to the Iraqi purchase of U.S. high-technology goods by suddenly approving large numbers of dual-use export licenses.[41] Then, in September, the administration signed a commercial, economic, and technical cooperation agreement with Iraq.[42]

Beginning in the summer of 1985, however, the White House suddenly began to work at cross-purposes with itself by engaging in surreptitious military cooperation with Iran. Despite the president's categorical declaration that he would "make no deals"[43] with terrorists, in August, Reagan allowed National Security Advisor Robert McFarlane to pursue a quid pro quo in which the White House would transfer U.S.-made arms to Iran via Israel in exchange for Iran's help in securing the release of the American hostages held by Iran-backed Shia terrorists in Beirut. In September, the first shipment of 508 TOW missiles was transferred from Israel to Iran, and the next day, one hostage was freed by the terrorists. In November, the conspiring officials agreed to sell the country 120 HAWK missiles in exchange for the release of all the remaining hostages. NSC aide Lieutenant Colonel Oliver North suggested adding an $850,000 surcharge to this sale, which would be transferred to the *contra* insurgent group that was fighting the leftist Sandinista government in Nicaragua. This move violated the 1984 Boland Amendment, which explicitly prohibited the United States from supporting military or paramilitary operations in Nicaragua. But the HAWK sale failed to elicit the anticipated hostage release, because the Iranians test-fired one of the missiles and judged it to be ineffective.[44]

During the next year, the conspirators directly and indirectly transferred to Iran thousands of additional TOW missiles, tons of arms and spare parts for Iran's U.S.-made warplanes and tanks, spare parts for its HAWK missiles, and even sensitive battlefield intelligence.[45] Although the Lebanese terrorists released two hostages, they took two more, making a mockery of the covert operation.[46] In any event, in November the gambit unraveled after a Beirut news magazine broke the arms-for-hostages story. The subsequent Congressional, public, and international furor brought the policy to a screeching halt. The affair dealt a "severe blow" to the administration's credibility with its Arab allies, which received the news of the operation with "shock and disbelief." Saddam personally drafted a letter to Reagan conveying the "intense anger and sense of betrayal" of the Iraqi people.[47]

In response to Iran's conquest of the Fao Peninsula and the embarrassing revelation of the arms-for-hostages operation, the Reagan administration strove to repair the severe damage that it had inflicted on the alliance with Iraq. On the economic front, the NAC approved its largest annual disbursements of CCC credits to Iraq yet, $652.5 million for fiscal year 1987 and $1.113 billion for fiscal year 1988. The latter figure accounted for no less than 25 percent of the entire CCC budget.[48] It also "considerably eased" the rules that governed the use of those credits by permitting Iraq (alone among CCC recipients) to use part of its allocation to offset freight costs.[49] In addition, the White House redoubled its efforts to facilitate the export of high-technology U.S. products to Iraq.[50] Meanwhile, in October 1987, President Reagan signed an executive order banning the import of all Iranian products, including oil.[51]

These attempts to strengthen the economic dimension of the alliance were overshadowed by even more dramatic U.S. initiatives in the military domain. First, in early 1987, the administration began handling "considerable quantities" of satellite and radar intelligence to the Iraqi regime, as "American intelligence officers plotted the movement of Iranian troops and planes and passed the information on to Iraq."[52] Second, in response to Iran's escalation of the tanker war in the Persian Gulf, in March the White House agreed to extend military protection to Kuwaiti oil tankers.[53] The Kuwaiti government subsequently proposed "reflagging" some of its tankers as U.S. vessels, thereby deepening the United States' commitment to defend them.[54] In May the White House acquiesced, and on July 21, the Pentagon launched Operation Earnest Will, the largest naval escort operation since World War II. Before long, the U.S. flotilla swelled to fifty ships, including an aircraft carrier, and was reinforced by thirty-four combat vessels from Britain, France, the Netherlands, Italy, and Belgium.[55] In late April, soon after U.S. forces launched a single-day operation that destroyed nearly all of Iran's remaining naval assets, the Pentagon announced that the United States Navy would defend all maritime vessels transiting the Gulf. This prompted a shell-shocked Iranian government to suspend all offensive operations there.[56]

INTRA-ALLIANCE DISPUTES BETWEEN THE UNITED STATES AND IRAQ

Even as the United States partnered with Iraq in an ultimately fruitful alliance of convenience against Iran, two serious national security–related disputes divided the fledgling allies. These were Iraq's sponsorship of international terrorism and its suspected efforts to develop nuclear weapons and the ballistic missiles to carry them.

The Reagan administration had a strong interest in securing Iraqi concessions on both issues. Over the course of the 1980s, the number and destructiveness of terrorist attacks around the globe escalated dramatically.[57] This ominous trend significantly raised concerns and fears on the part of the U.S. public. A 1986 survey conducted by the Chicago Council on Foreign Relations found that terrorism ranked only behind the nuclear arms race on the list of the U.S. public's foremost foreign policy concerns.[58] As a result, the desire to prevent international terrorist acts against U.S. citizens and interests abroad became "an important touchstone of the Reagan presidency."[59] In April 1986, Reagan ordered a bombing raid against military and political targets in Libya in retaliation for Libyan leader Mu'ammar Gaddhafi's sponsorship of multiple terrorist attacks against U.S. and other Western targets.[60] Iraq's programs to develop nuclear weapons and ballistic missiles also posed a serious danger to U.S. national security. With regard to nuclear weapons and ballistic missiles, as discussed in chapter 2, the administration adopted a firm stance in opposition to further proliferation, especially in the already volatile Middle East region.

Auspiciously for the White House, the strength of Iraq's interests in sponsoring terrorism and pursuing nuclear weapons had weakened following the outbreak of the Iran-Iraq War. First, Saddam's increasingly desperate need for assistance from the United States, the moderate Arab states, and Western Europe in order to feed his country's war machine rendered his extreme prewar position on the Arab-Israeli conflict a growing liability. Consequently, beginning in 1982, the Iraqi leader suddenly declared that he would accept a negotiated solution to Israel's dispute with the Palestinians. He then began to improve relations with both Egypt and the moderate wing of the PLO.[61]

Iraq's de facto abdication of its previous leadership of the rejectionist front of Arab states attenuated the rationale for its continued support for Palestinian terrorist organizations.[62] Among the most infamous terrorist leaders to receive sanctuary and succor in Iraq during the 1970s were Sabri al-Banna, or Abu Nidal, leader of the eponymous Abu Nidal Organization (ANO), and Dr. Wadi Haddad, founder of the Popular Front for the Liberation of Palestine. Both were responsible for orchestrating several of the most notorious terrorist attacks in the Middle East and Europe.[63] As will be discussed in more detail below, however, after the outbreak of the Iran-Iraq War, Saddam evinced a willingness to be at least somewhat more flexible on the terrorism front, as highlighted by his expulsion of Abu Nidal from Iraq in 1983.

Second, although Saddam was unquestionably determined to eventually develop nuclear weapons, in June 1981 Israeli F-16s bombed Iraq's Osiraq nuclear research reactor before it could become operational.[64] An interagency U.S. intelligence report disseminated less than a month after the raid speculated that it would take Iraq at minimum "several years to rebuild its nuclear facilities."[65] A follow-on CIA intelligence assessment disseminated in June 1983 claimed that the Israeli attack "clearly dealt a severe blow to the Iraqi nuclear program," which immediately prior to the Osirak attack was "still at a rudimentary stage."[66] This meant that Saddam was incapable of producing fission weapons for near-term use against Iran. Thus, concessions to the United States on the nuclear issue would have had no adverse impact on Iraq's ability to successfully engage in the war.[67]

RIVAL PREDICTIONS ON U.S. BARGAINING WITH IRAQ

According to the neorealist and tying hands hypotheses, the Reagan administration should have bargained successfully with Iraq on the issues of terrorism and proliferation. Conversely, the neoclassical realist hypothesis predicts passive and failed bargaining with Iraq.

The neorealist prediction is based on the extreme asymmetries of dependence and commitment within the alliance that overwhelmingly favored the United States. The asymmetry of dependence stemmed primarily from the United States' position as a global military and economic superpower, while Iraq was a small and underdeveloped regional power. This is evidenced by the vast disparity in the relative sizes of the U.S. and Iraqi economies: in 1982, the U.S. Gross National Product (GNP) stood at a towering $3.99 trillion, while that of Iraq amounted to a mere $51.54 billion. By 1988, this gap was even more yawning: U.S. GNP had soared to $5.07 trillion while that of Iraq had actually shrunk over the course of the war to $41.25 billion. Meanwhile, although reliable data on Iraqi military spending during the Iran-Iraq War is unavailable, the last year for which such data exist is 1979, when it spent $8.7 billion. By contrast, U.S. military spending between 1982 and 1988 grew from $248 billion to $305 billion.[68] In addition, whereas the United States was located thousands of miles away from the countries' common enemy, Iraq shared a lengthy land border with the far larger and more populous Iran. Therefore, whereas the Iranian threat to the United States was significant but distant, indirect, and limited, the threat it posed to Iraq was imminent, direct, and existential, with outnumbered Iraqi troops pitted against an Iranian adversary bent on toppling the Ba'ath regime from power in Baghdad.[69] This geopolitical asymmetry of dependence was compounded by an equally lopsided economic asymmetry. As the war ground on, Iraq's underdeveloped economy was battered by the combined effects of the war, a fall in world oil prices, and the drastic curtailing of Iraqi oil exports due to Syria's closure of its main oil pipeline.[70] Meanwhile, the United States, which was the world's largest and most advanced economy, engaged in a negligible amount of commerce with Iraq and did not import its oil in large quantities.[71] Further, much of the strategic assistance provided to Iraq was not easily replaceable. The United States was the only country able to provide Iraq with sensitive satellite intelligence on Iranian troop positions and economic targets and pressure its Arab and West European allies to both sell Iraq advanced U.S.-made weapons and restrict their arms transfers to Iran.[72]

The Iraq case also represents a bellwether by comparison with the United States' other Cold War–era alliances of convenience. In contrast to virtually all of the rest, Iraq was not recruited to confront the superpower Soviet Union or a Soviet proxy, but rather, a relatively weak nonaligned state (Iran). Therefore, Washington should have been less preoccupied with the need to maintain the alliance against the common enemy, and more highly motivated to secure concessions from Iraq on disputed issues than should have been the case in its anti-Soviet alliances of convenience.

The U.S.-Iraq alliance was also unusual insofar as it operated during a full-scale ground war in which the ally of convenience, but not the United States, was engaged in a life-or-death armed struggle against the shared threat. If the United States could not elicit substantial concessions from its ally of convenience under these exceptionally favorable circumstances, it is unlikely that it could have elicited them from its anti-Soviet allies, none of which were actually embroiled in full-scale war against the Soviet Union.

The United States' relatively low commitment to Iraq was reflected not only in the informal nature of the alliance, but also in the Carter and Reagan administrations' steadfast refusal to depart from an officially neutral posture toward the two belligerents at any point during the conflict. On this score, it is also noteworthy that U.S. officials maintained that their preferred outcome was not an Iraqi victory per se, but merely the prevention of an Iraqi defeat.[73]

These considerable asymmetries of dependence and commitment were evinced most vividly by the U.S. decisions to both covertly transfer arms to

Iran at the beginning of the war in order to forestall an Iraqi victory, and provide arms and intelligence to Iran later in the war to secure the release of the American hostages in Lebanon. Notably, when the latter operation was exposed by the media in late 1986, the otherwise highly mercurial Iraqi regime exhibited, in the words of one U.S. official, "considerable restraint" in its response.[74]

Tying hands theory similarly predicts successful U.S. bargaining with Iraq, but attributes this outcome to the vast gap in internal state strength between the United States, an internally weak state democracy, and Iraq, an internally strong state totalitarian dictatorship. This gap should have been magnified by the likelihood that the alliance with Iraq engendered controversy and resistance in Congress and the executive branch and among the general public. Meanwhile, in light of the gravity of the Iranian threat to Iraq and Iraq's heavy dependence on U.S. subvention, it would have been extremely risky, if not suicidal, for Baghdad to defect from the alliance on account of the stringency of U.S. conditions pertaining to issues unrelated to, and less urgent than, the war against Iran.

By contrast, neoclassical realist theory predicts feeble and failed U.S. bargaining with Iraq. It posits that a high level of domestic opposition to the alliance should have compelled senior leaders to try to keep it from unraveling by adopting a passive bargaining strategy aimed at casting its Iraqi ally in the best possible light.

IRAQ'S SPONSORSHIP OF INTERNATIONAL TERRORISM

DECEPTIVE FROM THE OUTSET: IRAQ'S REMOVAL FROM THE TERRORISM LIST

Although the Reagan administration's congressional liaison, Kenneth Duberstein, claimed publicly that the removal of Iraq from the State Department terrorism list on February 27, 1982 was precipitated by "Iraq's improved record" on terrorism and the need to "offer an incentive to continue this positive trend," U.S. officials were fully aware that Iraq's record had not actually improved. Noel Koch, the administration's director of counterterrorism programs at the Pentagon, would later claim "The real reason [for removing Iraq from the terrorism list] was to help them succeed in the war against Iran." Similarly, NSC Middle East specialist Geoffrey Kemp later recollected that the administration removed Iraq from the terrorism list because it was "terrified Iraq was going to lose the war."[75]

Iraq's reluctance to disassociate itself from international terrorism became amply evident in the months following the State Department's decision, as Saddam's regime continued to consort closely with Abu Nidal, the world's most notorious terrorist leader. In June 1982, Baghdad was directly implicated in the attempted assassination in London of Israel's ambassador to the United Kingdom by an ANO operative. The assailant was not only a deputy commander of the special operations section of the ANO, but also a colonel in the Iraqi intelligence service, and the British constabulary traced the hit man's firearm to Iraq's London embassy.[76] Two months later, at the behest of Saddam, ANO militants set off a bomb at a popular Jewish restaurant in Paris, killing six people and wounding over twenty.[77] Remarkably, during this period, the Iraqi government assured Washington that Abu Nidal was "no longer receiving Iraqi support subsequent to the Department's removal of Iraq from the 'terrorism list.'"[78]

It was hardly surprising that the State Department's decision elicited dissent in Congress. After all, a congressional outcry had led the previous administration to reverse its approval of the sale to Iraq of eight naval engine cores and five commercial aircraft.[79] Several legislators were openly skeptical of the claim made by multiple Reagan administration officials that its removal of Iraq from the terrorism list was warranted by Baghdad's recent behavior. For example, in an appearance before the Senate Foreign Relations Committee's Subcommittee on the Near East and South Asia, Deputy Assistant Secretary of State for Economic and Business Affairs Ernest Johnson Jr. testified, "In reaching our decision concerning Iraq, we took particular notice of the fact that in 1981 Iraq continued the patterns of recent years of reducing assistance to individuals and groups which employ terrorist means." Incredulous, Republican Senator Rudy Boschwitz of Minnesota demanded that Johnson present concrete evidence validating this claim, but Johnson refused to do so. Boschwitz countered Johnson's testimony by referring to a recent report prepared by the Congressional Research Service, which alluded to at least six attacks in 1981 by terrorist groups which "by their own admission" were linked to the Iraqi government. He also referred to "additional attacks which various intelligence sources attribute to Iraq-backed groups."[80] Boschwitz also blasted the White House for failing to consult Congress before taking the dramatic step of removing Iraq from the terrorism list, charging, "No case was made to Congress prior to the removal showing that Iraq has ended its support for terrorist groups."[81]

Unpersuaded by the administration's assurances, a bipartisan group of four senators, including Boschwitz, Paul Tsongas (D-MA), Edward Kennedy (D-MA), and Larry Pressler (R-SD), sponsored a resolution disapproving the administration's intended sale of six Lockheed L100 transport planes to Iraq and urging the State Department to immediately return Iraq to the terrorism list.[82] Despite this resolution, as well as the delivery of a letter to the president by ninety-seven members of Congress opposing the sale, the Commerce Department issued an export license to Lockheed, allowing it to proceed with the transaction.[83]

The Iraq terrorism controversy also played out during deliberations in both the House and Senate over the annual foreign aid bill. In May 1982, the House Foreign Affairs Committee voted by a substantial 17–11 margin to insert an amendment sponsored by Representative Jonathan Bingham (D-NY) placing Iraq back on the terrorism list. The Bingham Amendment even garnered the support of a number of the administration's most loyal Republican supporters in Congress, such as Representative Benjamin Gilman of New York.[84] The Republicans on the committee successfully watered down the amendment, however, by adding a provision allowing the president to waive it on national security grounds.[85] Meanwhile, in the Senate Foreign Relations Committee, Boschwitz proposed an amendment that would have reinstated export controls on Iraq. Opponents of the measure, led by Senator Charles Percy (R-IL), argued that its passage could undermine U.S. efforts to end the Iran-Iraq War, and mounted a successful campaign to weaken it.[86] The final version that passed the committee required merely that in future, the president notify Congress before removing any state from the State Department terrorism list. In any event, the foreign aid bill was dropped later that year for reasons unrelated to Iraq.[87]

Despite the administration's public insistence that Saddam's regime had curtailed its sponsorship of terrorism, it remained privately concerned about Iraqi behavior. A February 1983 briefing memorandum drafted for Secretary Shultz on the eve of his meeting with Iraqi foreign minister Saadoun Hammadi noted that Iraq's continuing support for international terrorists represented "the only major impediment to improved relations" with the United States. It also mentioned that the State Department had advised Iraq's Foreign Ministry that it would be "very useful" if Hammadi could bring some evidence that the Iraqi government was taking "active steps" to clamp down on terrorists operating out of Iraqi territory.[88]

By the fall of 1983, Iraq's lack of cooperation was posing a major problem for an administration that was extremely wary about domestic constraints on its ability to help Saddam fend off the Iranians. An internal State Department memo drafted for Undersecretary of State Lawrence Eagleburger in early October warned, "Congressional and public support for an overt tilt to Iraq would be difficult to obtain."[89] Another memo drafted a few months later for Secretary Shultz by the Department's Bureau of Near Eastern and South Asian Affairs and Bureau of Politico-Military Affairs reported that although the "depth of anti-Iranian and anti-Syrian public and Congressional sentiment has mitigated even some hardliners' reactions to our recent alleged 'tilt' [toward Iraq]," an Iraqi escalation of the war would "add to public and Congressional opposition" to Saddam's regime.[90]

In light of these concerns, the administration alternately dismissed and downplayed emergent allegations that contradicted its public position. In response to press inquiries, State Department spokesperson Alan Romberg insisted that the United States possessed no evidence that Iraq had supported terrorism since its removal from the terrorism list a year earlier. Although he conceded obliquely that members of one unnamed terrorist organization (i.e., the ANO) allegedly remained in Iraq, they were "apparently under certain constraints." Another administration official claimed anonymously that Abu Nidal's presence in Iraq was "not necessarily a matter of preference. He's not behind bars, but I think his freedom of movement, and communication, is sharply circumscribed."[91] Unnamed State

Department officials also informed the press that their reluctance to return Iraq to the terrorism list stemmed, among other things, from the desire to reward its growing moderation toward Israel and the Arab-Israeli peace process.[92] This logic was strained by the implication of the Iraqi regime in the attempted assassination of Israel's UK ambassador and Iraq's sponsorship of terrorist groups that were killing off moderate PLO diplomats and Jewish civilians throughout Europe.

These efforts failed to convince the administration's most ardent congressional critics. In 1983, Representative Howard Berman (D-CA.) inserted a tough provision into the House bill extending the 1979 Export Administration Act (EAA) that would immediately return Iraq to the terrorism list.[93] The administration "quietly and effectively" lobbied the Senate, however, to forestall the inclusion of an identical amendment in its companion bill. Under heavy pressure from the State Department, Senator Alan Dixon (D-IL) also agreed to water down an amendment on the same subject that he intended to bring to the Senate floor early the next year. According to an unnamed Senate aide, Dixon agreed to "leave room for the State Department to keep Iraq off the list"[94] by merely stipulating that the reinstatement be made within ninety days unless the president certified to Congress that Iraq no longer supported terrorism. In the end, Dixon's amendment was passed by the Senate.[95]

EXCEPTION TO THE RULE: IRAQ'S EXPULSION OF ABU NIDAL

As Congress debated the EAA bill, on November 4 Iraq made a major concession by expelling Abu Nidal and his senior associates from Baghdad.[96] On numerous occasions, State Department officials informed Representative Berman that they were able to use the threat of the EAA's passage to cajole Iraq into exiling Abu Nidal and cutting ties to terrorism more broadly.[97] This solitary instance of tough bargaining and at least tactical Iraqi compliance, which comports with the tying hands proposition, ultimately proved to be an aberration in an otherwise consistent pattern of U.S. deference to Iraq on the terrorism issue.[98] In any event, the salience of this high-profile expulsion was diminished by the subsequent acknowledgment by U.S. officials that Abu Nidal had been allowed to maintain an office and

property in Iraq.[99] As late as June 1990, the State Department was continuing to accuse Saddam's regime of maintaining contacts with the ANO.[100] In
addition, even as Saddam reduced Iraq's support for Abu Nidal, he compen-
sated by increasing it for the May 15 Organization and other radical Palestinian factions, and beginning to provide Arafat's PLO with heavy weaponry such as howitzers, antiaircraft guns, and armored combat vehicles.[101]

EASING THE PRESSURE ON SADDAM

Despite the salutary role that domestic pressure had apparently played in
Saddam's expulsion of Abu Nidal, the administration immediately labored
to weaken it. In late December 1983, Undersecretary of State Eagleburger
implored Eximbank chair William Draper to end the bank's prohibition
on lending to Iraq owing to "Iraq's [continuing] links to international terrorists." Eagleburger tried to allay this concern by referring to Saddam's
recent announcement of "the termination of all assistance to the principal
terrorist groups of concern" and the Abu Nidal expulsion.[102]

At the end of the year, though, Congress took additional steps to tighten
the screws on Iraq. On November 13, Representative Berman sent a letter
to Secretary Shultz objecting to the announced sale of forty-five Bell
214 ST helicopters to Iraq on the grounds that Baghdad had not appreciably
curbed its support for international terrorism. Reproving the administration's "mistaken attempt to woo Iraq by ignoring its support for terrorism,"
Berman charged that the State Department was misleading in claiming that
Baghdad had settled the issue because it had "cut" its support for *some* terrorist groups. Instead, he contended that the Saddam regime needed to
adopt "tough anti-terrorist policies similar to Egypt's, Jordan's, Kuwait's,
Saudi Arabia's and most other nations." He also castigated a State Department spokesperson who opposed the Senate's Iraq amendment to the EAA
on the grounds that "a nationalistic country like Iraq could not be expected
to make a commitment not to support terrorism."[103] Berman's claims echoed
the assessment of a defense estimative brief drafted by the Defense Intelligence Agency earlier that fall.[104]

In a written response to Berman, Assistant Secretary of State for Legislative and Intergovernmental Affairs W. Tapley Bennett Jr. took issue with

the lawmaker's assessment. Bennett misleadingly conveyed the department's concern that Iraq "not revert to its previous support for international terrorism," and vaguely alluded to "independent information" that supported Deputy Prime Minister Tariq Aziz's "categoric [*sic*] assurances to you" at Aziz's recent meeting with a Congressional delegation "that Iraq has severed ties to international terrorists." He concluded the correspondence by asserting that the personal channel established between Berman and Aziz would prove "far more" effective in favorably influencing Iraqi behavior "than new controls on U.S. non-military or 'dual use' exports to Iraq."[105]

A few months later, the administration turned its attention back to the long-gestating EAA legislation, which was nearing passage in both the House and Senate. In an April 1985 conversation with Tariq Aziz, U.S. Ambassador to Syria William Eagleton Jr. conveyed the administration's opposition to all legislative efforts to return Iraq to the terrorism list and promised that "our strongest efforts on the bill would be reserved for the time when it went to conference committee." Aziz replied that the Iraqi government had instructed its ambassador in Washington, Nizar Hamdoon, to meet with Undersecretary of State for Political Affairs Michael Armacost "in order to urge an intensification of our efforts to defeat the [congressional] measure."[106]

A House-Senate conference committee appointed to reconcile the two versions of the EAA bill tentatively adopted the less-stringent language on Iraq contained in the Senate bill, which mandated Iraq's return to the terrorism list after ninety days unless the president certified that Iraq had stopped supporting terrorism. In accordance with Eagleton's pledge to Aziz, the administration moved to quash even this attenuated measure. In a letter to Representative Berman on June 20, Secretary Shultz maintained that in recent years, the Saddam regime had taken "important steps" against terrorist groups operating in Iraqi territory, such as the ANO. He proceeded to claim that since Iraq had "effectively disassociated itself from terrorism," the conference committee needed to "recognize the [positive] steps that Iraq has already taken" and encourage further Iraqi concessions by scrapping the amendment. To this end, Shultz pledged that he would promptly return Iraq to the terrorism list if the State Department discovered that "any group based in or supported by Iraq is engaged in terrorist acts."[107]

Soon after Berman received Shultz's letter, he received another from Carl Schwensen, the executive vice president of the National Association of Wheat Growers. Schwensen informed Berman that his organization harbored "serious concerns" about the impending Iraq sanctions because the country had been "a very good customer for U.S. wheat and other agricultural commodities in recent years." He thereby cautioned Berman that the association would be "strongly opposed to any steps that needlessly jeopardized" U.S. trade with Iraq.[108] After receiving the admonitory letters from Shultz and Schwensen, the conference committee agreed to strike the Iraq amendment from the EAA bill.[109] Notably, in a major public address on terrorism the next month, President Reagan singled out Cuba, Iran, Libya, Nicaragua, and North Korea as state sponsors of terrorism but conspicuously omitted Iraq from the list.[110] Around this time, the U.S. embassy in Baghdad cabled the State Department to summarize a recent discussion between its chargé d'affaires and the first international director of Iraq's Ministry of Foreign Affairs, who was identified only by the surname Haddami. The chargé pointed out to the Iraqi official that the Reagan administration "had gone to considerable lengths" to prevent Iraq's being reinstated to the terrorism list, and that as a result, its "credibility was on the line." Haddami evinced little gratitude for these efforts, however, as he merely enunciated "the spurious Iraqi position that somehow giving refuge to Abu Nidal and his ilk did not equate with supporting terrorism."[111]

ABUL ABBAS AND THE *ACHILLE LAURO* HIJACKING

Within a matter of months, the administration's most recent assurances to Congress that Iraq had stopped sponsoring terrorism and that the State Department would return Iraq to the terrorism list in the event of recidivism were both exposed as hollow. On October 7, four armed members of the Palestinian Liberation Front (PLF), a radical splinter group of the PLO, hijacked the Italian cruise ship *Achille Lauro* in the waters off the coast of Port Said, Egypt. In return for the release of the ship's four hundred passengers and crew members, the hijackers demanded the release of fifty Palestinian militants incarcerated in Israel. When the ship was refused port rights, first in Syria and then in Cyprus, the hijackers returned the vessel to

Port Said. During this circuitous journey, the PLF operatives executed a wheelchair-bound American tourist, Leon Klinghoffer, and tossed his corpse and the chair into the Mediterranean Sea. From the outset of the operation, the terrorists were in frequent radio contact with Mohammed Abbad Zaidan, otherwise known as Abul Abbas, who led one of the two competing factions of the PLF. Both the U.S. and Israeli governments would later attest that Abbas had masterminded the operation. The Egyptian government agreed to provide safe passage out of Egypt for the four gunmen, as well as Abbas and Ozzudin Badrak Kan, the head of the PLF's military branch, provided that they freed the remaining hostages.[112]

The Egyptian airliner carrying the Palestinian terrorists was intercepted by American F-14 fighter jets scrambled from the aircraft carrier USS *Saratoga* and forced to land at the NATO air force base in Sigonella, Italy. The Egyptian officials on board the airliner turned over the four hijackers to the Italian police, but refused to give up Abbas and Kan on the grounds that they were guests of the Egyptian government and were therefore immune from arrest or investigation. After Abbas and Kan were moved to Rome, the U.S. District Court in the District of Columbia approved a petition by the Justice Department to charge Abbas and the four hijackers with the federal crimes of hostage-taking, piracy, and conspiracy to commit both offenses. The Italian authorities nevertheless allowed Abbas and Kan to board an Egyptian airliner bound for Yugoslavia.[113]

At this juncture, Iraq interceded to confound the administration's efforts to bring Abul Abbas to justice. On October 9, three days before Abbas fled to Yugoslavia, Secretary Shultz beseeched a visiting Arab League delegation, which included Iraq's deputy prime minister, Tariq Aziz, for their countries' support in bringing the perpetrators of the *Achille Lauro* attack to justice. Then, in the immediate aftermath of Abbas's departure from Rome, the State Department instructed U.S. Ambassador to Iraq David Newton to immediately deliver a démarche to the Iraqi government requesting its immediate withdrawal of Abbas's diplomatic passport and an agreement to extradite Abbas to the United States in the event that he sought refuge in Iraq. The cable also somewhat vaguely instructed Newton to inform the Iraqis that "should they give sanctuary to Abu[l] Abbas, a series of legal and administrative actions could be triggered which would do damage to the fabric of our expanding bilateral relations." Although the unidentified senior Iraqi official to whom Newton presented the démarche reaffirmed the 1934 extradition treaty between the United States and Iraq, he bluntly informed Newton that Abbas would "be welcome" in Iraq and that the Iraqi government would neither confiscate his diplomatic passport nor extradite him to the United States. The official added haughtily that he hoped that this would "not complicate our bilateral relations."[114]

Remarkably, on the very same day, Italian customs police apprehended two Arab men disembarking from an Iraqi Airways flight at Fiumicino Airport in Rome after explosives were detected in their luggage. One of the men confessed that they had arrived in Rome with orders to attack "any" American target. The Italian authorities subsequently informed the State Department that the same suspect had confessed to purchasing his airline ticket from a travel agent in Baghdad. Ambassador Newton conveyed to Iraqi officials the administration's "distress" and "grave concern" about the incident, and urged the Iraqi government to conduct an investigation into the matter. A subsequent State Department note relayed, "We have now raised this issue with the Iraqis at least five times through various channels; they have persisted in sticking with their original flimsy story" that the suspects were unknown to the Iraqi government.[115] The two Rome terrorists were soon identified as operatives of a radical offshoot of the Popular Front for the Liberation of Palestine, dubbed the May 15 Organization, which was based in Iraq.[116]

On October 25, Secretary of State Shultz sent a direct message to Aziz in which he asked the Iraqis to conduct a full investigation into the Rome incident and "reemphasized" the administration's concern about Iraq's willingness to provide sanctuary for Abul Abbas. In reply, Aziz denied any Iraqi connection with the Rome terrorists, avowed that Abbas possessed diplomatic "immunities" owing to his status as a member of the PLO Executive Committee, and insisted that Abbas was innocent of any involvement in the *Achille Lauro* hijacking. He proclaimed that, consequently, the Iraqi government could not "deal with the order of arrest issued against Abbas by the American authorities."[117]

Over the course of the next month, Iraq's involvement in the Abul Abbas controversy deepened. On November 11, Saddam Hussein publicly decried the Reagan administration's refusal to formally recognize the PLO and insisted that "in no way can we agree to describing the struggle maintained by the Palestinians as terrorism." He also condemned the U.S. military's diversion of the Egyptian airliner containing Abul Abbas and the *Achille Lauro* hijackers to Italy. Less than a week later, an American journalist in Baghdad informed the U.S. embassy that a PLO official based in the Iraqi capital had "confirmed Abbas' presence in Baghdad." On November 20, the *Christian Science Monitor* echoed that the Iraqi government "had allowed news to leak" that Abbas was in the capital.[118] Less than a week later, although the Justice Department announced a reward of up to $250,000 for information leading to the arrest, prosecution, and punishment of Abbas and others implicated in the *Achille Lauro* attack, an unnamed senior Iraqi official informed the *Washington Times* that the White House was not actively seeking Abbas's extradition. The same report made the troubling claim that, according to "Western diplomats," the White House was seeking to play down Abbas's presence in order to avoid damaging the bilateral relationship with Iraq.[119] At a press conference at the State Department on December 6, Secretary Shultz obliquely informed journalists that both the U.S. and Italian governments were "pursuing" Abbas but "so far we haven't been successful in getting him."[120] Later that month, at a joint press conference in Belgrade with the Yugoslav foreign minister, Raif Dizdarevic, Shultz declaimed angrily, "There must be no place to hide" for the *Achille Lauro* suspects. When a reporter asked what measures the administration was taking toward Iraq in order to win Abbas's extradition, however, Shultz replied tepidly, "I don't think we should feel every time we identify a problem we have to fire a gun or break diplomatic relations. There are all sorts of gradations."[121]

These developments caused a stir in Congress. Representative Berman began circulating a letter among his colleagues that requested an update from the administration on Abbas and the two suspected terrorists apprehended at the airport in Rome. In the Senate, William Proxmire (D-WI) introduced a resolution prohibiting all licenses for the export to Iraq of helicopters and fixed-wing aircraft, though the measure was dropped after it was referred to the Senate Banking Committee.[122]

Over the next few years, the adverse implications of the Reagan administration's lenient treatment of Iraq on the terrorism issue became clear to U.S. policymakers. A July 1986 report by the State Department's Bureau of Intelligence and Research (INR) acknowledged that Saddam's alleged retreat from terrorism "was painfully slow," and that "Iraq remains reluctant to cut completely its links to terrorist groups."[123] Three years later, the newly inaugurated administration of George H. W. Bush informed Baghdad that it was "disturbed by the continued presence in Iraq of Abu[l] Abbas."[124] From his Iraqi safe haven, Abbas planned and subsequently claimed responsibility for a plot by seventeen Palestinian terrorists to storm Tel Aviv's beaches in May 1989, which was foiled by Israeli authorities.[125] The administration also accused Iraq of harboring another Palestinian militant, Colonel Mahmoud al-Natour, (also known as Colonel Hawari). Hawari was suspected of orchestrating attacks on various U.S. targets in Europe, as well as the infamous 1986 bombing of a Trans World Airline passenger jet, which resulted in the death of four Americans.[126]

IRAQ'S WMD PROLIFERATION

Iraq's behavior also conflicted starkly with U.S. national security interests in the area of nuclear weapons proliferation. One scholar of Iraq's proliferation activities has judged that "based on the historical record . . . the intent of Iraq's nuclear program was to build nuclear weapons."[127] On September 8, 1975, Saddam Hussein, then Iraq's vice president, publicly announced that the Ba'ath regime's purchase of two nuclear reactors from France represented "the first actual step in the production of an Arab atomic weapon, despite the fact that the declared purpose for the establishment of the reactor is not the production of atomic weapons."[128] After Saddam deposed President Hasan al-Bakr four years later, he ordered the country's nuclear scientists to defy Iraq's commitments as a signatory to the Nuclear Non-Proliferation Treaty by embarking immediately on the construction of a fissile weapon.[129]

Israel's June 1981 airstrike against Iraq's French-made Osirak nuclear reactor further galvanized Iraq's motivation to develop nuclear weapons. In a publicized speech to his cabinet two weeks after the Israeli operation, Saddam enjoined "all peace-loving nations" to aid the Arab world "in one way or another to obtain the nuclear bomb in order to confront Israel's existing bombs." He further warned that "no power can stop Iraq from acquiring technological and scientific know-how to serve its national objectives."[130] At around the same time, Saddam released Iraq's foremost nuclear scientist, Jafar Dhia Jafar, from prison—where he had been incarcerated in 1979 on suspicion of involvement with the anti-Ba'ath opposition—and placed him in charge of the country's nuclear weapons program.[131] Saddam's post-Osirak quest for atomic weapons "went completely underground," and consisted of an increasingly elaborate program to secretly procure and enrich uranium to construct fissile weapons.[132] In the years following Osirak, Iraq's nuclear program expanded exponentially from 400 to 7,000 scientists and from $400 million to $10 billion in funding.[133]

A June 1983 CIA intelligence estimate titled "The Iraqi Nuclear Program: Progress Despite Setbacks" adjudged that the Israeli attack "dealt a severe blow to the Iraqi nuclear program, but does not appear to have altered Iraq's long-term plans for nuclear independence." It added that in the aftermath of the Israeli airstrike, Iraq "now appears resolved to get on with its nuclear program, but with more attention to covertness and physical security." The estimate additionally noted that Iraq "has made attempts to acquire a medium-range ballistic missile, possibly for a nuclear-warhead delivery system."[134] The next year, Iraq contracted with a West German company to design and build the Saad 16 industrial complex near Mosul, which upon completion would spearhead the regime's efforts to manufacture a ballistic missile arsenal.[135]

BUREAUCRATIC TUSSLING OVER DUAL-USE EXPORTS TO IRAQ

Iraq's suspected diversion of dual-use U.S. high-technology exports to its nuclear and missile programs touched off an internecine battle within the Reagan administration. On one side were the State Department and

Commerce Department, which generally sought to maximize U.S. exports of dual-use technologies to Iraq as part of the administration's wartime tilt to Saddam. On the other was the Defense Department, which tended to be extremely suspicious about Iraq's motives for acquiring several dual-use products. In this domain, however, the Pentagon's bureaucratic influence was relatively weak relative to the Commerce Department, which possessed the statutory authority to refer export license applications to other agencies for consultation as it saw fit and to ultimately approve or reject those applications.[136]

By early 1985, in conjunction with the administration's burgeoning wartime alliance with Iraq, Commerce began providing Iraq with a wide range of dual-use items, including those that were forbidden from being sold to the Soviet Union and its communist allies in Eastern Europe. It also stopped referring many suspect Iraqi license requests to other agencies for review. Of the small number of applications that it did refer, Commerce Department officials typically ignored those that were subsequently red-flagged by the recipient agencies.[137] Crucially, the State Department encouraged Commerce's permissive stance on Iraq. State's ardent position on the issue was reflected in a departmental memorandum drafted for Secretary Shultz in early 1984, which advocated a policy of "ceasing to discourage *any* non-controlled exports to Iraq, including those with military implications."[138] As a result, over $94 million worth of sophisticated computer hardware alone was eventually transferred to Iraq's unconventional weapons programs with the Commerce Department's express approval.[139]

The lax position of both departments toward Iraq became especially problematic in 1985, after Reagan instructed all U.S. government agencies to enforce the restrictions of the newly created Missile Technology Control Regime (MTCR). Instead of referring potentially suspect applications to the appropriate technical review agencies, Commerce officials instead cursorily "matched the items proposed for export with the new MTCR list [of proscribed technologies], and unless they found a direct hit, they approved the license."[140] In at least a dozen cases, Commerce approved licenses for Iraq even though the technologies in question perfectly matched those on the MTCR list. To cover its tracks, the department refrained from passing along those applications to the Pentagon for review.[141]

In a memorandum drafted for Shultz on April 29, Assistant Secretary for Near Eastern and South Asian Affairs Richard W. Murphy identified the Pentagon's International Security Policy (ISP) Directorate and its director, Assistant Secretary of Defense for International Security Policy Richard Perle, as the locus of bureaucratic opposition to dual-use exports bound for Iraq. Murphy specified that ISP "has used year-long delays and imposition of unworkable conditions . . . to 'kill' exports," and that those obstructive tactics were being perceived by "senior Iraqi officials . . . as a [negative] political signal." Assuring Shultz that no evidence existed to suggest that the Iraqis had provided the Soviets with access to U.S. high-technology exports or that the items that were held up by ISP were necessary for Iraq's nuclear program, Murphy warned that "[c]ontinued unwarranted denials, conditions, or delays will undermine our influence and interests in Iraq."[142]

On Murphy's recommendation, Shultz dispatched a letter to Secretary of Defense Caspar Weinberger the next day protesting ISP's dilatory behavior. Shultz insisted that an opportunity existed for the United States to "draw Iraq further away from the Soviets and help restrain its behavior," as well as to ensure that Iraq purchased high-technology goods from U.S. firms as opposed to rival foreign suppliers. He urged Weinberger to promote the "timely review of applications to export advanced U.S. technology to Iraq," warning that if the Pentagon continued to impede the licensing process for such items, including a pending application for a high-powered Sperry 1100/72 computer, it would "set back our political, commercial, nonproliferation and technology transfer interests." In order to ease Weinberger's concerns, Shultz contended that, according to a recent CIA study which he appended to the letter, no evidence existed to indicate that Iraq had diverted previous dual-use technology imports to the Soviet Union. Further, he maintained that "[t]he intelligence community also has no evidence that Iraq has yet embarked on a nuclear weapons program, or intends to do so."[143]

Perle determinedly countered Shultz in a July memo to Weinberger. First, he referred to a "body of evidence indicating that Iraq continues to actively pursue an interest in nuclear weapons," which paradoxically included the very CIA report Shultz had included in his letter to Weinberger. Second, Perle claimed that the "large number of Warsaw Pact nationals in

Iraq," made the diversion of high-technology imports from the United States "[a] real possibility." Third, he noted "in the past, Iraq has been somewhat less than honest in regard to the intended end-use of high-technology equipment." In a proposed reply to Shultz's missive, Perle explicated that the Pentagon had "by and large" recommended approval of exports to Iraq and that "certain conditions" needed to be imposed on some exports to protect U.S. national security interests. He reminded Weinberger that those conditions resembled the ones imposed on sales of such items to other countries that were not formal U.S. allies.[144]

Even as Shultz and Weinberger sparred over dual-use trade with Iraq, the Commerce Department's decision to grant an export license for the sale of a hybrid digital-analog computer to Iraq aroused the suspicions of Deputy Under Secretary of Defense for Trade Security Policy and Director of the Defense Technology Security Administration Stephen Bryen. The computer in question, which was manufactured by Electronic Associates Incorporated (EAI), was nearly identical to one it had previously sold to the White Sands missile test range in Nevada for the purpose of plotting ballistic missile trajectories. The EAI application was one of many that spring whose designated end-user was the Saad 16 research complex under construction outside Mosul. When Bryen's office advised that Commerce reject the application on national security grounds, the department ignored his recommendation and in late August gave its assent for the shipment.[145] The EAI case led Bryen to begin paying closer attention to applications for high-tech exports to Iraq.

In March 1986, Perle dispatched a memo to his immediate superior, Undersecretary of Defense for Policy Fred Charles Iklé, which addressed the risks of proceeding with two pending export license applications for Iraq. The applications in question were for the re-export of Datanet equipment from France to upgrade an existing Iraqi computer and the direct export of a Sperry 1100/72 high-speed computer. Perle reminded Iklé that it was "firm U.S. policy to deny dual-use exports to Iraq if the stated end-use involves nuclear activities," given that Iraq was "a problem country, at least in the mid-to-long term." He elaborated that "many if not all the elements of a substantial reprocessing capability are in place [in Iraq], and there are currently 40–45 kgs. of HEU [highly enriched uranium] in Iraq in fresh and spent reactor fuel." Consequently, he advised the interagency Subcommittee on Nuclear Export Controls (SNEC)—which was chaired by the State Department—to adopt precautionary measures on the pending export license applications. Perle recommended that approval of the two licenses, as well as of future applications for the export of advanced computer equipment, be rendered conditional on Iraq's provision of written nonnuclear assurances to the United States. Although the Iraqi regime had refused to provide such assurances in the past and the State Department "does not want to impose them," Perle countered that the U.S. government already required them for the export of similar computers to the considerably friendlier country of Israel.[146] Despite Perle's warnings, the applications were approved by the Commerce Department under the watered-down condition that the Iraqi government merely provide verbal assurances that the exports would not be diverted to military use.[147]

On April 3, the State Department released an internal memo originating from the Northern Gulf Affairs desk of the Near Eastern and South Asian Affairs Bureau in response to Perle's attempted intervention. Recalling that the Defense Department had lodged objections to three computer sales to Iraq on nonproliferation grounds the prior year, the unnamed author of the communiqué pointed out that the Pentagon "differs radically from all other agencies in its assessment of the proliferation threat from Iraq." Those other agencies believed that Iraq did not "have the resources for a nuclear weapons development program and will not have for the foreseeable future." The author concluded that Perle's argument also happened to be "convenient for DOD/ISP, which would like to block any high-tech sales to Iraq."[148]

THE PENTAGON'S LAST GASPS OF RESISTANCE

As Iraq's military position took a precarious turn in the months following Iran's seizure of the Fao Peninsula in early 1986, senior State Department officials chafed at the tight domestic constraints on their ability to directly support the Iraqi war effort. A July 1986 memo drafted by Assistant Secretary of State Richard Murphy for his boss, Undersecretary of State for Political Affairs Michael Armacost, conceded that due to the efforts of domestic opponents, bilateral relations with Iraq were "thin and likely to remain that way."[149] Another memo drafted by Murphy for Armacost later that year in the wake of the Iran-Contra revelations admonished that the United States "should not—and given Congressional opposition, we could not—move away from our policy of neutrality in the Gulf War by providing arms to Iraq."[150] A few months later, Armacost even advised Secretary Shultz against additional transshipments of U.S. weapons to Iraq via third countries, because, among other reasons, such a move "could provoke a strong negative reaction in Congress."[151] Domestic pressures would only continue to climb in 1987. Early in the year, the Export-Import Bank suspended its $200 million short-term credit line for Iraq because the Iraqi government had fallen behind in its payments. After the bank rebuffed a State Department request to rescind the decision, Vice President George Bush successfully petitioned the bank's chair, John A. Bohn Jr., to reverse the decision. The administration's announcement of the reflagging operation in the Gulf a few months later precipitated the introduction of a flurry of bills and amendments aimed at forestalling and constraining the operation. In the face of strenuous lobbying by the White House, however, none of these measures were enacted.[152]

In the July 1986 memo in which Murphy emphasized the tenuousness of the U.S. alliance with Iraq to Armacost, he urged the undersecretary to try to break the bureaucratic logjam on technology transfers to Iraq. In light of Iraq's dire military and economic straits, Murphy affirmed that strong policy intervention was necessary "to intensify U.S.-Iraqi relations and, in the process, add at the margins to the Iraqis' ability to carry on." Specifically, he identified the expansion of high-technology exports to Iraq as one of the few available "steps the US might take to bolster the Iraqi will to resist, both psychologically and militarily." On this front, Murphy fingered the Pentagon for "block[ing] the issuance of licenses to Iraq on several items of symbolic and practical importance . . . Sometimes this has been done through bureaucratic procedures, sometimes through personal intervention." He dismissed the Defense Department's objections to the licenses by referring to "the most recent determination by the intelligence community," which stated, "We have no evidence that Iraq has passed controlled Western dual-use equipment to the Soviets or has misdirected equipment

to non-authorized domestic users." Murphy advised that Armacost immediately convene a meeting of the NSC's deputy-level Crisis Pre-Planning
Group (CPPG) in order to expedite final decisions on outstanding Iraqi
export applications.[153] Armacost heeded Murphy's advice. At the meeting,
he joined with his counterparts from Commerce and Agriculture in
excoriating the Defense Department for its repeated "obstruction" of high-
technology export applications for Iraq.[154]

Following the July CPPG meeting, National Security Advisor John
Poindexter placed his thumb on the scales by issuing a directive ordering
all U.S. government agencies "to be more forthcoming" on the applications.[155] This new policy was reflected in a talking points memo prepared
by the State Department for Vice President Bush in advance of his
March 1987 meeting with Iraq's ambassador in Washington, Nizar
Hamdoon. Bush was advised to assure Hamdoon that "[e]xpanding trade
is an essential element in broadening and strengthening our relations" and
convey that the vice president personally "sympathize[d] with [Iraqi] concerns about delays in the issuance of export licenses for some high-tech
sales." The memo also suggested that Bush promise Hamdoon that the
administration would "cut down wherever we can on uncertainty for both
U.S. exporters and our trading partners, and we will be taking a special
look at Iraq."[156]

Despite Poindexter's broadside against the Pentagon dissenters, Bryen
and Perle continued to sound the claxon on Iraq. Infuriated by the continuing stream of U.S. exports making their way to recipients that included
Iraq's Atomic Energy Agency and the Iraqi Air Force, in September Bryen
dispatched a cautionary letter to Assistant Secretary of Commerce for Trade
Administration Paul Freedenberg. Bryen conveyed his specific opposition
to Commerce's decision to approve the export of a Gould high-speed computer to Iraq despite its inability to secure an assurance from the Iraqi government that the computer would be used exclusively for civilian purposes.
Instead, Commerce had allowed the sale to proceed on the less restrictive
condition that this assurance be provided by the applicant corporation, as
opposed to the Iraqi end-user. Bryen explained that after reviewing the
background to this case, he discovered that the end-user was the same Saad
16 research complex to which Commerce had granted an export license for

the EAI hybrid computer over the Pentagon's objections the previous year. The sheer vastness of the Saad 16 facility alone, consisting of "approximately 82 different laboratories, covering a broad gambit of scientific research, including fuels, electro-optic, navigation and control, atmospheric, and microwave development," strongly hinted that it was engaged in military research.[157] According to investigative journalist Kenneth Timmerman, by this juncture Bryen had discovered that Commerce had approved more than thirty licenses for exports to Saad 16 for such items as "advanced computers, test instruments, microwave communications and manufacturing equipment, satellite mapping devices, image enhancement, radio scaler, spectrum analyzers, and telemetry equipment."[158] Declaring that he was "very concerned that Commerce has taken such a casual attitude towards providing such sophisticated equipment for an end-use as ambiguous as this and with such military significance," Bryen urged Freedenberg to suspend the EAI license (as the computer had not yet been shipped to Iraq) and refer both the EAI and Gould applications to the interagency Technology Transfer Steering Group.[159]

In line with Bryen's suspicions, though the Ba'ath regime described Saad 16 as an innocuous university research complex, in actuality it was Iraq's "largest and most important site for missile and nonconventional weapons development."[160] By November 1986, the Defense Department was able to learn that it was the primary site used to develop the Condor II short-range ballistic missile. The Condor II was a joint project by the governments of Iraq, Argentina, and Egypt to develop a missile that when completed would possess a range of 965 kilometers (600 miles) and would be capable of carrying nuclear warheads.[161] The Condor II promised a "qualitative advance in [Iraq's] military ambition," as its deployment would place all of Iran, Israel, Kuwait, Saudi Arabia, Oman, and Bahrain within Iraq's crosshairs.[162] An August 1988 report drafted by the Pentagon's Office for Non-Proliferation adjudged that "almost all of the labs [at Saad 16] deal with areas applicable to missile research and production," and even more ominously reported that it contained "a lab for 'seismographic soil test' . . . possibly indicating nuclear research."[163] The U.S. intelligence community additionally reported that Saad 16 was heavily guarded and surrounded by several antiaircraft batteries, and that Iraqi intelligence agents constantly patrolled the site in armored cars possessing ground surveillance radars.[164] Emboldened by the administration's permissive new policy on trade with Iraq, however, Freedenberg ignored Bryen's letter.[165]

A desperate Perle tried to mount an end-run around the administration by appealing to sympathetic ears in Congress. In a letter sent to Senators John Glenn (D-OH), Sam Nunn (D-GA), and Barry Goldwater (R-AZ), Perle decried the reckless behavior of State and Commerce. Glenn was so incensed that he convened a hearing on the matter in February 1987, during which he accused Richard Kennedy, the State Department's ambassador-at-large for nuclear affairs, of increasingly circumscribing the Defense Department's access to State Department cables pertaining to nonproliferation.[166]

THE U.S.-IRAQ BUSINESS FORUM ENTERS THE SCENE

In late 1986, a formidable private interest group weakened the Defense Department's hand on Iraq still further. In May 1985, Marshall Wiley, a lawyer and ex–U.S. Foreign Service officer, established the U.S.-Iraq Business Forum to promote commerce between the two countries. By late 1986, the forum had attracted the membership of over forty domestic corporations, including oil heavyweights Amoco, Mobil, Exxon, and Occidental; defense contractors Lockheed, Bell Helicopter–Textron, and United Technologies; and other high-profile Fortune 500 companies such as AT&T, General Motors, Bechtel, and Caterpillar.[167] Wiley would later describe the forum's intermediary role in bilateral trade promotion: "The Iraqis set up meetings [with senior government officials] for us when we brought trade missions to Baghdad. In return, they would inform us ahead of time of their visits to Washington so we could set up meetings for them."[168] Iraq's U.S. ambassador, Nizar Hamdoon, bolstered the organization's influence by informing an assembly of major U.S. corporate chief executive officers that Iraq would bestow preferential treatment on businesses that joined the forum. It did not take long for the White House to begin viewing it as a vital partner in fending off domestic opponents of its Iraq policy. At a forum-sponsored conference in early 1988, an unnamed administration official informed attendees that the White House depended on them to "help preserve—and expand the overall U.S.-Iraqi relationship through its commercial side."[169] Wiley later attested that senior officials had assured him that "not only were our goals consistent with U.S. policy, but what we were endeavoring to do served to enhance their policy."[170]

At Wiley's direction, the forum dispatched letters to senior policymakers in the administration to apprise them of the considerable economic stakes attached to enhanced trade with Iraq. In a November 1986 letter to Secretary of State Shultz, the forum's board chair, A. Robert Abboud, stated that his organization was "very concerned that we not lose the forward momentum in our trade relations [with Iraq]." Abboud concluded the communication with a veiled reference to the recent Iran-Contra revelations, which he claimed had ironically presented the United States with a new opportunity to "show that it continues to value Iraq as a force for moderation and stability in the region."[171]

THE CONTROVERSY COMES TO A HEAD

Within weeks of Shultz's receipt of the letter from Abboud, the State Department took additional steps to expedite the export licensing process for Iraq. On December 12, Armacost sent a letter to Acting National Security Advisor Alton Keel Jr. complaining about the "long delays" associated with the issuance of export licenses for Iraq, which entailed "disruptive consequences both for American exporters and for our relations with Iraq." He beseeched Keel's staff to "review the handling of Commerce license applications for Iraq, with the goal of resolving long-pending license requests by the end of the year." Armacost argued (carefully) that the nation had "a strong interest in *maintaining our influence* with Iraq on terrorism and other issues, but only limited options for accomplishing that." He dismissed as "exaggerated" Pentagon concerns that high-tech exports would be diverted from Iraq to the Eastern Bloc, though he refrained from mentioning the Pentagon's additional concerns about Iraq's nuclear and missile programs.[172] A follow-on démarche to Assistant Secretary of Commerce Freedenberg from the State Department's Bureau of Near Eastern and South Asian Affairs stressed that "[t]angible steps in expanding commerce between the U.S. and Iraq are especially urgent right now," and that Iraq and other Arab

Gulf states "have made it clear that they consider U.S. high-tech exports one measure of U.S. seriousness."[173] Just a few months after this, Freedenberg's immediate superior, Undersecretary of Commerce for International Trade S. Bruce Smart Jr., received a similar letter from Abboud lamenting the "difficulties encountered in obtaining export licenses from your department."[174]

During the final months of the Iran-Iraq War, U.S. technology exports poured into Iraq despite increasingly unmistakable signs of covert Iraqi proliferation activities. On June 25, 1988, the United States Customs Service intercepted several goods bound for Iraq that were "entirely consistent with items necessary to support the manufacture of a ballistic missile."[175] Notwithstanding this ominous development, Commerce approved a series of export licenses for Iraq's Nassr State Establishment for Mechanical Industries (NASSR), even though it was known to be a military complex that by 1987, if not earlier, had been active in ballistic missile production. NASSR was the most important location for the manufacture of the al-Hussein modified Scud-B missile, which Saddam began to use against Iran in early 1988; the facility played an important role in the development of the Condor II. It was also the chief production location for the (ill-fated) 1,000-millimeter "Super Gun," a giant artillery piece capable of launching one-thousand-pound bombs with conventional or unconventional payloads. Most worrisome was that the facility was involved in Iraq's nuclear, chemical, and biological weapons programs.[176] Despite the Pentagon's July 1988 warning that NASSR was a "bad end-user" and a "subordinate to the Military Industry Commission and located in a military facility," Commerce approved several exports to the facility. The acting director of its Office of Export Licensing dispatched a memo to the Defense Department defending the sale of a consignment of computers "for a graphic design system used in tooling designs," on the grounds that NASSR was a "multifunctional complex."[177]

Commerce and State also turned a blind eye toward export license applications destined for another suspicious Iraqi recipient, the Ministry of Industry and Military Industrialization (MIMI). Saddam Hussein created MIMI in April 1988 to amalgamate several industrial concerns, including oil refineries, chicken farms, chemical plants, phosphate mines, and fertilizer and truck assembly factories. These entities served as a front for the clandestine production of weapons of mass destruction. MIMI procured equipment necessary for the development of the Condor II missile under the pretext that the imports were destined for a petrochemical complex. In addition, it purchased components for the construction of the "Super-Gun." The Reagan administration also acquired intelligence linking MIMI to nuclear, chemical, and biological weapons development programs. MIMI's salience was underscored by Saddam's appointment as its director of his son-in-law, Hussein Kamal, whom the CIA believed to be the second most powerful man in Iraq. Kamal also served as the director of the Special Security Organization, Saddam's personal intelligence agency.[178]

In sum, the Defense Department's opposition to the unbridled provision of dual-use export licenses for Iraq was effectively steamrolled by a formidable coalition comprising senior officials in the White House, State Department, and Commerce Department supported by a powerful private lobby group representing some of America's largest corporations. During the final two years of the Reagan administration, the Commerce Department approved 241 dual-use export license applications for products bound for Iraq and rejected a mere six. A 1990 State Department memo reported that the U.S. government granted no fewer than seventy-three dual-use export licenses to Iraq that were suspected of being diverted to proliferation-related end-users. Congressional investigators have similarly estimated that two of every seven licensed exports to Iraq between 1985 and 1990 were diverted to military uses. By comparison, Deputy Undersecretary Bryen claimed to have raised objections to approximately 40 percent of the license applications sent to the Pentagon for review by the Commerce Department.[179] By the time that the George H. W. Bush administration entered office, the implications of its predecessors' open-armed policy on dual-use exports were clear. In April 1989, the new administration's Acting Assistant Secretary of Energy for Defense Programs, Troy Wade II, wrote to Energy Secretary James Watkins in alarm, "Recent evidence indicates that Iraq has a major effort under way to produce nuclear weapons." Wade referred specifically to "recent evidence of Iraq[i] endeavors to procure both non-nuclear components for weapons, as well as items specific to producing nuclear materials."[180]

CONCLUSION

A number of scholars have treated America's relationship with Iraq during the Iran-Iraq War as relatively unproblematic, concurring tacitly with George Shultz's own description of U.S. policy during that period: "our support for Iraq increased in rough proportion to Iran's military successes: plain and simple, the United States was engaged in a limited form of balance of power policy."[181] Alexander George's highly influential book *Bridging the Gap*, which analyzes U.S. policy toward Iraq prior to the 1991 Persian Gulf War, devotes only a single paragraph to the discussion of the bilateral relationship during the entirety of the Iran-Iraq War. George mentions only that the United States "strongly tilted" toward Iraq during the war and cursorily asserts that the policy "was based on familiar balance-of-power considerations, and it was successful."[182] This is also the case with Stephen Rock's chapter on U.S. relations with Iraq between 1989 and 1990, in his book *Appeasement in International Politics*. Rock merely notes that the primary purpose of U.S. policy during the Iran-Iraq War was not to influence Iraq's foreign or domestic policy behavior but to support it in its war against Iran.[183] An only slightly more nuanced discussion can be found in Kenneth Juster's essay "The U.S. and Iraq: Perils of Engagement" in a 2000 edited volume on incentives and sanctions in foreign policy. Juster does note that the Reagan administration had multiple policy objectives relating to Iraq during the war, but, in a puzzling omission, refrains from mentioning the most important ones: curbing Iraq's support for terrorism and the proliferation of nuclear weapons and ballistic missiles.[184]

These interpretations of U.S. policy fail to note that the Reagan administration had multiple national security–related disputes with Iraq during the war and was well positioned to achieve all of them, given the United States' advantaged systemic position vis-à-vis Iraq. That it ultimately failed to do so was attributable to the thorny domestic politics of the alliance, which compelled senior administration officials to adopt a forgiving position toward the Saddam regime on terrorism and proliferation. As a result, Iraq emerged at the end of the conflict politically unreformed and unrepentant. In short order, it supplanted Iran as America's foremost adversary in the Gulf.

5

THE U.S. "SPECIAL RELATIONSHIP" ALLIANCE WITH THE UNITED KINGDOM, 1950–1953

The United States administration often behaves insufferably to its allies. Americans are apt to behave insufferably to each other. Their natural characteristics and their constitutional processes are what they are, and it does little good to get angry about them.

—SIR WILLIAM STRANG, UK PERMANENT UNDER-SECRETARY FOR
FOREIGN AFFAIRS, FOREIGN OFFICE MINUTE, JANUARY 3, 1951

THE THREE PREVIOUS chapters have provided strong support for the neo-classical realist (NCR) proposition that *if a systemically advantaged ally has an internally weak state, then it will bargain passively and unsuccessfully with a systemically disadvantaged ally of convenience* (Hypothesis 3). In this chapter, I test NCR's antipodal proposition: that *if a systemically advantaged ally has an internally weak state, then it will bargain aggressively and successfully with a systemically disadvantaged special relationship ally* (Hypothesis 2). It examines U.S. bargaining behavior toward its most intimate special relationship ally of the past century, the United Kingdom, during the Korean War (1950–1953). Although both neorealist and tying hands theories join NCR in making the same prediction, the case's inclusion is necessary to bolster confidence in NCR by avoiding the charge of selection bias. By restricting the research design to predicted cases of U.S. bargaining failure with ideologically and geopolitically hostile allies of convenience, I would have run the risk of selecting on the dependent variable. By adding a case in which the theory predicts the opposite outcome in U.S. bargaining with a friendly special relationship ally, I can show covariation between its purported independent and intervening variables, on the one hand, and the dependent variable, on the other. Specifically, if alliances of convenience produce high levels of domestic opposition that force U.S. leaders to adopt anemic and fruitless bargaining strategies, then more benign special relationship alliances should engender little domestic opposition, thereby enabling those leaders to bargain tenaciously and effectively.

Although the United States and United Kingdom agreed on the dangers posed by the North Korean invasion of South Korea and on the imperative of intervening militarily on Seoul's behalf, disagreements arose between them on several important national security–related issues. In Korea, the two allies clashed repeatedly on key decisions involving the U.S.-led coalition's prosecution of the war. Meanwhile, outside Korea, they disagreed on issues pertaining to the signing of a peace treaty with Japan to end the Pacific War, the command structure of the North Atlantic Treaty Organization (NATO), Iran's nationalization of the Anglo-Iranian Oil Company (AIOC), and Britain's rearmament program. At almost every juncture in which British officials expressed disagreement with their American counterparts, they ultimately backed down in the face of vociferous U.S. opposition.[1]

THE UNITED STATES, BRITAIN, AND THE UN INTERVENTION IN KOREA (1950–1953)

In the early hours of June 25, 1950, over one hundred thousand North Korean troops crossed the 38th parallel into South Korea, marking the outbreak of the first major interstate war since World War II. The North Korean People's Army (NKPA) made rapid progress against the poorly trained and outgunned Republic of Korea Army (ROKA), capturing the South Korean capital of Seoul in just three days. Although the Korean Peninsula was not considered of vital interest to either the United States or Britain, both governments strongly supported military intervention on behalf of the Republic of Korea (ROK). This stemmed in large measure from their erroneous belief that the Soviet Union had instigated the attack, and that failing to thwart it would therefore be tantamount to appeasing Moscow and inviting the Soviet Red Army to invade Western Europe.[2] The Truman administration exploited a temporary Soviet walkout from the United Nations Security Council to secure passage—with British support—of successive resolutions demanding an immediate cease-fire and North Korea's complete withdrawal from South Korea, enjoining all UN members to militarily assist the ROKA, and establishing a unified United Nations Command (UNC) under General Douglas MacArthur, the commander of U.S. forces in the Far East and overlord of occupied Japan.[3]

The war consisted of four temporal phases.[4] During the first, which spanned the conflict's first three months, the Soviet-supplied NKPA swept southward, culminating in its establishment of a front line just outside the southeast port city of Pusan. The second phase was inaugurated with MacArthur's daring amphibious invasion at Inchon on September 15, followed by UN forces' envelopment of the NKPA and rapid advance deep into North Korean territory. The expansion of UN war aims from the liberation of South Korea to the complete destruction of communist North Korea, formally known as the Democratic People's Republic of Korea (DPRK), brought UN troops to the Yalu River separating the DPRK from an increasingly anxious China. In late October, Chinese leader Mao Zedong dramatically inaugurated the third phase of the war by deploying nearly three hundred thousand Chinese People's Volunteer Army (CPVA) troops across the Yalu to repulse the UNC offensive. The CPVA pushed UN troops back below the 38th parallel in early January 1951 and recaptured Seoul just a few weeks later. The next month, UN forces managed to halt the counteroffensive and by mid-March had liberated Seoul. The stabilization of the front line at the 38th parallel helped pave the way for the inauguration of face-to-face armistice talks on June 10.[5]

The final and lengthiest stage of the war was characterized by a grinding stalemate on the battlefield and grueling negotiations at the peace table.[6] By March 1952, the belligerents settled all outstanding issues save the rules governing repatriation of prisoners of war (POWs).[7] The UNC held more than ten times as many POWs as the Communists, and the United States hewed to the principle of voluntary repatriation (i.e., that prisoners could choose whether to be sent back to their home country), while the

Communists insisted on an involuntary all-for-all exchange of POWs. Only after the issue was settled by the belligerents and President Eisenhower secured the acquiescence of obdurate South Korean president Syngman Rhee was a cease-fire finally concluded on July 27, 1953. After three hard years of fighting, millions of combat and civilian deaths, and the physical devastation of much of the Korean Peninsula, the war ended at virtually the exact same place that it had begun three years earlier.[8]

THE U.S.-UK ALLIANCE: A MOST SPECIAL RELATIONSHIP

At the time that the United States and Britain joined forces with South Korea, the relationship of the two states was characterized by relative—if not perfect—ideological and geopolitical harmony. Ideologically, both were liberal democracies, which rendered them "natural allies," according to a 1948 State Department policy statement.[9] Reinforcing the ideological kinship of the two countries was their shared history, culture, and language, which Churchill depicted succinctly in his landmark 1946 "Iron Curtain" speech in Fulton, Missouri as the "fraternal association of the English-speaking peoples."[10]

Since the end of the American revolutionary era in the early nineteenth century, the two countries have also possessed closely overlapping geopolitical interests, stemming from their shared position as offshore maritime powers concerned predominantly with maintaining a balance of power in both Europe and East Asia.[11] During the first half of the twentieth century, they fought on the same side in both world wars, and during World War II, they forged what is arguably the most intimate and cohesive military partnership in the history of modern warfare.[12] The relationship was briefly marred in the immediate aftermath of their victory by the Truman administration's abrupt decision in August 1945 to stop wartime lending to and bilateral military and nuclear cooperation with the United Kingdom, as well as its interference in British efforts to broker a peace deal between Jews and Arabs in Palestine.[13]

Rising tensions between the Western powers and the Soviet Union brought the formerly close allies back together. In 1946, Britain agreed to host nuclear-armed American B-29 bombers in the event of an emergency. The next year, the Truman administration both relieved the United Kingdom of the responsibility of defending Greece and Turkey from Communist encroachments and embarked on a massive economic reconstruction program for Western Europe, the Marshall Plan or European Recovery Program (ERP).[14] Britain received the largest portion, approximately $2.7 billion, of the $12 billion in total aid dispensed under the aegis of the ERP.[15] The Kremlin's sponsorship of a Communist coup in Czechoslovakia in February 1948 and its imposition of a blockade on West Berlin four months later lent extreme urgency to ongoing multilateral discussions on continental defense, culminating in the April 1949 North Atlantic Treaty, which created the NATO alliance.[16]

By the time of the outbreak of the Korean War, policymakers in both Washington and London were casting the bilateral relationship in lofty terms redolent of those used during its heyday in the early 1940s. On the U.S. side, an April 1950 State Department paper avowed, "No other country has the same qualifications for being our principal ally and partner as the UK . . . Most important, the British share our fundamental objectives and standards of conduct."[17] Across the Atlantic, the Labour government of Prime Minister Clement Attlee endorsed an August 1949 Foreign Office paper acknowledging that British and American "political interests coincide in most parts of the world" and that the UK "is the principal partner and ally on whom the USA can rely."[18]

DYNAMICS OF THE U.S.-UK ALLIANCE IN KOREA

The UN coalition that waged the war in Korea was led and dominated by the United States. At its peak strength, the U.S. ground force deployment reached a total of three hundred and thirty thousand troops. This was second only to the ROK itself, which at peak strength fielded five hundred and ninety thousand troops. Of the fifty-six additional countries that lent assistance to the UN coalition in one form or another, the most substantial contribution was made by the UK. Britain dispatched two infantry brigades totaling 14,200 troops, one aircraft carrier, two cruisers, four destroyers, one hospital ship, four frigates, and one headquarters ship to the war effort.[19]

INTRA-ALLIANCE DISPUTES BETWEEN
THE UNITED STATES AND UNITED KINGDOM

Over the course of the Korean War, the United States and United Kingdom disagreed on a number of national security–related matters. The war broke out just as the U.S.-led Western Bloc was in its earliest stages of organizing against the burgeoning Soviet threat.[20] This engendered a fluid situation in which several disputes between Washington and London emerged more or less simultaneously.

From the outset of the war until its conclusion three years later, the two allies repeatedly butted heads on a number of issues, pertaining to both the Korean War and broader Cold War. In Korea, British leaders recurrently complained that Washington was either not consulting sufficiently with them or was not taking Britain's interests sufficiently into account on a range of important tactical and strategic decisions.[21] Also, although both the U.S. and UK governments sought to keep the war limited by forestalling the full-scale intervention of the Soviet Union and China, Washington repeatedly proved far more risk-acceptant than London on this score.[22]

The allies also disagreed on four crucial matters related to the broader Cold War against the Soviet Union. First, the urgent process of negotiating a peace treaty with Japan to end the Pacific War sparked two separate rows over whether a postwar security guarantee for Australia and New Zealand should include the United Kingdom and whether Japan should conclude peace and establish formal diplomatic relations with the Nationalist Chinese regime in Taiwan or the Communist People's Republic of China (PRC). Whereas U.S. leaders favored Britain's exclusion from a prospective alliance with Australia and New Zealand and Japan's formal recognition of Taiwan as China's sovereign government, the British sought to be included in a South Pacific defense treaty and favored Japan's formal recognition of the PRC. Second, on the matter of NATO's prospective command arrangements, the United States favored and Britain opposed the appointment of an American admiral atop a unified Supreme Allied Command Atlantic and the establishment of a Mediterranean command that would be firmly subordinated to the Supreme Allied Commander Europe.

Third, after Iran nationalized the AIOC in early 1951, Washington pressed for the two allies' joint adoption of a conciliatory posture toward the recalcitrant Iranian regime in order to keep Iran out of the Soviet sphere of influence, while London favored a highly coercive approach. Fourth, the allies diverged on the subject of British defense spending, as the White House repeatedly urged British leaders to devote greater sums to the country's rearmament program while fending off their repeated requests for greater economic assistance on the program's behalf.

THREE HYPOTHESES ON U.S.-UK BARGAINING DURING THE WAR

All three of the rival theories of alliance bargaining tested in this book offer identical predictions of successful U.S. bargaining with the UK during the Korean War. Neorealism primarily bases this prediction on Britain's relatively high level of dependence for its security on the United States. Historians Steve Marsh and John Baylis depict the postwar balance of dependence between the two states as follows:

> The US came out of the war with enormous self-sufficiency, a monopoly over the atomic bomb, the world's most advanced industrial-military complex and a pre-eminent global economic position in which it held $20 billion of the world's $33 billion of gold reserves, manufactured over half of the world's goods and controlled over half of the world's shipping. Britain emerged economically exhausted and dislocated by its sustained war effort and dependence on overseas trade and investment . . . Britain's wartime dependence on the US lend-lease program in 1946 continued into peacetime through the highly controversial American loan [of $3.75 billion].[23]

During the Korean War, America's aggregate wealth and military power exponentially outstripped those of the United Kingdom. In 1950, the year that the war commenced, the United States' $381 billion Gross National

Product (GNP) exceeded Britain's GNP of $71 billion by a factor of five. Meanwhile, over the course of the war, annual U.S. military spending soared from six times that of the United Kingdom in 1950 ($14.5 billion versus $2.3 billion) to a staggering eleven times ($49.6 billion versus $4.5 billion) by 1953.[24]

In addition, although the United States was formally bound to the defense of Britain by dint of both states' membership in NATO, this commitment was not directly engaged during the Korean War. Article V of the 1949 North Atlantic Treaty stipulates that an "armed attack against one of more of [the signatories] *in Europe or North America* shall be considered an attack against them all."[25] Importantly, Article V also specifies that in the event of such an attack, each of the other alliance members are obliged to take only *"such action as it deems necessary, including the use of armed force,* to restore and maintain the security of the North Atlantic area."[26] The vagueness of this provision afforded the United States considerable wiggle-room in deciding how to respond to a prospective Soviet attack against Britain or any other NATO ally. In sum, neorealism predicts that, at least with respect to issues in which the balance of interests did not grossly favor the United Kingdom, favorable balances of dependence and commitment should have enabled U.S. leaders to bargain successfully with their British counterparts.

Tying hands attributes the predicted outcome of successful U.S. bargaining to America's slightly narrower win-set than that of the United Kingdom. Although both states are liberal democracies, senior executive branch leaders in Britain possess more centralized policymaking power than their American counterparts. In the British parliamentary system of government, the political party that wins a majority of seats in the House of Commons is empowered to form a government headed by a prime minister and cabinet with a five-year mandate. In his comparative study of U.S. and British foreign policymaking, Kenneth Waltz claims that the "fusion of the executive with its party in [the British] Parliament produces a situation in which he who wills the ends thereby wills the means. The policy of the government receives the support it may need from the legislative assembly."[27] Consequently, "Parliamentary government easily becomes Cabinet government, and Cabinet government in England has increasingly become Prime Ministerial government."[28]

Whereas in Britain the executive and legislative branches of governance are fused, they are constitutionally separated in the United States. The president is elected independently of members of Congress, in two respects. First, whereas congressional lawmakers are elected by subnational constituencies at either the state or substate level, the president is independently elected by a nationwide constituency. Second, members of the House are obliged to stand for reelection every two years and senators every six years, while the president serves a four-year term in office. Throughout U.S. history, this arrangement has frequently resulted in divided government, in which one party has controlled the White House and the other has held a majority in the House of Representatives, Senate, or both.[29] Even during the infrequent periods in which the national government has been unified, however, differences in electoral constituencies and calendars have produced invariable frictions between the White House and Congress.[30] Since the electoral fates of legislators are not tightly bound to that of the chief executive, as is the case in Britain, and the legislative branch possesses a range of constitutionally enshrined prerogatives and checks on the executive, Congress "can obstruct the President's program or force policies upon him."[31] In sum, because the U.S. president possesses less policymaking autonomy and a (slightly) narrower win-set than the British premier, tying hands theory proposes that the former will tend to bargain successfully with the latter.

In contrast to the examples in the previous three chapters, NCR makes the same prediction as its neorealist and tying hands rivals. It proposes that if the systemically advantaged ally possesses a weak extractive state, it will nevertheless bargain aggressively and successfully with the systemically disadvantaged partner if the partner is a special relationship ally. Although the foreign policy executive (FPE) of the systemically advantaged ally possesses little policymaking autonomy, domestic opposition to the alliance will be muted because the partner will be widely perceived as benign, friendly, and reliable. Since the FPE will not be preoccupied with cutting domestic slack on behalf of the alliance, it will be inclined to exploit its systemic advantage over the partner by adopting an aggressive bargaining strategy toward it on salient disputed issues. Thus, NCR predicts that senior officials in both the Truman and Eisenhower administrations should have encountered minimal domestic resistance to the special relationship alliance with the United Kingdom, enabling them to engage in heavy-handed and fruitful bargaining with Britain's leaders.

NCR joins with neorealism in proposing that the two administrations should have swayed their British interlocutors by stressing the United States' favorable international systemic position vis-à-vis the United Kingdom. Evidence showing that U.S. leaders leveraged British concessions by stressing their narrower domestic win-set, which more closely accords with tying hands theory, does not refute NCR in this instance, however. Whereas the FPE of an internally weak state will be unable to play tying hands with an ally of convenience due to its preoccupation with defusing domestic opposition to the alliance, it can entertain this option in negotiating with a much less controversial special relationship ally. In this particular case, since the systemically advantaged ally also happened to possess a narrower win-set than the disadvantaged partner, the former's FPE can be expected to have exploited both attributes in bargaining with the latter.

This case is a particularly useful one for NCR because, owing to the prevailing international systemic and domestic political conditions during the war, it constitutes a least likely one for the theory. From the vantage point of the international system, during the early years of the Cold War, Britain was by a wide margin the United States' most wealthy and powerful ally.[32] By the early 1950s, British arms production eclipsed that of all other European NATO partners combined, while Britain's economy was considerably larger in size that those of both West Germany and France, alone accounting for nearly one-third of total industrial production in Western Europe.[33] In addition, Britain was the world's most important overseas base for the U.S. Strategic Air Command's B-29 nuclear bombers, remained the predominant Western military power in the Middle East and Persian Gulf, and contributed the second largest number of troops to the Korean War after the United States.[34] Meanwhile, of America's European NATO allies, Britain was the least proximate to the Soviet adversary against which the alliance was directed and exclusively enjoyed a significant geographical buffer—namely, the English Channel—separating it from the rest of the continent. These factors rendered London less dependent on the United States than all of Washington's other allies, both formal and informal.

Additionally, the United States was contractually committed to the defense of Britain owing to both countries' membership in NATO. But even if the NATO alliance had never been concluded, it would have been unthinkable for Washington to allow Britain to succumb to the Soviets because the United Kingdom held a pivotal geopolitical position offshore of Western Europe and played an instrumental role in the Western capitalist economic system.[35] As a result, although the United States was the systemically favored ally in the dyad, the magnitude of its advantage should have been less than that which it enjoyed over all of its other alliance partners.

From a domestic political perspective, the case was also a least likely one because for most of the war (June 1950–January 1953), the United States was led by the politically embattled Democratic president Harry Truman. According to historian Steven Casey, the war "was an increasingly unpopular conflict, one that largely wrecked the Truman administration" following China's late 1950 intervention.[36] By February 1952, Truman's job approval bottomed out at a mere 22 percent, which led him to announce the next month that he would not seek or accept the nomination of the Democratic Party for a second presidential term.[37] In such adverse political conditions, the administration could have been expected to be highly disposed to bargain passively with the UK in order to keep the alliance from unraveling at the hands of domestic critics.

KOREAN WAR–RELATED DISPUTES

EARLY DISAGREEMENTS ON CONSULTATION AND UK GROUND FORCES

The earliest wartime disputes between the allies set the pattern for the rest of the war, as the United States gave way on a minor semantic issue but Britain conceded on several more important substantive matters. The first disagreement centered on the wording of one of the Security Council resolutions drafted by the Truman administration immediately after the North Korean invasion, which declared that the attack "makes amply clear centrally directed Communist Imperialism has passed beyond subversion in seeking to conquer independent nations."[38] Concerned that this inflammatory phrase foreclosed the possibility of enlisting Soviet cooperation in ending the war, Whitehall prevailed on the State Department to strike it from the resolution. At around the same time, however, British leaders were enraged by the administration's sudden arbitrary deployment of the U.S. Navy's Seventh Fleet to the Taiwan Strait in order to deter a Chinese invasion of Taiwan, as well as its brazen violation of a prior pledge not to conduct air strikes north of the 38th parallel.[39] These developments prompted British Minister of Defence Emmanuel Shinwell to lament that His Majesty's Government (HMG) possessed "very little information about American plans and intentions."[40]

The White House proved no more considerate on the matter of Britain's putative contribution to the war effort. On June 28, the Cabinet Defence Committee agreed to place the Far East fleet, consisting of a light fleet carrier, two cruisers, and five escort vessels, at the disposal of the UN Command for operations in Korea.[41] The fall of Seoul two days later spurred the White House to begin urging Britain to send an expeditionary force to the peninsula.[42] Lord Tedder, who headed Britain's Joint Services Mission in Washington, poured cold water on the request, explaining to Chairman of the Joint Chiefs of Staff General Omar Bradley that London had already drawn on overstretched UK forces in the Middle East and "meagre reserves in the UK"[43] to shore up its vulnerable positions in Hong Kong and the Federation of Malaya. Attlee overruled Tedder, however, and ordered the formation by November 1 of the 29 Brigade Group for deployment to Korea after he received a cable from Britain's U.S. ambassador, Sir Oliver Franks, warning that a rebuff of the U.S. request would "seriously impair" the bilateral relationship.[44] Unsatisfied, General MacArthur implored the British to deploy those troops to Korea "urgently now."[45] In response, Attlee both moved forward the date of the brigade's departure by one month and ordered the immediate transfer of two additional infantry battalions to Korea from Hong Kong.[46]

During this anxious period for the besieged UN coalition, some grumbling about the lack of allied contributions to the war was evident in the media and Congress. An assessment of newspapers across the country conducted by the State Department's Office of Public Affairs summarized their shared editorial position that "others should be sending their soldiers and equipment to fight [in Korea]."[47] This sentiment was echoed by several Republicans in Congress. The arrival of the first British troops in late August, however, "helped still some of this criticism," which died down in any event the next month after MacArthur's successful amphibious landing at Inchon.[48] As would prove to be the case for the rest of the war, to the extent that anti-NATO opposition occasionally flared up in Congress, it emanated from a hardline nationalist faction of the Republican minority in both chambers whose members routinely voted against the administration on foreign policy issues. The White House repeatedly mobilized a formidable coalition of Democrats and internationalist Republicans to defeat their efforts. Although several of the latter belonged to the so-called China Lobby, which regularly criticized the administration for its failure to stem the spread of Communism in East Asia, they did not oppose the U.S. commitment to NATO. Most of them "simply wanted the United States to commit an equal amount of resources to stopping communist expansion in Asia as it did to fighting the Cold War in Europe."[49]

THE KELLY-GROMYKO INCIDENT, OIL SANCTIONS AGAINST CHINA, AND THE UK BUFFER ZONE PROPOSAL

During the tense early weeks of the war, a spat also emerged between the allies in response to a British diplomatic initiative to tempt the Soviets into brokering a cease-fire in Korea. On July 6, Britain's ambassador to the Soviet Union, Sir David Kelly, cabled the Foreign Office that Soviet Deputy Foreign Minister Andrei Gromyko had conveyed to him the Kremlin's desire for a peaceful settlement of the war.[50] British Foreign Minister Ernest Bevin unintentionally sparked a row by conjecturing in a subsequent cable to U.S. Secretary of State Dean Acheson that in return for the USSR's help in ending the war, Soviet leader Joseph Stalin would almost certainly demand Taiwan's ejection from the UN and its replacement by the Communist PRC.[51] In a blistering reply, Acheson categorically ruled out any quid pro quo with the Soviets and instructed Lewis Douglas, the U.S. ambassador in London, to leave Bevin "in no doubt of the seriousness with which I view [the] implications of his message and their possible effect on our future relationship."[52] In response, Attlee spurned Gromyko's statement to Kelly on

July 17 that "an indispensable condition"[53] for ending the war was for the Security Council to convene with the participation of the PRC.

As the Kelly-Gromyko controversy unfolded, Britain further provoked the administration's ire by refusing to follow America's lead in imposing oil sanctions against China. Though HMG protested that Britain's oil exports to China were negligible, Deputy Assistant Secretary of State for Far Eastern Affairs Livingston Merchant warned a British embassy official that Americans would be furious if China were to intervene militarily in Korea using vehicles fueled by British petroleum. In the face of this warning, London reluctantly agreed to cease exporting oil to the PRC from Hong Kong.[54]

Reports in early November that large numbers of Chinese troops were sweeping into North Korea led the UK cabinet to call on UN forces to withdraw to a line running approximately along the 40th parallel between the North Korean cities of Hungnam and Chongju, creating a demilitarized buffer zone on the Korean side of the Manchurian border.[55] When Acheson learned that Bevin planned to formally introduce this buffer zone proposal to the Security Council, he instructed Britain's UN ambassador, Gladwyn Jebb, to inform Bevin that the United States "would be compelled to oppose such proposals if made."[56] On November 22, Bevin reluctantly scuttled the initiative.[57] Even as the British fatefully conceded to the Americans on the larger issue of the buffer zone, they prevailed on a subsidiary dispute over whether U.S. combat aircraft could enter Chinese airspace under certain narrowly circumscribed conditions. After MacArthur began petitioning the White House to allow U.S. warplanes to pursue Chinese combat aircraft operating in Korea back to their bases in Manchuria, the administration proposed the idea to London. When Bevin strongly objected to the proposal, however, the White House quietly demurred.[58]

A "NUCLEAR" PRESS CONFERENCE AND
THE TRUMAN-ATTLEE SUMMIT

As UN forces chaotically retreated down the length of the peninsula in late 1950, President Truman held a press conference during which he responded affirmatively to a reporter's question whether he would consider using nuclear weapons to secure U.S. military objectives in Korea.[59] Although the White House released a statement later that day clarifying that the president had not specifically authorized the UNC to use nuclear weapons, alarm bells nevertheless rang in London and other allied capitals, and Attlee urgently requested a face-to-face meeting with Truman.[60] The pivotal Truman-Attlee summit of December 4–8 consisted of a series of "tense and acrimonious"[61] meetings in Washington between the two leaders and their senior advisors. The first item discussed at the summit was whether the UNC should appeal to China for a negotiated end to hostilities. Whereas Attlee endorsed this option on the grounds that the allies should not "get so involved in the East as to lay ourselves open to attack in the West," Truman insisted that it was out of the question because the Chinese Communists were "complete satellites" of the USSR.[62] After Acheson insisted to Ambassador Franks that the American people "would not accept a surrender in the Far East in accord with the desire of some of our Allies and then cooperate in Europe with the same Allies who have urged us to be conciliatory in the Far East,"[63] the British delegation stood down. The joint communiqué released at the conclusion of the summit stipulated that both governments "were in complete agreement that there can be no thought of appeasement or rewarding [Chinese] aggression, whether in the Far East or elsewhere."[64]

Attlee proved no more successful when he broached the equally delicate matter of the administration's continuing reluctance to consult with Britain on the war. During a December 6 dinner meeting at the British embassy, Attlee told Acheson that there was a "feeling in Europe" that General MacArthur was "running the show and that the other participating countries had little to say in what was done." To ameliorate this problem, he requested the formation of "some sort of committee to direct the war." General Bradley rejoined brusquely that "a war could not be run by a committee" and added that "if others did not like what was going on, they should say so and they would be given assistance in withdrawing."[65]

Finally, as the conclusion of the summit neared, Truman and Attlee held a private one-on-one discussion regarding the nuclear issue that had precipitated Attlee's request for the meeting in the first place. Truman informed Attlee that by law only he could authorize the use of nuclear weapons, but reassured the premier that he had not authorized their use in Korea and he would not consider using the atom bomb without consulting London. When Attlee requested that Truman put this promise in writing, however, the president balked.[66] During the bilateral negotiations over their joint communiqué, the State Department instructed the British delegation to delete a passage from its formal minutes that noted that Truman had promised to "consult" the UK on the use of nuclear weapons.[67] Attlee justified his acceptance of Truman's oral promise to Foreign Minister Bevin, who did not attend the summit, on the grounds that the administration, and particularly Acheson, was "obviously under heavy fire" domestically.[68]

THE AGGRESSOR RESOLUTION

No sooner had Attlee returned to London than the stage was set for yet another intra-alliance quarrel, this time over whether the UN should formally brand China an aggressor in the war. On December 12, Acheson agreed to vote for a cease-fire resolution in the General Assembly that was supported by London on condition that if China rejected it, the United States would proceed to introduce a resolution condemning Chinese aggression in Korea and directing the United Nations to impose economic sanctions against the People's Republic. After China spurned the cease-fire resolution and PLA troops began descending south of the 38th parallel toward Seoul, Britain's panicked Permanent Under-Secretary of State for Foreign Affairs, Sir William Strang, drafted a memo counseling the government to ask Washington to dispense with the aggressor resolution and negotiate a cease-fire with Beijing. Strang pointedly conceded, however, that persuading America to abandon its reckless and dangerous course in Asia would not be an easy task. A sympathetic Kenneth Younger, who was minister of state at the Foreign Office (its second-highest-ranking official behind Bevin), persuaded Attlee to inform the U.S. administration that British support for the aggressor resolution could not be assumed.[69]

Acheson remonstrated that the UN's failure to condemn Chinese aggression would "create a wave of isolationism in this country which would jeopardize all that we are trying to do with and for the Atlantic Pact countries."[70] He then dismissed out of hand a compromise proposal devised by

Bevin that would have entailed disaggregating the aggressor resolution into two separate measures, one formally branding China an aggressor and the second imposing new sanctions.[71] Instead, the administration submitted the aggressor resolution, which contained a clause inviting the UN's Collective Measures Committee (CMC) to propose "additional actions" (i.e., economic sanctions) to the UN Political Committee to be taken against Beijing.[72] Attlee then proposed a last-ditch compromise to reword the offending section of the resolution so that it called for the consideration of additional action against China only in the event that a UN Good Offices Committee (GOC) created to negotiate an end to the Korean War failed in its mission.[73] Acheson blasted the proposed change as "completely unacceptable" and warned that an open split between the two allies would have "probable repercussions on US efforts to strengthen the NATO countries in view of current sensitive state of US public opinion."[74]

The debate over the aggressor resolution once again resulted in a small U.S. concession and a large British one. On January 27, Acheson informed Ambassador Franks that President Truman had permitted the insertion of language into the aggressor resolution stating that the CMC would be authorized to withhold its report if the GOC was judged to be making progress in securing an end to the war. He maintained, however, that this proposal represented the "end of his elasticity," in light of the U.S. Congress's extreme hostility toward Beijing.[75] In return, Attlee secured the cabinet's approval to vote in favor of the aggressor resolution, which passed the UN General Assembly by a wide margin on February 3.[76]

Notably, Attlee's frantic trip to Washington and the controversy over the aggressor resolution took place at the same time that Congress's wartime frustration with Britain (and America's other European allies) reached its zenith. On December 6, firebrand Republican senator James Kem of Missouri sponsored a resolution stipulating that any agreements reached during the Truman-Attlee summit "should, under the Constitution, be embodied in a treaty which should be submitted to the Senate for ratification."[77] However, Kem's resolution met with harsh and overwhelming scorn on the part of congressional Democrats. With the support of Republican senators Margaret Chase Smith (ME), Leverett Saltonstall (MA), and Chan Gurney (SD), the committee voted down the measure by a 30–45 margin.[78]

Later that month, the administration's plan to dispatch four additional divisions of troops to Europe to shore up NATO defenses triggered a major outcry by congressional Republicans. The subsequent "great debate" over the deployment centered on two congressional resolutions. The first, introduced by Frederic Coudert (NY) in the House of Representatives, held that no additional forces "be sent or maintained outside the United States . . . without the prior approval of Congress in each instance." The second, introduced in the Senate by Kenneth Wherry (NE), was less strident, merely stipulating that no additional U.S. ground forces could be deployed to Europe on NATO's behalf "pending the formulation of a policy with respect thereto by Congress."[79] It is important to note, however, that these measures were extremely unpopular. The State Department's Office of Public Affairs adjudged that "the preponderance of American opinion still appears to reject any suggestion for pulling out of Europe . . . All evidence continues to indicate support for large-scale rearmament and mobilization measures."[80] A January 1951 national opinion research poll found that 78 percent of Americans supported NATO and that public support for the provision of military aid to Europe had actually increased over the course of the previous year from 55 percent to 71 percent.[81] Meanwhile, even the most prominent exponents of the Republican position on the NATO troop deployment, former president Herbert Hoover and Senator Robert Taft (OH), still advocated the use of U.S. air and naval power to defend key overseas interests, including Britain.[82]

In the end, the nationalist Republicans lost the "great debate." A full-court press by the administration and a bipartisan coalition of internationalist legislators resulted in Congress's passage of a resolution approving the president's decision to dispatch the four divisions of troops to Europe by enormous margins (a 69–21 vote in the Senate and a 372–44 vote in the House).[83] The nationalists' pique at the allies' professed lack of military and diplomatic support for the UNC war effort in Korea did result, however, in the passage of two nonbinding amendments that exhorted America's NATO allies to provide "the major contribution" to the defense of Western Europe and opposed the dispatch of additional U.S. troops to Europe "without further congressional approval."[84]

MACARTHUR'S DISMISSAL AND THE AIR
RETALIATION PROPOSAL

The Communists' capture of Seoul and Inchon raised suspicions in London that MacArthur was seeking a pretext to withdraw from Korea and launch an all-out attack on China, perhaps even with nuclear weapons. Attlee dispatched Air Marshal Sir John Slessor, chief of staff of the Royal Air Force, and Field Marshal Sir William Slim, chief of the Imperial General Staff, to Washington in order to determine the Truman administration's actual intentions. In their meetings with the Joint Chiefs of Staff (JCS) at the Pentagon on January 15 and 16, Slessor and Slim inveighed against the "scanty and often conflicting information" that the administration had furnished to Britain and criticized MacArthur for being "too political and too independent of Washington's control."[85] Although Bradley reassured Slessor and Slim that the administration harbored no intention of withdrawing from Korea, he dismissed the British criticisms of MacArthur.[86] In a thinly veiled swipe at the British, Bradley referred to "a very strong feeling in U.S. public opinion . . . that America had been let in to the Korean campaign by the United Nations and that it was not receiving from the United Nations the support to which it was entitled."[87] In any event, on April 11, Truman sacked MacArthur after the general sent a letter to Congress railing against the administration's lack of resolve in confronting Communism in Asia.[88]

Whitehall's expectation that MacArthur's dismissal would produce a more risk-averse U.S. strategy in Korea was shattered immediately thereafter, when General Bradley revealed to Franks and Tedder that President Truman had approved a draft directive authorizing military retaliation in the event of an external attack against UN forces in Korea. Bradley ruled out the possibility of consulting with allied governments prior to such retaliation, on the grounds that this would allow the enemy to launch another major attack before a counterattack could be mustered.[89] On April 15, Assistant Secretary of State for Far Eastern Affairs Dean Rusk admonished Franks that if Britain continued to oppose UN retaliation against Chinese targets in Manchuria in the event of a large-scale Chinese air attack against coalition forces, the U.S. public would become so enraged that it would "break the alliance of our two countries."[90] The dubiousness of Rusk's threat was underscored by the results of a poll taken a few months later by the State Department's Office of Public Affairs that showed that 52 percent of the public supported continued economic aid to the European allies and 57 percent supported the deployment of U.S. troops to Europe.[91] On April 28, MacArthur's successor, General Matthew Ridgway, received formal authority from the JCS to attack China in the event of a major air attack against UN forces in Korea.[92] A few days later, after Acheson warned Attlee and Foreign Secretary Herbert Morrison, who had replaced Bevin the previous month, about "a strong wave of anti-British feeling in the United States," the cabinet reluctantly gave way on the retaliation issue.[93]

MORE FRICTIONS OVER BOMBING

Mere weeks after Winston Churchill replaced Attlee as prime minister in October 1951, the newly reinstalled Conservative prime minister was already complaining to Foreign Secretary Anthony Eden: "No one here knows what is going on in Korea or which side is benefiting in strength from the bombing and grimaces in Panmunjom [the site where armistice negotiations had resumed on October 25]. We must try to penetrate the American mind and purpose."[94] Churchill's concerns were validated by the U.S. Air Force's sudden initiation of heavy airstrikes against North Korean hydroelectric facilities in late June 1952. The targets included the power station at Suifeng/Supung (Suiho) on the Yalu River, the largest generating station in East Asia. The Suifeng/Supung station had previously been considered a politically sensitive target by the UNC because it supplied electricity to both China and the Soviet Union. British leaders had not been apprised in advance of the bombing raids, even though Defence Minister Lord Harold Alexander and Minister of State for Foreign Affairs Selwyn Lloyd had been in Korea a mere two weeks earlier for discussions with Commander Mark Clark (who had taken over command of the UNC from General Ridgway in May), and both were present in Washington at the time the bombings commenced. The White House poured salt on the wound by additionally ordering U.S. warplanes to bomb an oil refinery at Aoji, which was located only eight miles from Soviet territory and four miles from Manchuria, as well as a chemical plant located right on the Yalu River.[95]

THE MENON RESOLUTION

Churchill also battled the Truman administration over its proposed General Assembly resolution holding that POWs were exempt from forcible repatriation. Although the measure gleaned twenty co-sponsors, Britain and the Commonwealth states scrambled behind the scenes to scuttle it. Indian envoy Krishna Menon swept in to foil the United States by introducing a rival resolution. It called for the establishment of a commission of four neutral countries that would assume custody of all prisoners, classify them "as to nationality and domicile," and permit them to subsequently "return to their homelands" after an unspecified period of time.[96]

Acheson objected strongly to the Menon Resolution's deliberate vagueness. Although Menon agreed to insert a stipulation prohibiting the forced repatriation of POWs in the resolution's preamble, which satisfied the British and Commonwealth delegations, Acheson demanded that the reference be in the body of the draft and additionally specify that prisoners would be freed from the commission's control after a clearly specified and limited period of time. In a determined effort to restore support for the rival twenty-one-power resolution, Acheson exerted "enormous pressure"[97] on the British to abandon the Menon draft. He warned that the measure would pose "grave hazards" to the UNC as "[o]ur defensive position would be weakened after the armistice."[98] Acheson also warned that if London wavered on the resolution, it would be viewed by the incoming Eisenhower administration as unreliable and thereby sacrifice any leverage it might otherwise have had to divert the United States from a "get-tough policy" toward China.[99] The secretary of state cautioned Eden and Lloyd that failure to support the resolution would attenuate U.S. support for European defense, claiming that "divisions among us on this essential matter would bring grave disillusionment in the United States regarding collective security, which would not be confined to Korea but would extend to NATO and other arrangements . . . of the same sort."[100] In another encounter with Eden and Lloyd, Acheson even more bluntly threatened that if the British defected from the twenty-one-power resolution, "there would be no NATO, no Anglo-American friendship."[101]

Paradoxically, Acheson's apocalyptic threats were uttered against a backdrop of growing Republican support in Congress for Truman's internationalist grand strategy. Following Truman's dismissal of MacArthur and MacArthur's subsequent testimony before the Senate Foreign Relations Committee and House Armed Services Committee, several internationalist Republican senators, including Wayne Morse (OR), Leverett Saltonstall (MA), and Richard Russell (GA), rallied behind the president. Although the administration had made several mistakes in foreign policy, these Republicans conceded that its "fundamental strategy, both in Korea and Europe, remained sound."[102]

Although Acheson soon abandoned the twenty-one-power resolution, his pressure tactics yielded a major change to the Menon initiative. British (and Canadian) diplomats persuaded Menon to endorse the principal of non-forced repatriation of prisoners in the main body of the draft resolution. The amended resolution passed the General Assembly on December 3.[103]

A ROCKY ROAD TO THE ARMISTICE

The British expected that Dwight Eisenhower, the former Supreme Commander of the Allied Expeditionary Force in Europe during World War II and NATO's first Supreme Allied Commander in Europe (SACEUR), would be more yielding toward Britain than his predecessor. After Stalin's unexpected death in March 1953, Churchill asked Eisenhower to reconsider part of a major speech that the new president planned to deliver on April 16 that implored the new Soviet leadership to agree to the "immediate cessation of hostilities" and the "prompt initiation of political discussions leading to the holding of free elections in a united Korea."[104] He urged Eisenhower to wait until the intentions of the new Soviet regime became clearer before setting out such an extreme position on Korea. Eisenhower brushed aside Churchill's entreaty, and the Korea section remained unaltered in his otherwise conciliatory "Chance for Peace" address.[105]

Early the next month, the Foreign Office gingerly pressed the new administration to disown its predecessor's insistence on a joint U.S.-UK statement to be issued at the close of hostilities in Korea, which would threaten to impose "greater sanctions" against North Korea and China if they violated the terms of the armistice. In response, Undersecretary of State Walter Bedell Smith told the newly appointed British ambassador in Washington, Sir Roger Makins, that an "articulate minority on [Capitol H]ill" was suspicious of the United Kingdom and opposed to a compromise truce to end the war. If London wobbled on the "greater sanctions" statement, Smith predicted, "it would . . . certainly precipitate critical trouble in our [bilateral] relations." The Foreign Office immediately reversed itself, advising the cabinet that "we should not press our suggestion further but confirm our acceptance of the issue of the warning statement in the form originally agreed upon."[106]

Only two days after Smith's warning to Makins, Churchill endorsed the most recent Communist proposal in the armistice negotiations, which stipulated that a political conference to decide the fate of unrepatriated POWs should be convened after 120 days, not the 90 days mandated in the Menon Resolution.[107] This provoked Republican firebrands, whose voices were amplified in the wake of the election of Republican majorities in both houses of Congress in the November 1952 general election that also handed the presidency to a (nominal) Republican for the first time since 1928. Senator William Knowland of California, chair of the Republican Policy Committee, lamented that "our chief ally" was "urging a Far Eastern Munich," while infamous Wisconsin senator Joseph McCarthy exhorted that the United States should serve notice to the rest of the world "that we shall never supinely kneel and beg for allies."[108] Senator Everett Dirkson of Illinois piled on with the suggestion that Congress retaliate by slashing foreign aid. These incendiary remarks were countered, however, by the cautious counsel of more sober-minded voices in the party, particularly Senator Alexander Wiley (WI), the chair of the Foreign Relations Committee, and did not culminate in the introduction of any actual legislation.[109]

Eisenhower adopted a heavy-handed approach to breaking the impasse in Korea. On the one hand, as a sop to Britain and other weary allies, he made some concessions at Panmunjom. The most controversial of these was to accept a majority-vote decision rule by the five-state repatriation commission charged with deciding the fate of individual prisoners, as opposed to the previously advocated 4–1 rule. This raised the probability that unrepatriated prisoners would be returned involuntarily to their communist states of origin.[110] On the other hand, the president insisted that the Communists had one week to take or leave the final terms. If they rejected this final offer, the UNC would terminate the truce talks, release all unrepatriated POWs, and expand naval and air operations against North Korea. In privately conveying this ultimatum to the communist powers, the White House defied its allies, who were willing to make further concessions to reach an agreement. Eisenhower told Churchill that Britain's refusal to toe the U.S. line on the armistice ultimatum "would have the most adverse effects on the American public and Congressional opinion at this critical time."[111] In any event, the Communists' acceptance of the final UNC offer on June 4 forestalled additional U.S.-UK acrimony on the matter.

COLD WAR–RELATED DISPUTES

THE JAPAN PEACE TREATY

The outbreak of war in Korea lent considerable urgency to the task of drafting and ratifying a peace treaty between the allied victors of World War II and the defeated Axis power of Japan, which had been occupied by the United States since Tokyo's September 1945 surrender. In April 1950, Truman delegated the task of spearheading the peace negotiations to the hardline Republican lawyer and politician John Foster Dulles, whom the president appointed special consultant to the secretary of state. Following North Korea's invasion of South Korea and particularly in the wake of China's massive intervention in late 1950, Dulles became increasingly determined to secure a rapid and amicable peace settlement with Japan in order to ensconce it in the Western camp in the emerging Cold War.[112]

The first serious disagreement between the allies regarding the peace treaty centered on the preliminary task of easing Australia and New Zealand's fears of Japanese revanchism.[113] Dulles recognized that Japanese rearmament could not occur in the absence of firm security guarantees for these nations, which had narrowly avoided Japanese invasion during World War II. He sought to bar a militarily weakened Britain from participating in any such arrangement, however, even though the "Old Commonwealth" states of the South Pacific traditionally fell under its sphere of influence. In January 1951, the State Department introduced a blueprint for a Pacific Ocean pact that would extend a formal U.S. security guarantee to Australia and New Zealand, as well as Japan, the Philippines, and Indonesia.[114] Dulles remarked to British ambassador Oliver Franks that the United Kingdom would be a "valued consultant" to the alliance but would not be offered formal membership. Attlee's cabinet viewed Dulles's proposal as a slap in the face. It dismissed the plan as "unsound, both politically and militarily," and singled out its exclusion of mainland Southeast Asia, which included the restive British colony of Malaya, as "a source of special embarrassment."[115]

Although the administration refused to consider extending the State Department's island chain plan, which would have necessitated Britain's inclusion, it agreed to modify it in order to address British sensitivities. The amended plan, which consisted of a formal U.S. security guarantee only to Australia and New Zealand, nevertheless engendered much consternation in the cabinet, which reluctantly bowed to Attlee's insistence that continued British resistance to the arrangement "was not practicable."[116] The dispute was resolved in September 1951, when the governments of the United States, Australia, and New Zealand signed the ANZUS alliance treaty. Although Churchill mounted a vigorous campaign to secure the United Kingdom's accession to ANZUS after he returned to the premiership in late 1951, neither the outgoing Truman administration nor the incoming Eisenhower administration budged on the matter.[117]

While the two allies tangled over the contours of the South Pacific security guarantee in early 1951, the Attlee government lodged objections to two other positions struck by the Truman administration relating to the peace treaty: namely, that Japan should be permitted to renounce its sovereignty over Taiwan without prior specification of the island's legal status and that the People's Republic of China be excluded from the peace negotiations with Japan.[118] Dulles angrily rejoined that London had placed "two very large rocks on the road of progress," which might compel the administration to consider reaching a "unilateral arrangement with Japan."[119] In order to resolve the impasse, Dulles flew to London in early June. After considerable wrangling, he acquiesced to a formula in which neither the People's Republic nor President Chiang Kai-shek's Kuomintang (KMT) regime in Taiwan would participate in peace negotiations with Japan, and Tokyo would decide on its own after signing the peace treaty which of the two rival Chinas it would recognize formally. Dulles warned Foreign Secretary Morrison that this concession made ratification of the treaty by two-thirds of the U.S. Senate highly uncertain. Even if all of the Senate Democrats voted in the treaty's favor, it would still be necessary to gain the support of about half of the Republicans, a faction certain to lambaste him for excluding the KMT and yielding to British appeasement. Morrison successfully persuaded the cabinet, which still strongly favored the inclusion of the PRC in the peace negotiations, to accept the compromise. He argued that if the dispute over the peace negotiations with Japan was not settled, this would disrupt Anglo-U.S. relations on a host of even more important matters.[120]

On September 4, representatives of forty-nine countries assembled in San Francisco to sign the peace treaty formally ending the Pacific War. Dulles's strong concerns about the treaty's fate in the Senate—a September 12 letter from a bipartisan group of fifty-six senators warned that Japanese recognition of the PRC would be "adverse" to the interests of both the United States and Japan—prompted him to cable the Foreign Office demanding that the British sanctify the establishment of "reasonable relations" between Japan and Taiwan.[121] The new Conservative foreign secretary, Anthony Eden, exploded with rage when he read the cable and instructed the Foreign Office to reply that Japan should not be permitted to negotiate with Taiwan's Nationalist government until after the peace treaty's ratification.[122]

On December 18, Dulles presented for Japanese prime minister Shigeru Yoshida's consent a document stating that the Japanese government was prepared to sign a peace treaty with Taiwan's Nationalist government, led by President Chiang Kai-shek, and normalize diplomatic relations with Taipei.[123] Yoshida signed the letter on December 24 after Dulles simultaneously warned that failure to do so would endanger the peace treaty's passage by the Senate and promised that he would refrain from making it public until after a scheduled trip by Churchill and Eden to Washington the next month. On January 16, 1952, the day after the British delegation left Washington and the day that the Senate Foreign Relations Committee was scheduled to begin debating the peace treaty, Acheson and Dulles called on Yoshida to make the letter public. Yoshida's announcement stunned Eden and the Foreign Office issued a formal complaint to Acheson, who expressed regret over the incident and assured Eden that it had not been deliberately orchestrated. On March 20, the Senate ratified the treaty by a gaping 66–10 margin. A month later, the governments of Japan and Taiwan signed the bilateral peace treaty sought by the United States, which amounted to the formal recognition by Tokyo of the KMT as the sovereign government of China.[124]

NATO COMMAND-AND-CONTROL ARRANGEMENTS IN THE ATLANTIC AND MEDITERRANEAN

As Washington and London jointly prosecuted the limited war in Korea, they also hastily prepared plans alongside their NATO partners for waging unlimited war in Europe against the Soviet Red Army. These efforts laid bare additional differences between them regarding the structure of NATO's prospective command arrangements for the Atlantic Ocean and Mediterranean Sea.

Following the creation of NATO in 1949, U.S. military planning focused on the requisites for pursuing a strategy of forward defense in West Germany against invasion by the far larger Soviet-led Warsaw Pact forces. This strategy hinged on the United States' ability to safely and expeditiously transport a steady flow of troops and equipment across the Atlantic to the front at the Rhine River. American planners believed that in order to effectively protect trans-Atlantic supply lines from attack by Soviet submarines and orchestrate strike operations by carrier-based aircraft against Soviet naval forces, NATO had to establish a unified command structure for the North Atlantic theater of operations.[125]

Controversy erupted in February 1951 following a leak to the British media of U.S. plans for a unified Supreme Allied Command Atlantic (SACLANT), which would be headed by an American commander in chief.[126] This revelation touched off a firestorm of controversy within Britain, as SACLANT was a "highly emotive subject for a country that had a proud maritime heritage and depended on the seas for its lifeblood."[127] By the time that Attlee was replaced by Churchill, in October, the issue remained unresolved; it promised to become even more contentious owing to Churchill's emotional opposition to the American proposal.[128]

During a January 1952 summit meeting between Churchill and Truman in Washington, Churchill argued emphatically that unified command in the Atlantic was unnecessary and asked to be released from his predecessor's commitment to establishing it. On this front, he assured Truman that a joint U.S.-UK command would be just as effective in defending the ocean's sea lanes.[129] The premier added that the appointment of an American SACLANT would constitute "a deep injury to British feelings" and a "great blow [to the United Kingdom] when it was told not only that it would not have the command but that it would not even have an equal voice."[130] Administration officials, however, strongly favored the appointment of an American admiral as SACLANT, not only on the grounds that the United States possessed by far the largest and most powerful navy within NATO, but also because this would strongly signal Washington's commitment to the defense of its European alliance partners. At the conclusion of the summit, Secretary of Defense Robert Lovett definitively informed Churchill that he could not be freed from Attlee's commitments and that, in any event, SACLANT had been formally approved by the alliance, which meant it could not be amended or scuttled on a strictly bilateral basis.[131]

During this period, the two allies also debated NATO's prospective command structure in the Mediterranean. North Korea's aggression against South Korea stoked U.S. fears of a follow-on Soviet offensive in Europe, which focused American planners' attention on the responsibility of the

Navy's Sixth Fleet for supporting NATO's southern flank in Europe. While the White House fixated on the Cold War imperative of defending against a potential Soviet attack in Europe, Whitehall was concerned primarily with consolidating Britain's fragile sphere of influence in the Middle East.[132] In early 1951, the UK government proposed the establishment of a unified Mediterranean command under a British Supreme Commander, who would have control over all NATO naval forces operating in the Mediterranean and would hold equal status to the SACEUR and SACLANT. This proposal envisioned that the U.S. Sixth Fleet, which had grown to become the "most powerful force under [SACEUR] General Eisenhower's command,"[133] would be reallocated to the prospective British Supreme Commander, Mediterranean. Admiral Robert Carney, who was serving as both Commander in Chief, United States Naval Forces East Atlantic and Mediterranean (CINCNELM) and Commander in Chief, NATO Southern Flank (CINCSOUTH), objected: creating a separate command for NATO's Mediterranean forces was inadvisable due to the alliance's limited means and the fact that they comprised mainly U.S. naval, maritime aviation, and marine forces.[134]

As the impasse continued into 1952, London adopted a new position. British negotiators began to posit that that since there were two conceivable combat theaters in the Mediterranean, namely Southern Europe and the Middle East, naval forces at war there would have to support operations conducted by both commands. It would therefore be unwise for the naval commander in the Mediterranean to be subordinate to CINCSOUTH, which had no responsibility for combat operations in the Middle East. Instead, coordination among the different commands should be delegated to the NATO Standing Group, which would manage overall allied strategy and operations. The British also maintained that the naval Commander in Chief, Mediterranean (CINCMED) should be a British officer and vested with the authority to coordinate the activities of the Sixth Fleet with other naval and air operations in the Mediterranean. By contrast, U.S. officials continued to push for the formal subordination of a prospective Mediterranean naval commander to CINCSOUTH. They reminded London that President Truman had explicitly dispatched the Sixth Fleet to the Mediterranean in support of NATO's right flank in

Southern Europe, that General Eisenhower was insisting that the fleet remain under his direct command, and that NATO members France and Italy—as well as prospective members Greece and Turkey—were all committing their naval forces to the Mediterranean only on condition that they fall under the authority of the American CINCSOUTH.[135]

Matters came to a head at a November 1952 meeting in Washington of senior U.S., UK, and French military officials under the auspices of the NATO Standing Group, during which the alliance agreed to establish a Mediterranean command under the command of a Royal Navy officer who would be directly subordinate and responsible to the SACEUR. In return, the British delegation acquiesced to the U.S. demand that the heavy aircraft carriers and amphibious forces of the Sixth Fleet (i.e., its "Strike Force") be placed under the command of CINCSOUTH and utilized exclusively in support of land warfare in Southern Europe, unless otherwise directed by SACEUR. All other elements of the fleet would be allocated to Commander in Chief Mediterranean. On March 15, 1953, NATO's new Mediterranean Command was officially inaugurated and British Admiral Lord Louis Mountbatten was appointed the alliance's first Commander in Chief, Allied Forces Mediterranean.[136] According to historian Dionysios Chourchoulis, the appointment of a British officer to this post amounted to a "small consolation" for Britain, which had above all sought to use the Mediterranean Command issue as a "strategic lever in its efforts to retain its preponderance in the Middle East."[137]

THE IRAN CRISIS

The most contentious dispute between the two allies during the Korean War period involved a political crisis transpiring thousands of miles from the blood-soaked battlefields in Northeast Asia, in the oilfields of the Persian Gulf. It was rooted in the passage in 1947 of a bill in the Majlis, the lower house of the Iranian parliament, that called on Iran's government to negotiate a more favorable concession with the Anglo-Iranian Oil Company, in which the British government owned a 51-percent share.[138] This legislation resulted in the negotiation of a Supplemental Oil Agreement (SOA) between Tehran and the AIOC two years later. Many Iranians, including nationalist firebrand Mohammed Mossadegh's broad-based National Front organization, viewed the SOA as "a fraud perpetrated by traitors who wished to perpetuate British domination of the country."[139] Under Mossadegh's leadership, the nationalist faction in the Majlis obstructed floor debate on the agreement. The bill languished in legislative purgatory until June 1950, when Premier Ali Mansur announced the formation of a special legislative commission to preliminarily review the legislation.[140] Unfortunately for the AIOC, after the Majlis Oil Commission (MOC) convened, the government of Saudi Arabia concluded a concession deal with the U.S.-based Arabian-American Oil Company (ARAMCO) whose centerpiece was a fifty-fifty profit-sharing agreement. By contrast, the SOA merely increased Iran's share of the AIOC's oil export royalties to a maximum of 30 percent.[141] On November 25, the commission voted unanimously to reject the SOA and Mansur's successor, General Ali Razmara, quickly scuttled it.[142]

During the first half of 1951, the oil crisis reached a boiling point. On March 7, Razmara was assassinated by religious hardliners associated with the National Front, which spurred the commission to immediately begin drafting an oil nationalization plan. A week later, the Majlis unanimously endorsed the MOC's resolution for nationalization and granted it two months to devise a concrete implementation plan. As popular support swelled, on April 27 the MOC passed a resolution nationalizing the oil industry and creating an Iranian board to run the AIOC's operations. This development prompted the resignation of Razmara's successor, Hossein Ala. The Majlis installed Mossadegh in his place and voted unanimously to pass the resolution. After the bill received the unanimous approval of the Iranian Senate, on May 1 Iran's monarch, Shah Mohammad Reza Pahlavi, signed it into law.[143]

For London, the stakes at issue in Iran were inestimable. Economically, the AIOC's monopoly control over Iran's vast oil reserves and the continued operation of its refinery complex at Abadan, the largest in the world, constituted Britain's "most important single overseas investment."[144] During a period of financial straits for the United Kingdom, the AIOC was therefore an invaluable source of tax revenue for the British government, having filled its coffers with £250 million between 1945 and 1950. Britain's export of AIOC oil also alleviated the country's growing dollar shortage by providing London with the equivalent of £100 million per year in foreign exchange. Additionally, the AIOC's Iran operations directly provided the British economy with twenty-two million tons of oil products and seven million tons of crude oil per year, with the Royal Navy receiving 85 percent of its oil from AIOC at undisclosed, specially discounted prices.[145] The broader geopolitical implications of Iran's seizure of Abadan were, if anything, just as threatening. By the late 1940s, the only region in which Britain continued to exercise predominant influence was the Middle East, where the United Kingdom functioned "as an independent power between the two postwar giants [i.e., the United States and Soviet Union], to counter communism and to emphasize to the Americans the mutual importance of the Special Relationship."[146] If London were to lose its most important economic asset in the Middle East, its hegemonic regional position would collapse.[147]

Across the Atlantic, the Truman administration exhibited mounting anxiety about a possible Soviet bid to dominate Iran, or at least large segments of it, in order to gain direct access to the Persian Gulf. A February 1950 State Department paper warned that if the Kremlin achieved this aim, it would "acquire advance bases for subversive activities or actual attack against the vast contiguous area; obtain a base hundreds of miles nearer potential U.S.-UK lines of defense in the Middle East than any held at present; control part and threaten all of the Middle Eastern oil reservoir; control continental air routes across Iran and threaten those traversing adjacent areas; be in a position to menace shipping in the Persian Gulf; and undermine the will of all Middle Eastern countries to resist Soviet aggression."[148] The outbreak of the Korean War further elevated the importance of keeping Iran and its oil resources out of Soviet hands, as it dramatically increased demand for aviation gasoline and other fuels required to sustain the UN war effort against the North Korean and Chinese armies.[149] Reflecting the administration's growing worries about Iran's vulnerability to Soviet military aggression or a Soviet-fomented Communist revolution, in August Acheson blasted the AIOC for narrow-mindedly treating the SOA "as [a] commercial proposition without economic, political, and strategic considerations important to [the] outside world."[150]

The Iranian parliament's passage of the nationalization bill brought simmering tensions between the United States and Britain to a boil. Britain immediately retaliated by filing a petition with the International Court of Justice (ICJ), imposing trade sanctions against Iran, and initiating a phased evacuation of British personnel from Abadan.[151] Acheson fulminated that these moves reflected the "persistent and unusual stupidity of the [AIOC] and the British Government" and risked the "loss of Iran to [the] free world."[152] On September 5, Mossadegh threatened to cancel the residence permits of the remaining British technicians at Abadan unless London returned to the negotiating table with a set of new proposals. Attlee not only spurned this ultimatum but announced new economic sanctions against Iran, against which Mossadegh retaliated by announcing that British technicians at Abadan had one week to flee the country.[153] By this juncture, in the estimation of historian Steve Marsh, "Attlee's government knew that [military] inaction would be interpreted as weakness and that the implications for British prestige would be particularly grave."[154] During the first week of September, however, at the Japan Peace Treaty conference in San Francisco, Secretary of State Acheson explained to British leaders that the Truman administration could not provide a "blanket endorsement" of every action that the British government might take regarding Iran and sternly cautioned them not to "do anything which would make it difficult for Iran to resume negotiations."[155] On September 27, as more than a dozen Royal Navy warships conducted drills in the Persian Gulf, Attlee backed away from the precipice of war. In a rebuke to the hawks in his cabinet, the prime minister maintained that "in light of the United States attitude . . . force could not be used to hold the refinery and maintain the British employees of the [AIOC]. We could not afford to break with the United States on an issue of this kind."[156]

The next summer, a series of shocking developments in Iranian domestic politics reopened the rift between Washington and London. On July 17, after a dispute with the shah, Mossadegh abruptly resigned the premiership, only to be reappointed mere days later following the outbreak of mass protests in Tehran.[157] On July 31, Acheson dispatched an urgent telegram to London stating that the prevention of Iran's loss to the West necessitated

Britain's immediate acceptance of several conditions: the purchase by the AIOC of Iranian oil being held in storage at Abadan at commercial rates "less an appropriate discount," the creation of an arbitration panel to decide the matter of compensation for the AIOC's losses from Iran's oil nationalization, the initiation of bilateral UK-Iran negotiations to devise a permanent arrangement for the export of Iranian oil, and the U.S. provision to Iran of $10 million in emergency economic aid.[158] Although the Churchill cabinet expressed ferocious opposition to Acheson's proposal, Anthony Eden protested that its rejection would lead to unilateral American action in Iran, which in turn would devastate both the Anglo-U.S. special relationship and Britain's influence in the Middle East.[159]

In light of Eden's grave concerns about the consequences of a diplomatic breach with Washington, the cabinet acquiesced to Acheson's initiative, provided that certain conditions were met. Specifically, it held that U.S. aid to Iran be made contingent on Iran's agreement to convene negotiations on a permanent oil sales agreement, that oil purchases from Iran be delayed until Tehran arranged satisfactory terms of reference on compensating the AIOC for the loss of its concession and facilities, and that the ban on imports of Iranian oil be maintained until the conclusion of a final settlement with the British.[160] On August 12, Acheson telegraphed Eden that these "stringent" British conditions would be unacceptable to Mossadegh and in a message to Churchill the next week, Truman warned that if Iran went "down the communist drain," it would "place a strain on [the] gen[eral] Anglo-Amer[ican] relationships not pleasant to contemplate."[161]

Churchill responded subtly to Truman's demand by suggesting that the two leaders rework the original U.S. proposals and offer them jointly to Mossadegh. Truman agreed, so long as it did not commit his administration to follow a joint policy with Britain in the future. The joint cable presented to Iran on August 30 stipulated that if both the ICJ settled compensation claims for Britain and Iran concluded a deal with the AIOC to distribute and market Iranian oil, Iran would be permitted to manage and control its oil industry, Britain would loosen financial and trade sanctions against it, Washington would transfer the $10 million aid package, and the AIOC would sell the oil in storage at Abadan. Two weeks later, Mossadegh angrily rejected the joint proposal in a speech to the Majlis and severed Iran's diplomatic relationship with the UK.[162] In order to forestall Iran's political collapse, Truman agreed to provide Tehran with a $100 million advance against future oil sales and violated the British embargo by enlisting U.S. oil companies to purchase and market Iranian oil.[163] At a UN meeting in New York on November 20, Acheson told Eden that if Britain did not produce a "new and more vigorous effort"[164] to address the crisis, the U.S. State Department would act unilaterally to do so. Churchill temporized, anticipating that the incoming Eisenhower administration would adopt a less hostile position toward London.[165]

As it happened, however, the new administration unexpectedly distanced itself from the most recent proposal floated by Truman and Churchill, which had tilted the negotiating terms somewhat in London's favor, and demanded greater flexibility from London.[166] In response, Churchill retreated even further, to a position that Acting Secretary of State H. Freeman Matthews judged to be "relatively close to rock bottom."[167] Churchill conceded that Iranian compensation to Britain could not amount to more than 25 percent of Iran's annual oil earnings for a maximum period of twenty years, and that the remainder could be payable in the export of free oil to Britain. Eisenhower accepted Churchill's compromise, and it was passed along to Mossadegh on February 20.[168]

Mossadegh rejected the proposal a month later, leading Undersecretary of State Walter Bedell Smith to inform the British that the Eisenhower administration could no longer support of the existing Iranian government. On June 23, Churchill approved a CIA covert action plan to depose Mossadegh, dubbed Operation Ajax, which would be successfully orchestrated two months later by the head of the agency's operations in the Middle East, Kermit Roosevelt.[169] After Mossadegh's ouster, the Eisenhower administration offered the new Iranian government led by the moderate ex-general Fazlollah Zahedi $234 million in economic assistance and spearheaded negotiations alongside Britain and Iran to finally resolve the oil crisis. The administration's proposal to create a multinational consortium of oil companies to manage Iran's oil industry—of which the AIOC would possess the largest share—received the support of both the British and Iranian governments, was ratified by the Iranian parliament, and was signed by the shah on October 29, 1954.[170]

BRITISH REARMAMENT

The final spat between the allies dealt with British defense spending. Soon after the outbreak of the Korean War, the Truman administration declared to America's NATO allies that they would not qualify for U.S. military assistance unless they submitted proposals for dramatic expansions of their defense production.[171] In August 1950, Chancellor of the Exchequer Stafford Cripps submitted a proposal to the Attlee cabinet for £3.4 billion in defense spending over a three-year period, a substantial £1.1 billion increase over Britain's pre–Korean War spending, which already amounted to a staggering 8 percent of its GNP. His Majesty's Government informed Washington, however, that it could only afford to bear £2.85 billion of this sum without placing the country's still-fragile economic health at grave risk; this meant that the United States would have to provide the remaining £550 million (approximately $1.54 billion) in military aid to the United Kingdom. Further, it requested that at least £350 million (approximately $980 million) of the aid package should take the form of "free dollars" that could be used to add to Britain's currency reserves for the purpose of easing its balance-of-payments deficit.[172] Acheson unsympathetically rejoined that HMG would have to "reconsider its entire proposal," as under existing law, free dollars could not be granted on an unconditional basis and the prospect of securing an amendment from the current U.S. Congress permitting such a transfer was highly unlikely.[173]

Spurred into rapid action by the events in Korea, in September 1950 the U.S. Congress appropriated $4.5 billion in military aid under the aegis of the Mutual Defense Assistance Program. Although Attlee's government had increased its initial rearmament proposal by £200 million to a total of £3.6 billion, the administration allocated to Britain a meagre $112 million (approximately £40 billion) in assistance.[174] Then, adding insult to injury, it advised the British to consider an even more expansive rearmament plan. During Attlee's December 1950 summit trip to Washington, Acheson told him that unless Truman and Secretary of Defense George C. Marshall were "convinced that the British are doing all possible in the direction of their own defense effort, the British have not accomplished much here." If the

British could convince Truman and Marshall that they were doing all they could to bolster their defenses, it would "help a great deal in meeting [the] feeling in this country to the contrary."[175] In a private conversation with Attlee the next day, Special Assistant to the President W. Averell Harriman also cautioned that if London did not move ahead with "a substantially increased" rearmament program—he floated the astronomical figure of £6 billion as a benchmark—"the American people [might] . . . be inclined to withdraw [from Europe]."[176]

At a December 18 cabinet meeting, Attlee distributed a telegram from Ambassador Franks claiming that fulfillment of U.S. rearmament demands would "help the [Truman a]dministration's case domestically." He also professed that U.S. leaders' acceptance of the Anglo-U.S. relationship as "the mainspring of Atlantic defense" hinged on the degree to which Britain differentiated itself from the rest of the European pack in rearming to meet the growing Soviet threat.[177] Despite the strong reservations of several ministers, a majority of the cabinet voted to increase Britain's three-year defense program from £3.6 billion to £4.7 billion (a stunning 15 percent of British GNP).[178] The difficulty of this decision was underscored by the subsequent resignation of three Labour ministers in protest.[179]

The administration evinced little sympathy for Attlee's political and economic plight. In March 1951, the White House shocked London by announcing that it would abstain from seeking congressional authorization for any economic assistance to Britain under its proposed Mutual Security Program, created to fuse the U.S. economic and military assistance programs. This provoked panicked protests from British leaders, who stressed to their American counterparts that the most onerous part of the UK's rearmament program was the approximately £2 billion allocated to defense production. In order to meet this benchmark without crippling the country's terms of trade and thereby precipitating an economic collapse, extensive U.S. economic support was absolutely necessary. The White House reassured London that emergency subvention would be available if it proved necessary, but spurned a British request to enshrine that pledge in writing.[180] In a follow-on communiqué, the State Department added to British woes by stipulating that U.S. economic assistance could be used by recipient countries only for the purpose of "transferring real resources currently required by the countries . . . for the support of their defense efforts,"[181] and therefore not to increase their gold and dollar reserves. In a crushing conclusion, the communiqué conveyed the administration's view that Britain was fully capable of fulfilling its rearmament commitments in the absence of economic subvention.[182]

Attlee's government tried to make the best of a difficult situation by attempting to maximize its allocation of military aid in the form of funds to both facilitate defense production and purchase finished military hardware from the United States. With regard to the former, HMG communicated to Washington that the fulfillment of the indigenous defense production targets necessitated $332 million in U.S. export credits. It anticipated a shortfall of between £1.4 billion and £1.8 billion (out of £4.7 billion) in its ability to purchase finished items necessary to equip its armed forces.[183]

After Churchill returned to the premiership, he informed Truman during his January 1952 visit to Washington that the anticipated price tag for the UK rearmament program had swelled from £4.7 billion to £5.2 billion due to rising import costs. He reminded the president that when the program was initially conceived at a projected cost of £3.6 billion, Attlee's government had expected £550 million (approximately $1.54 billion) in U.S. aid, which had still not been committed by the administration.[184] Meanwhile, Churchill's close advisor, Paymaster-General Lord Cherwell, told Treasury Department officials that the combination of rising costs and intensifying export competition from a reviving West Germany had triggered a severe balance-of-payments crisis in the United Kingdom. As a result, Britain's dollar reserves had plummeted by nearly half from the previous year.[185]

When the dust settled, Britain's share of the $5.8 billion in aid budgeted under the aegis of the Mutual Security Appropriation Act passed by Congress in late 1951 ended up being just $650 million. Of this sum, $300 million took the form of interim aid for the purchase of specific goods from the United States in which a direct connection to defense could be demonstrated; the remaining $350 million was allocated exclusively to the purchase of end-use defense items only. This meant that HMG would receive no assistance for defense production.[186] In July 1952, Truman signed a follow-on appropriation for the MSA, which provided Britain with $350 million in military end-item credits and $416 million in credits that could be used to purchase goods for arms production. The 1953 Mutual Security Act established termination dates for economic and military assistance to Western Europe of June 30, 1956 and June 30, 1957, respectively, and drastically cut aid to the United Kingdom. It provided Britain with a mere $55 million (approximately £19.6 million) in credits to purchase agricultural commodities, $65 million (£23.2 million) in credits for nonagricultural commodities, and $85 million (£30.3 million) to support Britain's military aircraft production program. The reductions, which would become increasingly steep until the termination of the MSA, were a function of the belief in both the White House and Congress that America's NATO allies "had added steadily to their gold and dollar reserves since 1952 and were no longer in urgent need of even indirect military aid."[187]

According to historian Peter Boyle, over the course of the Korean War, Britain's rearmament program "in essence showed an acceptance of American pressure and American assumptions."[188] The UK's defense budget rose dramatically from £820 million in 1950 to £1.54 billion in 1953.[189] This exacted a substantial long-term toll on the British economy. Boyle claims that the program was a "factor of major importance in Britain's economic decline from a position of predominance among European nations in the late 1940s to a place in the lower ranks of the European economic league table after 1960."[190]

CONCLUSION

Whereas the previous three chapters have painted a distressing picture of the United States as a helpless giant, pathetically beseeching its diminutive allies of convenience to change their ways while nervously ignoring and downplaying their most audacious transgressions, this chapter paints a starkly different picture. In dealing with its most intimate, friendly, and well-regarded ally during the three years of the Korean War, the United States emerges contrarily as a dismissive, browbeating bully that repeatedly drove the hardest of bargains with its weaker and more vulnerable partner. Freed of the need to constantly defend and justify the alliance with Britain to domestic audiences, U.S. officials were paradoxically able to repeatedly threaten an end to the special relationship if British leaders refused to toe the American line on key issues relating to both the Korean War and the Cold War more generally. As one historian of the bilateral relationship during the Korean War's first two years remarks, "No one seemed to question whether an administration which went to war ostensibly to protect a corrupt regime in Seoul would easily abandon more compatible democratic governments in London or Paris. Though the Americans might regularly threaten a return to isolationism, they never came within an inch of doing so."[191]

American policymakers' willingness to apply the screws to their closest international ally in order to get their way would be demonstrated even more flagrantly three years later during the fateful Suez Crisis. In response to Egyptian strongman Gamal Abdel Nasser's decision to nationalize the Suez Canal in July 1956, British Prime Minister Anthony Eden conspired with the French and Israeli governments to launch a military invasion of Egypt to depose Nasser and restore the Canal to the Suez Canal Company, in which Britain held a controlling interest. The intervention, which was launched on November 1 against the backdrop of the Soviet invasion of Hungary, shocked and infuriated President Eisenhower. In response, the administration refused to assure Whitehall that the United States would defend Britain and France if the Soviets made good on their threat to "crush the aggressors."[192] It additionally deployed combat aircraft and submarines to harass the invasion fleet and initiated a massive selloff of British pounds at a discount while blocking a British request for a loan from the International Monetary Fund. In response to this toxic stew of U.S. military, diplomatic, and financial coercion, as well as Washington's promise of a $1 billion loan if London agreed to an immediate cease-fire, a humiliated Eden capitulated less than a week after launching the war.[193] Although Suez unquestionably marked the nadir of the bilateral relationship, the subsequent improvement in relations between the archetypal special relationship allies did not markedly reduce British submissiveness to the much stronger United States. Although Prime Minister Tony Blair would several decades later be castigated as President George W. Bush's "poodle" for unreservedly embracing Bush's reckless and catastrophic invasion of Iraq in 2003, his behavior proved no more submissive than that of his esteemed predecessors Attlee, Churchill, and Eden several decades earlier.[194]

CONCLUSION

After [Libyan President Mu'ammar Ghaddafi] abandoned his pur-
suit of weapons of mass destruction in 2003, many American officials
praised his cooperation. Visiting with a congressional delegation in
2009, Senator Joseph I. Lieberman, Independent of Connecticut told
the leader . . . that Libya was "an important ally in the war on
terrorism, noting that common enemies sometimes make better
friends."

—SCOTT SHANE, "WIKILEAKS CABLES DETAIL QADDAFI FAMILY'S EXPLOITS,"
NEW YORK TIMES, FEBRUARY 22, 2011

I N ARGUING THAT the United States has consistently failed to impose its will on much weaker allies of convenience, this book contributes to a literature in International Relations that focuses on the paradoxical influence exercised by small powers over great ones.[1] One particular subset of this literature examines what Robert Keohane referred to in a seminal 1971 article as "the big influence of small allies."[2] Keohane argued that a small ally could wrench concessions from the United States if it anticipated continued support given Washington's larger grand strategic ambitions, possessed a stronger vested interest in the outcome of the dispute(s) in question, cultivated agencies in the U.S. executive bureaucracy eager to perpetuate the alliance, and exploited influential domestic interest groups in the United States to mobilize public opinion on its behalf. In a more recent work, Stephen Walt has claimed that the last of these tactics, which he dubs domestic political "penetration," is most likely to succeed if the targeted ally (i.e., the United States) is secure and possesses a polity that is relatively open and accessible to foreign actors, if the two states enjoy a cultural affinity, and if the penetrating state (i.e., the small ally) can rely on a sympathetic group of supporters in the target state.[3]

The foregoing study supplements these analyses with the insight that even small allies that are widely disliked and distrusted within the United States can nevertheless exercise formidable bargaining power over Washington. Neoclassical realist theory stipulates that domestic political opposition to, rather than domestic support for, alliances of convenience struck with unfriendly autocratic allies compels U.S. officials to refrain from bargaining aggressively with them. The pressing need to mobilize shaky domestic support for alliances of convenience compels the foreign policy executive (FPE) to exaggerate those allies' compliance with U.S. preferences on important national security-related disputes. Although at times the activities of pro-alliance interest groups can reinforce this temptation, it is the broader context of domestic hostility that engenders it in the first place and enhances the FPE's reliance on those groups.

Whereas Walt claims that small allies that are culturally similar to the United States will enjoy a bargaining advantage, neoclassical realist theory argues contrarily that those allies most proximate to the United States in culture, ideology, and interests will actually be more likely to be bullied by Washington.[4] Since such allies will not ruffle feathers domestically, U.S. leaders will feel no compulsion to purvey an overly benign image of them to domestic audiences. They will therefore be inclined to fully exploit the gross asymmetries of dependence and commitment favoring the United States to wrest major concessions from those allies in emergent disputes.

Three implications for the practice of U.S. foreign policy follow from these findings.

POLICY IMPLICATION 1: ALLIANCES OF CONVENIENCE SHOULD ALWAYS BE A LAST RESORT

The most troubling implication is that an inverse relationship paradoxically holds between U.S. bargaining leverage and the relative troublesomeness of its small allies. Senior decision makers will be least able to modify the behavior of allies whose values and interests are most at odds with those of the United States, namely, allies of convenience. By contrast, they will have the greatest leverage over the behavior of allies whose values and interests already largely align with their own, namely special relationship allies. Thus, the United States will possess the least amount of bargaining leverage vis-à-vis those allies and in those circumstances in which it most needs it, and vice-versa.[5] Thus, to the extent that U.S. policymakers confront burgeoning adversaries via the establishment of ad hoc alliances of convenience, they will have to trade off their enhanced capacity to balance rising threats against their inability to control allies' behavior even as the United States markedly adds to their material power. In certain instances, the likely benefits associated with the former will overshadow the likely costs associated with the latter, but in others, this might not be the case. Prospective allies of convenience that are already great powers, such as the Soviet Union during World War II, or that are known proliferators of nuclear weapons, such as Pakistan and Iraq during the 1980s, pose the greatest potential long-term threats to U.S. interests.[6] Therefore, although alliances of convenience should always serve as a last-resort option for U.S. leaders, some of those partnerships will be even more inauspicious than others and should therefore be entered into with the utmost caution or not at all.

POLICY IMPLICATION 2: ALLYING BELOW THE DOMESTIC POLITICAL RADAR IS PREFERABLE

Even if there are no good alternatives to aligning with an adversary, officials can reduce the anticipated risks and costs by keeping the relationship covert and narrowly circumscribed. To the degree that strategic cooperation with an enemy state takes place below the radar of U.S. domestic politics, the FPE will be able to circumvent the domestic pressures that would otherwise tempt it into adopting an overly conciliatory bargaining stance vis-à-vis that state. At least two discrete strategies can accomplish this, which I refer to as clandestine security cooperation and parallel alignment.

CLANDESTINE SECURITY COOPERATION

In clandestine security cooperation, all bilateral contacts with an ally of convenience are secretly established and managed by a small number of senior officials. On the one hand, such partnerships are advantageous because Congress, the general public, and even much of the executive bureaucracy are unaware that they exist and therefore cannot attempt to constrain or obstruct them. The FPE will consequently experience little, if any, pressure to adopt a passive bargaining strategy toward the ally that is aimed at stanching domestic opposition. On the other hand, this type of partnership necessitates that the FPE refrain from attempting to extract material resources on behalf of the allied state from Congress and much of the executive bureaucracy.

Unless it resorts to illegal action, such as the Reagan administration's clandestine sale of arms to Iran in the mid-1980s, the FPE has little in the way of material resources that it can independently transfer to an ally. In the first place, Congress must authorize and appropriate funds to transfer foreign economic and military assistance.[7] Economic assistance funds are in turn dispensed by multiple cabinet departments, including State, Defense, Treasury, Agriculture, and Health and Human Services, as well as a number of independent government agencies, such as the United States Agency for International Development, the Export-Import Bank of the United States, and the Overseas Private Investment Corporation. The State Department is the lead agency providing policy guidance on security-related assistance (Foreign Military Financing, or FMF), which is implemented by the Defense Department.[8] Under the terms of the Arms Export Control Act of 1976, the administration is obliged to formally notify Congress in advance of major arms sales to all states excepting its NATO partners, Israel, Australia, Japan, South Korea, and New Zealand. Major commercial arms sales similarly require that the administration first secure an export license from the State Department's Bureau of Political-Military Affairs and then formally notify Congress thirty days before it issues the license for the sale. Congress may then block or modify the sale by passing a law or joint resolution forbidding the transaction.[9] Only in the material domain of intelligence can the FPE exercise considerable autonomy to clandestinely deliver assistance to an ally of convenience.[10]

In the absence of substantial material cooperation, clandestine alliances will be quite tenuous, consisting largely of secret diplomacy, intelligence sharing, and covert action operations. If the ally is highly dependent on U.S. material support, however, American officials can enjoin the ally to make significant concessions on disputed issues between the two countries as a prelude to their decision to go public with a full-fledged alliance policy. It will be easier for the FPE to mobilize extensive domestic support for the alliance if it can first make a credible case that the ally of convenience has already taken dramatic steps to reform its errant behavior and thereby deserves large-scale U.S. material support in the conflict against the shared enemy. The more aggressively U.S. negotiators bargain with the ally during the initial secret phase of the alliance, the more substantial the concessions delivered by the ally and the lower in turn the domestic opposition to the alliance after the FPE goes public with the relationship and the greater the FPE's subsequent bargaining leverage. This type of strategy was pursued with uncharacteristic adroitness by the George W. Bush administration after the 9/11 attacks, when it joined surreptitiously with Mu'ammar Gaddhafi's Libya in the fight against Al Qaeda. This exception proves the neoclassical realist rule of anemic U.S. bargaining with allies of convenience.[11]

Following the 1969 coup that marked his rise to power in Libya, Colonel Mu'ammar Gaddhafi emerged as a prominent enemy of the United States owing to his active sponsorship of terrorism, vociferous opposition to Israel, military aggression against neighboring Chad, and establishment of close relations with the Soviet Union.[12] In early 1986, his orchestration of the bombing of a Berlin nightclub frequented by U.S. military personnel prompted the Reagan administration to launch air strikes against Libyan military and government targets, including Gaddhafi's command center. Libyan terrorists retaliated in late 1988 by bombing a U.S. civilian airliner, Pan Am Flight 103, as it was passing over Lockerbie, Scotland, killing 270 passengers (189 of whom were American citizens).[13] Gaddhafi's refusal to extradite two Libyan intelligence operatives indicted by U.S.

and British courts in connection with the bombing led the UN Security Council to impose a range of stringent economic sanctions against Libya.[14] In addition, due in part to the political pressure exerted by the families of the Pan Am 103 victims, in 1996 Congress passed two major sanctions bills against Libya, the Iran-Libya Sanctions Act and the Antiterrorism and Effective Death Penalty Act.[15]

In part due to the crushing impact of these sanctions, during the 1990s the Libyan economy plunged into crisis, exacerbating the danger posed by homegrown Islamist radicals to Gaddhafi's hold on power. The largest and deadliest Islamist opposition movement was the Libyan Islamic Fighting Group (LIFG).[16] Several LIFG militants and other Libyan Islamists joined Osama Bin Laden's Al Qaeda organization, and some of them assumed senior positions in the Al Qaeda hierarchy.[17] These intense economic and political pressures compelled Gaddhafi to signal Washington that he desired to "come in from the cold"[18] by turning over the Pan Am 103 suspects to The Hague for trial in 1999.[19] In response, U.S. President Bill Clinton authorized the opening of secret back-channel talks in Europe among American, British, and Libyan diplomats in order to negotiate financial restitution for the families of the Lockerbie victims.[20]

When incoming members of the George W. Bush administration were briefed on the Libya back channel, they were "somewhat stunned these negotiations had been held and nervous about it," fearing that if the news were to be leaked to the Families of Pan Am 103 lobby, a political scandal would ensue.[21] Within days of Bush's January 2001 inauguration, however, the Hague tribunal found one of the two Libyan defendants guilty, sentencing him to life in prison. This development spurred the administration to resume the secret trilateral negotiations, during which the participants worked on a prospective agreement whereby the Libyan government would formally accept responsibility for Pan Am 103 and provide monetary compensation to the victims' families in return for the lifting of the UN sanctions.[22] At the same time, in August 2001 Congress approved a five-year extension of the soon-to-expire Iran-Libya Sanctions Act and tightened the Libya-related penalties contained within the legislation.[23]

The catastrophic terrorist attacks in New York and Washington just weeks later brought U.S. and Libyan interests into close alignment and the back-channel dialogue was quickly elevated into a covert alliance of convenience. Gaddhafi was one of the first international leaders to condemn Al Qaeda's "horrific and destructive" acts, while President Bush signed an executive order freezing LIFG assets in the United States.[24] More importantly, within weeks of the attacks, Gaddhafi sent his head of intelligence, Musa Kusa, to London to meet with Assistant Secretary of State for Near Eastern Affairs William Burns and a team of CIA officials, as well as representatives of British intelligence. Kusa furnished his interlocutors with the names of known LIFG operatives and other Libyan militants who had trained with Al Qaeda in Afghanistan, as well as those who were known to be living in the UK.[25] In December, the State Department added the LIFG to its terrorism exclusion list (thereby preventing identified members from entering the United States) on the grounds that it was planning attacks against the United States.[26] In 2003, the Bush administration formally designated the LIFG a terrorist organization in the State Department's annual *Patterns of Global Terrorism* report.[27]

At this pivotal juncture in bilateral relations, the administration found itself fiercely divided on Libya. In advance of Bush's January 2002 State of the Union address, John Bolton, the ultra-hawkish undersecretary of state for disarmament and arms control, pressed for the inclusion of Libya in what the president would dub in his speech the "axis of evil," the list of the world's most dangerous states. This effort was only thwarted when British Foreign Secretary Jack Straw and a top aide to Prime Minister Tony Blair, David Manning, persuaded Secretary of State Colin Powell and National Security Advisor Condoleezza Rice to veto the proposal in order to salvage the ongoing talks with the Libyans.[28] Undeterred, Bolton pushed for a greater role in those negotiations. Again, British officials "at the highest level"[29] successfully persuaded their American counterparts to hold him at bay. Meanwhile, in the aftermath of Bush's Axis of Evil speech, Secretary of Defense Donald Rumsfeld dispatched a memo to the president in which he affirmed his strident opposition to the lifting of the UN sanctions against Libya in light of Gaddhafi's suspected development of weapons of mass destruction (WMD).[30]

In August 2003, Gaddhafi completed his rehabilitation on the terror-ism issue by formally accepting responsibility for Pan Am 103 and agree-ing to pay out $2.7 billion in financial damages to the victims' families.[31] This decision, which resulted in the permanent lifting of the UN sanc-tions, followed on the heels of Gaddhafi's offer earlier that March, on the eve of the U.S. invasion of Iraq, to "clear the air" about Libya's WMD capabilities in return for a U.S. pledge to abstain from invading Libya to topple him from power.[32] This proposal sparked another series of secret trilateral negotiations, during which Libya admitted to possessing an active chemical weapons program but denied the existence of a nuclear weapons program.[33] In October, however, Italian authorities seized a German merchant vessel bound for Libya from Pakistan, which con-tained thousands of centrifuge components for the enrichment of ura-nium. This surprising development prompted Gaddhafi to come clean on his nuclear activities. A final round of secret negotiations produced a landmark agreement, which was announced by Libyan Foreign Minis-ter Abdel Rahman Shalqam on December 19, 2003.[34] It stipulated that Libya would completely eliminate its chemical weapons stockpiles and its nuclear weapons development programs and destroy all of its ballistic mis-siles proscribed by the Missile Technology Control Regime.[35] Crucially, Undersecretary of State Bolton was not apprised of the Libyans' planned WMD announcement until it was imminent. Although the White House proceeded to grant Bolton a leading role in implementing the agreement, his subsequent efforts to scuttle it persuaded the British to yet again convince the Bush administration to mitigate his involvement with the Libyan disarmament process.[36]

Libya's declaration marked a transition in U.S. policy from covert to overt cooperation. Beginning in April 2004, the administration began to retract the web of economic and diplomatic sanctions that had almost com-pletely estranged the two nations for the previous three decades. This process culminated in the full restoration of diplomatic relations between them in May 2006 and the decision by the White House a month later to remove Libya from the State Department's list of state sponsors of terrorism, thereby eliminating the last of the remaining U.S. economic sanctions against that country.[37] The renaissance in U.S.-Libyan relations was underscored by the visit undertaken to Tripoli by Secretary of State Condoleezza Rice in September 2008, during which she met personally with Gaddhafi.[38]

In sum, the relatively fruitful U.S. alliance with Libya was narrowly focused on secret counterterrorism cooperation and managed by an extremely small coterie of policymakers in the executive branch. By insulating security cooperation with Gaddhafi from opponents in the executive bureaucracy (with the notable exception of John Bolton), Congress, and the general public, the administration was able to drive a series of hard bargains on restitution for past Libyan terrorism and WMD proliferation. It was only after Gaddhafi committed to thoroughgoing concessions on these issues that the administration went public with the alliance.

PARALLEL ALIGNMENT

An alternative and even more tenuous strategy for operating below the radar of U.S. domestic politics is what can be called *parallel alignment*. If two states are threatened by a third, they do not necessarily have to actually form an alliance with one another in order to deter or defeat the shared enemy. Instead, they can in essence wage two separate and only minimally coordinated efforts to balance against the shared threat. For U.S. leaders, this strategy is attractive in at least two respects: it obviates the need to extract material resources on behalf of an unsavory autocracy and does not directly empower that state through the transfer to it of such resources. The strategy's chief disadvantage, though, is that since there will be virtually no cooperation between the United States and similarly endangered states, the former will be highly circumscribed in its capacity to directly help the latter fend off the third-party enemy.

In the nearly two decades since the 9/11 attacks, the United States has briefly pursued both "under the radar" strategies with the Islamic Republic of Iran, a state that has ranked at the very top of the list of America's global foes since the hostage crisis of 1979–1981.[39] First, the Bush administration cooperated clandestinely with Iran after its October 2001 invasion of Afghanistan to depose the Taliban regime that was providing sanctuary for Osama Bin Laden and Al Qaeda. During a multilateral dialogue convened under the aegis of the UN, the U.S. and Iranian delegates initiated a sub-group that met in Geneva to secretly discuss the American military inter-vention in Afghanistan.[40] This "Geneva Contact Group" proved useful to the U.S. war effort. Most notably, Tehran allowed American transport air-craft to stage from its airfields, agreed to perform search-and-rescue missions for American aircrews if they had to bail out over Iran, allowed an Ameri-can freighter to offload its humanitarian supplies at the Iranian port of Chah Bahar, persuaded the Tajik-dominated Northern Alliance resistance faction to cooperate with both United States and Pashtun opposition forces operating in southern Afghanistan, and apprehended at least one Al Qaeda leader who fled to Iran.[41] After the United States and allied Afghan factions succeeded in deposing the Taliban in November, Washing-ton and Tehran continued to quietly work together at a UN conference con-vened in Bonn, Germany to establish an interim Afghan government.[42]

Second, as the Bush administration prepared for war against Saddam Hussein's Iraq in late 2002, it engaged in parallel alignment with the Ira-nian regime. Although Iran's Ayatollah Ali Khamenei and President Mohammad Khatami both publicly expressed their opposition to a prospec-tive U.S. invasion of Iraq to topple Saddam from power, the Iranian Navy closed the country's waterways to vessels attempting to smuggle oil and other items out of Iraq. This had the effect of "help[ing] the United States tighten its embargo on Iraqi trade that [was] not specifically authorized" by existing Security Council sanctions against Iraq.[43]

Third and most recently, the United States again resorted to parallel alignment with Iran in order to crush the Islamic State of Iraq and Syria (ISIS), the radical Sunni terrorist and insurgent group that was an out-growth of Al Qaeda's notoriously vicious subsidiary in Iraq. ISIS emerged as a major threat to the regional interests of both the United States and Iran after it expanded from its base in civil war–torn Syria and rapidly conquered large swaths of northern and central Iraq, culminating in the conquest of Iraq's-second largest city, Mosul, in June 2014.[44] In response, Washington and Tehran intervened separately in both Iraq and Syria to roll back the Islamic State's self-declared caliphate. The Obama administration orga-nized a multinational coalition against the Islamic State, launched airstrikes against ISIS positions in Iraq and Syria, and deployed thousands of special operations troops into Iraq and hundreds into Syria to provide training and combat support for local forces battling ISIS fighters.[45] Meanwhile, Iran dispatched members of its elite Quds Force to train and equip Shia militias in Iraq, provided the Iraqi army with a range of heavy weapons, and deployed regular armored and mechanized army units into northern Iraq to battle ISIS alongside Kurdish *peshmerga* fighters. After the outbreak of the civil war in Syria in 2011, Tehran had also provided various forms of material subvention to Bashar al-Assad's embattled government. Most notably, it spearheaded an ambitious operation to train, arm, and transport thousands of Shia militia forces from the broader Middle East region to Syria in order to combat the various rebel forces threatening Assad's rule.[46]

Importantly, virtually no coordination took place between the U.S. and Iranian governments as they battled ISIS. Washington refused to invite Iran to join the Global Coalition Against Daesh (i.e., ISIS), which it founded in September 2014, and which currently includes seventy-five countries.[47] Meanwhile, following the creation of the anti-ISIS coalition, Iran's Supreme Leader Ayatollah Khamenei claimed that he had rebuffed multiple attempts by U.S. officials to better coordinate their respective military campaigns.[48] Although Obama administration officials asserted that they were not formally coordinating the anti-ISIS campaign with Iran, U.S. war planners closely monitored Iranian operations against the Islamic State in Iraq "through a range of channels, including conversations on radio frequencies that each side [knew] the other [was] monitoring." In addition, the U.S. and Iranian militaries "frequently [sought] to avoid conflict in their activities using Iraqi command centers as an intermediary."[49] These efforts allowed the two belligerents to loosely, though effectively, coordinate U.S.-led coalition airstrikes with Iranian-led ground assaults in order to recapture major Iraqi cities from ISIS.[50] These efforts produced a series of operational victories and eventually proved strategically successful. In November 2017, Iraqi Prime Minister Hadir al-Abadi officially declared military victory over ISIS in Iraq. Iranian President Hassan Rouhani announced mere hours later that ISIS had also been driven out of Syria.[51]

POLICY IMPLICATION 3: THE RISKS OF CONSTRUCTIVE ENGAGEMENT

The argument presented here implies that U.S. attempts to conditionally conciliate adversaries in the absence of overarching third-party threats will be even more prone to failure than its efforts to bargain with allies of convenience. Since the end of the Cold War, a number of scholars and analysts have advocated a policy of "constructive engagement" with Iran, North Korea, and other U.S. adversaries.[52] Proponents of engagement believe that a carefully calibrated strategy that deploys both carrots and sticks will be more likely to reform the behavior of "rogue states"[53] than one that relies on one or the other. This book's findings impart that such balanced strategies will be even more difficult to implement toward rogue state adversaries than they are toward allies of convenience. This is because the domestic political pressures that complicate bargaining with an ally of convenience should logically be magnified when the United States attempts to constructively engage an enemy in the absence of an overarching third-party threat. Consequently, the FPE will be even more susceptible to the temptation of pursuing a passive bargaining strategy with the target state. Alternatively, if the FPE resists that temptation by adopting a tough, aggressive bargaining strategy with the adversary state, this will dramatically raise the risk that domestic opponents will scuttle the engagement policy.[54] Meanwhile, the target of engagement will experience even less pressure to concede to U.S. demands than would an ally of convenience asymmetrically imperiled by a shared enemy.

Immediately following the dissolution of the alliances of convenience with China and Iraq that are discussed in this book, U.S. leaders misguidedly engaged America's former partners.[55] In each instance, the objectionable behavior of the target state that vexed Washington during the period of alliance worsened considerably. The first Bush administration's post–Tiananmen Square efforts to enhance diplomatic and economic contacts with China precipitated a frenzy of congressional opposition, even as Chinese foreign policy behavior became increasingly problematic. Beijing not only engaged in nuclear cooperation with both Algeria and Iran, but it also sold M-11 missiles to Pakistan. In response, the administration over-sold cosmetic Chinese concessions on missile proliferation, agreed to provide licenses for Chinese rockets to launch U.S. communications satellites, supported a restoration of World Bank lending to China, and rescinded a prohibition on the export of commercial satellite parts and high-speed computers to the People's Republic. Bush also vetoed a bill conditioning China's Most-Favored Nation (MFN) trade status to its human rights record.[56] Although Democratic candidate Bill Clinton lambasted Bush during the 1992 presidential campaign for "coddling dictators from Baghdad to Beijing,"[57] after his victory at the polls, Clinton approached China in an almost indistinguishable manner from his predecessor. Most infamously, in 1994, he reneged on his ostentatious announcement soon after his inauguration that he would only renew MFN status for China if he determined that it had made "overall significant progress"[58] on human rights. For the remainder of the decade, Clinton would side with an increasingly vocal domestic business community to block attempts by Congress to impose sanctions on China, notwithstanding Beijing's proliferation of nuclear and missile technologies in South Asia and the Middle East, coercive diplomacy toward Taiwan, and espionage against top-secret U.S. nuclear weapons facilities. Ultimately, just before leaving office, Clinton and his allies in the private sector mounted a full-court press to secure congressional ratification of permanent normal trade relations with China, which paved the way for its entry into the World Trade Organization.[59]

The outcome of U.S. efforts to constructively engage Iraq following the conclusion of the Iran-Iraq War was even more calamitous. Even though Iraq emerged from the war as the "dominant military power in the Persian Gulf"[60] and immediately launched a vicious campaign of bombarding its Kurdish population with chemical weapons, the Reagan administration refused to reorient U.S. policy toward its former ally of convenience. In response to the Senate's unanimous passage of the Prevention of Genocide Act, which imposed wide-ranging economic sanctions against Iraq, the administration and a constellation of business and agricultural interest groups mounted a strenuous campaign to forestall the bill's passage. It also approved a flood of dual-use exports for and dramatically increased oil purchases from Iraq and approved over $1 billion in Commodity Credit Corporation agricultural export credits for Saddam's regime.[61]

After succeeding Reagan in early 1989, George H. W. Bush unwisely continued to conciliate Iraq, notwithstanding rapidly mounting evidence of Iraqi bellicosity.[62] Throughout Bush's first year and a half in office, Saddam's debt-strapped government continued devoting enormous sums to its conventional and unconventional military capabilities, threatened to attack Israel with chemical weapons, expanded support for international terrorists, and even enjoined fellow Arab states to counter the United States.[63] During this period, senior officials scrambled to salvage the engagement policy in the face of intensifying efforts by Congress and segments of the executive bureaucracy to quash it by repeatedly pointing to alleged signs of moderation in Saddam's behavior.[64] One incredulous Democratic member of the House of Representatives responded to this campaign by excoriating its "'Alice in Wonderland' quality."[65] The policy reached its nadir when U.S. ambassador to Iraq April Glaspie received an audience with Saddam on July 25, 1990, as seventy-five thousand Iraqi troops massed ominously along the border with Kuwait.[66] At this now-infamous meeting, instead of issuing a firm deterrent threat against Iraq, Glaspie emboldened Saddam both by reassuring him that the U.S. government had benign intentions toward his country and avowing portentously that the administration had "no opinion on the Arab-Arab conflicts, like your border disagreement with Kuwait."[67] A week later, Iraq launched a full-scale invasion of Kuwait. This necessitated the formation of a U.S.-led military coalition to liberate the tiny oil-rich kingdom early the next year.[68]

LOOKING TO THE FUTURE

As long as the international system remains anarchic, states will periodically seek allies to bolster their security against rising threats, and some of these will of necessity be unsavory allies of convenience. It would behoove U.S. policymakers to better understand the dynamics associated with such alliances and why they so frequently engender national security problems as grave as those they resolve. The urgency of this task is likely to mount in the coming years, as America's hegemonic global position in relation to a speedily rising China continues to erode. As China emerges as a full-fledged peer competitor of the United States, no potential ally of convenience will loom larger in the calculations of American policymakers than Russia.

China is unique among America's great power competitors of the past century—including Wilhelmine and Nazi Germany, Imperial Japan, and the Soviet Union—because it alone has the potential to eclipse the United States in wealth and military power.[69] A recent RAND study of the Sino-U.S. military balance made the worrisome projection, "Over the next 5 to 15 years, if U.S. and PLA forces remain on roughly current trajectories, Asia will witness a progressively receding frontier of U.S. dominance." Importantly, its authors added that the United States "will probably not have the resources to prevent all further erosion of the balance of military power over the next decade."[70] If China even comes close to fulfilling its great power potential, the United States will therefore need all the security partners it can muster in order to effectively constrain its regional, if not global, expansion.

Although relations between China and Russia have been relatively friendly since the end of the Cold War, it is probable that the two states will eventually (once again) find themselves at odds.[71] The two states share a 4,200-kilometer border along which the Chinese population outnumbers that of Russia by a factor of eighteen (110 million versus just 6 million), and the Chinese government has invested far greater resources in basic infrastructure than has its Russian counterpart. Not only is the Russian Far East region immediately north of this border rich in natural resources such as oil, natural gas, and timber, but it also includes Russia's sole warm-weather port, Vladivostok, rendering it invaluable to Russia and tantalizing to China. Moreover, the region, which is approximately the size of Iran, used to be Chinese territory; the Russians seized it in accordance with the Treaties of Aigun (1858) and Convention of Beijing (1860), two of the "unequal treaties" imposed on the Qing dynasty by the European great powers in the nineteenth century.[72] Although China and Russia concluded several agreements between 1991 and 2008 to formally settle all outstanding border issues, a 2017 report claims that "many in China feel that as the Aigun Treaty and Convention of Beijing were unjust, China should at some point get back territories it ceded." The likelihood that the Russian Far East will become a geopolitical flashpoint between the two countries is only likely to grow as the far more dynamic Chinese economy, which is already ten times the size of Russia's, continues to expand while that of Russia continues to tread water.[73]

Russia will be an attractive though parlous ally of convenience for the United States. Irrespective of its lingering economic frailty, it remains a substantial military power armed with thousands of nuclear weapons.[74] In combination with America's burgeoning defense partnership with China's western neighbor, India—which also has a long-running border dispute with the PRC—a prospective alliance with Russia would force the People's Liberation Army to devote greater resources to those landed threats to China's west and north, at the expense of the People's Liberation Army Navy's ability to challenge America's maritime forces to its east.[75] However, Russia's steep descent into repressive authoritarianism under the leadership of Vladimir Putin, in combination with Putin's cyber-attacks against the United States, aggression in Ukraine, adventurism in the Middle East, and assorted provocations against America's NATO partners, have poisoned U.S. public and elite opinion against any rapprochement with the Kremlin in the short term.

Neoclassical realist theory suggests that a prospective U.S. attempt to ally with Russia in Asia will come at a steep price, most likely in terms of appeasing Moscow's geopolitical ambitions in Europe to some degree. It is worth recalling that the last time that Russia was recruited by Washington as an ally of convenience, the final defeat of the Axis powers in World War II entailed the concession to Stalin's Soviet Union of a sphere of influence encompassing all of Eastern Europe. Will future U.S. leaders sacrifice their nation's special relationships on one continent to reinforce a tenuous balance of power in another? This preliminary study of alliances of convenience offers a gloomy prediction, but the phenomenon necessitates further academic research commensurate with its considerable salience in U.S. national security policy.

NOTES

DNSA Afghanistan   *Digital National Security Archive (DNSA) Collection: Afghanistan: The Making of U.S. Policy, 1973–1990*. Proquest database.

DNSA China   *DNSA Collection: China and the U.S.: From Hostility to Engagement, 1960–1998*. Proquest database.

DNSA CIA   *DNSA Collection: CIA Covert Operations: From Carter to Obama, 1977–2010*. Proquest database.

DNSA Iran   *DNSA Collection: The Iran-Contra Affair: The Making of a Scandal, 1983–1988*. Proquest database.

DNSA Iraqgate   *DNSA Collection: Iraqgate: Saddam Hussein, U.S. Policy, and the Prelude to the Persian Gulf War, 1980–1994*. Proquest database.

DNSA Kissinger   *DNSA Collection: The Kissinger Transcripts: A Verbatim Record of U.S. Diplomacy, 1969–1977*. Proquest database.

DNSA Nuclear   *DNSA Collection: U.S. Nuclear Non-Proliferation Policy, 1945–1991*. Proquest database.

DNSA WMD   *DNSA Collection: U.S. Intelligence on Weapons of Mass Destruction: From World War II to Iraq*. Proquest database.

FRUS 1948 3   *Foreign Relations of the United States (FRUS), 1948*, Vol. 3: *Western Europe* (Washington, DC: United States Government Printing Office, 1948).

FRUS 1950 3   *FRUS, 1950*, Vol. 3: *Western Europe* (Washington, DC: United States Government Printing Office, 1950).

FRUS 1950 5   *FRUS 1950*, Vol. 5: *The Near East, South Asia, and Africa* (Washington, DC: United States Government Printing Office, 1950).

FRUS 1950 7   *FRUS, 1950*, Vol. 7: *Korea* (Washington, DC: United States Government Printing Office, 1950).

FRUS 1951 3   *FRUS, 1951*, Vol. 3, Part 1: *European Security and the German Question* (Washington, DC: U.S. Government Printing Office, 1951).

FRUS 1951 6	*FRUS, 1951*, Vol. 6, Part 1: *Asia and the Pacific* (Washington, DC: United States Government Printing Office, 1951).
FRUS 1951 7	*FRUS, 1951*, Vol. 7, Part 1: *Korea and China* (Washington: U.S. Government Printing Office, 1951).
FRUS 1952 7	*FRUS, 1952–1954*, Vol 7, Part 1: *Western Europe and Canada* (Washington, DC: U.S. Government Printing Office, 1952–1954).
FRUS 1952 10	*FRUS, 1952–1954*, Vol. 10: *Iran* (Washington, DC: United States Government Printing Office, 1952–1954).
FRUS 1952 15	*FRUS, 1952–1954*, Vol. 15, Part 1: *Korea* (Washington, DC: United States Government Printing Office, 1952–1954).
FRUS 1969 38	*FRUS, 1969–1976*, Vol. 38, Part 1: *Foundations of Foreign Policy, 1973–1976* (Washington, DC: U.S. Government Printing Office, 2012).
NSA China	*National Security Archive (NSA) Electronic Briefing Book: China, Pakistan, and the Bomb: The Declassified File on U.S. Policy, 1977–1997.*
NSA Negotiating	*NSA Electronic Briefing Book: Negotiating U.S.-Chinese Rapprochement: New American and Chinese Documentation Leading Up to Nixon's 1972 Trip.*
NSA New	*NSA Electronic Briefing Book: New Documents Spotlight Reagan-Era Tensions over Pakistani Nuclear Program.*
NSA Pakistan's	*NSA Electronic Briefing Book: Pakistan's Illegal Nuclear Procurement Exposed in 1987.*
NSA United	*NSA Electronic Briefing Book: The United States and the Pakistani Bomb, 1984–1985: President Reagan, General Zia, Nazir Ahmed Vaid, and Seymour Hersh.*

INTRODUCTION: ALLIANCES OF CONVENIENCE IN INTERNATIONAL POLITICS AND U.S. FOREIGN POLICY

1. Thucydides, *The History of the Peloponnesian War*, in *The Landmark Thucydides: A Comprehensive Guide to the Peloponnesian War*, ed. Robert B. Strassler (New York: Free Press, 1998), 16–37 (Book 1, 1.24–1.66).

2. Thucydides, *History*, 38–45 (Bk. 1, 1.67–1.78).

3. Thucydides, *History*, 45 (Bk. 1, 1.79).

4. Thucydides, *History*, 45–46 (Bk. 1, 1.80–1.82).

5. Quoted in Thucydides, *History*, 46 (Bk. 1, 1.82). The ancient Greeks used the term "barbarians" in reference to all peoples who did not speak Greek. Although the term often denoted a lack of civilization, this was not always the case. For instance, many Greeks considered the Persians to be culturally refined. Thucydides, *The Peloponnesian War: A New Translation, Backgrounds and Contexts, Interpretations*, trans. Walter Blanco, ed. Walter Blanco and Jennifer Tolbert Roberts (New York: Norton, 1998), 4, fn. 1.

6. Robert B. Strassler, "The Persians in Thucydides," in Strassler, *Landmark Thucydides*, 600–1; and Thucydides, *History*, 484–85 (Bk. 8, 8.5–8.6).

7. Victor Davis Hanson and David L. Berkey, "The Peloponnesian War and Sparta's Strategic Alliances," in *Grand Strategy and Military Alliances*, ed. Peter R. Mansoor and Williamson Murray (New York: Cambridge University Press, 2016), 214.

8. Thucydides, *History*, 128 (Bk. 2, 2.65).

9. Strassler, "Persians in Thucydides," 602; and Jennifer Roberts, *The Plague of War: Athens, Sparta, and the Struggle for Ancient Greece* (New York: Oxford University Press, 2017), 324–34.

10. Roberts, *Plague of War*, 334.

11. Roger Boesche, "Kautilya's Arthasastra on War and Diplomacy in Ancient India," *Journal of Military History* 67, no. 1 (January 2003): 9–38.

12. Kautilya, *The Arthashastra*, ed. and trans. R. P. Kangle (Delhi: Motilal Banardisass, 1992), book 6, chapter 2, p. 318, line 13. Parentheses in original.

13. S. C. Lee, R. G. Muncaster, and D. A. Zinnes, "'The Friend of My Enemy Is My Enemy': Modeling Triadic International Relationships," *Synthese* 100, no. 3 (September 1994): 357n1.

14. William Shakespeare, *The Tempest*, ed. J. M. Jephson (London: Macmillan, 1864), Act 2, scene 2, p. 34.

15. Shakespeare, *Tempest*, 35. Italics added for emphasis.

16. William Safire, *Safire's Political Dictionary* (New York: Oxford University Press, 2008), 707.

17. Safire, *Safire's*, 708.

18. This definition is obviously at odds with political scientist John Mearsheimer's broad claim that *all* military alliances are "marriages of convenience: today's alliance partner might be tomorrow's enemy, and today's enemy might be tomorrow's alliance partner." John J. Mearsheimer, *The Tragedy of Great Power Politics* (New York: Norton, 2001), 33.

19. Glenn H. Snyder, "Alliance Theory: A First Cut," *Journal of International Affairs* 44, no. 1 (Spring/Summer 1990): 108–9. Italics added for emphasis.

20. For example, Snyder defines alliances as "formal associations of states for the use (or non-use) of military force, intended for either the security or aggrandizement of their members, in specified circumstances, against states outside their own membership." Glenn H. Snyder, *Alliance Politics* (Ithaca, NY: Cornell University Press, 1997), 4. Notably, Stephen Walt is one of the few alliance scholars who has defined alliances more broadly, as "formal or informal commitment[s] for security cooperation between two or more states." Stephen M. Walt, "Why Alliances Endure or Collapse," *Survival* 39, no. 1 (Spring 1997): 157. See also Stephen M. Walt, *The Origins of Alliances* (Ithaca, NY: Cornell University Press, 1987), 1n1. In a more recent article, however, Walt reverts to Snyder's more restrictive definition of alliances: Stephen M. Walt, "Alliances in a Unipolar World," *World Politics* 61, no. 1 (January 2009): 86.

21. Mark Haas defines ideologies as "the principles upon which a particular leadership group attempts to legitimate its claim to rule and the primary institution, economic, and social goals to which it swears allegiance." Mark L. Haas, *The Ideological Origins of Great Power Politics, 1789–1989* (Ithaca, NY: Cornell University Press, 2005), 5. In this

book, Haas persuasively argues that the greater the ideological disparity between states, the more likely they will be to perceive one another as untrustworthy and threatening.

22. See Haas, *Ideological Origins*; John M. Owen, "How Liberalism Produces Democratic Peace," *International Security* 19, no. 2 (Fall 1994): 87–125; and Fareed Zakaria, "The Rise of Illiberal Democracy," *Foreign Affairs* 76, no. 6 (November/December 1997): 22–43.

23. Specifically, the operational indicators of pre-alliance geopolitical conflict include one or more of the following: (1) the partners were on opposing sides of a war or proxy war, the latter including cases in which one partner sponsored terrorist or insurgent organizations targeting the other; (2) the partners were members of rival peacetime alliances; (3) the partners staked rival claims of sovereignty or a sphere of influence over a given territory; or (4) one partner engaged in aggressive or destabilizing foreign policy activity that the other partner viewed as threatening to its national security. This last criterion includes a partner's recent efforts to proliferate Weapons of Mass Destruction (i.e., nuclear, chemical, or biological weapons and ballistic missiles), even though, strictly speaking, this behavior transpires largely within its own borders.

24. Walt construes threat as a compound variable consisting of aggregate capabilities, geographic proximity, offensive capabilities, and aggressive intentions. Walt, *Origins of Alliances*, 22.

25. Paul W. Schroeder, "Alliances, 1815–1945: Weapons of Power and Tools of Management," in Paul W. Schroeder, *Systems, Stability, and Statecraft: Essays on the International History of Modern Europe*, ed. David Wetzel, Robert Jervis, and Jack S. Levy (New York: Palgrave Macmillan, 2004), 195–222; and Patricia A. Weitsman, *Dangerous Alliances: Proponents of Peace, Weapons of War* (Stanford, CA: Stanford University Press, 2004), 21–24.

26. Winston S. Churchill, "The Sinews of Peace," in *Winston S. Churchill: His Complete Speeches, 1897–1963*, vol. 7, ed. Robert R. James (New York: Chelsea House, 1974), 7285–93.

27. The most comprehensive academic treatment is John Dumbrell and Axel Schäfer, eds., *America's "Special Relationships": Foreign and Domestic Aspects of the Politics of Alliance* (London: Routledge, 2009). Similar to my distinction between special relationship allies and allies of convenience, Raymond Aron distinguishes between what he refers to as permanent alliances and occasional alliances. Permanent allies are "those states that, whatever the conflict of some of their interests, do not conceive, in the foreseeable future, that they can be in opposite camps." Occasional allies, by contrast, "have no bond, other than a common hostility toward an enemy, a hostility capable of inspiring sufficient fear to overcome the rivalries that yesterday opposed and tomorrow will oppose again the temporarily allied states. Moreover, occasional allies, on a deeper level, may be permanent enemies: by this we mean states that are committed to conflict because of their ideology or their position on the diplomatic chessboard." Raymond Aron, *Peace and War: A Theory of International Relations* (New Brunswick, NJ: Transaction, 2003), 28.

28. Daniel Pipes and Adam Garfinkle, eds., *Friendly Tyrants: An American Dilemma* (New York: St. Martin's Press, 1991). Although the title of this edited volume accords with my

conception of ambivalent allies, some of its chapters examine relationships that I classify as alliances of convenience. John Lewis Gaddis uses the term "benign authoritarianism" to refer to those autocratic security partners of the United States during the Cold War that broadly shared America's anti-communist orientation: "Regimes like those of Somoza in Nicaragua or [Rafael] Trujillo in the Dominican Republic might be unsavory, but they fell into the benign category because they posed no serious threat to United States interests and in some cases even promoted them." John Lewis Gaddis, *We Now Know: Rethinking Cold War History* (New York: Oxford University Press, 1997), 35.

29. The alliance typology advanced here categorizes dyads of states at the moment they initiate security cooperation against a burgeoning threat. It is possible, however, that at some point following the formation of an alliance, major changes in the domestic ideology or foreign policy behavior of one or both of the partners effectively changes the alliance from one type to another. For example, America's ambivalent alliances with the anticommunist autocracies of South Korea and Taiwan during the Cold War ostensibly resembled alliances of convenience during the 1970s when both states undertook programs to develop nuclear weapons. On these nuclear programs and U.S. efforts to stanch them, see Nicholas L. Miller, *Stopping the Bomb: The Sources and Effectiveness of US Nonproliferation Policy* (Ithaca, NY: Cornell University Press, 2018), 109–12, 171–92.

30. Samuel P. Huntington, "American Ideals versus American Institutions," *Political Science Quarterly* 97, no. 1 (Spring 1982): 1–37.

31. Colin Dueck, *Reluctant Crusaders: Power, Culture, and Change in American Grand Strategy* (Princeton, NJ: Princeton University Press, 2006), 22.

32. Dueck, *Reluctant Crusaders.*

33. Mark Grimsley, "The Franco-American Alliance during the War of Independence," in Mansoor and Murray, *Grand Strategy*, 256–58; and Claude Van Tyne, "French Aid before the Alliance of 1778," *American Historical Review* 31, no. 1 (October 1925): 37–40.

34. Grimsley, "Franco-American," 255.

35. Grimsley, "Franco-American," 255.

36. Grimsley, "Franco-American," 254–55. See also Howard H. Peckham, *The Colonial Wars, 1689–1762* (Chicago: University of Chicago Press, 1965); and Fred Anderson, *Crucible of War: The Seven Years War and the Fate of Empire in British North America, 1754–1766* (New York: Vintage Press, 2000).

37. Grimsley, "Franco-American," 262, 265–66, 270.

38. Grimsley, "Franco-American," 272–75.

39. Grimsley, "Franco-American," 275.

40. Stephen M. Walt, *Revolution and War* (Ithaca, NY: Cornell University Press, 1996), 129–209.

41. Quoted in Robert Dallek, *Franklin D. Roosevelt and American Foreign Policy, 1932–1945*, (New York: Oxford University Press, 1995), 209.

42. Franklin D. Roosevelt, "Address to the Delegates of the American Youth Congress," Washington, DC, February 10, 1940, available at Gerhard Peters and John T. Wooley's American Presidency Project website, University of California at Santa Barbara: http://www.presidency.ucsb.edu/ws/?pid=15918.

43. Winston S. Churchill, *The Second World War*, vol. 3, *The Grand Alliance* (New York: Houghton-Mifflin, 1986 [1950]).

44. John J. Mearsheimer, *Why Leaders Lie: The Truth about Lying in International Politics* (New York: Oxford University Press, 2011), 78–79.

45. Mark A. Stoler, *Allies in War: Britain and America Against the Axis Powers* (New York: Oxford University Press, 2005), 215.

46. Mark A. Stoler, "The Grand Alliance in World War II," in Mansoor and Murray, *Grand Strategy*, 162; Gerhard L. Weinberg, *A World at Arms: A Global History of World War II* (New York: Cambridge University Press, 1994), 890; Adam B. Ulam, *Expansion and Coexistence: Soviet Foreign Policy 1917–73* (Fort Worth: Holt, Rinehart and Winston, 1974), 395; and Ward Wilson, "The Winning Weapon? Rethinking Nuclear Weapons in Light of Hiroshima," *International Security* 31, no. 4 (Spring 2007): 163–67.

47. Melvyn P. Leffler, *A Preponderance of Power: National Security, the Truman Administration, and the Cold War* (Stanford, CA: Stanford University Press, 1992).

48. Lorraine M. Lees, *Keeping Tito Afloat: The United States, Yugoslavia, and the Cold War* (University Park: Pennsylvania State University Press, 1997).

49. Michael Wines, "US Used Romania to Get Soviet Arms," *New York Times*, May 7, 1990, A7.

50. See chapter 2.

51. See chapter 3.

52. Theodore J. Lowi, "Bases in Spain," in *American Civil-Military Relations: A Book of Case Studies*, ed. Harold Stein (Tuscaloosa: University of Alabama Press, 1963), 669–705; Boris Liedtke, "Spain and the United States, 1945–1975," in *Spain and the Great Powers in the Twentieth Century*, ed. Sebastian Balfour and Paul Preston (London: Routledge, 1999), 229–44; Rachel Bronson, *Thicker Than Oil: America's Uneasy Relationship with Saudi Arabia* (New York: Oxford University Press, 2006), 14–203 (chaps. 1–10); Raymond L. Garthoff, *Détente and Confrontation: American-Soviet Relations from Nixon to Reagan* (Washington, DC: Brookings Institution Press, 1994), 686–718; Steven David, "Realignment in the Horn: The Soviet Advantage," *International Security* 4, no. 2 (Fall 1979): 69–90; Study Commission on U.S. Policy toward Southern Africa, *South Africa: Time Running Out* (Berkeley: University of California Press, 1981), 340–66; and Alex Thomson, *Incomplete Engagement: U.S. Foreign Policy towards the Republic of South Africa, 1981–1988* (Aldershot, UK: Avebury Press, 1996).

53. See chapter 4.

54. Bronson, *Thicker Than Oil*, 191–203, 219–21; Richard Swain, "The Gulf War, 1990–1991: A Coalition of Convenience in a Changing World," in Mansoor and Murray, *Grand Strategy*, 343–75; Spencer C. Tucker, "Desert Storm, Operation, Coalition Ground Forces," in *The Encyclopedia of Middle East Wars: The United States in the Persian Gulf, Afghanistan, and Iraq Conflicts*, vol. 1, ed. Spencer C. Tucker (Santa Barbara, CA: ABC-CLIO, 2010), 363–65; and Patricia A. Weitsman, *Waging War: Alliances, Coalitions, and Institutions of Interstate Violence* (Stanford, CA: Stanford University Press, 2014), 60.

55. On Libya, see this book's conclusion. On Sudan, see Veronica Nmoma, "The Shift in United States–Sudan Relations: A Troubled Relationship and the Need for Mutual Cooperation," *Journal of Conflict Studies* 26, no. 2 (Winter 2006): 54–59.

56. Kenneth Pollack, *The Persian Puzzle: The Conflict between Iran and America* (New York: Random House, 2005), 346–49.

57. Bronson, *Thicker Than Oil*, 232–47.

58. Jeffrey Goldberg, "The Obama Doctrine," *The Atlantic*, April 2016: 84.

59. Kathleen J. McInnis, "Coalition Contributions to Countering the Islamic State," *Congressional Research Service Report*, August 26, 2016, 1, 10.

60. Goldberg, "The Obama Doctrine," 84.

61. Phil Stewart, "U.S. Military Strikes Yemen after Missile Attacks on U.S. Navy Ship," Reuters, October 13, 2016, https://www.reuters.com/article/us-yemen-security -missiles/u-s-military-strikes-yemen-after-missile-attacks-on-u-s-navy-ship-idUSKCN 12C294; and Doug Bandow, "America Should Quit Saudi Arabia's War in Yemen: The Senseless Killing Must Stop," *Forbes*, October 25, 2016, https://www.forbes.com/sites /dougbandow/2016/10/25/america-should-quit-saudi-arabias-war-in-yemen-the-sense less-killing-must-stop.

62. Michael Crowley, "Trump's Praise of Russia, Iran, and Assad Regime Riles GOP Experts," *Politico*, October 10, 2016, http://www.politico.com/story/2016/10/trump -praise-russia-iran-assad-criticism-229546.

63. Michael R. Gordon, Helene Cooper, and Michael D. Shear, "Dozens of U.S. Missiles Hit Air Base in Syria," *New York Times*, April 6, 2017, https://www.nytimes.com/2017 /04/06/world/middleeast/us-said-to-weigh-military-responses-to-syrian-chemical -attack.html; Helene Cooper, Thomas Gibbons-Neff, and Ben Hubbard, "U.S., Britain and France Strike Syria over Suspected Chemical Weapons Attack," *New York Times*, April 13, 2018, https://www.nytimes.com/2018/04/13/world/middleeast/trump-strikes -syria-attack.html; and Mark Landler, "Trump Abandons Iran Nuclear Deal He Long Scorned," *New York Times*, May 8, 2018, https://www.nytimes.com/2018/05/08/world /middleeast/trump-iran-nuclear-deal.html.

64. Eliza Mackintosh, "How Trump's First Foreign Trip Compares with Past Presidents," CNN, May 20, 2017, http://edition.cnn.com/2017/05/19/world/donald-trump-first -foreign-presidential-trips/index.html; Alex Ward, "What America's New Arms Deal with Saudi Arabia Says about the Trump Administration," *Vox*, May 27, 2017, https:// www.vox.com/2017/5/20/15626638/trump-saudi-arabia-arms-deal; Bruce Riedel, "The $110 Billion Arms Deal to Saudi Arabia Is Fake News," Markaz Middle East Politics and Policy Blog, Brookings Institution, June 5, 2017, https://www.brookings.edu/blog /markaz/2017/06/05/the-110-billion-arms-deal-to-saudi-arabia-is-fake-news/; and Alexia Fernández Campbell, "Trump Says Selling Weapons to Saudi Arabia Will Create a Lot of Jobs. That's Not True," *Vox*, November 20, 2018, https://www.vox.com /policy-and-politics/2018/10/17/17967510/trump-saudi-arabia-arms-sales-khashoggi.

65. David A. Graham, "Why Does Trump Still Refuse to Criticize Putin?," *The Atlantic*, August 11, 2017, https://www.theatlantic.com/politics/archive/2017/08/why-wont

-trump-criticize-putin/536556/; Office of the Director of National Intelligence, Intelligence Community Assessment (Declassified Version), "Assessing Russian Activities and Intentions in Recent US Elections," ICA 2017–01D, January 6, 2017, 1–15, https://www.dni.gov/files/documents/ICA_2017_01.pdf; and Brian Stelter, "Trump Says This Is All a Hoax. Mueller, Congress, and Facebook Disagree," CNN, September 22, 2017, http://money.cnn.com/2017/09/22/media/trump-facebook-russia/index.html. In July 2017, Congress passed sanctions legislation against Russia by overwhelming, veto-proof majorities, though Trump proceeded to delay its full implementation. Peter Baker and Sophia Kishkovsky, "Trump Signs Russian Sanctions into Law, with Caveats," *New York Times*, August 2, 2017, https://www.nytimes.com/2017/08/02/world/europe/trump-russia-sanctions.html; and Alex Ward, "Trump Just Decided Not to Sanction Russia for Its Election Meddling," *Vox*, January 30, 2018, https://www.vox.com/world/2018/1/30/16949878/trump-russia-sanction-list-oligarch-congress.
66. Johann Wolfgang von Goethe, "The Sorcerer's Apprentice," trans. Paul Dyssen, 1878, reproduced at the website of Professor Robert Godwin-Jones, Virginia Commonwealth University: https://germanstories.vcu.edu/goethe/zauber_e4.html.

1. CONTENDING THEORIES OF U.S. BARGAINING WITH ALLIES OF CONVENIENCE

1. Jeremy Pressman, *Warring Friends: Alliance Restraint in International Politics* (Ithaca, NY: Cornell University Press, 2008). On the informal U.S. alliance with Israel, see also John J. Mearsheimer and Stephen M. Walt, *The Israel Lobby and U.S. Foreign Policy* (New York: Farrar, Straus, and Giroux, 2007).
2. Jason W. Davidson, *America's Allies and War: Kosovo, Afghanistan, and Iraq* (New York: Palgrave Macmillan, 2011).
3. Stefanie von Hlatky, *American Allies in Time of War: The Great Asymmetry* (New York: Oxford University Press, 2013).
4. David P. Auerswald and Stephen M. Saideman, *NATO in Afghanistan: Fighting Together, Fighting Alone* (Princeton, NJ: Princeton University Press, 2014).
5. Gene Gerzhoy, "Alliance Coercion and Nuclear Restraint: How the United States Thwarted West Germany's Nuclear Ambitions," *International Security* 39, no. 4 (Spring 2015): 91–129.
6. Adam Garfinkle and Daniel Pipes, eds., *Friendly Tyrants: An American Dilemma* (New York: Macmillan, 1991); and Ernest R. May and Philip D. Zelikow, eds., *Dealing with Dictators: Dilemmas of U.S. Diplomacy and Intelligence Analysis, 1945–1990* (Cambridge, MA: MIT Press, 2007).
7. David F. Schmitz, *Thank God They're on Our Side: The United States and Right-Wing Dictatorships, 1921–1965* (Chapel Hill: University of North Carolina Press, 1999); and David F. Schmitz, *The United States and Right-Wing Dictatorships, 1965–1989* (New York: Cambridge University Press, 2006).

8. Schmitz, *The United States and Right-Wing Dictatorships*, 1. Schmitz argues in this second volume that during the Vietnam War, the Cold War consensus in American politics shattered and U.S. policy toward right-wing dictators became increasingly contested.

9. Douglas J. MacDonald, *Adventures in Chaos: American Intervention for Reform in the Third World* (Cambridge, MA: Harvard University Press, 1992); and Victor D. Cha, *Powerplay: The Origins of the American Alliance System in Asia* (Princeton, NJ: Princeton University Press, 2016).

10. The third case study surveyed by Cha, of the negotiation of the U.S. alliance with Japan, also meets the criteria for classification as an ambivalent alliance, but in the opposite respect. Unlike South Korea and Taiwan, postwar Japan was a democratizing state, but it was a recent geopolitical adversary of the United States.

11. Alexander Cooley, *Base Politics: Democratic Change and the U.S. Military Overseas* (Ithaca, NY: Cornell University Press, 2008); and Tongfi Kim, *The Supply Side of Security: A Market Theory of Military Alliances* (Stanford, CA: Stanford University Press, 2016).

12. Cooley, *Base Politics*, 56–64, 74–80, 89–94.

13. Kim, *Supply Side of Security*, 153–57. Kim's discussion of the alliance during Franco's reign is extremely brief, however, and he does not examine the domestic politics of the alliance from the U.S. side. Although I do not study this case in this book, my neoclassical realist theory of alliance bargaining predicts contrarily that U.S. bargaining with Franco on key national security issues should have been passive and generally unsuccessful.

14. William C. Wohlforth, "The Stability of a Unipolar World," *International Security* 24, no. 1 (Summer 1999): 5–41; Stephen G. Brooks and William C. Wohlforth, "American Primacy in Perspective," *Foreign Affairs* 81, no. 4 (July/August 2002), 20–33; Stephen G. Brooks and William C. Wohlforth, *World out of Balance: International Relations and the Challenge of American Primacy* (Princeton, NJ: Princeton University Press, 2008); Stephen G. Brooks and William C. Wohlforth, *America Abroad: The United States' Global Role in the 21st Century* (New York: Oxford University Press, 2016); Michael Beckley, *Unrivaled: Why America Will Remain the World's Sole Superpower* (Ithaca, NY: Cornell University Press, 2018); and Øystein Tunsjø, *The Return of Bipolarity in World Politics: China, the United States, and Geostructural Realism* (New York: Columbia University Press, 2018).

15. Glenn H. Snyder, "Alliance Theory: A Neorealist First Cut," *Journal of International Affairs* 44, no. 1 (Spring/Summer 1990): 113.

16. Although each of the three theories that I bring to bear on this question predicts uniformly successful or failed U.S. bargaining with post-1945 allies of convenience, it is possible that in any given case, the bargaining outcome may be mixed (i.e., the United States gets its way on some issues and the ally on others). If this outcome is more frequent than anomalous, it casts doubt on the predictive strength of all three theories.

17. These predictions are both retrodictions and forecasts. In other words, they "predict" both past and future U.S. foreign policy behavior. On predictions about past and future events, see Colin Elman, "Horses for Courses: Why Not Neorealist Theories of Foreign Policy?," *Security Studies* 6, no. 1 (Fall 1996): 7–53, 13n16.

18. International Relations scholars have diverged on the question of whether neorealist theories may be used to explain and predict the foreign policy behavior of individual states. See Elman, "Horses for Courses"; Kenneth N. Waltz, "International Politics Is Not Foreign Policy," *Security Studies* 6, no. 1 (Fall 1996): 54–57; Colin Elman, "Cause, Effect, and Consistency: A Response to Kenneth Waltz," *Security Studies* 6, no. 1 (Fall 1996): 58–61; and John J. Mearsheimer, *The Tragedy of Great Power Politics* (New York: Norton, 2001).

19. Elman, "Horses for Courses," 18–21; Kenneth N. Waltz, *Theory of International Politics* (Reading, MA: Addison-Wesley, 1979), 79–101; and Thomas J. Christensen, *Useful Adversaries: Grand Strategy, Domestic Mobilization, and Sino-American Conflict, 1947–1958* (Princeton, NJ: Princeton University Press, 1996), 11–14.

20. Glenn H. Snyder, *Alliance Politics* (Ithaca, NY: Cornell University Press, 1997), 165–200 (chap. 6). Snyder stipulates that his theory of alliance politics is primarily intended to apply to multipolar international systems because multipolarity has been the systemic norm for most of international political history and is likely to be the systemic configuration in the foreseeable future. He notes, however, that alliance patterns in bipolar and unipolar systems "can be easily accommodated from a multipolar base" (3).

21. Snyder, *Alliance Politics*, 166; and Snyder, "Alliance Theory," 113–14.

22. Snyder, *Alliance Politics*, 166–67. Snyder, in turn, conceives of need as a product of the "extent to which the state's actual and potential military resources fall short of the resources of its potential adversary and the probability of war with the adversary" (167).

23. Waltz, *Theory of International Politics*, 118.

24. Waltz, *Theory of International Politics*, 165.

25. Waltz, *Theory of International Politics*, 165–66.

26. Waltz, *Theory of International Politics*, 118, 168.

27. Waltz, *Theory of International Politics*, 168.

28. Stephen M. Walt, "Alliances in a Unipolar World," in *International Relations and the Consequences of Unipolarity*, ed. G. John Ikenberry, Michael Mastanduno, and William C. Wohlforth (New York: Cambridge University Press, 2011), 108–9.

29. Walt, "Alliances in a Unipolar World," 112.

30. Walt, "Alliances in a Unipolar World," 112.

31. Walt, "Alliances in a Unipolar World," 112–13.

32. Snyder, *Alliance Politics*, 169.

33. Snyder, *Alliance Politics*, 168–69.

34. Snyder, *Alliance Politics*, 170–72

35. Waltz, *Theory of International Politics*, 161–93; Mearsheimer, *The Tragedy of Great Power Politics*, 355–56; Brooks and Wohlforth, *World Out of Balance*; and Brooks and Wohlforth, *America Abroad*.

36. Brooks and Wohlforth, "American Primacy in Perspective," 24; Christopher Layne, *The Peace of Illusions: American Grand Strategy from 1940 to the Present* (Ithaca, NY: Cornell University Press, 2006), 19–23; and Stephen M. Walt, *Taming American Power: The Global Response to U.S. Primacy* (New York: Norton, 2005), 39–40.

37. Nicholas John Spykman, *America's Strategy in World Politics: The United States and the Balance of Power* (New York: Harcourt, Brace, 1942); Hans J. Morgenthau, "The Mainsprings of American Foreign Policy: The National Interest vs. Moral Abstractions," *American Political Science Review* 44, no. 4 (December 1950): 833–54; Mearsheimer, *Tragedy of Great Power Politics*, 238–61; Robert J. Art, *A Grand Strategy for America* (Ithaca, NY: Cornell University Press, 2003); and Barry R. Posen, *Restraint: A New Foundation for US Grand Strategy* (Ithaca, NY: Cornell University Press, 2014).

38. For a similar argument, see Snyder, "Alliance Theory," 118–23.

39. Walt, "Alliances in a Unipolar World." The only partial exception to this assertion is that the United States did not establish a formal alliance with Saudi Arabia despite that country's enormous economic significance as the world's largest producer of oil.

40. Robert D. Putnam, "Diplomacy and Domestic Politics: The Logic of Two-Level Games," *International Organization* 42, no. 3 (Summer 1988): 427–60. This article was reprinted as Robert D. Putnam, "Diplomacy and Domestic Politics: The Logic of Two-Level Games," in *Double-Edged Diplomacy: International Bargaining and Domestic Politics*, ed. Peter B. Evans, Harold K. Jacobson, and Robert D. Putnam (Berkeley: University of California Press, 1993), 431–68.

41. Putnam, "Diplomacy and Domestic Politics," 436.

42. Thomas C. Schelling, *The Strategy of Conflict* (Cambridge, MA: Harvard University Press, 1960), 19.

43. Putnam, "Diplomacy and Domestic Politics," 441.

44. Putnam, "Diplomacy and Domestic Politics," 440–41; and Schelling, *Strategy of Conflict*, 28.

45. Schelling, *Strategy of Conflict*, 28.

46. Putnam, "Diplomacy and Domestic Politics," 450.

47. Stephen D. Krasner, *Defending the National Interest: Raw Materials Investments and U.S. Foreign Policy* (Princeton, NJ: Princeton University Press, 1978), 61.

48. Thomas E. Mann, "Making Foreign Policy: President and Congress," in *A Question of Balance: The President, the Congress, and Foreign Policy*, ed. Thomas E. Mann (Washington, DC: Brookings Institution Press, 1990), 4–5.

49. Mann, "Making Foreign Policy," 65–66.

50. Theodore J. Lowi, *The End of Liberalism: The Second Republic of the United States*, 2nd ed. (New York: Norton, 1979), 155.

51. Krasner, *Defending the National Interest*, 63. Krasner's definition of the U.S. state is found on p. 62.

52. Putnam, "Diplomacy and Domestic Politics," 449. See also Schelling, *Strategy of Conflict*, 28.

53. Gideon Rose, "Neoclassical Realism and Theories of Foreign Policy," *World Politics* 51, no. 1 (October 1998): 144–77.

54. Rose, "Neoclassical Realism," 152.

55. Rose, "Neoclassical Realism," 146.

56. Jeffrey W. Taliaferro, Steven E. Lobell, and Norrin M. Ripsman, "Neoclassical Realism, the State, and Foreign Policy," in *Neoclassical Realism, the State, and Foreign Policy*, ed. Steven E. Lobell, Norrin M. Ripsman, and Jeffrey W. Taliaferro (New York: Cambridge University Press, 2009), 4. See also Norrin M. Ripsman, Jeffrey W. Taliaferro, and Steven E. Lobell, *Neoclassical Realist Theory of International Politics* (New York: Oxford University Press, 2016), 18–20. In the latter book, the authors claim (80–98) that neoclassical realist theories of great power foreign policy behavior can also explain the long-term international political outcomes generated by the interaction of multiple great powers.

57. Rose, "Neoclassical Realism," 147.

58. For simplicity's sake, I will subsequently refer to bargaining between two allies, though conceivably the theory could apply to multilateral alliances.

59. This theory is a Type I neoclassical realist theory as identified by Ripsman, Taliaferro, and Lobell, as it invokes domestic political variables to explain patterns of foreign policy behavior that are considered anomalous from a structural perspective. *Neoclassical Realist Theory*, 28–29.

60. Snyder, "Alliance Theory," 108–9.

61. Taliaferro, Lobell, and Ripsman, "Neoclassical Realism, the State," 25.

62. Taliaferro, Lobell, and Ripsman, "Neoclassical Realism, the State," 25.

63. Taliaferro, Lobell, and Ripsman, "Neoclassical Realism, the State," 38.

64. According to Krasner (*Defending the National Interest*, 56), the weakest kind of state is "completely permeated by pressure groups" and thereby unable to pursue "the general aims of the citizenry as a whole," while the strongest "is able to remake the society and political culture in which it exists—that is, to change economic institutions, values, and patterns of interaction among private groups." For other neoclassical realist theories that focus on variations in the extractive capacity of states or of the same state over time in order to explain variations in foreign policy behavior, see Christensen, *Useful Adversaries*; Randall L. Schweller, *Unanswered Threats: Political Constraints on the Balance of Power* (Princeton, NJ: Princeton University Press, 2006); Fareed Zakaria, *From Wealth to Power: The Unusual Origins of America's World Role* (Princeton, NJ: Princeton University Press, 1998); Norrin M. Ripsman, *Peacemaking by Democracies: The Effect of State Autonomy on the Post–World War Settlements* (University Park: Pennsylvania State University Press, 2002); Jeffrey W. Taliaferro, "State Building for Future Wars: Neoclassical Realism and the Resource-Extractive State," *Security Studies* 15, no. 3 (July–September 2006): 464–95; and Lobell, Ripsman, and Taliaferro, *Neoclassical Realism, the State*.

65. Similarly, Alexander George argues that it was difficult for President Nixon to secure domestic legitimacy for his nuanced détente policy toward the Soviet Union. The policy required domestic audiences to perceive the USSR as a limited rather than

thoroughgoing adversary whose behavior would be most effectively modified via a delicate combination of carrots and sticks, rather than sticks alone. Alexander L. George, "Domestic Constraints on Regime Change in U.S. Foreign Policy: The Need for Policy Legitimacy," in *American Foreign Policy: Theoretical Essays*, 6th ed., ed. G. John Ikenberry (Boston: Wadsworth/Cengage Learning, 2011), 335. This essay was originally published in Ole Holsti, Randolph M. Siverson, and Alexander L. George, eds., *Change in the International System* (Boulder, CO: Westview Press, 1980), 233–62.

66. Andrew Moravcsik, "Integrating International and Domestic Theories of International Bargaining," in Evans, Jacobson, and Putnam, *Double-Edged Diplomacy*, 28.

67. Signal works on the use of deception in U.S. foreign policy are: John J. Mearsheimer, *Why Leaders Lie: The Truth about Lying in International Relations* (New York: Oxford University Press, 2011), and John M. Schuessler, *Deceit on the Road to War: Presidents, Politics, and American Democracy* (Ithaca, NY: Cornell University Press, 2015).

68. Lowi, *End of Liberalism*, 139.

69. Norrin M. Ripsman, "Neoclassical Realism and Domestic Interest Groups," in Lobell, Ripsman, and Taliaferro, *Neoclassical Realism, the State, and Foreign Policy*, 170–93; Tony Smith, *Foreign Attachments: The Power of Ethnic Groups in the Making of American Foreign Policy* (Cambridge, MA: Harvard University Press, 2005); Mearsheimer and Walt, *Israel Lobby*; and John W. Dietrich, "Interest Groups and Foreign Policy: Clinton and the China MFN Debates," *Presidential Studies Quarterly* 29, no. 2 (June 1999): 280–96.

70. Both neorealism and tying hands theories predict implicitly that the systemically advantaged ally and the ally with the narrower win-set, respectively, will adopt an aggressive bargaining strategy toward the partner.

71. Alexis de Toqueville, *Democracy in America*, vol. 1, trans. Henry Reeve, 3rd American ed. (New York: George Adlard, 1839), 231; George F. Kennan, *American Diplomacy: Sixtieth Anniversary Expanded Ed.* (Chicago: University of Chicago Press, 2012), 70; and Walter Lippmann, *The Public Philosophy* (New Brunswick, NJ: Transaction, 2009), 20.

72. Krasner, *Defending the National Interest*, 63. George Tsebelis similarly asserts that a greater number of domestic political veto players biases policy outcomes toward the status quo. Thus, in a weak state characterized by a multiplicity of veto players, such as the United States, major shifts in policy should be very difficult to achieve. See George Tsebelis, "Decision Making in Political Systems: Veto Players in Presidentialism, Parliamentarism, Multicameralism, and Multipartyism," *British Journal of Political Science* 25, no. 4 (October 1995): 289–325.

73. Stephen D. Krasner, "United States Commercial and Monetary Policy: Unravelling the Paradox of External Strength and Internal Weakness," in *Between Power and Plenty: Foreign Economic Policies of Advanced Industrial States*, ed. Peter J. Katzenstein (Madison: University of Wisconsin Press, 1978), 61.

74. On process-tracing, see Alexander L. George and Andrew Bennett, *Case Studies and Theory Development in the Social Sciences* (Cambridge, MA: MIT Press, 2004), 6.

75. Colin Dueck, *Hard Line: The Republican Party and U.S. Foreign Policy since World War II* (Princeton, NJ: Princeton University Press, 2010). This perception continued well into the post–Cold War era, at least until the final years of the George W. Bush administration. Hannah Goble and Peter M. Holm, "Breaking Bonds? The Iraq War and the Loss of Republican Dominance in National Security," *Political Research Quarterly* 62, no. 2 (June 2009): 215–29.

76. Dueck, *Hard Line*, chaps. 5 and 6 (pp. 142–231). It has become a cliché among foreign policy analysts that "only Nixon could go to China." This implies that, as two leading diplomatic historians attest, Nixon "knew that his own anti-communist stridency, though it had mellowed as the 1960s progressed, provided him with important cover on the domestic front, immunizing him against charges of 'appeasement' and being 'soft on the Reds.'" Campbell Craig and Frederik Logevall, *America's Cold War: The Politics of Insecurity* (Cambridge, MA: Belknap Press of Harvard University Press, 2009), 264. The more moderate Republicans Gerald Ford and George H. W. Bush were president for approximately three years of the alliance with China (August 1974–January 1977; January–June 1989) and Democrat Jimmy Carter was president for another four (January 1977–January 1981).

77. Harry Eckstein, "Case Studies and Theory in Political Science," in *Handbook of Political Science*, vol. 7, ed. Fred Greenstein and Nelson Polsby (Reading, MA: Addison-Wesley, 1975), 113–23. See also Jack S. Levy, "Case Studies: Types, Designs, and Logics of Inference," *Conflict Management and Peace Science* 25, no. 1 (February 2008): 12.

78. Of the presidents who managed the alliance with China, only Carter had the ostensible advantage of unified government, as his Democratic Party held majorities in both the House of Representatives and the Senate during his single term in office. By contrast, the Republican Nixon confronted Democratic majorities in both chambers for the entirety of his presidency, while the Republican Reagan faced a Democratic House for both of his two terms in office and a Democratic Senate for the final two years of his second term (January 1987–January 1989). Because, as the case studies demonstrate, all three presidents met heavy and bipartisan congressional opposition to the alliances of convenience in question, the existence of unified or divided government does not appear to have been a salient factor. Data on the party composition of Congress were obtained from the websites of the U.S. House of Representatives (https://history.house.gov/institution/Party-Divisions/Party-Divisions) and U.S. Senate (www.senate.gov/history/partydiv.htm).

79. I do not examine any of the several alliances of convenience that the United States has struck with the kingdom of Saudi Arabia since the end of World War II because, from the vantage point of neorealist theory, they are the least likely of America's post-1945 alliances of convenience to have resulted in successful U.S. bargaining. Although Saudi Arabia is similar to America's other allies of convenience insofar as it has been much weaker militarily than the United States, the asymmetry of dependence has been considerably less favorable to Washington because of Saudi Arabia's unique and vital global role as its "swing producer" of oil. Since it holds approximately one-quarter of the world's known oil resources and possesses approximately eighty-five percent of the

Organization of Petroleum Exporting Countries' spare capacity, Saudi Arabia has been able to disproportionately influence the global price of oil and place massive amounts of petroleum on the market during times of crisis. This attribute has arguably rendered Riyadh considerably less dependent on the United States than all of Washington's other allies of convenience and generated a strong inherent interest on the part of the United States in guaranteeing the kingdom's security. It also explains why the U.S. government has so frequently allied with the Saudis against the kingdom's various enemies. On the U.S.-Saudi relationship, see Rachel Bronson, *Thicker Than Oil: America's Uneasy Partnership with Saudi Arabia* (New York: Oxford University Press, 2006) and Bruce Riedel, *Kings and Presidents: Saudi Arabia and the United States since FDR* (Washington, DC: Brookings Institution Press, 2018).

80. On the methodological value of maximizing the number of observations in political science research, see Gary King, Robert O. Keohane, and Sidney Verba, *Designing Social Inquiry: Scientific Inference in Qualitative Research* (Princeton, NJ: Princeton University Press, 1994), 24, 29–31, 120–21, 123.

81. National Security Archive website: https://nsarchive.gwu.edu/digital-national-security -archive.

82. See conclusion.

83. Barbara Geddes, "How the Cases You Choose Affect the Answers You Get: Selection Bias in Comparative Politics," *Political Analysis* 2 (1990): 134. For a dissenting view on the taboo associated with selecting cases on the dependent variable, see George and Bennett, *Case Studies and Theory Development*, 23–25.

84. This book does not test the theory's Hypothesis 4, which proposes that if the systemically advantaged ally possesses an internally weak state, it will bargain passive-aggressively and partially successfully with an ambivalent ally. It makes a preliminary examination of cases in which the causal and dependent variables adopt extreme values: that is, for the causal variables, alliances of convenience generating high levels of domestic opposition in the systemically advantaged, internally weak state ally and special relationship alliances generating low levels of domestic opposition in the systemically advantaged, internally weak state ally; and for the dependent variable, a passive bargaining strategy producing bargaining failure and an aggressive bargaining strategy producing bargaining success. A mid-range assessment of ambivalent alliances producing a mixed bargaining strategy on the part of a systemically advantaged, internally weak ally and yielding a partially successful outcome awaits a future work. Because this book focuses on the bargaining behavior of the United States, an internally weak state, it also does not test Hypothesis 1, which proposes that a systemically advantaged ally that possesses an internally strong state will bargain aggressively and successfully with all types of systemically disadvantaged allies.

85. For the duration of the Korean War, both Truman and Eisenhower presided over a unified government in which the Democrats and Republicans, respectively, held majorities in both chambers of Congress. https://history.house.gov/institution/Party-Divisions /Party-Divisions; and www.senate.gov/history/partydiv.htm.

2. THE U.S. ALLIANCE WITH THE PEOPLE'S REPUBLIC OF CHINA, 1971–1989

1. Quoted in Richard M. Nixon, *RN: The Memoirs of Richard Nixon* (New York: Grosset & Dunlap, 1978), 560.

2. Robert L. Suettinger, *Beyond Tiananmen: The Politics of U.S.-China Relations, 1990–2000* (Washington, DC: Brookings Institution Press, 2003), 7.

3. Henry Kissinger, *On China* (New York: Penguin Press, 2011), chap. 4.

4. Kissinger, *On China*, chap. 12; Suettinger, *Beyond Tiananmen*, 15.

5. Suettinger, *Beyond Tiananmen*, 18–19.

6. Lorenz M. Luthi, *The Sino-Soviet Split: Cold War in the Communist World* (Princeton, NJ: Princeton University Press, 2008), 30–31.

7. Wang Zhongchun, "The Soviet Factor in Sino-American Normalization, 1969–1979," in *Normalization of U.S.-China Relations: An International History*, ed. William C. Kirby, Robert S. Ross, and Gong Li (Cambridge, MA: Harvard University Press, 2005), 148–49.

8. Robert S. Ross, *Negotiating Cooperation: The United States and China 1969–1989* (Stanford, CA: Stanford University Press, 1995), 10.

9. Seyom Brown, *Faces of Power: Constancy and Change in United States Foreign Policy from Truman to Obama* (New York: Columbia University Press, 2015), 70–72.

10. Robert Accinelli, "In Pursuit of a Modus Vivendi: The Taiwan Issue and Sino-American Rapprochement, 1969–1972," in Kirby, Ross, and Li, *Normalization of U.S.-China Relations*, 15.

11. Luthi, *The Sino-Soviet Split*, 304–7, 316–20.

12. Ross, *Negotiating Cooperation*, 13.

13. Harry Harding, *A Fragile Relationship: The United States and China Since 1972* (Washington, DC: Brookings Institution Press, 1992), 30.

14. Harding, *Fragile Relationship*, 31.

15. Campbell Craig and Frederik Logevall, *America's Cold War: The Politics of Insecurity* (Cambridge, MA: Harvard University Press, 2012), 261.

16. Brown, *Faces of Power*, 232–34.

17. Zhongchun, "Soviet Factor," 157.

18. Brown, *Faces of Power*, 249–68; and Salim Yaqub, "The Weight of Conquest: Henry Kissinger and the Arab-Israeli Conflict," in *Nixon in the World: American Foreign Relations, 1969–1977*, ed. Frederik Logevall and Andrew Preston (New York: Oxford University Press, 2008), 227–48.

19. Zhongchun, "Soviet Factor," 150, 157–58.

20. Zhongchun, "Soviet Factor," 151; and Ross, *Negotiating Cooperation*, 24.

21. Patrick Tyler, *A Great Wall: Six Presidents and China: An Investigative History* (New York: Public Affairs, 2000), 73; and Zhongchun, "Soviet Factor," 152–53.

22. Quoted in Tyler, *Great Wall*, 66.

23. Tyler, *Great Wall*, 98.

24. James Mann, *About Face: A History of America's Curious Relationship with China, from Nixon to Clinton* (New York: Vintage Books, 2000), 35–36.

25. Quoted in Mann, *About Face*, 35.

26. "The Shanghai Communique, February 27, 1972," in Harding, *Fragile Relationship*, 376.

27. Memorandum from the President's Assistant for National Security Affairs (Kissinger) to President Nixon, "My Trip to China," March 2, 1973, in *FRUS 1969 38*, 7.

28. Quoted in Tyler, *Great Wall*, 158, 159.

29. Tyler, *Great Wall*, 162.

30. Mann, *About Face*, 74, 76.

31. Quoted in Hugo Meijer, "Balancing Conflicting Security Interests: U.S. Defense Exports to China in the Last Decade of the Cold War," *Journal of Cold War Studies* 17, no. 1 (Winter 2015): 9.

32. Quoted in Harding, *Fragile Relationship*, 89.

33. Harding, *Fragile Relationship*, 89.

34. Ross, *Negotiating Cooperation*, 137–38, 146.

35. Mann, *About Face*, 100.

36. Mann, *About Face*, 111.

37. Harding, *Fragile Relationship*, 92.

38. Quoted in Meijer, "Balancing Conflicting Security Interests," 10.

39. Meijer, "Balancing Conflicting Security Interests," 10–11.

40. Meijer, "Balancing Conflicting Security Interests," 11–12; Tyler, *Great Wall*, 285.

41. Secret Department of Defense Memorandum for Assistant Secretary of Defense for International Security Affairs Franklin Kramer, "Military Sales to China," February 23, 1981, quoted in Meijer, "Balancing Conflicting Security Interests," 12.

42. Meijer, "Balancing Conflicting Security Interests," 15–16.

43. Meijer, "Balancing Conflicting Security Interests," 17–18.

44. Meijer, "Balancing Conflicting Security Interests," 25–27.

45. Meijer, "Balancing Conflicting Security Interests," 28–31.

46. Meijer, "Balancing Conflicting Security Interests," 36.

47. Meijer, "Balancing Conflicting Security Interests," 34.

48. Suettinger, *Beyond Tiananmen*, 63–68, 83–85.

49. Raymond L. Garthoff, *The Great Transition: American-Soviet Relations and the End of the Cold War* (Washington, DC: Brookings Institution Press, 1994), 375–408.

50. Garthoff, *Great Transition*, 644–56.

51. Vitaly Kozyrev, "Soviet Policy Toward the United States and China, 1969–1979," in Kirby, Ross, and Li, *Normalization of U.S.-China Relations*, 264.

52. Kozyrev, "Soviet Policy," 266–67.

53. Kozyrev, "Soviet Policy," 269.

54. Garthoff, *Great Transition*, 713.

55. Ross, *Negotiating Cooperation*, 12–13.

56. Ross, *Negotiating Cooperation*, 14–15.

57. Quoted in Lien-Hang T. Ngyuen, "Waging War on All Fronts: Nixon, Kissinger, and the Vietnam War, 1969–1972," in Logevall and Preston, *Nixon in the World*, 186.

58. Ngyuen, "Waging War on All Fronts," 187–98.

59. Craig and Logevall, *America's Cold War*, 258.

60. Tyler, *Great Wall*, 51.

61. Li Danhui, "Vietnam and Chinese Policy toward the United States," in Kirby, Ross, and Li, *Normalization of U.S.-China Relations*, 206.

62. "The President's News Conference," June 16, 1981, in *DNSA Nuclear*, Doc. NP01900, p. 521. According to Francis Gavin, the effort to inhibit the global spread of nuclear weapons has represented "an independent and driving feature of U.S. national security policy for more than seven decades." Gavin concedes that some presidents have pursued nuclear inhibition more zealously than others, but he "arguably" places Reagan in the former category, alongside Harry Truman, John Kennedy, Lyndon Johnson, Jimmy Carter, and all post–Cold War presidents, as opposed to the latter category, where he places Dwight Eisenhower and Richard Nixon. Francis J. Gavin, "Strategies of Inhibition: US Grand Strategy, the Nuclear Revolution, and Nonproliferation," *International Security* 40, no. 1 (Summer 2015): 11, 34. Nicholas Miller argues that in general, the U.S. government began to consistently pay greater attention to nuclear nonproliferation only after the Chinese and Indian nuclear tests of 1964 and 1974, respectively. Nicholas L. Miller, *Stopping the Bomb: The Sources and Effectiveness of US Nonproliferation Policy* (Ithaca, NY: Cornell University Press, 2018), chaps. 1 and 2 (pp. 40–94).

63. "United States Non-Proliferation and Peaceful Nuclear Cooperation Policy, July 16, 1981," National Security Decision Directive No. 6, in Online Database of Presidential Directives and Executive Orders, ed. John Pike, located on the Federation of American Scientists website: http://www.fas.org/irp/offdocs/nsdd/23-1468t.gif.

64. John L. Gaddis, *Strategies of Containment: A Critical Appraisal of American National Security Policy During the Cold War*, revised and expanded ed. (New York: Oxford University Press, 2005), 357–62.

65. State Department Secret Cable from State Department to American Embassy, Beijing, "[Four Briefing Papers on Missile Proliferation for Use in U.S.-Chinese Arms Control Discussions]," July 29, 1988, in *DNSA China*, Doc. CH00969, p. 9.

66. Kenneth R. Timmerman, *The Death Lobby: How the West Armed Iraq* (Boston: Houghton-Mifflin, 1991), 208–9; and "Nuclear Capable Missile Technology Transfer Policy, November 30, 1982," National Security Decision Directive No. 70, in Online Database of Presidential Directives and Executive Orders: http://www.fas.org/irp/offdocs/nsdd/nsdd-070.htm.

67. U.S. Arms Control and Disarmament Agency, *World Military Expenditures and Arms Transfers 1971–1980* (Washington, DC: U.S. Government Printing Office, 1983), 44, 71; and U.S. Arms Control and Disarmament Agency, *World Military Expenditures and Arms Transfers 1990* (Washington, DC: U.S. Government Printing Office, 1991), 58, 85. The 1971 figures are in constant 1979 U.S. dollars and the 1989 figures in constant 1989 U.S. dollars.

68. Zhongchun, "Soviet Factor," 150.

69. Zhongchun, "Soviet Factor," 150–51; Chi Su, "The Strategic Triangle and China's Soviet Policy," in *China, the United States, and the Soviet Union: Tripolarity and Policy Making in the Cold War*, ed. Robert S. Ross (Armonk, NY: M. E. Sharpe, 1993), 45.

70. Robert S. Norris and Hans M. Kristensen, "Global Nuclear Weapons Inventories, 1945–2010," *Bulletin of Atomic Scientists* 66, no. 4 (July/August 2010): 81–82.

71. Ross, *Negotiating Cooperation*, 8.

72. Richard Bernstein, *China 1945: Mao's Revolution and America's Fateful Choice* (New York: Knopf, 2014).

73. State Department Secret Memorandum from Marshall Green to Eliot L. Richardson, "Next Steps in China Policy," October 6, 1969, in *DNSA China*, Doc. CH00079, pp. 2, 4; and Mann, *About Face*, 19.

74. Secret State Department Cable from Secretary of State William P. Rogers to U.S. Embassy, Poland, "Guidance for 135th Sino-U.S. Ambassadorial Meeting," January 17, 1970, in *DNSA China*, Doc. CH00115, pp. 6–7, 10.

75. State Department Secret Action Memorandum from Marshall Green to William P. Rogers, "How to Deal with the Question of a Higher-Level Meeting with the Chinese [Includes Attachments: Memorandum for the President; U.S. Strategy in Current Sino-U.S. Talks; A Higher Level Sino-U.S. Meeting in Peking; Tactical Factors Relating to our Response to the Chinese on a Move From Warsaw to Peking]," March 5, 1970, in *DNSA China*, Doc. CH00148.

76. Tyler, *Great Wall*, 88.

77. Mann, *About Face*, 25.

78. Harding, *Fragile Relationship*, 40.

79. Quoted in *New York Times*, April 20, 1971, 1; and Tyler, *Great Wall*, 92.

80. Secretary of State Rogers was apprised of the trip, albeit only after Kissinger was already en route to China. Accinelli, "In Pursuit of a Modus Vivendi," 29.

81. Ross, *Negotiating Cooperation*, 37.

82. Accinelli, "In Pursuit of a Modus Vivendi," 26.

83. Accinelli, "In Pursuit of a Modus Vivendi," 26–27.

84. Tyler, *Great Wall*, 99.

85. Accinelli, "In Pursuit of a Modus Vivendi," 36.

86. Accinelli, "In Pursuit of a Modus Vivendi," 28; and Tyler, *Great Wall*, 100–1.

87. Quoted in Accinelli, "In Pursuit of a Modus Vivendi," 29.

88. Quoted in Chris Tudda, *A Cold War Turning Point: Nixon and China, 1969–1972* (Baton Rouge: Louisiana State University Press, 2012), 121.

89. Conversation between President Nixon and National Security Adviser Kissinger, followed by Conversation among Nixon, Kissinger, and UN Ambassador George Bush, September 30, 1971, in *NSA Negotiating*, No. 70, posted May 22, 2002: https://nsarchive2.gwu.edu/NSAEBB/NSAEBB70/, Doc. 6, p. 2.

90. George H. W. Bush with Victor Gold, *Looking Forward* (New York: Doubleday, 1987), 112–13.

91. Quoted in Tyler, *Great Wall*, 113.

92. Accinelli, "In Pursuit of a Modus Vivendi," 37–38.

93. Tyler, *Great Wall*, 117.

94. Top Secret Memorandum of Conversation, "President's Visit, Taiwan, and Japan [Meeting with Zhou Enlai]," October 21, 1971, in *DNSA Kissinger*, Doc. KT00369, pp. 20, 21, 28, 29.

95. Top Secret Memorandum of Conversation, Kissinger and Zhou, "Korea, Japan, South Asia, Soviet Union, Arms Control," October 22, 1971, 4:15–8:28 p.m. Top Secret/Sensitive /Exclusively Eyes Only, in *NSA Negotiating*, Doc. 13, p. 33. Italics added.

96. Top Secret Memorandum of Conversation, Haig and Zhou, January 7, 1972, 11:45 p.m., Great Hall of the People, Top Secret/Sensitive/Exclusively Eyes Only, in *NSA Negotiating*, Doc. 25, pp. 6–7.

97. Top Secret Memorandum of Conversation, Haig and Zhou, January 7, 1972. Italics added for emphasis.

98. Quoted in Richard Reeves, *President Nixon: Alone in the White House* (New York: Simon and Schuster, 2001), 455.

99. Top Secret Memorandum of Conversation, "[President Nixon's Meeting with Zhou Enlai]," February 22, 1972, in *DNSA Kissinger*, Doc. KT00435, pp. 5–6; and Top Secret Memorandum of Conversation, "[President Nixon's Meeting with Zhou Enlai]," February 24, 1972, in *DNSA Kissinger*, Doc. KT00440, p. 11.

100. Quoted in Tyler, *Great Wall*, 139–40.

101. "The Shanghai Communique, Feb. 27, 1972," in Harding, *Fragile Relationship*, 376.

102. Mann, *About Face*, 47.

103. Harding, *Fragile Relationship*, 43–44. Harding nevertheless concludes that "both sides made significant concessions" on Taiwan in the communiqué.

104. Richard Nixon, "Remarks at Andrews Air Force Base on Returning from the People's Republic of China," February 28, 1972, *American Presidency Project* web archive, http://www.presidency.ucsb.edu/ws/index.php?pid=3756.

105. Accinelli, "In Pursuit of a Modus Vivendi," 50.

106. Accinelli, "In Pursuit of a Modus Vivendi," 50.

107. Table A-1, "U.S. Public Opinion of China," in Harding, *Fragile Relationship*, 363.

108. Top Secret State Department Memorandum of Conversation, "[Meeting with Deng Xiaoping and Chinese Officials]," November 26, 1974, in *DNSA Kissinger*, Doc. KT01426, pp. 3–13; and Secret State Department Draft Memorandum of Conversation, "[Conversation with Deng Xiaoping in Peking]," November 28, 1974, in *DNSA Kissinger*, Doc. KT01431, p. 14.

109. Tyler, *Great Wall*, 199.

110. Harding, *Fragile Relationship*, 363.

111. Quoted in Tyler, *Great Wall*, 202.

112. Tyler, *Great Wall*, 214.

113. Quoted in Mann, *About Face*, 71.

114. Ross, *Negotiating Cooperation*, 85.

115. Cyrus Vance, *Hard Choices* (New York: Simon & Schuster, 1983), 79.

116. Quoted in Tyler, *Great Wall*, 245.

117. Quoted in Mann, *About Face*, 76.

118. Zbigniew K. Brzezinski, *Power and Principle: Memoirs of the National Security Advisor 1977–1981* (New York: Farrar, Straus, and Giroux, 1985), 196.

119. Mann, *About Face*, 85.

120. Mann, *About Face*, 86–91.

121. Tyler, *Great Wall*, 252–56.

122. Quoted in Brzezinski, *Power and Principle*, 224.

123. Jimmy Carter, *Keeping Faith: Memoirs of a President* (New York: Bantam Books, 1982), 197; and Harding, *Fragile Relationship*, 84.

124. Non-Classified Statement, "Diplomatic Relations between the United States and the People's Republic of China," December 15, 1978, in *DNSA China*, Doc. CH00448. During the one-year period of advance notice prior to formal withdrawal that was stipulated in Article 10 of the MST, Carter agreed to a prohibition on any new weapons sales to Taiwan. Tyler, *Great Wall*, 262–63.

125. Mann, *About Face*, 91.

126. Quoted in Tyler, *Great Wall*, 273.

127. Harding, *Fragile Relationship*, 85.

128. George Bush, "Our Deal with Peking: All Cost, No Benefit; Even the Chinese Now Know We Cannot Be Relied on Too Much," *Washington Post*, December 24, 1978, D1.

129. Quoted in Harding, *Fragile Relationship*, 85; Ross, *Negotiating Cooperation*, 142.

130. "Taiwan Relations Act," in Ross, *Negotiating Cooperation*, 274.

131. Harding, *Fragile Relationship*, 87.

132. Quoted in Mann, *About Face*, 116.

133. Mann, *About Face*, 120.

134. Mann, *About Face*, 120.

135. Tyler, *Great Wall*, 316.

136. Mann, *About Face*, 124–25; and Jaw-ling Joanne Chang, "Negotiation of the 17 August 1982 U.S.-PRC Arms Communique: Beijing's Negotiating Tactics," *China Quarterly* 125 (March 1991): 48.

137. Mann, *About Face*, 124; and Tyler, *Great Wall*, 318–21.

138. Don Oberdorfer, "U.S. Views Discussion with Peking on Taiwan Arms Sale as 'A Success,'" *Washington Post*, January 14, 1982, A22.

139. Quoted in Mann, *About Face*, 125.

140. Quoted in Mann, *About Face*, 128, 129.

141. Mann, *About Face*, 129.

142. Tyler, *Great Wall*, 324–25.

143. Quoted in Tyler, *Great Wall*, 325.

144. Quoted in Mann, *About Face*, 126.

145. Harding, *Fragile Relationship*, 116.

146. "Documents on U.S. Arms Sales to Taiwan, August 17, 1982," in Harding, *Fragile Relationship*, 384.

147. Harding, *Fragile Relationship*, 117.

148. Quoted in Harding, *Fragile Relationship*, 117.

149. Harding, *Fragile Relationship*, 116–17.
150. Harding, *Fragile Relationship*, 154–62.
151. Ross, *Negotiating Cooperation*, 3.
152. Quoted in Tyler, *Great Wall*, 81.
153. Tyler, *Great Wall*, 52.
154. Quoted in Li, "Vietnam and Chinese Policy," 182.
155. Mann, *About Face*, 33.
156. Li, "Vietnam and Chinese Policy," 190.
157. Quoted in Li, "Vietnam and Chinese Policy," 190–91.
158. Quoted in Li, "Vietnam and Chinese Policy," 191.
159. Quoted in Li, "Vietnam and Chinese Policy," 191.
160. Ross, *Negotiating Cooperation*, 49; and Albin Krebs, "David K. E. Bruce, Diplomat, Dies," *New York Times*, December 6, 1977, 1, 42.
161. Memecon, Haig and Zhou, January 3, 1972, in *NSA Negotiating*, pp. 3–5.
162. Memecon, Haig and Zhou, January 7, 1972, p. 3.
163. Quoted in Ross, *Negotiating Cooperation*, 49.
164. Quoted in Tyler, *Great Wall*, 126.
165. Quoted in Tyler, *Great Wall*, 15.
166. Quoted in Li, "Vietnam and Chinese Policy," 197.
167. Li, "Vietnam and Chinese Policy," 197.
168. Li, "Vietnam and Chinese Policy," 201.
169. Quoted in Li, "Vietnam and Chinese Policy," 202.
170. Quoted in Li, "Vietnam and Chinese Policy," 202.
171. Jussi M. Hanhimäki, *The Flawed Architect: Henry Kissinger and American Foreign Policy* (New York: Oxford University Press, 2004), 244.
172. Top Secret Memorandum of Conversation, "[Dinner Meeting with Quio Guanha, Huang Ha, and Nelson Rockefeller]," November 13, 1972, in *DNSA Kissinger*, Doc. KT00597, pp. 20–23.
173. Top Secret Memorandum of Conversation, "[Discussion of Vietnam Peace Negotiations with Chinese Ambassador Huang Zhen]," November 25, 1972, in *DNSA Kissinger*, Doc. KT00611, p. 9.
174. Quoted in Hanhimäki, *Flawed Architect*, 255, 256.
175. Quoted in Hanhimäki, *Flawed Architect*, 256.
176. Hanhimäki, *Flawed Architect*, 256.
177. Nixon, *RN*, 568.
178. Li, "Vietnam and Chinese Policy," 205.
179. Li, "Vietnam and Chinese Policy," 205.
180. China's nuclear cooperation with Pakistan is covered from the vantage point of the United States' concurrent alliance of convenience with Pakistan in chapter 3.
181. U.S. Embassy China Cable 17090 to State Department, "Arms Control and Disarmament," December 17, 1982, in *NSA China*, No. 114, https://nsarchive2.gwu.edu/NSAEBB/NSAEBB114/press.htm, posted on March 5, 2004, Doc. 8, p. 2.

182. U.S. Embassy China Cable 17168 to State Department, "U.S.-PRC Nuclear Cooperation— or the Lack of It," December 18, 1982, Secret, in *NSA China*, Doc. 9, p. 3.

183. State Department Cable 348835 to U.S. Embassy Pakistan, "Newsweek Article on Chinese Nuclear Cooperation with Pakistan," December 18, 1982, Confidential, in *NSA China*, Doc. 10.

184. Secret State Department Briefing Paper, "The Pakistani Nuclear Program," June 23, 1983, in *DNSA Nuclear*, Doc. NP02057, pp. 1, 7 (original document is incorrectly numbered). According to Adrien Levy and Catherine Scott-Clark, some of the drawings that the Pakistanis were providing to prospective foreign suppliers of various nuclear components included notes and an operations manual that were written in Chinese. Adrian Levy and Catherine Scott-Clark, *Deception: Pakistan, the United States and the Global Nuclear Weapons Conspiracy* (London: Atlantic Books, 2007), 93.

185. Levy and Scott-Clark, *Deception*, 94.

186. George P. Shultz, *Turmoil and Triumph: My Years as Secretary of State* (New York: Charles Scribner's Sons, 1993), 382.

187. Levy and Scott-Clark, *Deception*, 100n6.

188. Mark Holt and Mary Beth Nikitin, "U.S.-China Nuclear Cooperation Agreement," *Congressional Research Service Report*, May 6, 2015, p. 11.

189. U.S. Embassy China Cable 00644 to State Department, "Premier Zhao's Statement on Non-Proliferation Published in Beijing," January 12, 1984, Confidential, in *NSA China*, Doc. 13.

190. Leonard Spector, *Nuclear Proliferation Today* (New York: Vintage Books, 1984), 324.

191. Quoted in Levy and Scott-Clark, *Deception*, 99n1.

192. Quoted in Levy and Scott-Clark, *Deception*, 107.

193. Quoted in Leslie H. Gelb, "Pakistan Tie Imperils U.S.-China Nuclear Pact," *New York Times*, June 22, 1984, A1.

194. Levy and Scott-Clark, *Deception*, 107–8.

195. "Hold the Toasts to Nuclear Trade," editorial, *New York Times*, July 10, 1984, A22.

196. Quoted in Qingshan Tan, "U.S.-China Nuclear Cooperation Agreement: China's Nonproliferation Policy," *Asian Survey* 29, no. 9 (September 1989): 876.

197. Qingshan Tan, "U.S.-China Nuclear Cooperation Agreement," 877.

198. See, for example, "Proposed Nuclear Cooperation Agreement with the People's Republic of China," Hearing and Markup before the Committee on Foreign Affairs, House of Representatives, 99th Congress, 1st Session, on H.J. Res. 404, July 31; Nov. 13, 1985 (Washington, DC: U.S. Government Printing Office, 1987), 53–137.

199. Daniel Horner and Paul Leventhal, "The U.S.-China Nuclear Agreement: A Failure of Executive Policymaking and Congressional Oversight," *Fletcher Forum* 11, no. 1 (Winter 1987): 113.

200. Horner and Leventhal, "U.S.-China Nuclear Agreement," 120.

201. Quoted in Bernard Gwertzman, "Cranston Assails U.S.-China Accord," *New York Times*, October 22, 1985, A1.

202. Horner and Leventhal, "U.S.-China Nuclear Agreement," 117.

203. Quoted in Patrick E. Tyler, "China Pact Restriction Is Dropped: Senate Wanted Curb on Nuclear Sales," *Washington Post*, December 12, 1985, A27.

204. Eden Y. Woon, "Chinese Arms Sales and U.S.-China Military Relations," *Asian Survey* 29, no. 6 (June 1989): 604–5. During the war, China also reportedly sold Iraq tanks, artillery, ammunition, MiG-21 fighter jets, TU-16 bombers, and both surface- and air-launched versions of the Silkworm missile.

205. Don Oberdorfer, "U.S. Warns Tehran on Missile Menace," *Washington Post*, March 20, 1987, A27.

206. Oberdorfer, "U.S. Warns Tehran"; and Woon, "Chinese Arms Sales," 604. Iran received its first of several shipments of Silkworms from China during the summer of 1986. Timothy V. McCarthy, *A Chronology of PRC Missile Trade and Developments* (n.pl.: International Missile Proliferation Project, Monterey Institute of International Studies, 1992), 5.

207. Quoted in Edward A. Gargan, "Major Deals Cited in China-Iran Arms," *New York Times*, June 11, 1987, A8. One report claims that North Korea also began selling its own Silkworms to Iran in July 1987. McCarthy, *Chronology*, 5.

208. Clyde H. Farnsworth Jr., "U.S. Will Penalize China on Missiles," *New York Times*, October 23, 1987, A1; Woon, "Chinese Arms Sales," 611–12.

209. Woon, "Chinese Arms Sales," 611.

210. Woon, "Chinese Arms Sales," 612.

211. McCarthy, *Chronology*, 6.

212. Meijer, "Balancing Conflicting Security Interests," 28.

213. Quoted in Molly Moore and David Ottaway, "U.S. Reacts to China's Silkworm Sale; Technology Transfer Delayed," *Washington Post*, October 23, 1987, A32.

214. State Department Confidential Telegram from American Embassy, China, to the State Department, "Background Statement on U.S. Export Controls Policy for China," December 18, 1987, in *DNSA China*, Doc. CH00904, p. 1.

215. Telegram from American Embassy, China, to the State Department, December 18, 1987, 2.

216. Edward A. Gargan, "China Says It Will Stop Arms for Iran," *New York Times*, November 4, 1987, A3.

217. McCarthy, *Chronology*, 6–7.

218. Unclassified cable from Department of State to American Embassy, Beijing, "Proposed Demarche on Silkworms, Arms Sales to Iran, UNSC Res. 598 and Wu Visit," February 3, 1988, in *DNSA China*, Doc. CH00911, pp. 2–3. Italics added for emphasis.

219. State Department Secret Cable from U.S. Embassy, China, to the State Department, "Foreign Minister Wu Visit: Handling Chinese Arms Sales to Iran," February 4, 1988, in *DNSA China*, Doc. CH00912.

220. Quoted in Don Oberdorfer, "U.S. to Lift Sanctions against Beijing; Chinese Agree to Accept Peace Corps," *Washington Post*, March 10, 1988, A41.

221. Jim Mann, "China Said to Offer More Missiles to Iran," *Los Angeles Times*, February 14, 1989, 5.

222. Mann, *About Face*, 168.
223. John M. Goshko and Don Oberdorfer, "Chinese Sell Saudis Missiles Capable of Covering the Middle East," *Washington Post*, March 18, 1988, A1. An April 1988 intelligence report by the Joint Chiefs of Staff noted that the missiles delivered to China had been modified to improve their accuracy. United States Joint Chiefs of Staff Intelligence Information Report, "[Excised] Export of the CSS-2 to Saudi Arabia," April 29, 1988, in *DNSA China*, Doc. CH00942, p. 3.
224. Rachel Bronson, *Thicker Than Oil: America's Uneasy Relationship with Saudi Arabia* (New York: Oxford University Press, 2006), 188.
225. Bronson, *Thicker Than Oil*, 188; Woon, "Chinese Arms Sales," 613; and Meijer, "Balancing Conflicting Security Interests," 30.
226. Bronson, *Thicker Than Oil*, 188.
227. Mann, *About Face*, 169.
228. Woon, "Chinese Arms Sales," 610.
229. Mann, *About Face*, 170; and Secret State Department Testimony, "[Chinese Missile Transfers to Saudi Arabia: Bilateral Dialogue]," April 20, 1988, in *DNSA China*, Doc. CH00937.
230. Mann, *About Face*, 170; and Evan S. Madeiros, *Reluctant Restraint: The Evolution of China's Nonproliferation Policies, 1980–2004* (Stanford, CA: Stanford University Press, 2007), 109–10.
231. Nonclassified letter from U.S. House of Representatives to George P. Shultz, "[Alleged Chinese Sale of Ballistic Missiles to Syria]," July 14, 1988, in *DNSA China*, Doc. CH00958.
232. Quoted in Mann, *About Face*, 171. Chinese leaders also rebuffed Shultz's proposal of "international consultations" to prevent additional missile proliferation. Quoted in McCarthy, *Chronology*, 9.
233. Unclassified State Department Cable, "Dole Resolution on Chinese Arms Sales," July 28, 1988, in *DNSA China*, Doc. CH00966.
234. Secret letter from Acting Secretary of State John C. Whitehead to The Hon. Mel Levine, August 1, 1988, in *DNSA China*, Doc. CH00972, p. 1.
235. Quoted in Mann, *About Face*, 171.
236. Mann, *About Face*, 171.
237. Anthony H. Cordesman, "Syrian Weapons of Mass Destruction: An Overview," Center for Strategic and International Studies, June 2, 2008, http://www.csis.org, p. 10.
238. McCarthy, *Chronology*, 20.
239. Thomas J. Christensen, *The China Challenge: Shaping the Choices of a Rising Power* (New York: Norton, 2015); and Ramon Myers and Linda Chao, *The First Chinese Democracy: Political Life in the Republic of China on Taiwan* (Baltimore, MD: Johns Hopkins University Press, 1998).
240. Richard K. Betts, *American Force: Dangers, Delusions, and Dilemmas in National Security* (New York: Columbia University Press, 2012), 186.

3. THE U.S. ALLIANCE WITH PAKISTAN, 1981–1988

1. Carter administration National Security Council staff member Thomas Thornton, quoted in Dennis Kux, *Disenchanted Allies: The United States and Pakistan, 1947–2000* (Washington, DC: Woodrow Wilson Center Press, 2001), 245.

2. Don Oberdorfer, *From the Cold War to a New Era: The United States and the Soviet Union, 1983–1991,* updated ed. (Baltimore: Johns Hopkins University Press, 1998), 235.

3. Raymond Garthoff, *Détente and Confrontation: American-Soviet Relations from Nixon to Reagan,* revised ed. (Washington, DC: Brookings Institution Press, 1994), 977–1075.

4. Kux, *Disenchanted Allies,* 252. The administration persuaded the Saudi royal family to match the U.S. contribution to the insurgency dollar for dollar, which it did for the duration of the war. China and Egypt also provided arms to the rebels. Steve Coll, *Ghost Wars: The Secret History of the CIA, Afghanistan, and Bin Laden, from the Soviet Invasion to September 10, 2001* (New York: Penguin Books, 2004), 58.

5. White House National Security Decision Directive Number 166: "U.S. Policy, Programs and Strategy in Afghanistan," March 27, 1985, p. 1. Obtained from online database of National Security Decision Directives maintained by the Federation of American Scientists, Intelligence Resource Program: www.fas.org. See also Coll, *Ghost Wars,* 58, 89, 102, 151, 216.

6. Coll, *Ghost Wars,* 150.

7. Artemy M. Kalinovsky, *A Long Goodbye: The Soviet Withdrawal from Afghanistan* (Cambridge, MA: Harvard University Press, 2011), 1.

8. Ian Talbot, *Pakistan: A Modern History* (New York: Palgrave Macmillan, 2009), 185–244.

9. Kux, *Disenchanted Allies,* 234; and Robert G. Wirsing, *Pakistan's Security Under Zia, 1977–1988: The Policy Imperatives of a Peripheral Asian State* (New York: St. Martin's Press, 1991), 105.

10. Craig Baxter, "The United States and Pakistan: The Zia Era and the Afghan Connection," in *Friendly Tyrants: An American Dilemma,* ed. Daniel Pipes and Adam Garfinkle (New York: St. Martin's Press, 1991), 484–89.

11. Kux, *Disenchanted Allies,* 244.

12. Quoted in Kux, *Disenchanted Allies,* 245.

13. Kux, *Disenchanted Allies,* 51–114; and "U.S. Signs Agreements of Cooperation with Turkey, Iran, and Pakistan," *Department of State Bulletin,* 40, No. 1030 (March 23, 1959): 416–17.

14. Kux, *Disenchanted Allies,* 115–77, 178–99.

15. Kux, *Disenchanted Allies,* 219.

16. Kux, *Disenchanted Allies,* 235; Warren H. Donnelly, "Pakistan's Nuclear Activities: A Chronology of Four Eras," *Congressional Research Service,* March 8, 1987, p. 19; and Richard P. Cronin, "Pakistan's Nuclear Program: U.S. Foreign Policy Considerations," *Congressional Research Service Issue Brief,* Updated January 13, 1988, p. 6.

17. Adrian Levy and Catherine Scott-Clark, *Deception: Pakistan, the United States and the Global Nuclear Weapons Conspiracy* (London: Atlantic Books, 2007), 35, 54–55.

18. Kux, *Disenchanted Allies*, 236, 239.

19. President Jimmy Carter, 1980 State of the Union Address, Jan. 23, 1980, Jimmy Carter Presidential Library website: http://www.jimmycarterlibrary.gov/documents/speeches /su8ojec.phtml.

20. Kux, *Disenchanted Allies*, 252; and Garthoff, *Détente and Confrontation*, 1054–75.

21. Quoted in Kux, *Disenchanted Allies*, 246–47.

22. Wirsing, *Pakistan's Security Under Zia*, 38–39.

23. Quoted in John M. Goshko, "U.S. Forging Ahead on Aid to Pakistan; U.S. Going Ahead with Aid That Zia Called 'Peanuts'; 'Peanuts' Remark by Zia Dismissed by Carter Aides," *Washington Post*, January 19, 1980; and William Branigan, "Pakistan Seeks Billions in U.S. Aid," *Washington Post*, January 23, 1980.

24. Kux, *Disenchanted Allies*, 250, 255.

25. U.S. House of Representatives, Committee on Foreign Affairs, *Congress and Foreign Policy 1981* (Washington, DC: U.S. Government Printing Office, 1982), 107.

26. Kux, *Disenchanted Allies*, 259; and Central Intelligence Agency, Directorate of Intelligence, Secret Intelligence Assessment, "Pakistan-United States: Dynamics of the Relationship," September 1985, in *NSA United*, No. 531, http://nsarchive.gwu.edu/nukevault /ebb531-U.S.-Pakistan-Nuclear-Relations,-1984–1985/, Posted October 14, 2015, Doc. 16, p. 1.

27. The follow-on six-year package was split 43–57 in terms of the proportions of military and economic assistance, respectively. Kux, *Disenchanted Allies*, 282–83.

28. Kux, *Disenchanted Allies*, 308.

29. In an October 1984 national security decision directive (NSDD 147) setting out U.S. policy toward India and Pakistan, Reagan prescribed actions to address the nuclear issue only. Secret National Security Decision Directive 147, "U.S. Policy towards India and Pakistan," Oct. 11, 1984, in *DNSA CIA*, Doc. CO01568, p. 1, 3. Similarly, in a July 1986 memo to President Reagan, Secretary of State George Shultz referred to the nuclear proliferation issue alone as a "serious threat to [the U.S.-Pakistan] relationship." Confidential State Department Memorandum from Secretary of State George F. Shultz to President Reagan, "Your Meeting with Pakistan Prime Minister Mohammed Khan Junejo (July 16, 10:30)," in *DNSA Nuclear*, Doc. NP02306, p. 1.

30. Secret State Department Memorandum from Secretary of State George P. Shultz to President Ronald W. Reagan, "How Do We Make Use of the Zia Visit to Protect Our Strategic Interests in the Face of Pakistan's Nuclear Weapons Activities," Nov. 26, 1982, in *DNSA CIA*, Doc. CO01227, pp. 1, 4.

31. Statement of Robert A. Peck, Deputy Assistant Secretary of State, Bureau of Near Eastern and South Asian Affairs, Department of State, before the Subcommittee on Asia and Pacific Affairs, House Foreign Affairs Committee, March 5, 1987, in *DNSA Afghanistan*, Doc. AF01942, p. 11.

32. Quoted in Zulfikar Ali Bhutto, *The Myth of Independence* (Karachi: Oxford University Press, 1969), 153; Wirsing, *Pakistan's Security Under Zia*, 113.

33. Richard B. Cronin, "Pakistan's Nuclear Program: U.S. Foreign Policy Considerations," *Congressional Research Service Issue Brief* no. IB87227, Updated January 13, 1988, pp. 8–9.

34. Secret National Security Council Memorandum from Shirin Tahir Kheli to Robert Oakley, "Dealing with Pakistan's Nuclear Program: A U.S. Strategy," July 23, 1987, in *NSA Pakistan's*, No. 446, http://nsarchive.gwu.edu/nukevault/ebb446/, Posted November 22, 2013, Doc. 9, p. 4.

35. Joseph S. Nye Jr., "Pakistan's Bomb Could Kill Us All," *Washington Post*, November 9, 1986, H1. Or Rabinowitz and Nicholas Miller argue that U.S. nuclear bargaining with Pakistan during the 1980s was successful insofar as the Reagan administration dissuaded Zia from violating the most crucial of its nuclear "redlines," namely, conducting a hot nuclear test. The evidence presented in this chapter demonstrates that Rabinowitz and Miller damn the administration with faint praise: in light of the lopsided balances of dependence and commitment that favored the United States over Pakistan during the Afghanistan war and the strong U.S. interest in counterproliferation, tougher bargaining by the White House should have been able to secure more extensive Pakistani nuclear concessions. Or Rabinowitz and Nicholas L. Miller, "Keeping the Bombs in the Basement: U.S. Nonproliferation Policy toward Israel, South Africa, and Pakistan," *International Security* 40, no. 1 (Summer 2015): 78–83. Their argument is also countered by the U.S. intelligence community's discovery in 1983 that China had provided Pakistan with a complete design for a 20-kiloton nuclear bomb, which Beijing had already tested at Lap Nor. This rendered unnecessary a Pakistani hot test of the weapon. Jeffrey T. Richelson, *Spying on the Bomb: American Nuclear Intelligence from Nazi Germany to Iran and North Korea* (New York: Norton, 2007), 342.

36. U.S. Arms Control and Disarmament Agency, *World Military Expenditures and Arms Transfers 1990* (Washington, DC: U.S. Government Printing Office, 1992), 36, 38, 76, 85.

37. President Jimmy Carter, 1980 State of the Union Address, January 23, 1980. See also White House National Security Decision Directive Number 166, p. 1.

38. Central Intelligence Agency, Directorate of Intelligence Secret Intelligence Appraisal, "Pakistan: Tough Choices on Afghanistan [REDACTED]," July 1982, in *DNSA CIA*, Doc. CO01178, p. 1. A September 1983 CIA report claimed that Pakistani leaders worried that, even short of an all-out Indo-Soviet military invasion of Pakistan, the two adversaries would attempt to "neutralize and dismember Pakistan [via their deployment of] a combination of external military pressure and subversive meddling in Pakistan's unstable domestic politics." Central Intelligence Agency, Directorate of Intelligence, "Pakistan: Steadfastness on Afghanistan," September 14, 1983, in *DNSA CIA*, Doc. CO01340, p. 1.

39. Central Intelligence Agency, Directorate of Intelligence, Secret Intelligence Appraisal, "Current Soviet Strategy on Afghanistan," September 2, 1987, in *DNSA CIA*, Doc. CO01957, p. 2; and Wirsing, *Pakistan's Security Under Zia*, 35.

40. CIA Secret Special National Intelligence Estimate, SNIE 32–82, "Pakistan: The Next Years," November 8, 1982, Key Judgments, p. 9, in *DNSA CIA*, Doc. CO01217. See also Secret Cable from U.S. Ambassador to Pakistan Ronald Spiers to Secretary of State George Shultz, "Pakistan Nuclear Issue: Meeting With General Zia," October 17, 1982,

in *NSA New*, Doc. 14A, p. 3; and Unclassified Memorandum from Hugh Montgomery, Director, Bureau of Intelligence and Research, U.S. Department of State, to Ambassador Ronald Spiers, February 17, 1984, enclosing "India-Pakistan Pressures for Nuclear Proliferation," INR Report 778-AR, Feb. 10, 1984, in *NSA New*, Doc. 18, p. ii.

41. CIA, "Pakistan-United States: Dynamics of the Relationship," 14. According to Levy and Scott-Clark, Pakistan's nuclear program was also paradoxically dependent on continued U.S. aid. They claim that, according to Saudi and European intelligence sources, as well as a British diplomat who was privy to the relevant intelligence, Pakistan's secret uranium enrichment operation was able to make forward progress during the 1980s only by skimming hundreds of millions of dollars from the U.S. aid that was flowing into the country for the ostensible purposes of sponsoring the Afghan insurgency and supporting Pakistan's economic development. Levy and Scott-Clark, *Deception*, 125–26.

42. CIA, "Pakistan-United States: Dynamics of the Relationship," 13.

43. "It is even possible that a US aid cutoff would force Zia to resign or be removed by a military coup." CIA, "Pakistan-United States: Dynamics of the Relationship," 17.

44. Confidential Briefing Memorandum from Roberts Owen to Office of Deputy Secretary of State Warren Christopher, "U.S. Obligations under the 1959 U.S.-Pakistan Agreement of Cooperation," January 23, 1980, in *DNSA Afghanistan*, Doc. AF00819, pp. 1–2.

45. Department of State Telegram from U.S. Embassy in Islamabad to the Secretary of State, "Zia's Remarks to US Newsmen on US Aid Offer, Bilateral Agreement," January 18, 1980, in *DNSA Nuclear*, Doc. NP01720, p. 3; and Wirsing, *Pakistan's Security Under Zia*, 107.

46. CIA, "Pakistan-United States: Dynamics of the Relationship," 12.

47. Beginning in 1985, Zia slightly loosened his tight grip on Pakistani politics by agreeing to hold national parliamentary elections, appointing a new prime minister, Mohammed Khan Junejo, and lifting martial law. Kux, *Disenchanted Allies*, 279–80.

48. For examples of the U.S. intelligence community warning of possible Pakistani defection, see Central Intelligence Agency, Directorate of Intelligence, Secret Intelligence Memorandum, "Pakistan: Challenges in the Next Year," July 20, 1984, in *DNSA CIA*, Doc. CO01512, pp. 5–6; Central Intelligence Agency, Directorate of Intelligence, Top Secret Intelligence Appraisal, "Pakistan: Soviet Policy Options," August 28, 1984, in *DNSA CIA*, Doc. CO01525, p. 3; and Statement of Deputy Assistant Secretary of Defense for Near Eastern and South Asian Affairs, Robert H. Pelletreau Jr., before the Subcommittee on Asian and Pacific Affairs, Committee on Foreign Affairs, U.S. House of Representatives, March 5, 1987, in *DNSA Afghanistan*, Doc. AF01941, p. 19. On Pakistan's low likelihood of defection, see Claiborne Pell, "Get Tough with Pakistan," *Washington Post*, August 5, 1987, A23; Stuart Auerbach, "Pakistan's Rejection of U.S. Aid Laid to American Miscues," *Washington Post*, March 17, 1980, A19; and John Glenn, "Pakistan's Bomb and the Mujaheddin; We Can Discourage One and Still Help the Other," *Washington Post*, November 4, 1987, A23.

49. Kux, *Disenchanted Allies*, 246; Wirsing, *Pakistan's Security Under Zia*, 35.

50. Department of State, Bureau of Intelligence and Research Report, "India-Pakistan: Pressures for Nuclear Proliferation," February 10, 1984, in *DNSA WMD*, Doc. WM00285, p. 5.

51. "Pakistan's Nuclear Activities: A Chronology of Four Eras," *Congressional Research Service Report*, March 8, 1987, in *DNSA Afghanistan*, Doc. AF01944, pp. 15–16; Letter from Sen. Alan Cranston to Secretary of State Alexander Haig, February 18, 1981, p. 1, in *DNSA Nuclear*, Doc. NP01864.

52. Quoted in Levy and Scott-Clark, *Deception*, 82.

53. Levy and Scott-Clark, *Deception*, 82; Kux, *Disenchanted Allies*, 256.

54. Kux, *Disenchanted Allies*, 260.

55. U.S. Department of State, Secret Talking Points, "Talking Points on Pakistan [Pakistani Nuclear Capabilities]," c. March 1, 1981, in *DNSA Nuclear*, Doc. NP01867, pp. 3–4.

56. U.S. Department of State, Bureau of Near Eastern and South Asian Affairs, Secret Report, "Near East and South Asia Overview—Nuclear Non-Proliferation Policy in NEA," Dec. 1, 1980, in *DNSA Nuclear*, Doc. NP01854, p. 8.

57. Senator Alan Cranston, remarks on the floor of United States Senate, June 25, 1984, in *Congressional Record—Senate*, 130, part 14 (June 26–28, 1984): 18564; "Cranston Says Pakistan Can Make Bomb," *New York Times*, June 21, 1984, A14.

58. Department of State Secret Cable from Secretary of State Alexander M. Haig Jr. to U.S. Embassy, Pakistan, "Buckley Briefing of House Foreign Affairs Committee on Pakistan," July 2, 1981, in *DNSA Afghanistan*, Doc. AF01216, pp. 2–3. During this period, the White House also met staunch opposition from senior officials in the CIA, Pentagon, and Office of Management and Budget to its plan to sell Pakistan cutting-edge F-16 fighter-bombers. Meanwhile, congressional resolutions barring the sale were only narrowly defeated in the SFRC and HFAC. Memorandum from Deputy CIA Director John N. McMahon to Deputy Secretary of Defense Frank Carlucci, "Risks Assessment of the Sale of AN/ALR-69 Radar Warning Receiver to Pakistan," Nov. 8, 1982, in *NSA New*, Doc. 15-B.

59. Staff Report to the Committee on Foreign Relations, U.S. Senate, *Nuclear Proliferation in South Asia: Containing the Threat*, August 1988, p. 10; Warren H. Donnelly, "Pakistan's Nuclear Activities: A Chronology of Four Cases," *Congressional Research Service Report*, March 8, 1987, in *DNSA Afghanistan*, Doc. AF01944, p. 13.

60. Terry Jones, Office of Nonproliferation and Export Policy, Department of State, to J. Devine et al., enclosing summaries of State Department cable traffic during 1981–1982 relating to démarches on attempted purchase of sensitive nuclear-related products, June 17, 1982, in *NSA New*, Doc. 12; Note for [NAME EXCISED] from [NAME EXCISED], "State/INR Request for Update of Pak SNIE and Assessment of Argentine Nuclear Program," June 4, 1982, in *NSA New*, Doc. 11.

61. Secret Cable from Ambassador Vernon Walters to Secretary of State Shultz, "My First Meeting with President Zia," July 5, 1982, in *NSA New*, Doc. 13A, p. 2.

62. Walters–Shultz cable, p. 2.

63. "Pakistan Nuclear Issue: Meeting With General Zia," p. 1; Secret Memorandum from Secretary of State George P. Shultz to President Ronald W. Reagan, "How Do We Make Use of Zia Visit to Protect Our Strategic Interests in the Face of Pakistan's Nuclear Weapons Activities," November 26, 1982, in *DNSA CIA*, Doc. CO01227, p. 2.

64. Shultz-Reagan memorandum, 3.

65. Top secret memorandum from Kenneth Adelman, director, Arms Control and Disarmament Agency, to the Assistant to the President for National Security Affairs, "Pakistan's Nuclear Weapons Program and U.S. Security Assistance," p. 1.

66. Quoted in Bernard Weinraub, "Zia Tells Reagan He Won't Build Atomic Weapon," *New York Times*, December 8, 1982, A1. During his visit, Zia also met with members of the SFRC. In response to "often-hostile queries regarding Pakistan's nuclear program and its human rights record," he professed that Pakistan was not pursuing nuclear weapons and was in the process of moving toward a more democratic political system. Kux, *Disenchanted Allies*, 268.

67. Secret State Department Briefing Paper, "The Pakistani Nuclear Program," June 23, 1983, in *DNSA Nuclear*, Doc. NP02057, 5–6; Levy and Scott-Clark, *Deception*, 93–94.

68. Levy and Scott-Clark also refer to another U.S. intelligence source, who affirmed that the Pakistani regime had already converted the highly enriched uranium transferred by Beijing into a metal core that would subsequently be inserted into a Chinese bomb design under construction by Pakistani scientists and technicians. Levy and Scott-Clark, *Deception*, 94.

69. Kux, *Disenchanted Allies*, 272–73.

70. Quoted in Levy and Scott-Clark, *Deception*, 106.

71. Levy and Scott-Clark, *Deception*, 101–2; Kux, *Disenchanted Allies*, 275.

72. Cranston-Glenn amendment wording quoted in Levy and Scott-Clark, *Deception*, 115.

73. Quoted in Levy and Scott-Clark, *Deception*, 116.

74. Levy and Scott-Clark, *Deception*, 106.

75. Quoted in Cranston, *Cong. Record—Senate*, 18564.

76. William E. Burrows and Robert Windrem, *Critical Mass: The Dangerous Race for Superweapons in a Fragmented World* (New York: Simon and Schuster, 1994), 74.

77. Burrows and Windrem, *Critical Mass*, 74.

78. Wirsing, *Pakistan's Security Under Zia*, 111–12.

79. Kux, *Disenchanted Allies*, 277; and Donnelly, "Pakistan's Nuclear Activities: A Chronology of Four Eras," 5.

80. Quoted in Levy and Scott-Clark, *Deception*, 116.

81. Cranston, *Congressional Record—Senate*, 18562–67.

82. Cranston, *Congressional Record—Senate*, 18564.

83. Cranston, *Congressional Record—Senate*, 18564.

84. Cranston, *Congressional Record—Senate*, 18564, 18566, 18567.

85. The three men were indicted by a federal grand jury on July 20. Levy and Scott-Clark, *Deception*, 109–10; and Rick Atkinson, "Use in Arms Feared; Nuclear Parts Sought by Pakistan," *Washington Post*, July 21, 1984, A1.

86. Quoted in Seymour M. Hersh, "Pakistani in U.S. Sought to Ship A-Bomb Trigger," *New York Times*, February 25, 1985, A1. At Vaid's arrest U.S. Customs officers seized letters connecting Vaid to high-ranking officials at the Pakistani Atomic Energy Commission (PAEC). In September, the Justice Department subpoenaed telex records that constituted smoking-gun evidence connecting Vaid to the PAEC. Vaid's arrest followed closely on the heels of the conviction of two Pakistani citizens by a Canadian court for also attempting to smuggle U.S.-made equipment that could be used in the production of nuclear weapons. Kux, *Disenchanted Allies*, 275.

87. Top Secret Agenda from Robert C. "Bud" McFarlane to President Reagan, "Meeting With the National Security Planning Group," August 30, 1984, in *DNSA CIA*, Doc. CO01528, p. 2.

88. U.S. National Security Council, National Security Planning Group, Top Secret Minutes, "Pakistan and NSDD-99 Work Program," September 7, 1984, in *DNSA CIA*, Doc. CO01547, pp. 2, 4, 5.

89. Letter from President Ronald W. Reagan to His Excellency, General Mohammed Zia-ul-Haq, President of the Islamic Republic of Pakistan, Sept. 12, 1984, in *NSA United*, No. 531, Doc. 7A, p. 2.

90. Letter from President Zia to President Reagan, November 7, 1984, in *NSA United*, Doc. 9, p. 5.

91. Zia–Reagan letter.

92. Poindexter handwritten notes in Zia–Reagan letter, p. 2.

93. "Pakistan Protests Afghan Airspace Violations," *United Press International*, March 14, 1985.

94. Levy and Scott-Clark, *Deception*, 114.

95. Hersh, "Pakistani in U.S."

96. Hersh, "Pakistani in U.S."

97. Hersh, "Pakistani in U.S.," 117–18.

98. Hersh, "Pakistani in U.S.," 116.

99. Section 670(a)(2) of the Foreign Assistance Act of 1961, as quoted in Non-Classified Presidential Determination No. 88–5, "Determination Pursuant to Section 670(a) and Section 620E(d) of the Foreign Assistance Act, as Amended," January 15, 1988, in *DNSA Nuclear*, Doc. NP02588.

100. Secret Briefing Memorandum from Assistant Secretary of State for Near Eastern and South Asian Affairs Richard Murphy to Secretary of State George Shultz, "Scope Paper: Official Visit of Pakistan Prime Minister Mohammed Khan Junejo—15–22 July 1986," circa July 1, 1986, in *DNSA Nuclear*, Doc. NP02308, pp. 2, 4.

101. Quoted in Don Oberdorfer, "Nuclear Issue Clouds Visit by Junejo; White House Warns Pakistan Leader against Weaponry," *Washington Post*, July 17, 1986, A21.

102. Stuart Auerbach, "U.S. Eyes Technology Agreement; Exports to Pakistan Tied to Weapons Ban," *Washington Post*, July 16, 1986, A19.

103. Quoted in Burrows and Windrem, *Critical Mass*, 76.

104. Adelman, "Pakistan's Nuclear Weapons Program and US Security Assistance," 1–3.

105. Levy and Scott-Clark, *Deception*, 147.

106. Quoted in Levy and Scott-Clark, *Deception*, 148.

107. Quoted in Levy and Scott-Clark, *Deception*, 148.

108. Bob Woodward, "Pakistan Reported Near Atom Arms Production; Acquisition of Weapon Could Halt U.S. Aid," *Washington Post*, November 4, 1986, A1.

109. Quoted in Levy and Scott-Clark, *Deception*, 167.

110. Levy and Scott-Clark, *Deception*, 167.

111. Unclassified State Department Cable from Kent Obee, U.S. Embassy, Pakistan to United States Information Agency, "Text Ambassador Deane R. Hinton's Speech on Nuclear Non-Proliferation at the Institute of Strategic Studies in Islamabad," circa Feb. 16, 1987, in *DNSA Nuclear*, Doc. NP02423, p. 7.

112. Kux, *Disenchanted Allies*, 284. Citing Khan's declaration, Senator Glenn dispatched a letter to President Reagan urging the suspension of all U.S. military aid to Pakistan pending "reliable assurances from the Pakistanis that they have ceased producing nuclear explosive materials." Quoted in David B. Ottaway, "Pakistan's Nuclear Intentions Called into Doubt; State Department Says U.S. Lacks 'Reliable Assurances' That Arms Production Isn't Planned," *Washington Post*, March 6, 1987, A29.

113. Zia interview in *Time*, March 30, 1987, 42, quoted in Kux, *Disenchanted Allies*, 285.

114. Prepared Statement of Robert A. Peck, Deputy Assistant Secretary of State, Bureau of Near Eastern and South Asian Affairs, Department of State, for the Subcommittee on Asian and Pacific Affairs of the Committee on Foreign Affairs, House of Representatives, "Foreign Assistance Legislation for Fiscal Years 1988–89 (Part Five)," hearings and markup, 100th Cong., 1st sess., February 25 and March 3, 4, 5, 11, 12, 17, and 18, 1987, p. 422.

115. Testimony of Robert A. Peck in above statement, p. 473.

116. Quoted in Steven R. Weisman, "Pakistan Stiffens on Atom Program," *New York Times*, March 22, 1987, A15.

117. Secret State Department Memorandum from Richard W. Murphy, Assistant Secretary for Near Eastern and South Asian Affairs, to Secretary of State George Shultz, "Action Plan on Pakistan Nuclear and Security Problems," date unknown, enclosed in Fred McGoldrick, Acting Director, Office of Nonproliferation and Export Policy, to John Negroponte, Assistant Secretary of State for Environment, Oceans, and Fisheries, "Pakistan," April 9, 1987, in *NSA New*, Doc. 23, p. 1.

118. Murphy–Shultz memorandum, 2.

119. Murphy–Shultz memorandum, 3.

120. Murphy–Shultz memorandum, 2, 3.

121. Murphy–Shultz memorandum, 4.

122. Don Oberdorfer, "Senate Committee Votes Pakistan Aid; Funds Approved Despite Nuclear Arms Project," *Washington Post*, April 24, 1987, A1.

123. Adam Scheinman and Warren Donnelly, "Pakistan: Non-Proliferation Conditions for Future U.S. Economic and Military Aid," *Congressional Research Service Issue Brief*, August 12, 1987, pp. 4–5.

124. Quoted in Oberdorfer, "Senate Committee"; and Elaine Sciolino, "Pakistan Aid Foes Vow Fight," *New York Times*, April 25, 1987, A5.

125. Levy and Scott-Clark, *Deception*, 156–57; and Don Oberdorfer, "Pakistani Native Charged with Nuclear-Export Plot; Alleged Effort to Aid Weapons Program Triggers Demand to Cut off U.S. Aid," *Washington Post*, July 15, 1987, A19.

126. Quoted in Michael R. Gordon, "Pakistani Seized by U.S. in a Plot on A-Arms Alloy," *New York Times*, July 15, 1987, A1

127. Gordon, "Pakistani Seized"; and Levy and Scott-Clark, *Deception*, 156–57.

128. Barbara Crossette, "Pakistan Denies Any Link to Atom Arms Plot in U.S.," *New York Times*, July 17, 1987, A2; Don Oberdorfer, "2 Indicted in Pakistani Nuclear-Export Case; U.S. May Request Extradition of 1 Suspect," *Washington Post*, July 29, 1987: A10; and Don Oberdorfer, "U.S. Asks Pakistan to Stop Producing Bomb-Grade Uranium; Outside Inspections Also Requested," *Washington Post*, July 23, 1987, A37.

129. Quoted in Don Oberdorfer, "Lawmakers Say Aid to Pakistan Is in Jeopardy; Two Senators Reportedly Reconsider Their Votes Following Nuclear Export Charges," *Washington Post*, July 22, 1987: A15.

130. Letter from Don Bonker, Chair, Subcommittee on International Economic Policy and Trade of the House Foreign Affairs Committee, and Dante B. Fascall, Chair, House Foreign Affairs Committee, U.S. House of Representatives, to President Ronald Reagan, July 22, 1987, in *NSA Pakistan's*, Doc. 10.

131. Quoted in Hearing before the Subcommittees on Asian and Pacific Affairs and on International Economic Policy and Trade of the Committee on Foreign Affairs, House of Representatives, "Pakistan's Illegal Nuclear Procurement in the United States," 100th Cong, 1st Session, July 22, 1987, p. 1.

132. Quoted in Gordon, "Pakistani Seized."

133. Secret Memorandum from Kenneth Adelman, Director, United States Arms Control and Disarmament Agency, to Michael Armacost, Undersecretary of State for Political Affairs, "Your Meeting with Ambassador Marker," July 14, 1987, in *NSA Pakistan's*, Doc. 4.

134. Secret Memorandum from Kenneth Adelman, Director, Arms Control and Disarmament Agency, to Michael Armacost, Undersecretary of State for Political Affairs, "The Pakistani Procurement Cases," July 23, 1987, in *NSA Pakistan's*, Doc. 8. Also see Note 34, Kheli–Oakley memorandum, "Dealing with Pakistan's Nuclear Program," 1, 4.

135. Unnamed administration official quoted in Michael R. Gordon, "U.S. Pressing Pakistan on Export Plot," *New York Times*, July 16, 1987, A3.

136. Quoted in Gordon, "U.S. Pressing Pakistan."

137. Hearing, "Pakistan's Illegal Nuclear Procurement in the United States," pp. 13, 15

138. Einsel testimony recalled by Barlow in Levy and Scott-Clark, *Deception*, 160; Barlow is quoted in Seymour M. Hersh, "On the Nuclear Edge," *New Yorker*, March 29, 1993, 35.

139. Quoted in Levy and Scott-Clark, *Deception*, 161–62.

140. Quoted in Levy and Scott-Clark, *Deception*, 162.

141. Levy and Scott-Clark, *Deception*, 162–64. According to these authors, a similar incident occurred "just before" the Einsel/Barlow blow-up, during a congressional

briefing on Pakistan conducted by Undersecretary of State for Security Assistance, Science, and Technology William Schneider. At the briefing, Assistant Secretary Robert Gallucci was disturbed by inaccuracies in Schneider's presentation and proceeded to articulate "a much darker description of the situation regarding that country" (163).

142. S. I. Waxman, "Foreign Aid Packaged for Fiscal '88; House Subcommittee Would Penalize Pakistan for Nuclear Activities," *Washington Post*, July 30, 1987, A17.

143. Quoted in Waxman, "Foreign Aid."

144. Text of Senate Resolution 266 obtained from: https://www.congress.gov/bill/100th -congress/senate-resolution/266. The House passed the same resolution on August 2. Text of H.R. 239 obtained from: https://www.congress.gov/bill/100th-congress/house -resolution/239. Also, on July 29, Arshad Pervez and Inam ul-Haq were indicted by a federal grand jury. Michael R. Gordon, "2 Charged in Plan on Pakistan's Bomb," *New York Times*, July 29, 1987, A11.

145. Department of State Secret Telegram to the Embassy in Islamabad, "Under Secretary Armacost Meeting with Zia," August 7, 1987, in *NSA Pakistan's*, Doc. 14C, p. 5.

146. Department of State secret telegram, 5–10. Armacost mentioned that the available evidence "suggested a long relationship between General Inam and the Khan research labs" (p. 5).

147. Department of State secret telegram, 12.

148. Department of State secret telegram, 6.

149. Department of State secret telegram, 10–11.

150. Michael Getler and Richard M. Weintraub, "Pakistan Strikes Defiant Tone on Nation's Nuclear Program; Prime Minister Rules Out Further Assurances to U.S.," *Washington Post*, October 13, 1987, A16.

151. Quoted in Kux, *Disenchanted Allies*, 285–86.

152. David K. Shipler, "U.S. Presses Pakistan on Atom Plants," *New York Times*, September 22, 1987, A15.

153. Quoted in Don Oberdorfer, "U.S. Aid to Pakistan Ends as Waiver of Nuclear Laws Expires," *Washington Post*, October 1, 1987, A23.

154. Testimony of Hon. Richard T. Kennedy, Ambassador at Large and Special Advisor to the Secretary of State on Non-Proliferation and Nuclear Energy Affairs, before the Subcommittees on Arms Control, International Security, and Science; and Asian and Pacific Affairs; and International Economic Policy and Trade, of the Committee on Foreign Affairs, House of Representatives, "Pakistan and United States Nuclear Nonproliferation Policy," Hearing, 100th Congress, 1st Session, Oct. 22, 1987 (Washington, DC: Government Printing Office, 1988), pp. 3, 4.

155. Testimony of Hon. Richard T. Kennedy, p. 3. Levy and Scott-Clark note that, contrary to this assurance, in early 1985 a select group of senior Pakistani officials had begun to explore the possible sale of their country's nuclear technology to other states, particularly Iran, Syria, and Libya. Then, in 1987, Zia and A. Q. Khan laid the groundwork for a sale to Iran of material for the construction of two thousand nuclear centrifuges. Zia's army chief, Gen. K. M. Arif, later explained in an interview that

Pakistan's leaders were unconcerned about the consequences of possible discovery of this initiative by the United States: "Having seen the US so flexible in the past, everyone doubted that it would sanction us at all." Quoted in Levy and Scott-Clark, *Deception*, 133, 142.

156. Testimony of Hon. Richard T. Kennedy, p. 34.

157. Testimony of Hon. Richard T. Kennedy, p. 34.

158. Testimony of Hon. Richard T. Kennedy, p. 35.

159. Testimony of Hon. Richard T. Kennedy, pp. 46–47.

160. Testimony of Hon. Richard T. Kennedy, pp. 40–41. In a November 4 op-ed in the *Washington Post*, Senator Glenn proposed that Congress only grant a six-year waiver of the Symington Amendment if Pakistan agreed to provide the United States with reliable assurances "backed up by tough means of verification (with on-site inspections if necessary)" that Pakistan had stopped producing highly enriched uranium. Short of this, Glenn urged Congress to suspend military aid to Pakistan and only provide economic aid on a year-by-year basis. Glenn, "Pakistan's Bomb and the Mujaheddin."

161. Secret Memorandum from Kenneth Adelman, Director, United States Arms Control and Disarmament Organization, to Michael Armacost, Undersecretary of State for Political Affairs, "A Strategy on Pakistan," in *NSA Pakistan's*, Doc. 20, p. 1.

162. Secret Memorandum from Kenneth Adelman, Director, United States Arms Control and Disarmament Organization, to President Ronald W. Reagan, "Certification on Pakistan," in *NSA Pakistan's*, Doc. 22.

163. Letter from President Reagan to The Honorable Jim Wright, Speaker, United States House of Representatives, December 17, 1987, in *NSA Pakistan's*, Doc. 24, p. 1.

164. Reagan–Wright letter, pp. 1–2.

165. Don Oberdorfer, "Conferees Won't Penalize Pakistan; Role in Afghanistan Overrides Atom Issue," *Washington Post*, December 18, 1987, A10. Congress's passage of new aid for Pakistan precipitated yet another dissenting memo to Armacost from the ACDA leadership. This time, Acting Director Norman Wulf pleaded that the president should hold off on the sale to Pakistan of advanced Airborne Warning and Control System (AWACS) surveillance aircraft until Zia stopped enriching uranium beyond 5 percent. Secret Memorandum from Norman A. Wulf, Acting Director, United States Arms Control and Disarmament Agency, to Michael Armacost, Undersecretary of State for Political Affairs, "Next Steps on Pakistan—Solarz and Symington," December 21, 1987, in *NSA Pakistan's*, Doc. 25, pp. 1–5.

166. Hedrick Smith, "A Bomb Ticks in Pakistan," *New York Times*, March 6, 1988, F38.

167. Secret Memorandum from Morton I. Abramowitz, Director, State Department Bureau of Intelligence and Research, to Michael Armacost, Undersecretary of State for Political Affairs, "Pakistan—Pervez Case and Solarz Amendment," December 29, 1987, in *NSA Pakistan's*, Doc. 26, p. 3.

168. Abramowitz–Armacost memorandum, pp. 1, 2.

169. Neil A. Lewis, "U.S. Unsure Pakistan Seeks 2d A-Fuel Plant," *New York Times*, January 10, 1988, A8.

170. "Presidential Determination No. 88–5 of January 15, 1988: Determination Pursuant to Section 670(a) and Section 620E(d) of the Foreign Assistance Act, as Amended," *Federal Register* 83, no. 24 (February 5, 1988), 3325.

171. "White House Statement on Continuation of Military Aid to Pakistan, January 15, 1988," *Public Papers of the President of the United States, Ronald Reagan, 1988*, Book I (Washington, DC: Government Printing Office, 1990), p. 46.

172. "The Implications of the Arshad Pervez Case for U.S. Policy toward Pakistan," Hearing before the Subcommittees on Asian and Pacific Affairs and on International Economic Policy and Trade of the Committee on Foreign Affairs, House of Representatives, 100th Congress, 2nd Session, February 17, 1988 (Washington, DC; Government Printing Office, 1989), p. 34.

173. Levy and Scott-Clark, *Deception*, 171–72.

174. David B. Ottaway, "Pakistan May Lose U.S. Aid; 'No Atom Bomb' Certification Is Unlikely," *Washington Post*, January 28, 1989, A1.

175. Levy and Scott-Clark, *Deception*, 173.

176. See Rabinowitz and Miller, "Keeping the Bombs in the Basement," 50; Baxter, "The United States and Pakistan," 505; Samina Ahmed, "Pakistan's Nuclear Weapons Program: Turning Points and Nuclear Choices," *International Security* 23, no. 4 (Spring 1999): 184; and Glenn Chafetz, "The Political Psychology of the Nuclear Nonproliferation Regime," *Journal of Politics* 57, no. 3 (August 1995): 756.

177. Kux, *Disenchanted Allies*, 343–48.

178. Kux, *Disenchanted Allies*, 351–56.

179. Levy and Scott-Clark, *Deception*, chaps. 12–20 (pp. 214–449); Alexander H. Montgomery, "Ringing in Proliferation: How to Dismantle an Atomic Bomb Network," *International Security* 30, no. 2 (Fall 2005): 171; and Bruce Riedel, *Deadly Embrace: Pakistan, America, and the Future of the Global Jihad* (Washington, DC: Brookings Institution Press, 2011), 72–74.

4. THE U.S. ALLIANCE WITH IRAQ, 1982–1988

1. Michael R. Gordon and Bernard E. Trainor, *The Generals' War: The Inside Story of the Conflict in the Gulf* (New York: Little, Brown, 1995); and Michael R. Gordon and Bernard E. Trainor, *Cobra II: The Inside Story of the Invasion and Occupation of Iraq* (New York: Vintage, 2006).

2. Pierre Razoux, *The Iran-Iraq War*, trans. Nicholas Elliott (Cambridge, MA: Belknap Press, 2015), 61.

3. Razoux, *Iran-Iraq War*, 62.

4. Geoff Simons, *Iraq: From Sumer to Saddam* (London: Palgrave Macmillan, 1994), 274; and Williamson Murray and Kevin Woods, *The Iran-Iraq War: A Military and Strategic History* (Cambridge, UK: Cambridge University Press, 2014), 12.

5. Murray and Woods, *Iran-Iraq War*, 49, 100–31; and Razoux, *Iran-Iraq War*, 10, 22–44, 121–46, 216.

6. Razoux, *Iran-Iraq War*, 217–20, 319–31, 345–78, 420–32.

7. Razoux, *Iran-Iraq War*, 439–72.

8. Kenneth M. Pollack, *The Threatening Storm: The Case for Invading Iraq* (New York: Random House, 2002), 7–11; and Kanan Makiya, *Republic of Fear: The Politics of Modern Iraq* (Berkeley: University of California Press, 1998).

9. Bruce W. Jentleson, *With Friends Like These: Reagan, Bush, and Saddam, 1982–1990* (New York: Norton, 1994), 31; and Richard M. Preece, *United States–Iraqi Relations*, Congressional Research Service (CRS) Report for Congress (Washington, DC: Library of Congress, July 30, 1986), Report No. 86-142F, pp. 9–10.

10. Preece, *United States–Iraqi Relations*, 19–21; Razoux, *Iran-Iraq War*, 69.

11. Preece, *United States–Iraqi Relations*, 22–23.

12. Pollack, *Threatening Storm*, 15–16; and Stephen M. Walt, *Revolution and War* (Ithaca, NY: Cornell University Press, 1996), 212–16.

13. Pollack, *Threatening Storm*, 16.

14. Memorandum for Geoffrey Kemp, Senior Staff, National Security Council, from Henry S. Rowen, Chairman, National Intelligence Council, July 20, 1982, in *Becoming Enemies: U.S.-Iran Relations and the Iran-Iraq War, 1979–1988*, eds. James G. Blight, Janet M. Lang, Hussein Banai, Malcolm Byrne, and John Tirman (New York: Rowman & Littlefield, 2012), Appendix 2, Doc. 3-3, pp. 311–12.

15. George P. Shultz, *Turmoil and Triumph: My Years as Secretary of State* (New York: Charles Scribner's Sons, 1993), 235, 240.

16. Blight et al., *Becoming Enemies*, 108.

17. Murray and Woods, *Iran-Iraq War*, 33–35.

18. Quoted in Murray and Woods, *Iran-Iraq War*, 205.

19. Jimmy Carter, "Situation in Iraq and Iran, Remarks Concerning the Conflict, September 24, 1980," American Presidency Project website, ed. Gerhard Peters and John T. Wooley, University of California at Santa Barbara: http://www.presidency.ucsb.edu/ws/?pid=45129.

20. Secret cable from Secretary of State Alexander M. Haig Jr. to U.S. Interests Section, Iraq, "Secretary's Message to Iraqi Foreign Minister," April 8, 1981, in *DNSA Iraqgate*, Doc. IG00046; and "Secret Cable from William L. Eagleton, U.S. Interests Section, Iraq, to the Secretary of State, "Meetings in Baghdad with Foreign Minister Hammadi," April 12, 1981, in *DNSA Iraqgate*, Doc. IG00047.

21. "The Israeli Raid on Iraqi Nuclear Facilities: Statement by the Representative at the United Nations (Kirkpatrick) before the UN Security Council, June 19, 1981," and "Resolution 487 (1981), Adopted by the UN Security Council, June 19, 1981: Condemnation of the Israeli Raid on the Iraqi Nuclear Reactor," in *American Foreign Policy Current Documents, 1981* (Washington, DC: Department of State, 1984), 687–88, 689.

22. Seymour M. Hersh, "U.S. Secretly Gave Aid to Iraq Early in Its War against Iran," *New York Times*, January 26, 1992, A1; and Trita Parsi, *The Treacherous Alliance: The Secret Dealings of Israel, Iran, and the U.S.* (New Haven, CT: Yale University Press, 2007), 105–6.

23. Jentleson, *With Friends Like These*, 42. In December 1979, the Carter administration had placed Iraq on the newly inaugurated terrorism list, which was mandated by the 1979 Export Administration Act. See Bernard Gwertzman, "U.S. May Let Iraq Buy Jets despite Terrorism Questions," *New York Times,* August 6, 1980.

24. Associated Press, December 18, 1982.

25. Unnamed administration official quoted in Hersh, "U.S. Secretly Gave Aid."

26. Howard Teicher and Gayle Radley Teicher, *Twin Pillars to Desert Storm: America's Flawed Vision in the Middle East From Nixon to Bush* (New York: William Morrow, 1993), 207.

27. Hersh, "U.S. Secretly Gave Aid"; Murray Waas, "What Washington Gave Saddam for Christmas," in *The Iraq War Reader: History, Documents, Opinions*, ed. Micah L. Sifry and Christopher Cerf (New York: Touchstone, 2003), 30–32; Confidential Cable from William A. Brown, United States Embassy, Israel, to the Secretary of State and Secretary of Defense, May 24, 1982, in *DNSA Iraqgate*, Doc. IG00072. Importantly, the Arms Export Control Act of 1976 prohibited the transfer of U.S.-supplied arms to a third party in the absence of congressional notification. Steven Hurst, *The United States and Iraq since 1979: Hegemony, Oil, and War* (Edinburgh: Edinburgh University Press, 2009), 45.

28. Confidential Cable, William L. Eagleton Jr., to State Department, "Sale of Hughes Helicopters to Iraq," December 16, 1982, in *DNSA Iraqgate*, Doc. IG00085; and Confidential Cable, George P. Shultz to United States Embassy, Italy, "Hughes Civil Helicopter Sale to Iraq," February 18, 1983, in *DNSA Iraqgate*, Doc. IG00111.

29. For Official Use Only, Letter, from David W. Culver, Director, Program Development Division, Export Credits, United States Department of Agriculture, Foreign Agricultural Service, to Robert S. Watson, Secretary, National Advisory Council on International Monetary and Financial Policies, Department of the Treasury, Dec. 18, 1982, in *DNSA Iraqgate*, Doc. IG00087; and Minutes, Extract, U.S. National Advisory Council on International Monetary and Financial Policies, "National Advisory Council Staff Committee, Minutes Meeting 82-52, 21 December 1982," December 21, 1982, in *DNSA Iraqgate*, Doc. IG0088.

30. Kenneth R. Timmerman, *The Death Lobby: How the West Armed Iraq* (Boston: Houghton Mifflin, 1991), 138–39; and Mark Phythian, *Arming Iraq: How the U.S. and Britain Secretly Built Saddam's War Machine* (Boston: Northeastern University Press, 1997), 36.

31. United States General Accounting Office (GAO), Testimony, Statement of Allan I. Mendelowitz, Director, International Trade, Energy, and Finance Issues, National Security and International Affairs Division, before the Subcommittee on Department Operations, Research, and Foreign Agriculture, Committee of Agriculture, House of Representatives, "Iraq's Participation in the Commodity Credit Corporation's GSM-102/103 Export Credit Guarantee Programs," March 14, 1991, p. 14, GAO website: https://www.gao.gov/products/143407.

32. Secret Cable from George P. Shultz to United States Embassy, Korea (Republic) et al., "Staunching Iran's Imports of Western Arms and Urging Restraint on Iraq," December 14, 1983, in *DNSA Iraqgate*, Doc. IG00152. In the recollection of then–Secretary of Defense Caspar Weinberger, Operation Staunch proved "an excellent means for

slowing the flood of weapons to Iran to a more tolerable level." Caspar Weinberger, *Fighting for Peace: Seven Critical Years in the Pentagon* (New York: Warner Books, 1990), 422. On the effectiveness of Operation Staunch, also see Kenneth Timmerman, "Europe's Arms Pipeline to Iran," *The Nation*, July 18–25, 1987: 47.

33. State Department Secret Cables from U.S. Embassy, United Kingdom to State Department, "Rumsfeld Mission: December 20 Meeting with Iraqi President Saddam Hussein" (1 of 6)," December 21, 1983, p. 2; and "Rumsfeld Mission: December 20 Meeting with Iraqi President Saddam Hussein (3 of 6)," p. 2, in *DNSA Iraqgate*, Doc. IG00156; and Hurst, *United States and Iraq*, 46–47.

34. Timmerman, *Death Lobby*, 142.

35. State Department Unclassified Action Memorandum from Acting Assistant Secretary of State for Near Eastern and South Asian Affairs David T. Schneider and Assistant Secretary of State for Political-Military Affairs Jonathan T. Howe to the Secretary of State, "Easing Restrictions on Exports to Iraq," January 30, 1984, in *DNSA Iraqgate*, Doc. IG00168, p. 5; and State Department Confidential Memorandum from Deputy Assistant Secretary of State for Near Eastern and South Asian Affairs Arnold Raphel to Director, Near Eastern and South Asian Affairs, Northern Gulf Affairs Peter Burleigh, "U.S. Heavy Trucks for Iraq," April 22, 1986, in *DNSA Iraqgate*, Doc. IG00324.

36. Quoted in Hurst, *United States and Iraq*, 47.

37. In June, the Eximbank also approved a massive package of $484 million in credits to subsidize the construction of a $1.1 billion pipeline from Iraq to Jordan, but Saddam later scuttled the project for fear that the Israelis would sabotage it. Jentleson, *With Friends Like These*, 42–43, 47; Timmerman, *Death Lobby*, 218–19; GAO, Statement of Allan I. Mendelowitz, "Iraq's Participation," p. 12.

38. Jentleson, *With Friends Like These*, 47–48; Razoux, *Iran-Iraq War*, 320–24; and Dilip Hiro, *The Longest War: The Iran-Iraq Military Conflict* (New York: Routledge, 1991), 160.

39. National Security Council Note from Alton G. Keel to William A. Cockell, "Iran Game Plan," November 21, 1986, in *DNSA Iraqgate*, Doc. IG00363.

40. State Department Confidential Cable from David G. Newton, U.S. Embassy, Iraq, to Agriculture Department, Foreign Agricultural Service, "FAS Administrator Smith's Meeting with Iraq's Minister of Trade Hassan Ali," January 16, 1985, in *DNSA Iraqgate*, Doc. IG00236; GAO, Statement of Allan I. Mendelowitz, "Iraq's Participation," p. 12.

41. Timmerman, *Death Lobby*, 202.

42. Commerce Department Briefing Memorandum, "Visit of Iraqi Minister of Trade Dr. Mohammed Mahdi Salih, from 11:00 a.m. to 2:00 p.m. on August 26 at the Department of Commerce," August 26, 1987, in *DNSA Iraqgate*, Doc. IG00458, p. 3.

43. Quoted in U.S. Congress, Senate, Select Committee on Secret Military Assistance to Iran and the Nicaraguan Opposition and House, Select Committee to Investigate Covert Arms Transactions with Iran, *Iran-Contra Affair*, Report 100-216, 100th Congress, 1st Session, November 1987, pp. 160–61.

44. Hiro, *Longest War*, 216–17; Jentleson, *With Friends Like These*, 58; "Iran-Contra Hearings; Boland Amendments: What They Provided," *New York Times*, July 10, 1987, A9;

and Tim Weiner, *Legacy of Ashes: The History of the CIA* (New York: Anchor Books, 2008), 468.

45. Hurst, *United States and Iraq*, 62; Hiro, *Longest War*, 217–18; Central Intelligence Agency Cable from John N. McMahon to Director of Central Intelligence, "Present Status in Saga Regarding the Movement of TOW Missiles," January 25, 1986, in *DNSA Iraqgate*, Doc. IG00302.

46. Central Intelligence Agency Top Secret Transcript, "[Transcript of October 6–8, 1986, Discussions with Iranian Intermediaries]," October 8, 1986, in *DNSA Iran*, Doc. IC03560.

47. Hiro, *Longest War*, 219–20; and State Department Secret Action Memorandum from Richard W. Murphy to Michael H. Armacost, "U.S.-Iraqi Relations: Picking Up the Pieces," December 5, 1986, in *DNSA Iraqgate*, Doc. IG000380, p. 1.

48. GAO, Statement of Allan I. Mendelowitz, "Iraq's Participation," p. 12.

49. John Roberts, "Iraq: More Banks Brought in for U.S. Commodity Finance," *Middle East Economic Digest* 20 (February 1988): 21.

50. Phythian, *Arming Iraq*, 43.

51. Walt, *Revolution and War*, 228.

52. John Simpson, *From the House of War: John Simpson in the Gulf* (London: Hutchinson, 1991), 44.

53. Jentleson, *With Friends Like These*, 61–62.

54. Kuwait initially approached both the U.S. and Soviet governments for protection of its merchant ships. In response, the Reagan administration temporized, but sprang immediately into action after discovering that Moscow had offered to cooperate fully with Kuwait. Jentleson, *With Friends Like These*, 62; and U.S. Congress, Senate, Committee on Foreign Relations, *War in the Persian Gulf: The U.S. Takes Sides*, Committee Print 100-60, 100th Congress, 1st Session, Nov. 1987, p. 37.

55. Razoux, *Iran-Iraq War*, 420–22; and Shultz, *Turmoil and Triumph*, 926.

56. Razoux, *Iran-Iraq War*, 444–48.

57. Tim Zimmerman, "Coercive Diplomacy and Libya," in *The Limits of Coercive Diplomacy*, 2nd ed., ed. Alexander L. George and William E. Simons (Boulder, CO: Westview, 1994), 223 fn. 2.

58. John E. Reilly, "America's State of Mind," *Foreign Policy*, no. 66 (Spring 1987): 42.

59. Zimmerman, "Coercive Diplomacy and Libya," 201.

60. Zimmerman, "Coercive Diplomacy and Libya," 213–16.

61. Preece, *United States-Iraqi Relations*, 23–24. Iraq supported the moderate Arab League plan for Arab-Israeli peace proposed in its 1982 summit at Fez; the next year, it refrained from voicing opposition to a U.S.-brokered peace treaty between Israel and Lebanon. Jentleson, *With Friends Like These*, 48.

62. Some sources have suggested that Saddam's escalated support for terrorism during the 1980s represented a desperate effort to kindle a new Arab-Israeli war that would persuade Iran to end its war with Iraq and join forces with Iraq against Israel. Timmerman, *Death Lobby*, 114; Jentleson, *With Friends Like These*, 52; and Hiro, *Longest War*, 63. Even if this was the case, it was clearly a long shot at best, and it would be

highly unlikely that Saddam would push ahead with this gambit in the face of a credible threat by the United States and its allies to retract their wartime support for Iraq.

63. Con Coughlin, *Saddam: His Rise and Fall* (New York: Harper Perennial, 2004), 140–43.

64. Dan Reiter, "Preventive Attacks against Nuclear Programs and the 'Success' at Osirak," *Nonproliferation Review* 12, no. 2 (July 2005): 357.

65. Secret Interagency Intelligence Assessment, "Implications of Israeli Attack on Iraq," July 1, 1981, p. 3. On CIA website: https://www.cia.gov/library/readingroom/docs /DOC_0000211961.pdf.

66. Top Secret Intelligence Assessment, Central Intelligence Agency, Directorate of Intelligence, "The Iraqi Nuclear Program: Progress Despite Setbacks," June 1983, in Malcolm Byrne and Christian F. Ostermann, eds., *The Iran-Iraq War, 1980–1988: Reader of Declassified U.S. Documents*, prepared for the conference "The Origins, Conduct, and Impact of the Iran-Iraq War, 1980–1988," Woodrow Wilson International Center for Scholars, Washington, DC, July 19–20, 2004, Doc. 25, pp. 6, 7. See also Jeremy Tamsett, "The Israeli Bombing of Osirak Reconsidered: Successful Counterproliferation?" *Nonproliferation Review* 11, no. 3 (Fall/Winter 2004): 71.

67. CIA Intelligence Assessment, "The Iraqi Nuclear Program: Progress Despite Setbacks." During the war, the administration also voiced objection to the Ba'ath regime's flagrant use of chemical weapons against Iranian troops and Iraqi Kurds, as well as its suspected diversion of certain dual-use U.S. exports to its conventional military. I do not include these disputes in the case study because it could be plausibly argued that the administration's interest in securing concessions from Iraq on these matters was probably quite low, as they would have adversely affected Iraq's war effort against Iran. For more on these three disputes, see Evan N. Resnick, "Ties That Bind or Ties That Blind? Assessing Engagement as an Instrument of U.S. Foreign Policy" (unpublished Ph.D. diss., Columbia University, 2005), 260–73.

68. All of these figures are in constant 1989 dollars. United States Arms Control and Disarmament Agency, *World Military Expenditures and Arms Transfers 1990* (Washington, DC: U.S. Government Printing Office, 1991), pp. 67, 85.

69. Most worryingly from Washington's perspective, an Iranian victory would increase the potential for the radical and rabidly anti-American Iranian regime to fix the rate of extraction and price of Persian Gulf oil on which the economies of the United States and its allies depended. Hiro, *Longest War*, 263.

70. Jentleson, *With Friends Like These*, 81.

71. Only in the final year of the war did U.S. oil imports from Iraq begin to rise dramatically, ballooning to 126 million barrels, which represented one-quarter of Iraq's total oil exports. Jentleson, *With Friends Like These*, 81–82.

72. Jentleson claims that merely by virtue of the economic benefits that Iraq was receiving from the United States, the Reagan administration "should have been able to hold Iraq to its commitment not to threaten the interests of its new and vital supporter." Bruce W. Jentleson, "Iraq: Failure of a Strategy," in *Reversing Relations with Former Adversaries:*

U.S. Foreign Policy after the Cold War, ed. C. Richard Nelson and Kenneth Weisbrode (Gainesville: University Press of Florida, 1998), 131–32.

73. Cable, State Department to American Embassy Amman, "Kittani Call on Under Secretary Eagleburger," Secret, March 24, 1984, pp. 1–2; and Briefing Papers, State Department, "Gulf War Update: U.S. Attitude toward Iran; the Gulf War," Secret, February 27, 1986, in Byrne and Ostermann, *Iran-Iraq War*, Docs. 61 and 93, respectively. The neorealist hypothesis could be challenged by the contention that U.S. dependence on and commitment to the alliance with Iraq were heightened by the fear that Saddam would gravitate more closely toward the Soviet bloc. In July 1983 President Reagan signed National Security Decision Directive No. 99, which stipulated that the "most serious threats to our vital interests and objectives in the [Near East and South Asia] region are the power, influence, and activity of the Soviet Union." "United States Security Strategy for the Near East and South Asia, July 12, 1983," National Security Decision Directive No. 99, in Online Database of Presidential Directives and Executive Orders, ed., John Pike, https://fas.org/irp/offdocs/nsdd/nsdd-99.pdf. In an April 1985 letter to Secretary of Defense Weinberger, Secretary of State Shultz referred to the imperative of "expanding our political and commercial influence in Iraq . . . as directed by NSDD-99, to counter Soviet influence in Southwest Asia." Action Memorandum, State Department, Office of the Assistant Secretary for Near Eastern and South Asian Affairs, "Letter to Secretary Weinberger on U.S.-Iraqi Relations and Advanced Technology Exports to Iraq," Secret, April 29, 1985, in *DNSA Iraqgate*, Doc. IG00250, p. 1 of attached letter from George Shultz to Caspar Weinberger. An August 1983 CIA assessment cast doubt on the possibility that Iraq would drift into the Soviet orbit, however, referring to "some important constraints on the improvement in Soviet-Iraqi relations," namely, the existence of high levels of distrust between the two governments, the USSR's aversion to antagonizing its Syrian proxy, and the Soviet desire to improve relations with Iran. Due to these constraints, the Soviet Union's share of Iraq's arms purchases declined significantly, from 97 percent during the period 1970–1975 to 85 percent during the period 1975–1980 to 55 percent during the period 1980–1985. Intelligence Assessment, CIA Directorate of Intelligence, "Moscow's Tilt toward Baghdad: The USSR and the War between Iran and Iraq," Top Secret, August 1983, in Byrne and Ostermann, *Iran-Iraq War*, Doc. 29. For similar assessments, see "DIA Defense Estimative Brief, 'Prospects for Iraq,' Classification Unknown, September 25, 1984" in Byrne and Ostermann, *Iran-Iraq War*, Doc. 76; and "Intelligence Assessment, CIA Directorate of Intelligence, 'Is Iraq Losing the War?'" in Byrne and Ostermann, *Iran-Iraq War*, Doc. 97. In fact, the only occasion in which the administration clearly acted out of a credible fear of being outbid by the Soviets was its decision to reflag Kuwaiti merchant vessels in 1987. This decision, however, had little to do with Iraq directly, as it was motivated primarily by the desire to prevent the Soviet Union from "playing a key maritime role in the [Persian] Gulf." Shultz, *Turmoil and Triumph*, 926.

74. State Department Memorandum, Richard W. Murphy to Under Secretary Armacost, "U.S.–Iraqi Relations: Picking Up the Pieces," Secret, December 5, 1986, in Byrne and Ostermann, *Iran-Iraq War*, Doc. 110.

75. Quoted in Guy Gugliotta, Charles R. Babcock, Benjamin Weisner, and Lucy Shackleford, "At War, Iraq Courted U.S. into Economic Embrace," *Washington Post*, September 16, 1990.

76. Jentleson, *With Friends Like These*, 52; Hiro, *Longest War*, 63.

77. Jentleson, *With Friends Like These*, 52; Timmerman, *Death Lobby*, 130.

78. State Department Information Memorandum, Bureau of Intelligence and Research to Secretary Shultz, "Iraq's Retreat from International Terrorism," July 1, 1986, in *DNSA Iraqgate*, Doc. 341, p. 2.

79. David A. Flores, "Export Controls and the U.S. Effort to Combat International Terrorism," *Law and Policy in International Business* 13, no. 2 (Spring 1981): 567–75.

80. Quoted in Carl Hartman, "Administration Defends Easing of Restrictions," Associated Press, March 18, 1982.

81. Quoted in Juan J. Walte, "Congress Told Iraq No Longer a Prime Supporter of Terrorism," United Press International, March 18, 1982. Similar claims about Iraq's alleged reduced support for terrorism were made to members of Congress by William Root, director of the State Department's Office of East-West Trade. William Chapman, "House Committee Votes to Restore Trade Curbs on Iraq, South Africa," *Washington Post*, May 14, 1982, A2.

82. John M. Goshko, "U.S. Moves to Sell Aircraft Parts to Taiwan; Iraq Permitted to Buy Planes," *Washington Post*, April 14, 1982, A1.

83. Barry Schweid, "Iraq Seeking to Buy 45 US Helicopters," *Associated Press*, October 16, 1984.

84. Chapman, "House Committee Votes to Restore."

85. Chapman, "House Committee Votes to Restore."

86. W. Dale Nelson, "Washington Dateline," Associated Press, October 16, 1984.

87. Pamela Fessler, "Congress' Record on Saddam: Decade of Talk, Not Action," *Congressional Quarterly Weekly Review*, April 27, 1991, 1069.

88. Secret State Department Briefing Memorandum from Nicholas A. Veliotes, State Department, to George P. Shultz, "Your Meeting with Iraqi Minister of State Dr. Saddoun Hammadi, February 14, 1983, at 2:30–3:00 p.m.," February 7, 1983, in *DNSA Iraqgate*, Doc. IG00103, p. 3. See also, Cable, State Department to U.S. Interests Section, Baghdad, "Message from the Secretary for FONMIN Tariq Aziz: Iraqi Support for Terrorism," Secret, May 23, 1983, in Byrne and Ostermann, *Iran-Iraq War*, Doc. 24.

89. State Department Secret Information Memorandum from Office of Assistant Secretary for Near Eastern and South Asian Affairs and Bureau of Politico-Military Affairs to Lawrence S. Eagleburger, "Iran-Iraq War, Analysis of Possible U.S. Shift from Position of Strict Neutrality," October 7, 1983," in *DNSA Iraqgate*, Doc. IG00139, p. 7.

90. Unclassified State Department Action Memorandum from Bureau of Politico-Military Affairs and Office of Assistant Secretary of State for Near Eastern and South Asian Affairs to George P. Shultz, "Easing Restrictions on Exports to Iraq," January 30, 1984," in *DNSA Iraqgate*, Doc. IG00168, p. 2.

91. Quoted in Ian Black, "U.S. Doesn't See Iraq as Backing Terrorists," *Washington Post*, October 8, 1983, A25.

92. Black, "U.S. Doesn't See Iraq."

93. Black, "U.S. Doesn't See Iraq."

94. "Congress Wrestles over Iraq," *Washington Report on Middle East Affairs*, December 12, 1983, 4.

95. Letter from Howard L. Berman to George P. Shultz, "[Export of Bell Helicopters to Iraq]," November 13, 1984, in *DNSA Iraqgate*, Doc. IG00225, p. 1.

96. Bureau of Intelligence and Research to Secretary Shultz, "Iraq's Retreat from International Terrorism"; Jentleson, *With Friends Like These*, 52; Hiro, *Longest War*, 63; Timmerman, *Death Lobby*, 130; and Patrick Seale, *Abu Nidal, A Gun for Hire: The Secret Life of the World's Most Notorious Arab Terrorist* (London: Hutchinson, 1992), 111.

97. Fessler, "Congress' Record on Saddam," 1069, 1072; and Preece, *United States-Iraqi Relations*, 27.

98. Seale, *Abu Nidal*, 111, 123.

99. Elaine Sciolino, *The Outlaw State: Saddam Hussein's Quest for Power and the Gulf Crisis* (New York: Wiley & Sons, 1991), 164.

100. Secret State Department Cable from Secretary of State James A. Baker III to U.S. Embassy, Baghdad, "Iraq and Terrorism [Cover Memorandum Attached]," June 27, 1990, in *DNSA Iraqgate*, Doc. IG01441.

101. Baker–U.S. Embassy cable; and "Iraq Supplies PLO Army Units," *Washington Times*, February 8, 1985.

102. "Letter from Lawrence S. Eagleburger to William Draper, Secret, December 24, 1983," in Byrne and Ostermann, *Iran-Iraq War*, Doc. 45.

103. Berman, "[Export of Bell Helicopters to Iraq]," 1.

104. Defense Intelligence Agency, Intelligence Brief DEB-85-84, "Defense Estimative Brief: Prospects for Iraq," p. 5.

105. Letter from W. Tapley Bennett Jr. to Howard L. Berman, "[Reply to Representative Berman's Letter Regarding Export of Bell Helicopters to Iraq]," Dec. 6, 1984, in *DNSA Iraqgate*, Doc. IG00230, pp. 2, 3.

106. State Department Cable from U.S. Embassy, Syria, to State Department, "Iraqi Concerns about Congressional Passage of the Export Administration Act," April 23, 1985, in *DNSA Iraqgate*, Doc. IG00249, p. 1.

107. "Legislative History, P.L. 99-64: Export Administration Amendments of 1985 [Letter from George Shultz to Representative Howard Berman, Dated June 20, 1985, Attached]," circa June 27, 1985, in *DNSA Iraqgate*, Doc. IG00260, pp. 109, 110.

108. Letter from Carl F. Schwensen, Executive Vice President of the National Association of Wheat Growers, to Rep. Howard L. Berman, June 24, 1985, quoted in Jentleson, *With Friends Like These*, 55.

109. "Legislative History, P.L. 99-64," 109.

110. Ronald Reagan, "Remarks at the American Bar Association's Annual Convention," July 8, 1985, American Presidency Project, www.presidency.ucsb.edu/ws/index.php ?pid=38854.

111. State Department Confidential Cable from U.S. Embassy, Iraq to State Department, "U.S. Iraqi Relations: The EAA List on State-Supported Terrorism," July 18, 1985, in *DNSA Iraqgate*, Doc. IG00267.

112. Tracey E. Madden, "An Analysis of the United States: Response to the Achille Lauro Hijacking," *Boston College Third World Law Journal* 8, no. 1 (1988): 137–38; and Gregory V. Gooding, "Fighting Terrorism in the 1980s: The Interception of the *Achille Lauro* Hijackers," *Yale Journal of International Law* 12, no. 1 (1987): 158.

113. Gooding, "Fighting Terrorism in the 1980s," 166–68.

114. Secret State Department Chronology, "Chronology: October 4 through December 6, 1985," in *DNSA Iraqgate*, Doc. IG00291, p. 1.

115. State Department, "Chronology," 2.

116. State Department Bureau of Intelligence and Research, "Iraq's Retreat from International Terrorism [Excised]," in *DNSA Iraqgate*, Doc. IG00341, p. 2.

117. State Department Bureau of Intelligence and Research, "Iraq's Retreat," 2.

118. Quoted in State Department, "Chronology," 3. This document notes that on November 13, a redacted source had "reported that [redacted] Abbas had been in Baghdad."

119. State Department, "Chronology," 5

120. "News Conference of December 6," *Department of State Bulletin* 86, no. 2107 (February 1986): 51.

121. Quoted in "Shultz Says He Was Angry 'For American People,'" *New York Times*, December 19, 1985, A14.

122. "News Conference of December 6," 4; Preece, *United States–Iraqi Relations*, 28; and "Legislative History of S. 1897: A Bill to Amend the Export Administration Act of 1979 to Prohibit the Export to Yugoslavia or Iraq of Certain Articles or Technology," On Library of Congress website: http://icreport.loc.gov.

123. State Department, "Iraq's Retreat," 1–3.

124. Secret State Department Briefing Memorandum from Paul J. Hare, Bureau of Near Eastern and South Asian Affairs, to Secretary of State James A. Baker III, "Meeting with Iraqi Under Secretary Nizar Hamdun, March 24, 1989 at 2:00 pm [Talking Points Attached]," March 23, 1989, in *DNSA Iraqgate*, Doc. IG00828, p. 2 of attached talking points.

125. The Abul Abbas saga did not end until 2003, when U.S. special operations forces captured him on the outskirts of Baghdad during the U.S.-led invasion of Iraq. Abbas died while in the custody of the U.S. military just under a year later. Bruce Hoffman, *The Ultimate Fifth Column: Saddam Hussein, International Terrorism, and the Crisis in the Gulf* (Santa Monica, CA: RAND, 1990), 3; David Ensor, "U.S. Captures Mastermind of Achille Lauro Hijacking," *CNN.com*, April 16, 2003, http://edition.cnn.com/2003/WORLD/meast/04/15/sprj.irq.abbas.arrested/; and "Obituaries: Abu Abbas," *Daily Telegraph*, March 11, 2004, http://www.telegraph.co.uk/news/obituaries/1456489/Abu-Abbas.html.

126. Barry M. Rubin, *Revolution until Victory? The Politics and History of the PLO* (Cambridge, MA: Harvard University Press, 1994), 156.

127. Tamsett, "Israeli Bombing of Osirak Reconsidered," 74.

128. Quoted in Dan Reiter, "Preventive Attacks against Nuclear Programs and the 'Success' at Osirak," *Nonproliferation Review* 12, no. 2 (July 2005): 357.

129. Reiter, "Preventive Attacks against Nuclear Programs," 357.

130. Quoted in R. Jeffrey Smith and Glenn Frankel, "Saddam's Nuclear Weapons Dream: A Lingering Nightmare," *Washington Post*, October 31, 1991, A1.

131. Reiter, "Preventive Attacks against Nuclear Programs," 361–62.

132. Tamsett, "Israeli Bombing of Osirak Reconsidered," 78.

133. Reiter, "Preventive Attacks against Nuclear Programs," 362.

134. CIA Intelligence Assessment, "Iraqi Nuclear Program: Progress Despite Setbacks," 7, 14.

135. Concurrent with Iraq's efforts to develop nuclear weapons and ballistic missiles were its equally ambitious programs to develop chemical and biological weapons. Hurst, *United States and Iraq*, 54–56; and Central Intelligence Agency Report, "Status of the Condor II Ballistic Missile Program," Nov. 1, 1991, located at CIA Electronic Reading Room: https://www.cia.gov/library/readingroom/docs/DOC_0001175541.pdf.

136. Ian F. Ferguson and Paul K. Kerr, "The U.S. Export Control System and the President's Reform Initiative," Congressional Research Service Report for Congress R41916, January 13, 2014, 2–4.

137. Timmerman, *Death Lobby*, 203.

138. State Department Unclassified Action Memorandum from Acting Assistant Secretary of State for Near Eastern and South Asian Affairs David T. Schneider and Assistant Secretary of State for Political-Military Affairs Jonathan T. Howe to the Secretary of State, "Easing Restrictions on Exports to Iraq," January 30, 1984, in *DNSA Iraqgate*, Doc. IG00168, p. 3.

139. Timmerman, *Death Lobby*, 203.

140. Timmerman, *Death Lobby*, 203, 208.

141. Timmerman, *Death Lobby*, 208–9.

142. State Department Secret Action Memorandum from Assistant Secretary of State for Near Eastern and South Asian Affairs Richard W. Murphy to the Secretary of State, "Letter to Secretary Weinberger and U.S.-Iraqi Relations and Advanced Technology Exports to Iraq [Letter from George Shultz to Caspar Weinberger Attached]," April 29, 1985, in *DNSA Iraqgate*, Doc. IG00250, pp. 1, 2.

143. Murphy–Weinberger memo, attached letter, pp. 1, 2.

144. Secret Defense Department Action Memorandum from Assistant Secretary for International Security Policy Richard N. Perle to the Secretary of Defense, "High Technology Dual-Use Export to Iraq [Letter from George P. Shultz to Caspar W. Weinberger, Dated April 30, 1985 Attached]," July 1, 1985, in *DNSA Iraqgate*, Doc. IG00262.

145. Timmerman, *Death Lobby*, 204–5.

146. Secret Defense Department Memorandum, "Computers for Iraq," March 10, 1986, in *DNSA Iraqgate*, Doc. IG00313.

147. Jentleson, *With Friends Like These*, 51.

148. Secret State Department Memorandum from Bureau of Near Eastern and South Asian Affairs, Northern Gulf Affairs Desk, to Bureau of Near Eastern and South Asian Affairs, "Computers for Iraq: DOD's Proliferation Concerns," April 3, 1986, in *DNSA Iraqgate*, Doc. IG00319.

149. State Department Secret Briefing Memorandum from Assistant Secretary of State for Near Eastern and South Asian Affairs Richard W. Murphy to Under Secretary of State for Political Affairs Michael H. Armacost, "Iraq: CPPG Meeting of Wednesday, July 23," circa July 23, 1986, in *DNSA Iraqgate*, Doc. IG00346, p. 5.

150. State Department Secret Action Memorandum from Assistant Secretary of State for Near Eastern and South Asian Affairs Richard W. Murphy to Under Secretary of State for Political Affairs Michael H. Armacost, "U.S.-Iraqi Relations: Picking Up the Pieces," December 5, 1986, in *DNSA Iraqgate*, Doc. IG00380, p. 1.

151. State Department Secret Information Memorandum from Office of Assistant Secretary of Near Eastern and South Asian Affairs and Office of Assistant Secretary for Politico-Military Affairs to George P. Shultz, "U.S. Policy on Third-Country Transfers of U.S. Arms to Iraq," February 4, 1987, in *DNSA Iraqgate*, Doc. IG00312, p. 2.

152. Jentleson, *With Friends Like These*, 55–56, 60–61.

153. State Department, "Iraq: CPPG Meeting," 1, 2, 6.

154. Timmerman, *Death Lobby*, 241.

155. Quoted in Timmerman, *Death Lobby*, 241.

156. Confidential State Department Memorandum from State Department Executive Secretary Melvyn Levitsky to Donald P. Gregg, National Security Advisor to Vice President George H. W. Bush, "The Vice President's March 2 Meeting with Iraqi Ambassador Nizar Hamdoon [Background Papers and Talking Points Attached]," Feb. 26, 1987, in *DNSA Iraqgate*, Doc. IG00410.

157. Letter from Deputy Under Secretary of Defense for Trade Security Policy Stephen D. Bryen to Assistant Secretary of Commerce for Trade Administration Paul Freedenberg, "[Regarding Export Licenses for Computers Destined for Iraq]," September 19, 1986, in *DNSA Iraqgate*, Doc. IG00359.

158. Timmerman, *Death Lobby*, 205.

159. Bryen–Freedenberg letter, "[Regarding Export Licenses]."

160. Jentleson, *With Friends Like These*, 63.

161. Timmerman, *Death Lobby*, 156; and Statement by Representative Henry Gonzales, *Congressional Record—House*, 102nd Congress, 2nd Session, February. 3, 1992, p. 1176.

162. Phythian, *Arming Iraq*, 23.

163. Quoted in Timmerman, *Death Lobby*, 207.

164. Timmerman, *Death Lobby*, 157–59.

165. Quoted in Timmerman, *Death Lobby*, 205.

166. Timmerman, *Death Lobby*, 266–67.

167. Timmerman, *Death Lobby*, 220; Jentleson, *With Friends Like These*, 84.

168. Quoted in Timmerman, *Death Lobby*, 220.

169. Quoted in Jentleson, *With Friends Like These*, 85.

170. Quoted in Murray Waas, "What We Gave Saddam for Christmas," *Village Voice*, December 18, 1990: 36.

171. Letter from A. Robert Abboud, Chairman of the Board, U.S.-Iraq Business Forum, to Secretary of State George P. Shultz, November 20, 1986, in *DNSA Iraqgate*, Doc. IG 00375, pp. 2, 3.

172. Confidential Letter from Under Secretary of State for Political Affairs Michael H. Armacost to Acting Assistant to the President for National Security Affairs Alton G. Keel Jr., "[Export Licenses for Iraq; Cover Memo from Arnold Raphel to Michael Armacost Attached]," December 12, 1986, in *DNSA Iraqgate*, Doc. IG00382, pp. 1, 2 (italics added for emphasis).

173. State Department Confidential Memorandum from Deputy Assistant Secretary of State for Near Eastern and South Asian Affairs to Assistant Secretary of Commerce for Trade Administration Paul Freedenberg, "[Excised] Application for License to Export to Iraq [Talking Points Attached]," December 19, 1986, in *DNSA Iraqgate*, Doc. IG00387, p. 2.

174. Letter from A. Robert Abboud, Chairman of the Board, United States-Iraq Business Forum, to S. Bruce Smart Jr., "[Requests Clarification of U.S. Export Licensing Policy for Iraq; Membership List Attached]," March 10, 1987, in *DNSA Iraqgate*, Doc. IG00412.

175. Defense Intelligence Agency, "Assessment of the Activities of Abdul Kader Helmy, et al., and the Egyptian/Iraqi Condor Missile Program," September 19, 1989, filed with the U.S. Attorney, Eastern District of California, U.S. Courthouse, Sacramento, California, submitted by Rep. Henry Gonzalez (D-TX) to *Congressional Record—House*, 102nd Congress, 2nd Session, February 3, 1992, pp. 1179–80.

176. Statement by Rep. Henry Gonzalez, *Congressional Record—House*, 102nd Congress, 2nd Session, August 10, 1992, p. H7873.

177. Quoted in Jentleson, *With Friends Like These*, 64, 89.

178. Jentleson, *With Friends Like These*, 64; Statement by Rep. Henry Gonzalez, *Congressional Record*, August 10, 1992, p. H7872; "United States Exports of Sensitive Technology to Iraq," 4; and Statement by Rep. Henry Gonzales, *Congressional Record—House*, 102nd Cong., 2nd sess., July 21, 1992, p. H6339.

179. Statement by Rep. Henry Gonzales, July 21, 1992, H6341, H6342.

180. Energy Department Memorandum from Acting Assistant Secretary of Energy Troy E. Wade II to Secretary of Energy James D. Watkins, "Recommendations to Strengthen U.S. Nuclear Nonproliferation Policy [Memorandum from Roger Heusser and Bryan Siebert to Charles Gilbert Attached]," April 17, 1989, in *DNSA Iraqgate*, Doc. IG00853.

181. Shultz, *Turmoil and Triumph*, 237.

182. Alexander L. George, *Bridging the Gap: Theory and Practice in Foreign Policy* (Washington, DC: United States Institute of Peace Press, 1993), 33.

183. Stephen R. Rock, *Appeasement in International Politics* (Lexington: University Press of Kentucky, 2000), 104–6.

184. Kenneth I. Juster, "The United States and Iraq: Perils of Engagement," in *Honey and Vinegar: Incentives, Sanctions, and Foreign Policy*, ed. Richard N. Haass and Meghan L. O'Sullivan (Washington, DC: Brookings Institution Press, 2000), 52. Juster claims that in addition to buttressing Iraq as a counterweight to Iran, the Reagan administration sought to modify Saddam's attitude toward the Middle East peace process, open up a new market for U.S. exports, and loosen Iraq's relationship with the USSR (52–54). In

contrast to George, Rock, and Juster, Bruce Jentleson devotes significant attention to the U.S.-Iraq relationship during the Iran-Iraq War in his book *With Friends Like These* (chap. 1). Specifically, he notes that although the shared Iranian threat brought both countries together in an alliance of convenience, Iraq's continued sponsorship of terrorism and its expanding military ambitions remained "points of tension" (67).

5. THE U.S. "SPECIAL RELATIONSHIP" ALLIANCE WITH THE UNITED KINGDOM, 1950–1953

1. Rosemary Foot, *A Substitute for Victory: The Politics of Peacemaking at the Korean Armistice Talks* (Ithaca, NY: Cornell University Press, 1990), 6; and Larry Blomstedt, *Truman, Congress, and Korea: The Politics of America's First Undeclared War* (Lexington: University Press of Kentucky, 2015), 24.

2. Rosemary Foot, *The Wrong War: American Policy and the Dimensions of the Korean Conflict, 1950–1953* (Ithaca, NY: Cornell University Press, 1985), 59.

3. Callum A. MacDonald, *Britain and the Korean War* (Cambridge, MA: Blackwell, 1990), 18–19; Thomas Hennessey, *Britain's Korean War: Cold War Diplomacy, Strategy and Security, 1950–53* (Manchester, UK: University of Manchester Press, 2013), 12–14; and Max Hastings, *The Korean War* (New York: Simon & Schuster, 1987), 55.

4. William Stueck, "The Korean War," in *The Cambridge History of the Cold War*, vol. 1, *Origins*, ed. Melvyn Leffler and Odd Arne Westad (New York: Cambridge University Press, 2010), 277–83.

5. Stueck, "Korean War," 277–79.

6. William Stueck, *The Korean War: An International History* (Princeton, N.J.: Princeton University Press, 1997), 237–38.

7. Stueck, *Korean War*, 279–81.

8. Stueck, *Korean War*, 281–83.

9. Secret Department of State Policy Statement, Washington, June 11, 1948, in *FRUS 1948* 3, 1091, 1092.

10. Quoted in David Reynolds, "A 'Special Relationship'? America, Britain, and the International Order since the Second World War," *International Affairs* 62, no. 1 (Winter 1985/86): 6. Britain's election of a socialist Labour government in 1945 engendered some suspicion and consternation in the United States, especially during the congressional debate over a postwar loan to London in late 1945, but historian Bradford Perkins notes that this "never became an important theme." Bradford Perkins, "Unequal Partners: The Truman Administration and Great Britain," in *The "Special Relationship": Anglo-American Relations Since 1945*, ed. William Roger Louis and Hedley Bull (Oxford, UK: Clarendon Press, 1986), 46.

11. Reynolds, "Special Relationship," 5; John J. Mearsheimer, *The Tragedy of Great Power Politics*, updated ed. (New York: Norton, 2014), chap. 7; and Walter Russell Mead, *God and Gold: Britain, America, and the Making of the Modern World* (New York: Vintage Books, 2008). Between 1896 and 1903, Britain resolved all outstanding territorial

disputes with the United States in the Western Hemisphere by capitulating to Washington on all of them. Specifically, London agreed to submit a border dispute between its colony of British Guiana and Venezuela to international arbitration, formally accepted the Monroe Doctrine, ended its opposition to a U.S.-built and -fortified transisthmian canal in Central America, and accepted the U.S. position relating to the border between Alaska and the Canadian Yukon. Stephen R. Rock, *Appeasement in International Politics* (Lexington: University Press of Kentucky, 2000), 25–76.

12. Mark A. Stoler, *Allies in War: Britain and America against the Axis Powers, 1940–1945* (London: Hodder Arnold, 2005).

13. Kathleen Burk, *Old World, New World: Great Britain and America from the Beginning* (New York: Atlantic Monthly Press, 2008), 565–67, 573–74; Perkins, "Unequal Partners," 49–51; and John Baylis, *Anglo-American Defence Relations 1939–1980: The Special Relationship* (London: Macmillan, 1981), 23–26.

14. Baylis, *Anglo-American Defence Relations*, 28–31; Ritchie Ovendale, *Anglo-American Relations in the Twentieth Century* (New York: St. Martin's Press, 1998), 65; and Reynolds, "Special Relationship," 11.

15. Peter G. Boyle, "Britain, America, and the Transition from Economic to Military Assistance, 1948–51," *Journal of Economic History* 22, no. 3 (July 1987): 525.

16. Perkins, "Unequal Partners," 591.

17. "Paper Prepared in the Department of State," April 19, 1950, in *FRUS 1950 3*, 870, 878.

18. PUSC (51) Final, "Anglo-American Relations: Present and Future," Report of the PUSC, 24 August 1949, Public Record Office, FO 371/76385, in *Anglo-American Relations since 1939: The Enduring Alliance*, ed. John Baylis (Manchester, UK: Manchester University Press, 1997), 52, 53, 57; and Anthony Adamthwaite, "Britain and the World, 1945–9: The View from the Foreign Office," *International Affairs* 61, no. 2 (April 1985): 229.

19. James I. Matray and Donald W. Boose Jr., eds., *The Ashgate Research Companion to the Korean War* (Surrey, UK: Ashgate, 2014), 287, 289.

20. Michael J. Turner, *British Power and International Relations during the 1950s: A Tenable Position?* (Lanham, MD: Lexington Books, 2009), chap. 1.

21. Foreign and Commonwealth Office, "Korea: Britain and the Korean War (1950–51)," *History Notes*, no. 1 (June 1990): 3.

22. Foot, *Wrong War*, 92.

23. Steve Marsh and John Baylis, "The Anglo-American 'Special Relationship': The Lazarus of International Relations," *Diplomacy and Statecraft* 17, no. 1 (2006): 176.

24. Paul Kennedy, *The Rise and Fall of the Great Powers: Economic Change and Military Conflict from 1500 to 2000* (New York: Vintage Books, 1989), 364, 384. GNP figures are in 1964 dollars.

25. "The North Atlantic Treaty, Washington, D.C., 4 April 1949," on North Atlantic Treaty Organization website: https://www.nato.int/cps/ic/natohq/official_texts_17120 .htm. Italics added for emphasis.

26. "North Atlantic Treaty." Italics added.

27. Kenneth N. Waltz, *Foreign Policy and Democratic Politics: The American and British Experience* (Boston: Little, Brown, and Company, 1967), 20.

28. Waltz, *Foreign Policy and Democratic Politics*, 37.

29. David R. Mayhew, *Divided We Govern: Party Control, Lawmaking, and Investigations, 1946–2002* (New Haven, CT: Yale University Press, 2005).

30. These frictions are abetted by the extensive patronage opportunities that members of Congress enjoy which are "within the provenance of the Congress itself," rather than the White House. By contrast, patronage opportunities for members of the British parliament are almost exclusively dispensed by the prime minister. Waltz, *Foreign Policy and Domestic Politics*, 43.

31. Waltz, *Foreign Policy and Domestic Politics*, 39.

32. Steve Marsh, *Anglo-American Relations and Cold War Oil: Crisis in Iran* (New York: Palgrave Macmillan, 2003), 34.

33. Baylis, *Anglo-American Defence Relations*, 43.

34. Baylis, *Anglo-American Defence Relations*, 34–35; and Marsh, *Anglo-American Relations and Cold War Oil*, 35.

35. Marsh, *Anglo-American Relations and Cold War Oil*, 35.

36. Steven Casey, *Selling the Korean War: Propaganda, Politics, and Public Opinion in the United States, 1950–1953* (New York: Oxford University Press, 2008), 5.

37. Blomstedt, *Truman, Congress, and Korea*, 193–94.

38. Quoted in Michael F. Hopkins, *Oliver Franks and the Truman Administration: Anglo-American Relations 1948–1952* (London: Frank Cass, 2002), 159.

39. Sean Greenwood, "'A War We Don't Want': Another Look at the British Labour Government's Commitment in Korea, 1950–51," *Contemporary British History* 17, no. 4 (2008): 1-6.

40. Quoted in Greenwood, "A War We Don't Want," 6.

41. Hastings, *The Korean War*, 70.

42. Michael F. Hopkins, "The Price of Cold War Partnership: Sir Oliver Franks and the British Military Commitment in the Korean War," *Cold War History* 1, no. 2 (January 2001): 36; and Hopkins, *Oliver Franks and the Truman Administration*, 160–61.

43. Quoted in Hopkins, "The Price of Cold War Partnership," 36.

44. Hennessey, *Britain's Korean War*, 50–54. Franks quoted in Hennessey, *Britain's Korean War*, 52.

45. Quoted in Hennessey, *Britain's Korean War*, 54.

46. Hennessey, *Britain's Korean War*, 54.

47. Quoted in Casey, *Selling the Korean War*, 90.

48. Casey, *Selling the Korean War*, 90.

49. Blomstedt, *Truman, Congress, and Korea*, 12.

50. Hennessey, *Britain's Korean War*, 21–27.

51. Hennessey, *Britain's Korean War*, 30.

52. Top Secret Telegram from the Secretary of State to the Embassy in the United Kingdom, July 10, 1950, in *FRUS 1950* 7, 351–52.

53. Quoted in Hennessey, *Britain's Korean War*, 38.

54. Victor S. Kaufman, *Confronting Communism: U.S. and British Policies toward China* (Columbia: University of Missouri Press, 2001), 47–48.

55. Peter N. Farrar, "Britain's Proposal for a Buffer Zone South of the Yalu in November 1950: Was It a Neglected Opportunity to End the Fighting in Korea?" *Journal of Contemporary History* 18 (1983): 331–33.

56. Top Secret Telegram, The Secretary of State to the Embassy of the United Kingdom, November 21, 1950, in *FRUS 1950 7*, 1212–13.

57. "Secret Telegram, The British Secretary of State for Foreign Affairs (Bevin) to the British Ambassador (Franks), November 23, 1950, in *FRUS 1950 7*, 1218.

58. Top Secret Telegram, The Secretary of State to the Embassy in the United Kingdom, Nov. 13, 1950, in *FRUS 1950 7*, 1144, 1145; and Secret Message, The British Embassy to the Department of State, "From Mr. Bevin to Sir Oliver Franks," Nov. 16, 1950, in *FRUS 1950 7*, 1172.

59. "Editorial Note," in *FRUS 1950 7*, 1261–62.

60. Seventy-six Labour Members of Parliament signed a letter protesting Truman's statement and threatening to withdraw their support for the government if Britain endorsed war against China. Rosemary J. Foot, "Anglo-American Relations in the Korean Crisis: The British Effort to Avert an Expanded War, December 1950–January 1951," *Diplomatic History* 10, no. 1 (Winter 1996): 45.

61. Foot, "Anglo-American Relations in the Korean Crisis," 47.

62. "Top Secret United States Delegation Minutes of the First Meeting of President Truman and Prime Minister Attlee," December 4, 1950, in *FRUS 1950 7*, 1368, 1369.

63. Top Secret Memorandum of Conversation, by the Director of the Executive Secretariat (McWilliams), December 5, 1950, in *FRUS 1950 7*, 1383.

64. "[Annex] Communique Issued at the Conclusion of the Truman-Attlee Discussions," in *FRUS 1950 7*, 1477.

65. Top Secret Memorandum by Mr. Lucius D. Battle, Special Assistant to the Secretary of State, of a Meeting Held on December 6, 1950, in *FRUS 1950 7*, 1431.

66. Top Secret Memorandum for the Record by the Ambassador at Large (Jessup), December 7, 1950, in *FRUS 1950 7*, 1462.

67. Top Secret Memorandum for the Record, by R. Gordon Arneson, Special Assistant to the Secretary of State, January 16, 1951, in *FRUS 1950 7*, 1464; and Hennessey, *Britain's Korean War*, 130.

68. Quoted in Hennessey, *Britain's Korean War*, 128.

69. Stueck, *Korean War*, 138–42; and M. L. Dockrill, "The Foreign Office, Anglo-American Relations and the Korean War, June 1950–June 1951," *International Affairs* 62, no. 3 (Summer 1986), 466–68.

70. Top Secret Priority Telegram, The Secretary of State to the Embassy in the United Kingdom, Jan. 5, 1951, in *FRUS 1951 7*, 28.

71. Hennessey, *Britain's Korean War*, 151.

72. Quoted in Hennessey, *Britain's Korean War*, 152. A concurrent telegram to Franks composed by Younger and signed by Bevin castigated America's continuing aversion to consulting with allies and its "steamroller" bargaining tactics. Quoted in Peter Lowe, "The Significance of the Korean War in Anglo-American Relations, 1950–53," in *British*

Foreign Policy, 1945–56, ed. Michael Dockrill and John W. Young (New York: Macmillan, 1989), 132.

73. Hennessey, *Britain's Korean War*, 161.

74. Secret Telegram from the Secretary of State to the Embassy in the United Kingdom, January 27, 1951, p. 143.

75. Memorandum of Telephone Conversation, by Lucius D. Battle, Special Assistant to the Secretary of State, January 29, 1951, in *FRUS 1951 7*, 136, 137.

76. Hennessey, *Britain's Korean War*, 165.

77. Quoted in Casey, *Selling the Korean War*, 179.

78. Casey, *Selling the Korean War*, 180.

79. Quoted in Blomstedt, *Truman, Congress, and Korea*, 112.

80. Quoted in Casey, *Selling the Korean War*, 181.

81. Casey, *Selling the Korean War*, 182.

82. Casey, *Selling the Korean War*, 181–82.

83. Casey, *Selling the Korean War*, 197.

84. Quoted in Casey, *Selling the Korean War*, 198.

85. Quoted in Peter Lowe, "An Ally and a Recalcitrant General: Great Britain, Douglas MacArthur, and the Korean War 1950–51," *English Historical Review* 105, no. 416 (July 1990): 640.

86. Lowe, "Ally and a Recalcitrant General," 641.

87. Quoted in Lowe, "Ally and a Recalcitrant General," 641–42.

88. Historian Laura Belmonte claims that U.S. archival documents show conclusively that Truman fired MacArthur for his own reasons and not to pacify the British. "Anglo-American Relations and the Dismissal of MacArthur," *Diplomatic History* 19, no. 4 (Fall 1995): 664.

89. Top Secret Memorandum of Conversation, by the Director of the Policy Planning Staff (Nitze), April 12, 1951, in *FRUS 1951 7*, 339.

90. Quoted in Hennessey, *Britain's Korean War*, 191.

91. Casey, *Selling the Korean War*, 258.

92. Top Secret Urgent Telegram, The Commander in Chief, Far East (Ridgway) to the Joint Chiefs of Staff, April 27, 1951 in *FRUS 1951 7*, 385–86; and Top Secret Eyes Only Telegram, The Joint Chiefs of Staff to the Commander in Chief, Far East (Ridgway), April 28, 1951, in *FRUS 1951 7*, 386–87.

93. Quoted in Belmonte, "Anglo-American Relations and the Dismissal of MacArthur," 665; Hennessey, *Britain's Korean War*, 194–96.

94. Quoted in Hennessey, *Britain's Korean War*, 204.

95. While meeting General Clark, Alexander and Lloyd tentatively raised the possibility of appointing a British delegate to the truce negotiations. Clark spurned this proposal, permitting only the appointment of a British deputy chief of staff to his headquarters. Hennessey, *Britain's Korean War*, 215; MacDonald, *Britain and the Korean War*, 75; and Foot, *Wrong War*, 216.

96. Secret Telegram, the Secretary of State to the Department of State, Nov. 8, 1952, in *FRUS 1952 15*, 585.

97. Foot, *Wrong War*, 185.

98. Secret Memorandum of Conversation by the Secretary of State, Oct. 29, 1952, in *FRUS 1952 15*, 567–68.

99. Quoted in Foot, *Wrong War*, 185.

100. Quoted in Foot, *Wrong War*, 185–86.

101. Quoted in Stueck, *Korean War*, 299.

102. Casey, *Selling the Korean War*, 262.

103. Stueck, *Korean War*, 298–306.

104. Quoted in Hennessey, *Britain's Korean War*, 227.

105. "The Chance for Peace," Address Delivered before the American Society of Newspaper Editors, April 16, 1953, on the Dwight D. Eisenhower Presidential Library website: https://www.eisenhower.archives.gov/all_about_ike/speeches/chance_for_peace.pdf, p. 4.

106. Quoted in Hennessey, *Britain's Korean War*, 229, 230. Ultimately, the United States did agree to delay the timing of the release of the "Greater Sanctions" statement. Instead of issuing it immediately following the conclusion of the armistice, the Eisenhower administration agreed to include it in General Clark's final report to the UN, which was not presented until August 7, 1953. MacDonald, *Britain and the Korean War*, 92.

107. This proposal was rejected by the United States because it remained overly ambiguous regarding the fate of unrepatriated POWs. Stueck, *Korean War*, 314.

108. Quoted in Stueck, *Korean War*, 321.

109. Stueck, *Korean War*, 321.

110. Stueck, *Korean War*, 322–23.

111. Top Secret, The Acting Secretary of State to the Embassy in Pakistan, May 22, 1953, in *FRUS 1952 15*, 1080.

112. Howard Schonberger, "Peacemaking in Asia: The United States, Great Britain, and the Japanese Decision to Recognize Nationalist China, 1951–52," *Diplomatic History* 10, no. 1 (January 1996): 60; and Peter Lowe, *Containing the Cold War in East Asia: British Policies towards Japan, China and Korea, 1948–53* (Manchester, UK: Manchester University Press, 1997), 15–34.

113. Lowe, *Containing the Cold War in East Asia*, 28.

114. Lowe, *Containing the Cold War in East Asia*, 36; and Steve Marsh, "Anglo-American Relations, 1950–51: Three Strikes for British Prestige," *Diplomacy and Statecraft* 23, no. 2 (2012): 309.

115. Quoted in Lowe, *Containing the Cold War in East Asia*, 36.

116. Quoted in Marsh, "Anglo-American Relations, 1950–51," 321.

117. Marsh, "Anglo-American Relations, 1950–51," 321.

118. Lowe. *Containing the Cold War in East Asia*, 62.

119. Quoted in Lowe. *Containing the Cold War in East Asia*, 41.

120. The White House also largely won the day on a series of additional disagreements with the British regarding specific provisions of the treaty. First, whereas Whitehall sought the inclusion of tight restrictions on Japanese rearmament, Washington firmly opposed their imposition. In the end, on June 7, the Cabinet agreed to drop its demand for the

inclusion of specific rearmament limitations in the treaty. Second, the British pushed for the transfer of Japan's gold holdings to the allies as reparations, while Dulles claimed that they were necessary for Japan's economic stabilization. On June 14, Morrison and Chancellor of the Exchequer Hugh Gaitskill persuaded the Cabinet to drop their demands on the reparations issue. Third, the British sought the imposition of significant reductions in Japanese shipbuilding capacity outside the framework of the peace treaty, while the United States claimed that such restrictions would counterproductively inhibit Japan's postwar economic rehabilitation. By mid-August, Britain finally relented on the shipbuilding issue in the face of unstinting U.S. obduracy. The only dispute pertaining to the treaty in which British preferences won the day was by far the least salient, as it involved the extension of Japan's trade privileges in Africa, as mandated by the 1885 Congo Basin treaties and 1919 Versailles peace treaty. Britain sought to rescind these privileges while the United States sought to restore them. On June 14, Younger happily informed the Cabinet that Dulles had agreed that Japan's rights under the treaties in question should be terminated. Lowe, *Containing the Cold War in East Asia*, 51–61; Secret Draft Joint Statement of the United Kingdom and United States Governments, June 19, 1951, in *FRUS 1951 6*, 1134.

121. Quoted in "56 in Senate Bar Tokyo-Peiping Ties," *New York Times*, September 14, 1951, 3; and Lowe, *Containing the Cold War in East Asia*, 74.

122. Lowe, *Containing the Cold War in East Asia*, 74.

123. Copy of Draft Letter Handed the Prime Minister of Japan [Yoshida] by the Consultant to the Secretary [Dulles], Dec. 18, 1951, in *FRUS 1951 6*, 1445.

124. Schonberger, "Peacemaking in Asia," 69–78; and Treaty of Peace between the Republic of China and Japan, April 28, 1952, Taiwan Documents Project website: http://www .taiwandocuments.org/taipei01.htm.

125. Joel J. Sokolsky, *Seapower in the Nuclear Age: The United States Navy and NATO 1949–80* (Annapolis, MD: Naval Institute Press, 1991), 16.

126. Marsh, "Anglo-American Relations 1950–51," 310–11.

127. Marsh, "Anglo-American Relations 1950–51," 311.

128. Marsh, "Anglo-American Relations 1950–51," 322.

129. Marsh, "Anglo-American Relations 1950–51," 322–23.

130. Quoted in Marsh, "Anglo-American Relations 1950–51," 324.

131. Marsh, "Anglo-American Relations 1950–51," 322–24.

132. Dionysios Chourchoulis, "High Hopes, Bold Aims, Limited Results: Britain and the Establishment of the NATO Mediterranean Command, 1950–1953," *Diplomacy and Statecraft* 20, no. 3 (2009): 437.

133. Lisle Rose, *Power at Sea*, vol. 3, *A Violent Peace, 1946–2006* (Columbia: University of Missouri Press, 2007), 44.

134. The Commander in Chief of Allied Forces in Southern Europe (Carney) to the Supreme Commander of Allied Forces in Europe (Eisenhower), March 8, 1951, *FRUS 1951 3*, 481.

135. Chourchoulis, "High Hopes, Bold Aims," 439–41.

136. Chourchoulis, "High Hopes, Bold Aims," 447–48.

137. Chourchoulis, "High Hopes, Bold Aims," 450.

138. Mary Ann Heiss, *Empire and Nationhood: The United States, Great Britain, and Iranian Oil, 1950–1954* (New York: Columbia University Press, 1997), 5–9.

139. Heiss, *Empire and Nationhood*, 13.

140. Heiss, *Empire and Nationhood*, 13–14.

141. Ian Speller, "A Splutter of Musketry? The British Military Response to the Anglo-Iranian Oil Dispute, 1951," *Contemporary British History* 17, no. 1 (Spring 2003): 41.

142. Heiss, *Empire and Nationhood*, 40–43.

143. Heiss, *Empire and Nationhood*, 45–63; and David Painter, "The United States, Great Britain, and Mossadegh," Case 332, Part A, Instructor Copy, Institute for the Study of Diplomacy, Georgetown University (1993), p. 1.

144. 1949 Foreign Office minutes quoted in Steve Marsh, "The Special Relationship and the Anglo-Iranian Oil Crisis, 1950–4," *Review of International Studies* 24, no. 4 (1998): 536.

145. Heiss, *Empire and Nationhood*, 12, 58.

146. Marsh, *Anglo-American Relations and Cold War Oil*, 24.

147. Heiss, *Empire and Nationhood*, 11.

148. Secret Paper Prepared in the Bureau of Near Eastern, South Asian, and African Affairs, "Political and Economic Factors Involved in Military Assistance to Iran in FY 1951," undated, in *FRUS 1950 5*, 466. In the aftermath of World War II, the Soviets had both refused to withdraw Red Army forces from Iran and stop supporting secessionist rebels in the Iranian province of Azerbaijan unless the USSR received an oil concession in northern Iran. This dispute was one of the first that was taken up by the nascent United Nations, but Tehran rendered UN action unnecessary by complying with the Soviet demand. Heiss, *Empire and Nationhood*, 8.

149. Heiss, *Empire and Nationhood*, 57–59; and Marsh, *Anglo-American Relations and Cold War Oil*, 53–54.

150. Secret Priority Telegram, The Secretary of State to the Embassy in the United Kingdom, August 7, 1950, in *FRUS 1950 5*, 577.

151. Marsh, *Anglo-American Relations and Cold War Oil*, 63–64.

152. Dean G. Acheson, *Present at the Creation: My Years in the State Department* (New York: Norton, 1969), 501; and Top Secret Telegram, the Secretary of State to the U.S. Embassy in Tehran, May 10, 1951, in *FRUS 1952 10*, 50.

153. Marsh, *Anglo-American Relations and Cold War Oil*, 75, 210 fn. 89.

154. Marsh, *Anglo-American Relations and Cold War Oil*, 75.

155. "Editorial Note," in *FRUS 1950 5*, 155.

156. Quoted in Marsh, "Anglo-American Relations, 1950–51," 318; Painter, "The United States, Great Britain, and Mossadegh," 4.

157. Marsh, *Anglo-American Relations and Cold War Oil*, 117.

158. Top Secret Priority Telegram, The Secretary of State to the Embassy in Iran, July 31, 1952, in *FRUS 1952 10*, 429.

159. Marsh, *Anglo-American Relations and Cold War Oil*, 119.

160. *FRUS 1952 10*, 119–20; and Heiss, *Empire and Nationhood*, 139–40.

161. Secret Telegram, The Acting Secretary of State to the Embassy in the United Kingdom, August 18, 1952, in *FRUS 1952 10*, 447.

162. Marsh, *Anglo-American Relations and Cold War Oil*, 120–24; and Heiss, *Empire and Nationhood*, 140–50.

163. Top Secret Memorandum by the Secretary of State to the President, "Decisions Necessary If We Are to Move Forward toward a Solution of the Iranian Dispute," November 7, 1952, *FRUS 1952 10*, 518.

164. Quoted in Heiss, *Empire and Nationhood*, 155.

165. Steve Marsh, "Continuity and Change: Reinterpreting the Policies of the Truman and Eisenhower Administrations toward Iran, 1950–1954," *Journal of Cold War Studies* 7, no. 3 (Summer 2005), 99.

166. In its final days in office, the Truman administration bent to London's demands to substitute international arbitration for a lump-sum compensation scheme, render the $100 million U.S. advance conditional on successful arbitration, and grant the AIOC the right to market Iranian oil. Marsh, "Continuity and Change," 99–100.

167. Secret Priority Telegram, The Acting Secretary of State to the Embassy in the United Kingdom, Feb. 3, 1953, in *FRUS 1952 10*, 661. Peter Romsbotham, Head of Britain's Oil Desk at the Economic Relations Department of the Foreign Office, confirmed Mathews' claim with the declaration, "We are, in fact, now down to our last principle, viz.: impartial arbitration on the amount of compensation due for the loss of the concession." Quoted in Marsh, *Anglo-American Relations and Cold War Oil*, 149.

168. Heiss, *Empire and Nationhood*, 171.

169. Marsh, "Continuity and Change," 117.

170. Painter, "The United States, Great Britain, and Mossadegh," 16–18; Heiss, *Empire and Nationhood*, 181–219; and Marsh, *Anglo-American Relations and Cold War Oil*, 157–68.

171. Turner, *British Power and International Relations During the 1950s*, 92–93; and Dan Keohane, *Security in British Politics, 1945–99* (New York: St. Martin's Press, 2000), 119.

172. Top Secret Telegram, The Ambassador in the United Kingdom (Douglas) to the Secretary of State, August 2, 1950, in *FRUS 1950 3*, 1670; and Jihang Park, "Wasted Opportunities? The 1950s Rearmament Programme and the Failure of British Economic Policy," *Journal of Contemporary History* 32, no. 3 (July 1997): 358.

173. Top Secret Telegram, The Secretary of State to the Embassy in the United Kingdom, Aug. 11, 1950, in *FRUS 1950 3*, 1679.

174. Helen Leigh-Phippard, *Congress and US Military Aid to Britain: Interdependence and Dependence, 1949–56* (New York: St. Martin's Press, 1995), 63–66.

175. Top Secret Memorandum by Mr. Lucius D. Battle, Special Assistant to the Secretary of State, December 7, 1950, in *FRUS 1950 3*, 1759.

176. Quoted in Geoffrey Warner, "Anglo-American Relations and the Cold War in 1950," *Diplomacy and Statecraft* 22, no. 1 (2011): 56. Also see Boyle, "Britain, America and the Transition," 534.

177. Quoted in Hopkins, *Oliver Franks and the Truman Administration*, 189.

178. Hopkins, *Oliver Franks and the Truman Administration*, 189; and Park, "Wasted Opportunities?," 358.

179. Turner, *British Power and International Relations During the 1950s*, 93; and Warner, "Anglo-American Relations and the Cold War in 1950," 57–58.

180. Leigh-Phippard, *Congress and US Military Aid to Britain*, 83–85.

181. Quoted in Leigh-Phippard, *Congress and US Military Aid to Britain*, 85.

182. Leigh-Phippard, *Congress and US Military Aid to Britain*, 85.

183. Leigh-Phippard, *Congress and US Military Aid to Britain*, 69–72.

184. Top Secret United States Delegation Minutes of the First Formal Meeting of President Truman and Prime Minister Churchill, The White House, January 7, 1952, 11 a.m.–1 p.m., in *FRUS 1952 7*, 748, 750.

185. Confidential Memorandum of a Luncheon Meeting at the Department of the Treasury, January 8, 1952, in *FRUS 1952 7*, 787–88.

186. Leigh-Phippard, *Congress and US Military Aid to Britain*, 72, 81, 86. Ultimately, the Mutual Security Agency bent slightly to British preferences on the matter of interim aid. First it offered to place those monies in a Federal Reserve Bank account. The UK could draw on those funds to meet the cost of future defense-related projects, but in the interim they would count toward Britain's dollar reserves. In June, despite some reservations about the scheme, HMG agreed to the deposit of $110 million of interim aid. In addition, taking advantage of a Mutual Security Appropriation Act provision allowing a small percentage of military aid to be reprogrammed as economic aid, in March the MSA agreed to extend $47.9 million in economic aid to the UK via a promissory loan agreement (p. 88).

187. Leigh-Phippard, *Congress and US Military Aid to Britain*, 95.

188. Boyle, "Britain, America and the Transition," 534.

189. Central Statistical Office, National Income and Expenditure 1958 (London: Her Majesty's Stationary Office, 1958), p. 41, table 44. The figures for the years 1951 and 1952 are £1.09 billion and £1.45 billion, respectively.

190. Boyle, "Britain, America and the Transition," 534–35.

191. Greenwood, "A War We Don't Want," 20.

192. Quoted in Raymond Dawson and Richard Rosecrance, "Theory and Reality in the Anglo-American Alliance," *World Politics* 19, no. 1 (October 1966): 39.

193. Dawson and Rosecrance, "Theory and Reality," 38–40; and Richard E. Neustadt, *Alliance Politics* (New York: Columbia University Press, 1970), chap. 2.

194. Stephen M. Walt, *Taming American Power: The Global Response to American Primacy* (New York: Norton, 2005), 192–93.

CONCLUSION

1. Andrew Mack, "Why Big Nations Lose Small Wars: The Politics of Asymmetric Conflict," *World Politics* 27, no. 2 (January 1975): 175–200; T. V. Paul, *Asymmetric Conflicts: War Initiation by Weaker Powers* (New York: Cambridge University Press, 1994); Ivan

Arreguin-Toft, *How the Weak Win Wars: A Theory of Asymmetric Conflict* (New York: Cambridge University Press, 2006); Robert O. Keohane, "Lilliputians' Dilemmas: Small States in International Politics," *International Organization* 23, no. 2 (Spring 1969): 291–301; Robert O. Keohane, "The Big Influence of Small Allies," *Foreign Policy*, no. 2 (Spring 1971): 161–82; Robert O. Keohane and Joseph S. Nye, *Power and Interdependence*, 3rd ed. (New York: Longman, 2000); John J. Mearsheimer and Stephen M. Walt, *The Israel Lobby and U.S. Foreign Policy* (New York: Farrar, Straus, and Giroux, 2007); and Stephen M. Walt, *Taming American Power: The Global Response to U.S. Primacy* (New York: Norton, 2005).

2. Keohane, "The Big Influence of Small Allies."

3. Walt, *Taming American Power*, 194–217. See also Mearsheimer and Walt, *The Israel Lobby*.

4. Walt, *Taming American Power*, 198.

5. An anonymous reviewer questioned whether this is truly a paradoxical or counterintuitive implication, on the grounds that the shadow of the future looms larger in U.S. alliances with friendly democracies as opposed to those with unfriendly autocracies. As a result, it should not be surprising that the former will be more inclined than the latter to make big concessions to the United States. Although this is an astute critique, I reply that highly conflictual U.S. alliances with unfriendly allies of convenience, in which mutual trust is low and the shadow of the future is small, can be logically expected to be managed on a highly transactional tit-for-tat basis, which Robert Keohane has referred to as "strict reciprocity." By contrast, relatively amicable U.S. alliances with friendly special relationship allies can be expected to be conducted on a more relaxed and less transactional basis, which Keohane referred to as "diffuse reciprocity." In addition, the United States should be more highly motivated to secure major concessions from allies of convenience than special relationship allies because the former are much more likely to become dangers to the United States after the alliance is disbanded. On Keohane's distinction between strict and diffuse reciprocity, see Robert O. Keohane, "Reciprocity in International Relations," *International Organization* 40, no. 1 (Winter 1986): 1–27.

6. For a highly controversial argument that the U.S. entry into World War II and its alliance of convenience with the Soviet Union did not appreciably enhance America's national security because it merely enabled the Soviet Union to supplant Nazi Germany as a peer competitor, see Bruce M. Russett, *No Clear and Present Danger: A Skeptical View of the United States' Entry into World War II* (New York: Harper & Row, 1972).

7. Curt Tarnoff and Marian L. Lawson, "Foreign Aid: An Introduction to U.S. Programs and Policy," *Congressional Research Service Report*, April 25, 2018, pp. 30–31.

8. Tarnoff and Lawson, "Foreign Aid," 23–28.

9. Paul K. Kerr, "Arms Sales: Congressional Review Process," *Congressional Research Service Report*, July 25, 2017, pp. 1–7; and "U.S. Arms Sales and Defense Trade, Fact Sheet, Bureau of Political-Military Affairs," located at United States Department of State website: https://www.state.gov/t/pm/rls/fs/2018/280506.htm.

10. Jeffrey T. Richelson, "The Calculus of Intelligence Cooperation," *International Journal of Intelligence and Counterintelligence* 4, no. 3 (1990): 307–23; and Derek S. Reveron, "Old Allies, New Friends: Intelligence-Sharing in the War on Terror," *Orbis* 50, no. 3 (Summer 2006): 453–68.

11. A similar case from the Cold War period would be the U.S. alliance of convenience with Romania, which consisted of the secret transfer of tens of millions of dollars from Washington to Bucharest in exchange for advanced Soviet weapons. Michael Wines, "US Used Romania to Get Soviet Arms," *New York Times*, May 7, 1990, A7.

12. Robert S. Litwak, *Regime Change: U.S. Strategy through the Prism of 9/11* (Washington, DC: Woodrow Wilson Center Press, 2007), 171–72.

13. The next year, Libyan agents also bombed a French Union des Transports Aeriens (UTA) airliner over Niger, killing 170 passengers. Litwak, *Regime Change*, 173–77; and Randall Newnham, "Carrots, Sticks, and Bombs: The End of Libya's WMD Program," *Mediterranean Quarterly* 20, no. 3 (Summer 2009): 83–84.

14. Litwak, *Regime Change*, 173.

15. Bruce W. Jentleson and Christopher A. Whytock, "Who 'Won' Libya? The Force-Diplomacy Debate and Its Implications for Theory and Policy," *International Security* 30, no. 3 (Winter 2005/06): 65; Meghan L. O'Sullivan, *Shrewd Sanctions: Statecraft and State Sponsors of Terrorism* (Washington, DC: Brookings Institution Press, 2003), 183.

16. Jentleson and Whytock, "Who 'Won' Libya?," 65–67; John C. K. Daly, "Libya and al-Qaeda: A Complex Relationship," in *Unmasking Terror: A Global Review of Terrorist Activities*, ed. Christopher Heffelfinger (Washington, DC: The Jamestown Foundation, 2005), 124–125; Gary Gambill, "The Libyan Islamic Fighting Group (LIFG)," in Heffelfinger, *Unmasking Terror*, 128–31; and Alison Pargeter, "Political Islam in Libya," in Heffelfinger, *Unmasking Terror*, 135–36.

17. Gambill, "Libyan Islamic Fighting Group," 131; Daly, "Libya and al-Qaeda," 126.

18. Ray Takeyh, "The Rogue Who Came in from the Cold," *Foreign Affairs* 80, no. 3 (May/June 2001): 62–72.

19. After Gaddhafi turned over the Lockerbie suspects, the Security Council suspended its sanctions against Libya. O'Sullivan, *Shrewd Sanctions*, 207–11.

20. Jentleson and Whytock, "Who 'Won' Libya?," 70–71.

21. Barbara Slavin, "Libya's Rehabilitation in the Works since Early '90s," *USA Today*, April 27, 2004, 7A.

22. Litwak, *Regime Change*, 183.

23. Ronald Bruce St. John, "'Libya Is Not Iraq': Preemptive Strikes, WMD, and Diplomacy," *Middle East Journal* 58, no. 3 (Summer 2004): 393.

24. Quoted in Yahia H. Zoubir, "The United States and Libya: From Confrontation to Normalization," *Middle East Policy* 13, no. 2 (Summer 2006): 57; Daly, "Libya and al-Qaeda," 125.

25. Gambill, "Libyan Islamic Fighting Group," 131.

26. Ronald Bruce St. John, "Libyan Foreign Policy: Newfound Flexibility," *Orbis* 47, no. 3 (Summer 2003): 474.

27. Ronald Bruce St. John, "Libya and the United States: A Faustian Pact?," *Middle East Policy* 15, no. 1 (Spring 2008): 136.

28. Jentleson and Whytock, "Who 'Won' Libya?," 72.

29. Michael Hirsh, "Bolton's British Problem," *Newsweek*, May 2, 2005, 30.

30. Barbara Slavin, "Rivalry Can Make US Policy Look Shaky," *USA Today*, June 14, 2002, 14A.

31. Litwak, *Regime Change*, 184.

32. Quoted in Judith Miller, "From the Shores of Tripoli," *National Interest*, no. 89 (May/June 2007), 27.

33. Miller, "From the Shores of Tripoli," 27; Litwak, *Regime Change*, 185.

34. Litwak, *Regime Change*, 185; Miller "From the Shores of Tripoli," 27.

35. White House, "Fact Sheet: The President's National Security Strategy to Combat WMD—Libya's Announcement," December 19, 2003, formerly on the White House website: www.whitehouse.gov/news/release/2003/12/print/20031219-8.html.

36. Jentleson and Whytock, "Who 'Won' Libya?," 76. Gaddhafi also agreed to declare all of Libya's past nuclear activities to the International Atomic Energy Agency (IAEA), accede to the IAEA's Additional Protocol for especially intrusive inspections, and formally ratify the Chemical Weapons Convention.

37. Newnham, "Carrots, Sticks, and Bombs," 92. Gaddhafi subsequently frustrated the Bush administration by sponsoring an assassination attempt against Saudi Crown Prince Abdullah and refusing to transfer the final tranche of financial restitution to the Pan Am 103 victims' families. In response, the House Appropriations Committee passed a new sanctions amendment against Libya and a number of Democratic senators announced that they would not vote in favor of the administration's nominee as U.S. ambassador to Libya. After another round of secret bilateral negotiations, however, Gaddhafi's regime accepted a Comprehensive Claims Settlement Agreement that would establish a fund to redress all outstanding financial claims pertaining to past terrorist attacks against American citizens. Mathew Wald, "Sanctions Lifted, Libya Withholds Final Lockerbie Payment," *New York Times*, July 8, 2006, A1; Christopher M. Blanchard and Jim Zanotti, "Libya: Background and U.S. Relations," *Congressional Research Report for Congress*, February 25, 2011, 33–34.

38. Helene Cooper, "Rice, in North Africa, Visits a Tent and Many Tables," *New York Times*, September 8, 2008, A11. Although the precise date when counter-terrorism cooperation between the United States and Libya came to an end is not known, there is no question that it ceased by March 2011, when the United States and its North Atlantic Treaty Organization allies initiated a military intervention against Gaddhafi. The intervention, which consisted of the alliance's establishment of a no-fly zone over Libya and launching of airstrikes against Libyan ground forces, was a response to the regime's alleged threats to massacre civilians in the country's second-largest city, Benghazi. Seven months later, with NATO's help, Libyan rebels consolidated their hold over the country and killed Gaddhafi. Alan J. Kuperman, "A Model Humanitarian Intervention? Reassessing NATO's Libya Campaign," *International Security* 38, no. 1 (Summer 2013), 105–36.

39. Litwak, *Regime Change*, chap. 6.

40. Kenneth M. Pollack, *The Persian Puzzle: The Conflict between Iran and America* (New York: Random House, 2004), 346.

41. Pollack, *Persian Puzzle*, 346–47.

42. Pollack, *Persian Puzzle*, 347.

43. Michael R. Gordon with Neil MacFarquhar, "Threats and Responses: Diplomacy: Iraq's Neighbors Seem to be Ready to Support a War," *New York Times*, December 2, 2002, A1.

44. Ahmed S. Hashim, *The Caliphate at War: Operational Realities and Innovations of the Islamic State* (New York: Oxford University Press, 2018), chap. 6.

45. Roberta Rampton, "Obama Sends More Special Forces to Syria in Fight against IS," *Reuters*, April 15, 2016, https://www.reuters.com/article/us-mideast-crisis-usa-syria /obama-sends-more-special-forces-to-syria-in-fight-against-is-idUSKCN0XL0ZE; and Michael S. Schmidt and Mark Landler, "U.S. Will Deploy 560 More Troops to Iraq to Help Retake Mosul from ISIS," *New York Times*, July 12, 2016, A8.

46. Ben Hubbard, Isabel Kershner, and Anne Bernard, "Iran, Deeply Embedded in Syria, Expands 'Axis of Resistance,'" *New York Times*, February 19, 2018, A1.

47. See the official Global Coalition against Daesh website. http://theglobalcoalition.org /en/home/. See also Dina Esfandiary and Ariane Tabatabai, "Iran's ISIS Policy," *International Affairs* 91, no. 1 (January 2015): 1.

48. Esfandiary and Tabatabai, "Iran's ISIS Policy," 11.

49. Helene Cooper, "U.S. Strategy in Iraq Increasingly Relies on Iran," *New York Times*, March 6, 2015, A1. In addition, U.S. and Iranian officials reportedly engaged in some discussions concerning ISIS during the 2014 multilateral negotiations in Vienna regarding Iran's program. Esfandiary and Tabatabai, "Iran's ISIS Policy," 10.

50. Helene Cooper, "A U.S. Concession to Reality in the Battle against the Islamic State," *New York Times*, April 4, 2015, A4.

51. Alex Lockie, "ISIS Has Been Militarily Defeated in Iraq and Syria," *Business Insider U.S.*, November 21, 2017, https://www.businessinsider.sg/isis-military-defeat -iraq-syria-2017-11/?r=US&IR=T.

52. Representative works include Richard N. Haass and Meghan O'Sullivan, eds., *Honey and Vinegar: Incentives, Sanctions, and Foreign Policy* (Washington, DC: Brookings Institution Press, 2000); Miroslav Nincic, *The Logic of Positive Engagement* (Ithaca, NY: Cornell University Press, 2011); and Victor D. Cha and David C. Kang, *Nuclear North Korea: A Debate on Engagement Strategies* (New York: Columbia University Press, 2003).

53. Robert S. Litwak, *Rogue States and U.S. Foreign Policy: Containment After the Cold War* (Baltimore: Johns Hopkins University Press, 2000).

54. The Obama administration's nuclear negotiations with Iran exemplify this risk. The administration generally refrained from either overselling Iranian concessions or concealing and misrepresenting continuing Iranian misbehavior in other domains such as terrorism and missile proliferation. This left the July 2015 Joint Comprehensive Plan of Action (JCPOA) agreement on fragile ground domestically, as evidenced by Obama's refusal to submit it to the U.S. Senate for ratification as a formal international treaty. As

it was, Obama was barely able to muster the forty-one Senate votes necessary to filibuster a Republican resolution disapproving the deal. Consequently, his Republican successor Donald Trump was able to summarily withdraw the United States from the agreement. On the negotiation of the JCPOA, see Trita Parsi, *Losing an Enemy: Obama, Iran, and the Triumph of Diplomacy* (New Haven, CT: Yale University Press, 2017).

55. By contrast, the George H. W. Bush administration adopted a relatively hardline approach toward Pakistan following the Soviet military withdrawal from Afghanistan. After the Pakistani government defied a pledge to freeze its nuclear program, in October 1990 Bush refused to certify that Pakistan was in compliance with the Pressler Amendment. In so doing, he suspended the delivery not only of $564 million in military and economic aid to Islamabad, but also of military equipment and thirty F-16 fighter-jets purchased by Pakistan the previous year. Dennis Kux, *Disenchanted Allies: The United States and Pakistan 1947–2000* (Washington, DC: Woodrow Wilson Center Press, 2001), 299–331.

56. Robert L. Suettinger, *Beyond Tiananmen: The Politics of U.S.-China Relations, 1990–2000* (Washington, DC: Brookings Institution Press, 2003), chap. 4.

57. Quoted in Suettinger, *Beyond Tiananmen*, 155.

58. Executive Order 12850 of May 28, 1993, "Conditions for Renewal of Most-Favored Nation Status for the People's Republic of China in 1994," *Federal Register* 58, no. 103 (June 1, 1993), https://www.archives.gov/files/federal-register/executive-orders/pdf/12850.pdf.

59. Suettinger, *Beyond Tiananmen*, chaps. 5–9.

60. Secret Internal Department of State Paper, "Overview of U.S.-Iraqi Relations and Potential Pressure Points," September 9, 1988, in *DNSA Iraqgate*, Doc. IG00632, p. 1.

61. Bruce W. Jentleson, *With Friends Like These: Reagan, Bush, and Saddam, 1982–1990* (New York: Norton, 1994), 77–92.

62. This policy was codified in NSD-26, which was signed by Bush in October 1989. Unclassified White House National Security Decision Directive, "National Security Directive 26: U.S. Policy toward the Persian Gulf [Cover Sheet Attached]," October 2, 1989, p. 2, on Federation of American Scientists website: https://fas.org/irp/offdocs/nsd/nsd26.pdf.

63. Jentleson, *With Friends Like These*, chaps. 3–4.

64. Zachary Karabell, "Backfire: US Policy Toward Iraq, 1988–2 August 1990," *Middle East Journal* 49, no. 1 (Winter 1995): 34–44.

65. U.S. Congress, House of Representatives, Committee on Foreign Affairs, Subcommittee on Europe and the Middle East, U.S.-Iraq Relations, Hearing, 101st Congress, 1st Session, April 26, 1990, p. 5.

66. Amatzia Baram, "U.S. Input into Iraqi Decisionmaking, 1988–1990," in *The Middle East and the United States: A Historical and Political Reassessment*, ed. David W. Lesch (Boulder: Westview Press, 1996), 331.

67. Quoted in "Confrontation in the Gulf: Excerpts from Iraqi Document on Meeting with U.S. Envoy," *New York Times*, September 23, 1990, A19.

68. Michael R. Gordon and Bernard E. Trainor, *The Generals' War: The Inside Story of the Conflict in the Gulf* (New York: Little, Brown, 1995).

69. For figures demonstrating that Germany, Japan, and the Soviet Union were never able to generate more than a fraction of U.S. wealth during the twentieth century, see Paul Kennedy, *The Rise and Fall of the Great Powers: Economic Change and Military Conflict from 1500 to 2000* (New York: Vintage Books, 1989), 201, 202, 436; and John J. Mearsheimer, *The Tragedy of Great Power Politics* (New York: Norton, 2001), 220. According to the World Bank, in 2015 China's Gross Domestic Product (GDP) equaled 61 percent of U.S. GDP. According to the International Monetary Fund and the Economist Intelligence Unit, when GDP is measured in terms of purchasing power parity, by 2014, Chinese GDP ($18.22 trillion) had already exceeded that of the United States ($17.39 trillion). These figures are replicated in Graham Allison, *Destined for War: Can America and China Escape Thucydides's Trap?* (London: Scribe Publications, 2017), 6, 9.

70. Eric Heginbotham, Michael Nixon, Forrest E. Morgan, Jacob L. Heim, Jeff Hagen, et al., *The U.S.-China Military Scorecard: Force, Geography, and the Evolving Balance of Power 1996–2017* (Santa Monica, CA: RAND Corporation, 2015), xxxi.

71. Tom Røseth, "Moscow's Response to a Rising China," *Problems of Post-Communism*, forthcoming, published online March 23, 2018, pp. 1–19, https://doi.org/10.1080/10758216.2018.1438847.

72. Peter Zeihan, "Analysis: Russia's Far East Turning Chinese," *ABC News*, July 14, 2000, https://abcnews.go.com/International/story?id=82969&page=1; Chris Farnham, "Reading Room: Russia's Far East," review of *Russia's Far East: New Dynamics in Asia Pacific and Beyond* by Rensselaer Lee and Artyom Lukin, *Australian Outlook*, August 15, 2016, https://www.internationalaffairs.org.au/australianoutlook/review-russias-far-east/; and "Chinese in the Russian Far East: A Geopolitical Time Bomb?," *South China Morning Post*, July 8, 2017, https://www.scmp.com/week-asia/geopolitics/article/2100228/chinese-russian-far-east-geopolitical-time-bomb.

73. "Chinese in the Russian Far East."

74. Defense Intelligence Agency, *Russia Military Power: Building a Military to Support Great Power Aspirations*, DIA-11-1704-161, 2017, on Defense Intelligence Agency website: http://www.dia.mil/Portals/27/Documents/News/Military%20Power%20Publications/Russia%20Military%20Power%20Report%202017.pdf?ver=2017-06-28-144235-937.

75. Stephen Burgess, "The US Pivot to Asia and Renewal of the US-India Strategic Partnership," *Comparative Strategy* 34, no. 4 (2015), 367–79.

INDEX